THE YOGIN AND THE MADMAN

SOUTH ASIA ACROSS THE DISCIPLINES

SOUTH ASIA ACROSS THE DISCIPLINES

EDITED BY MUZAFFAR ALAM, ROBERT GOLDMAN,
AND GAURI VISWANATHAN

DIPESH CHAKRABARTY, SHELDON POLLOCK,
AND SANJAY SUBRAHMANYAM, FOUNDING EDITORS

Funded by a grant from the Andrew W. Mellon Foundation and jointly published by the University of California Press, the University of Chicago Press, and Columbia University Press

For a list of books in the series, see page 315.

The Yogin & the Madman

READING THE BIOGRAPHICAL CORPUS

OF TIBET'S GREAT SAINT MILAREPA

ANDREW QUINTMAN

COLUMBIA UNIVERSITY PRESS   NEW YORK

Columbia University Press
Publishers Since 1893
New York   Chichester, West Sussex
cup.columbia.edu

Library of Congress Cataloging-in-Publication Data
Quintman, Andrew (Andrew H.)
The yogin and the madman : reading the biographical corpus of Tibet's great saint Milarepa /
Andrew Quintman.
pages   cm. — (South Asia across the disciplines)
Includes bibliographical references and index.
ISBN 978-0-231-16414-6 (cloth : alk. paper) — ISBN 978-0-231-16415-3 (pbk.) —
ISBN 978-0-231-53553-3 (electronic)
1. Mi-la-ras-pa, 1040-1123 2. Lamas—Tibet Region—Biography—History and criticism.
3. Biography as a literary form. I. Title.
BQ7950.M557Q56   2013
294.3'923092—dc23
2012049297

Columbia University Press books are printed on permanent and durable acid-free paper.
This book is printed on paper with recycled content.
Printed in the United States of America
c 10 9 8 7 6 5 4 3 2 1
p 10 9 8 7 6 5 4 3 2

Cover design: Jordan Wannemacher
Cover images: Karma Losang of Dolpo; Dolpo, northwestern Nepal; mid or late 17th century;
Rubin Museum of Art, New York, F1997.11.2

For my parents

✻ ✻ ✻

CONTENTS

ACKNOWLEDGMENTS

T HIS BOOK is truly an example of interdependence, and I am happy to have an opportunity to acknowledge all those who contributed to its coming into being.

Although my fascination with the traditions of Milarepa's life began more than two decades ago, this book grew out of my doctoral dissertation at the University of Michigan. A Fulbright-Hays Doctoral Dissertation fellowship in Nepal allowed for a year of otherwise unencumbered research and translation in 2004 and 2005. The Rackham School of Graduate Studies at the University of Michigan generously provided me with a Predoctoral Fellowship to support the write-up. Princeton University's Society of Fellows served as an academic sanctuary while I revised the manuscript; it is hard to imagine a more collegial or inspiring setting for such an endeavor. The Department of Religious Studies at Yale University has provided a welcoming and supportive institutional home for finishing the text. I also gratefully acknowledge the support of the Frederick W. Hilles Publication Fund of Yale University.

My thanks first go to Donald S. Lopez, Jr., whose critical and creative approaches to Tibetan and Buddhist traditions shaped this project from a very early stage. Over the years he has continued to offer constructive feedback and counsel on all manner of things from Abhidharma to Zappa, extending far beyond the call of duty. Janet Gyatso helped direct my undergraduate thesis long ago and later gave substantive advice on the dissertation; I am thankful for the encouragement I have received from her since then. At the University of Michigan, this project also benefited from conversations with a host of other scholars, including Luis Gómez, Tomoko Masuzawa, James Robson, Robert Sharf, and Gareth Sparham.

I owe a particular debt of thanks to the late E. Gene Smith for his encouragement and for sharing with me his incomparable knowledge of Tibetan literature over the years. He provided several important manuscripts and offered innumerable helpful leads, as he has for nearly everyone in the field of Tibetan Studies. This project would not have been possible without his pioneering work on Milarepa's biographical tradition. For their assistance in locating and procuring key texts, I am indebted to Burkhard Quessel, Curator of the Tibetan Collections at the British Library; Valrae Reynolds, former Curator of the Asian Collections at the Newark Museum; and Jeff Watt, Director of Himalayan Art Resources. I am also thankful for the assistance I received in Tibet from Khamtrul Sonam Dondrup, Karma Delek, and Sherab Zangpo.

A number of other scholars have offered assistance, guidance, and support over the years. Hubert Decleer sparked my interest in the traditions of Milarepa while I was an undergraduate and has continued to share his fascination with them. He introduced me to the joys of research in books and on the ground, and taught me the importance of not only having a good story but also telling it well. I have also received helpful feedback on aspects of this project from Mathew Akester, Benjamin Bogin, Bryan Cuevas, Jacob Dalton, David DiValerio, Helmut Eimer, Roger Jackson, Stefan Larsson, Dan Martin, Sheldon Pollock, Peter Roberts, and especially Kurtis Schaeffer, who has long shared my interest in Milarepa and Tsangnyön Heruka.

There are many individuals in Nepal whose assistance I would like to acknowledge. Their efforts may not be immediately observable in the text that follows, but this project would have been much impoverished without their help. At Thrangu Tashi Choling Monastery, Khenpo Jigme generously read through sections of some manuscripts with me, and Khenpo Karma Gendun shared his interest and excitement about texts and manuscripts of all kinds. At Karma Lekshey Ling, Lama Phuntsok assisted me in answering a number of questions, while Khenpo Karma Namgyal assisted with many of the materials in this book. Khenpo Sherab Gyaltsen graciously shared his library and his expansive knowledge of Tibetan literary traditions. I would like to thank Dragomir Dimitrov, former Director of the Nepal Research Center in Kathmandu, for his help in tracking down many texts in their microfilm archives and for providing such a hospitable work environment. Conversations with Kashinath Timod were always stimulating, as he opened the floodgates of his incredible knowledge of Newar language and history. I am indebted to Punya Prasad Parajuli, who lent his considerable talents as a translator for numerous Nepalese materials. Harsha Ratna Shakya opened up his home and shared with me his family's stewardship of the Lhasa Paku cave in Bhaktapur and its long history of fostering Newar–Tibetan relations. Dawa Phuntsok Lama and Dharma Ratna Shakya Trisuli likewise lent their knowledge of the religious history of numerous sites in Rasuwa. With a true passion for Newar history and religion, Sarvajnya Vajracarya spent a number of days with me helping to track down obscure traces of Milarepa's presence in Kathmandu.

Over the years, I have received support from a number of traditional Tibetan Buddhist teachers whose knowledge has informed my reading of many materials studied in this book. Khenpo Karthar Rinpoche and Bardor Tulku Rinpoche remain continual sources of inspiration in their dedication to preserving and promoting the traditions that stem from Milarepa's life and teachings. I am indebted to the Venerable Thrangu Rinpoche, who encouraged me to take on this topic more than a decade ago. And it was Khenpo Tsultrim Gyatso, a true embodiment of Milarepa's activities, who first suggested long ago that I read the yogin's life story, not once but "many, many times." Over the years, they have offered guidance and encouragement for which I am both honored and grateful.

My thanks go to the editorial board of the South Asia Across the Disciplines series and the CUP staff for their support of this project. I am also grateful to Alexandra Kaloyanides and William McGrath for their assistance during the late stages of preparing the manuscript.

I have saved for last those most deserving of my gratitude. My parents, Larry and Judies, and my sisters, Debbie and Gail, have been unwavering in their support over the years even when I took to my own path. To Analis I am indebted most of all for her clarity and patience, and for continually bringing me back to what is most important. My daughter, Maya, was not born when I started this project, but she is now old enough to ask, "Isn't it done yet?" At last I have an answer for her. The better parts of this book bear the mark of these people; I thank them all.

Andrew Quintman
New Haven, CT

THE YOGIN AND THE MADMAN

INTRODUCTION

Whether with particles of heavenly fire,
The God of Nature did his soul inspire;
Or earth, but new divided from the sky,
And, pliant, still retain'd th'ethereal energy:
Which wise Prometheus temper'd into paste,
And, mix't with living streams, the godlike image caste . . .
From such rude principals our form began;
And earth was metamorphosed into man.

—Ovid, *Metamorphoses*

FROM ONE LIFE TO MANY: A BIOGRAPHICAL CORPUS

THIS BOOK traces the literary transformations of a seminal Tibetan life story—that of Milarepa (1028/1040–1111/1123), Tibet's eleventh-century Lord of Yogins—from its fragmentary origins to the standard version published nearly four centuries later. It is a life that has long served as a model for yogic virtuosi on the Himalayan plateau, a record for the birth of a religious tradition and the founding of its spiritual lineage, a tale of an individual's life of solitude and realization. It is a story that has been told in numerous forms: inscribed by authors, adapted by dramatists, illuminated by artisans, and proclaimed by wandering bards. It is a narrative that has become ingrained within the Tibetan religious and cultural landscape, a key element of the entity known as Tibetan Buddhism.

The late fifteenth century brought a version of Milarepa's life and collected songs that would form the authoritative record of the yogin's deeds. Written by the iconoclastic tantric master Tsangnyön Heruka (1452–1507), the self-proclaimed "Madman of Western Tibet," it has since served as the measure against which all other representations are judged.

In Tibetan monasteries and American classrooms alike, the portrait of Milarepa's spiritual career is founded almost exclusively upon this single narrative tradition. Indeed, few Tibetan literary works have attracted the attention, or the near universal acclaim, of this standard account of Milarepa's life and songs, works that had a profound influence on the development of Buddhism in Tibet and later served as a primary source for the Western study of Tibet's religions. Largely based upon this life story, itself hailed as a singular masterpiece of world literature, Milarepa became known as Tibet's most famous saint.

At the same time, the Madman's version of the yogin's life has most often been viewed in isolation from its origins, trajectories, and wider influences, like a narrative orphan long separated from its literary parents. Milarepa's life story was, however, founded upon the gradual production of an extensive biographical tradition, built up from a multitude of texts and narratives extending back some four hundred years. The present study is thus not simply of a life composed of events flowing from human birth to awakened *parinirvāṇa*; rather, it encompasses the confluences—and occasional collisions—of an entire body of biographical works predating the standard version, created over the course of many centuries. These works span the earliest fragmentary records written by direct disciples to the extensive biographical studies encompassing both life story and song collection and purportedly drawing upon hundreds of distinct sources. By emphasizing the interplay of these texts and the narrative representations they record, this book aims to illuminate the various forms in which the yogin's life story has been reimagined and rewritten, together with the broader historical and religious conditions that allowed for such forms of literary production.

The various texts of Milarepa's biographical tradition were never traditionally gathered together and were seldom, if ever, discussed as a unified whole, yet these works collectively form a literary corpus,[1] an extensive and varied body of writings, closely related in the common task of recording the yogin's life. But the corpus also signifies the means through which the life story's constituent parts coalesced in their representation of the yogin and his life. We might understand the biographical tradition as a process of embodying the yogin in literature, the means through which the life became manifest within the life story.

Milarepa's death brought with it a biographic birth, and soon the yogin's followers repeated and rewrote the life, copying stories or drawing upon new accounts. As authors began joining together these narratives, an image of the yogin came into view, first fragmented and skeletal, later incorporating literary structures as muscles and sinews binding together the body's inner frame. Comprehensive accounts later added layers of flesh, forming an increasingly lifelike representation. Finally, in the madman's hands, like Pygmalion's Galatea from the cold grain of ivory, the yogin's portrait embodied in the biographical corpus was brought to life. And in this living form, the madman's narrative was capable of both eclipsing four hundred years of literary development and reshaping Tibet's religious landscape.

The transformations within Milarepa's biographical tradition might be thought of as a gradual process of embodiment. This book undertakes an analogous process of biographical forensics, slicing through the outer layers of the standard work to expose and dissect the visceral structures within. Like a true anatomical dissection, the book aims not merely to carve the corpus into constituent pieces, but rather to identify its underlying structures and their systemic relationships through which the body coalesced. By mapping the anatomy of the literary corpus, it uncovers the reinvention of one of Tibet's preeminent literary traditions. It illuminates the madman's conflation of biographical subject and autobiographical voice to create the yogin's narrative form anew, as an autohagiography, a complex life story that is at once false but understood as highest truth. It further exposes the literary context that allowed such a transformation to take place. In the process, this book seeks to broaden received notions of what constitutes Tibetan sacred biography, guided by a series of related questions: How are lives recorded and transmitted? What are their limits and forms? How does form affect the reading and understanding of content? How has the writing and reading of sacred life stories transformed over time? And perhaps most important, how might a literary production—a body ultimately cast in words and stories—be brought to life?

OVERVIEW OF MILAREPA'S LIFE AND LIFE STORY

Milarepa, the meditator and poet whose very name refers to the simple cotton robes (ras, pronounced ré) of his yogic attire, is esteemed throughout the Himalayan Buddhist world as an exemplary religious figure. The principal themes associated with his life story—purification of past misdeeds, faith and devotion to the guru, ardor in meditation, and the possibility of attaining liberation in a single lifetime—have had a profound impact on the development of Buddhism across the region. In its best-known version, the *Life* describes how Milarepa was born in the early eleventh century to a prosperous family in the Mangyul region of southwest Tibet.[2] At a young age, after the death of his father, he was forced to live with his mother and sister under the care of his paternal uncle. Although the father's will stipulated that his estate would return to the boy upon his reaching majority, the uncle and his wife—portrayed as selfish and greedy—instead seized the wealth for themselves, forcing young Mila and his family into a life of abject poverty. At his mother's insistence, the boy set out to train in black magic and hail-making in order to avenge his family's treatment at the hands of their malicious relatives.

Reaching central Tibet, Milarepa encountered a number of teachers renowned for their skill in the black arts. He received their instructions, applied himself to their practice, and quickly attained signs of success. He returned to his homeland, and with his new powers caused his uncle's house to collapse, murdering dozens of people gathered for a wedding celebration inside. Only the aunt and uncle were spared to tell the tale of Milarepa's terrible revenge. The surviving relatives conspired to kill his mother in retaliation, so Milarepa once again returned, this time raining down great hailstorms that laid waste to the village's newly ripened crops.

Realizing the magnitude of his misdeeds, Milarepa sought to redeem himself from their inevitable karmic effects. Securing the support of his former magic instructor, he set out in search of a Buddhist master, promising to devote his life to the Dharma. He briefly studied in the systems of Tibet's Nyingma sect, including the meditation practices of Great Completion (*rdzogs chen*). Eventually, Milarepa met his principal guru, Marpa (1012–97), a celebrated translator of Indian texts and an important figure in the latter promulgation of the Buddhist teachings in Tibet. Known for his aggressive and quick-tempered personality, Marpa did not immediately teach his new disciple but instead subjected him to repeated abuse including, most famously, the trial of constructing immense stone towers.

Pushed to the brink of despair, Milarepa contemplated escape, and later suicide; but Marpa finally revealed the trials to be a skillful method for purifying the sinful deeds of his past. He explained that Milarepa was, from the beginning, a disciple prophesied by Marpa's own guru, the Bengali adept Nāropa (ca. 956–1040). Milarepa received the tantric transmissions Marpa had carried from India and translated, including those of Mahāmudrā and the famed Six Doctrines of Nāropa, which would form the core of his new lineage. He departed with his guru's final advice to persevere against all hardship and live out his life meditating in solitary caves and mountain retreats.

Milarepa is said to have spent the rest of his life practicing meditation and teaching small groups of disciples, mainly through spontaneous poetry and songs of realization. He traveled widely across Tibet's southern borderlands, on many occasions crossing into Nepal. By the time of his death, the yogin had staked out a new Buddhist landscape along the borderlands of southern Tibet, converted hosts of nonhuman spirits to the Dharma as protectors of the religion, and taught dozens (and in some accounts, hundreds if not thousands) of disciples. And, of course, he had sung the innumerable songs of spiritual realization for which he would become renowned.

Most traditions hold that Milarepa's death left behind no physical remains. But if the yogin's followers lacked a reminder of his life in the form of corporeal relics, that empty space was soon filled with literary records of his life and teachings. Milarepa's close disciples, who would promulgate their guru's teachings as a tradition later known as the Kagyu or "Oral Transmission" sect, wrote the first biographical works that appeared shortly after his death. Some were little more than narrative fragments; others, discrete but finely crafted vignettes. It is likely that one of the more comprehensive biographies appeared within a generation after Milarepa's passing. Another stratum of biographies developed in the generations following his death, texts this study calls "proto-Life/ Songs" in reference to a burgeoning literary structure encapsulating both a life story and a song collection. These were often, though not exclusively, incorporated into works known as "golden rosaries" (gser 'phreng), collective biographies documenting the vitae of a dozen or more masters in a particular lineage of doctrinal transmission. But the works that had the greatest influence on the corpus of Milarepa's tradition were the biographical compendia that record the yogin's life story by developing, both broadly and in detail, the themes for which the master would become famous. Here for the first time, the life story is plotted out as a broad, continuous narrative. And largely based upon these works, Tsang-nyön Heruka crafted the narratives that would eclipse all other forms of the life story and become recognized as the standard versions of both life and songs.

STRUCTURES AND FUNCTIONS OF TIBETAN LIVES

Life writing, including biography and autobiography, is common to religious traditions throughout Asia, from accounts of great Jain teachers in

India to the lives of eminent monks in China.[3] Narratives describing the deeds of the Buddha (in both his former and final incarnations) appear early in the Pāli canon. Authors of extensive Mahāyāna compositions later presented grand narratives describing their founder's birth, religious practice, and eventual awakening. Indeed, the life of Śākyamuni is central to Buddhism in each of its geographic manifestations, where the tale served as a principal motif for literary and visual expression, for ritual practice, and for the interpretation of religious doctrine.

In Tibet, the stories of religious masters assumed a particularly prominent role, and forms of life writing rapidly proliferated. The production of biographies and autobiographies throughout the Tibetan cultural world would eventually comprise thousands of individual texts. Early stories, including several of those examined in this book, might span only a dozen or so pages; later works were hundreds of times longer. According to one preliminary estimate, 20 percent of biographical texts produced in the nineteenth century were greater than 200 folios in length; nearly 10 percent exceeded 300.[4] In some cases, Tibetan life writing reached dizzying extremes of prolixity: the famed autobiography of the Fifth Dalai Lama (1617–82), for example, spanned some 900 folios and was later expanded to more than double that length by his regent, Desi Sangyé Gyatso (1653–1705). The various forms of Tibetan life writing include *vitae* of distant founders, such as the eleventh-century Milarepa. But they also cover a wide array of more historical figures, a cohort that includes yogins and scholars, monastics and laymen, aristocrats and village commoners, political rulers at the center of power and religious teachers on the margins of the Tibetan landscape. In many ways, biographical writing lies at the heart of Tibetan religious expression, and it is to stories such as *The Life of Milarepa* that Tibetans continually return.

Nearly all of the biographical texts discussed in this study are titled with the Tibetan word *namtar* (*rnam thar*), literally "complete liberation," signifying a literary genre that typically recounts the lives of religious figures with an emphasis on their practice of the Buddhist path and eventual spiritual awakening. *Namtar* is defined in *The Great Tibetan Dictionary* as "stories of the deeds and conduct of eminent individuals or a work that is a biographical narrative."[5] Here the final term rendered "biographical narrative" is of particular interest. *Tokjö* (*rtogs brjod*), literally "expression of realization" or "realization narrative," was used by Tibetan translators to render the name of a traditional Indian Buddhist form of biographical literature: the *avadāna*. Many such works recount the former lives of the Buddha and his disciples; others focus on the legends surrounding figures such as the emperor Aśoka. Some were translated into Tibetan and preserved as canonical works.[6] Tibetan authors occasionally recorded the lives of Indian and Tibetan masters under the title of "realization narratives," especially the extended works that began to appear in the seventeenth and eighteenth centuries. But it was largely in the form of *namtar* that Tibetan biographical writing developed and later flourished.[7]

While its definition invokes a traditional form of biographical literature, *namtar* renders the Sanskrit *vimokṣa*, which is not a literary genre but the state of a bodhisattva's final awakening itself. Franklin Edgerton, however, glosses *vimokṣa* with the form *bodhisattva-vimokṣa*, defined as "a Mahāyāna method of salvation"; this is cited from the *Gaṇḍavyūha Sūtra*, itself a renowned Mahāyāna narrative tracing the spiritual career and eventual liberation of Sudhana over the course of many lifetimes.[8] Here, the term *vimokṣa* seems to refer to the means through which liberation is gained and, by extension, to the practice of such means over the course of a life or lifetimes.[9]

The Tibetan word *namtar* draws upon these multiple meanings.[10] In its most common formulation, the term refers to texts that not only record the life stories of great masters traversing the Buddhist path and gaining liberation but also encompass the means for attaining liberation itself. Indeed, some versions of Milarepa's biography catalogued his songs according to a traditional formulation: the view, meditation, action, and fruition of Buddhist practice. Even today, masters continue to draw upon these songs as part of the core tradition of Tibetan Buddhist teaching and practice. Later chapters will describe how some literature of Milarepa's biographical tradition explicitly refers to itself as constituting tantric instructions, central to the religious praxis of the yogin's own lineage.

Scholars and translators of Tibetan literature have rendered *namtar* in a variety of ways to reflect these different shades of meaning: "sacred biography," "religious biography," "hagiography," "liberative life story," "liberation tale," "life story," and simply "biography." Although such accounts refer almost exclusively to the lives of religious figures, the Tibetan genre of *namtar* is neither homogeneous nor monolithic, and it allows for a wide range of literary structures and narrative content. In certain instances, *namtar* also appears to deemphasize the "graph" in biography, referring not just to a literary record but to the broad span of a life (*bios*)—in the sense of a life lived or even a lifestyle—more generally.[11] Previous studies of Tibetan life writing have tended to emphasize the discontinuities between the various forms of biographical literature, or have at least emphasized one over the others. This investigation instead adopts a systemic approach, examining the interrelationships among various biographical forms.

Tibetan life writing could be filled with visions and wonder working or with the tediously quotidian details of a religious vocation; many stories of "complete liberation" say very little about liberation at all. The traditional taxonomy of outer biography (*phyi'i rnam thar*), inner biography (*nang gi rnam thar*), and secret biography (*gsang ba'i rnam thar*) commonly found in Tibetan literature gives some indication of this diversity. While an outer biography might recount an individual's mundane affairs, such as places visited and people met, inner biographies could focus on the subject's spiritual career, recording long lists of teachings and initiations received and meditation retreats undertaken. In this case, the latter forms a subgenre of biographical literature known as "receipt records" (*thob yig*, or its honorific form *gsan yig*), long lists that document the multitude of textual, ritual, and oral transmissions received over the course of an individual's religious career.[12] Secret biographies frequently record the esoteric visions and inner yogic experiences gained through meditation practice and retreat. Although Milarepa's biographical tradition did not typically adopt this system, individual works show some resemblance to each of the three categories. Tibetan literature also preserves numerous examples of autobiographical writing (*rang rnam*), but as we shall see, the line between self- and other-written lives was not always firmly established or maintained.[13]

The texts forming the corpus of Milarepa's biographical tradition exemplify Tibet's diverse forms of life writing. The initial works, among Tibet's earliest biographical literature, are little more than character sketches, lacking any sense of a coherent life lived over time. Later versions developed increasingly complex narratives to emphasize the full arc of the yogin's life, spanning his birth, renunciation, training, liberation, teaching career, and death. Themes such as the search for a guru or the practice of austerities ground the story in extended narratives, and through narrative ground the life in the passing of time. In such cases, the life story forms a broad, contiguous sweep, not merely a conglomeration of unrelated anecdotes.

Other forms of life writing central to Milarepa's biographical corpus deemphasize the passage of time. Song collections formed an integral

Mirada doesn't change the saint's present

part of Mila's biographical tradition—first in proto-form and later as fully developed catalogues—documenting a major portion of the yogin's spiritual career. In nearly every instance, these song collections constituted a substantial part of the biography itself—nearly three-quarters of the written text. Although they are clearly biographical in nature and describe the yogin's mature teaching career, as will be discussed in detail in chapter 3, they lack the chronological structures that usually support narrative discourse. The song cycles are themselves narrative vignettes, but as part of a larger collection they are free-standing and atemporal; in subsequent versions, they were frequently edited, spliced, and rearranged while maintaining the desired effect of representing the yogin's later life and activities. The song collections might thus be better understood as forming biographical networks: structures of largely synchronic units contributing to the life story's overall representation while lacking any definite sense of relationship in time.

If the stories of Milarepa's biographical tradition vary greatly in terms of content and form, so also do they vary in function. Biographers typically claim the bodhisattva's motivation for crafting their work, aspiring to benefit beings by leading them to the state of a buddha. One of the biographical compendia concludes with a verse illustrating this tradition, referring to the yogin by his tantric initiation name, Zhepa Dorjé:

> Through the roots of virtue from composing this authentic Dharma,
> When the appearances of this life begin to fade,
> May sentient beings of the six migrations, headed by my mother and
>   father,
> Encounter the great Jetsün Zhepa Dorjé
> In the pure realm of Abhirati to the east
> And then swiftly achieve buddhahood.[14]

The author of another compendium states that the text, identified as part of an important tantric instruction cycle, "Has been put into writing according to the lama's words / For fear it might be forgotten by those of inferior minds / For future holders of the family line."[15] In this case, the preservation of the life story for the benefit of the subject's followers is offered as the author's principal motivation.

But as is now well known, religious biographies also promoted a range of polemical agendas that need to be understood within the contexts of their individual religious, social, and political climates. In its best-known formulation, Tibetan life writing supported the representation of figures considered founders of religious transmissions and institutions. Among the earliest extensive biographies in Tibet are those describing the lives of such charismatic founding figures as Atisha (982–1054), Padmasambhava (active late 8th c.), and Milarepa. The works of Tsangnyön Heruka, discussed in chapter 4, mark a concerted attempt at reinvigorating and reimagining the representations of the early founders from which his own tradition had sprung.

If Tibetan biography could emphasize the lives of individual founder figures, another important function was to record the lineages of transmission stemming from them. In a religious culture where the notion of unbroken lineage originating from an authoritative source was of paramount importance, such lineage biographies served a powerful legitimizing function. Chapter 2 discusses numerous works from Milarepa's biographical tradition in which the yogin's representation is subordinated to the representation of the lineage; individual members are important insofar as they represent links in an unbroken chain of transmission. In some instances, such works were situated at the beginning of an author's Collected Works as a means of authorizing the central body of writing that followed. On other occasions, lineage histories formed independent texts in the subgenre known as "golden rosary" (gser 'phreng) texts, symbolizing the strand of lives following one after the next as beads on a rosary, meant to document the lineage as a whole.

Works in Milarepa's biographical tradition were also used to make specific claims on the institution of reincarnation. In the nine hundred years since Milarepa's death, an overwhelming majority of authors described the yogin as a miraculous emanation of an enlightened figure, and several claimed to be his reincarnation (a phenomenon addressed later in the book). In chapter 3, we shall see how a religious community chose to reproduce a particular version of Milarepa's life story in order to support the identification of its principal teachers as reembodiments of Milarepa and his disciple Zhiwa Ö. Conversely, chapter 4 will address Tsangnyön Heruka's direct and unmistakable claim that viewing the guru as an incarnation of a previous master or an emanation of an enlightened buddha instead forms a major impediment to spiritual practice. This last point carries a note of irony since, as we will see in chapter 5, Madman Tsangnyön occasionally presented himself as Yogin Milarepa's reembodiment, and his disciples continued to promote this view in their own biographical writings.

MILAREPA UNDER THE MICROSCOPE

This book is concerned primarily with the figure of Milarepa, his representation, and his biographical tradition as they evolved inside Tibet, under the direction of Tibetan authors, for Tibetan audiences. It is, however, also a manifestation of the West's long-standing fascination with the yogin's life and spiritual career, and therefore carries traces of a tradition that has variously looked upon Milarepa and his life story as a cultural symbol, a religious icon, a historical datum, linguistic source material, and—with Buddhism's spread beyond the Himalayan borders—the source of great spiritual affinity and devotion. Therefore, I situate this study first by surveying briefly the entrance of Milarepa's corpus into both popular and academic Western discourse.

Illustrating the widespread practice of asceticism in Tibet, the seventeenth-century Jesuit missionary Ippolito Desideri noted a "certain ancient hermit of Thibet whose name I have forgotten, but whose life, written in most elegant Thubettan, is as follows."[16] This mendicant

> studied magic, and among other things could cause hail to fall when and where he pleased. But one day seeing the damage done to so many he reflected that hell would be his portion after death and decided to lead a holy life. . . . He wore no clothes to shield him from the bitter cold, only a skin over that part of the body which decency demands should be covered. He slept on the bare ground and his food was a handful of nettles, fresh or dried and boiled in water.[17]

The account Desideri records is, of course, the life of Milarepa, and "every hermit," the Jesuit continues, "has a copy of this book and professes to imitate him." Although Desideri describes the work's beauty, a refrain repeated by critics and commentators for centuries, it is perhaps noteworthy that one of Tibet's most famous books entered the Western imagination with little more than a whisper, its subject lacking even so much as a name.

Nearly a century passed before Milarepa resurfaced, this time in the writings of Alexander Csoma de Kőrös, Hungarian father of Tibetology, in 1834. And once again, the yogin's entrée into Western literature was somewhat lackluster: Milarepa's name appears only once, buried within an appendix of Kőrös's Tibetan grammar.[18]

Perhaps the earliest independently published discussion of the saint's life appeared in 1869, in a German article by the Moravian missionary

H. A. Jäschke.[19] His dictionary, published in 1881, glosses Milarepa as "a mendicant friar, [who] instructed the people by his improvisations delivered in poetry and song . . . whose legends, written not without wit and poetical merit, are still at present day the most popular and widely circulated book in Tibet."[20]

The last quarter of the nineteenth and early twentieth centuries saw a flurry of publications devoted to the standard biography by Tibet scholars such as Sarat Chandra Das, William Rockhill, Graham Sandberg, and Berthold Laufer.[21] The literary quality of Tsangnyön Heruka's work was quickly recognized, and it served as a standard reference for linguistic usage and style in the first Tibetan-English dictionaries, such as those by Jäschke and Das. Selections from the account were incorporated into the Indian government's high-proficiency examination for Tibetan. In *The Buddhism of Tibet*, published in 1895, L. A. Waddell described Milarepa as "a person of importance in Lāmaism," and included a somewhat prosaic summary of the life story (though relegated to a footnote), together with a hand-drawn reproduction of a biographical scroll painting.[22]

For the most part, these writings were uncritical translations of excerpted passages from the Collected Songs, and although their descriptions presented little in the way of a human life, the stories of Milarepa's career had clearly caught the Western imagination. The romantic mood was captured by Sandberg, an author "long smitten with the Tibetan hobby," in his turn-of-the-century piece on the yogin entitled "A Tibetan Poet and Mystic": "One result of the current taste for things Tibetan has been to direct attention, not only to the weird geography of the snowgirt land, but also to its literary treasures, which are known still less than its physical wonders."[23]

The view of Tibetan literature was complex in nineteenth-century Europe. Tibetan writing was generally seen first as a perversion of "original Buddhism" and later as the repository of stultifying and musty books of philosophy (which were, ironically, Tibetan versions of the canonical Indian texts that formed "original Buddhism").[24] Milarepa's life story, filled with unvarnished religious poetry, was received as a break from this: inspired, refreshing, pure, resonant of some inner mystical truth.

Writing in 1906, Sandberg notes in a chapter fully devoted to the yogin that Milarepa's songs are "composed in language differing considerably from the stilted artificial style of the [canonical] Kangyur treatises."[25] Two decades later Sir Charles Bell—British Political Officer stationed in Sikkim and friend of the Thirteenth Dalai Lama—observed, "As literature, [the songs of Milarepa] give us the real literature of Tibet, far more living and redolent of the soil, than the Scriptures and the Commentaries, these so-called classical works, which are but close-fitting translations from Sanskrit originals."[26]

Pioneering Italian Tibetologist Guiseppe Tucci was slightly more circumspect in his *Tibetan Painted Scrolls*, although he maintained the general mood of the times, noting that Milarepa's poetry "is frequently eclipsed by esoterical abstruseness or by the technicalities of yoga, but on the other hand it does sometimes break loose from such patterns and soars in perfect purity on the wings of fancy."[27] He later describes the *Life* and *Songs* as "noble masterpieces breathing a fresh, serene and robust poetic spirit."[28]

The earliest translation of Milarepa's life story into a foreign language was a Mongolian edition produced in 1618 from Tsangnyön Heruka's standard version, although it was only printed a century and a half later under the auspices of Changkya Rolpé Dorjé (1717–1786).[29] French scholar Jacques Bacot published the first extensive (though abridged) European translation of the *Life* in 1925 as *Le poète tibétain Milarépa: ses crimes, ses épreuves, son Nirvāna*. This was one of the earliest full-length accounts of a Tibetan Buddhist figure in a European language, and Bacot read the story as a modern psychological tale that spoke, if in a foreign tongue, at least with a familiar voice. Introducing the text, he wrote,

> Les peuple tibétain est plus friand de l'histoire qui est un roman psychologique et un roman de moeurs. Les premiers chapitres, dépourvus de ce qu'il est convenu d'appeler le caractère oriental, ont cette originalité qu'ils pourraient être vécus dans notre Europe contemporaine, sans trop d'anachronisme ni trop d'invraisemblance.[30]

This was followed by a complete English version by the Sikkimese translator Kazi Dawa-Samdup, and later published under the editorial direction of the eccentric American spiritual seeker and would-be scholar W. Y. Evans-Wentz. Dawa-Samdup worked intermittently on his translation between 1902 and 1917, well before Bacot's edition appeared, and he independently produced one chapter of the *Life* in 1914.[31] Evans-Wentz met Dawa-Samdup in 1919, during their collaboration on the *Bardo Tödröl* (*Bar do thos grol*), the so-called "Tibetan Book of the Dead" that constituted his first literary production. But it was only after the translator died in 1922 that Evans-Wentz took an interest in the text of Milarepa's life. He received Dawa-Samdup's manuscript translation from the latter's family in 1924 and published it four years later (in 1928) as *Tibet's Great Yogī Milarepa*.[32]

Major W. L. Campbell—British political officer in Gangtok, Sikkim, and amateur Tibetologist—had supplied Evans-Wentz with many of his Tibetan woodblock prints, including a copy of the *Bardo Tödröl*.[33] Major Campbell also collaborated with Dawa-Samdup on the translation of Milarepa's life story and described the text in a letter to Evans-Wentz dated July 14, 1919:

> I am helping [Dawa-Samdup] to correct his translation of Milarepa's Biography and getting it retyped in Calcutta in the hope of finding a publisher. It is one of the best known biographies in Tibet and would have the advantage of being about the first really Tibetan book to be translated—it is also extremely readable and ought to sell. When you come to think of it there is very little literature in the Tibetan classics which was not originally translated from Sanscrit [sic], but Milarepa is real Tibetan stuff.[34]

Indeed, *The Life of Milarepa* was arguably the first Tibetan book to be translated into English, and Campbell was certainly prescient in noting that the story was readable, that an audience beyond the Himalaya would see Milarepa as "real Tibetan stuff," and above all that the book would sell.[35] Oxford University Press recently released the third edition of Evans-Wentz's version, three-quarters of a century after its original publication. *The Life of Milarepa* was translated into Japanese in 1931 by the intrepid Tibet explorer Ekai Kawaguchi, and then into Chinese in 1949.[36] Garma C. C. Chang rendered the entire *Hundred Thousand Songs of Milarepa* into English for the first time in 1962. That same year, Laurence Michael Dillon, a British physician who studied Buddhism with a number of Western and Asian teachers, published a condensed account of Milarepa's life based on Evans-Wentz's version under the pen name Lobzang Jivaka. Dillon was also a transsexual and the first to undergo female-to-male sex reassignment surgery. It seems that his experience with the fluid nature of self-identity led him to embrace the Buddhist ideal of no-self exemplified in Milarepa's biography.[37] Lobsang Lhalungpa, a former official in Tibet's traditional government prior to exile, produced a new English edition of the *Life* fifteen years later, finally eclipsing Dawa-Samdup's pioneering efforts. In 2010 my own translation of *The Life of Milarepa* was published by Penguin Classics. Both the *Life* and the *Songs* have recently been translated into a host of other European languages; Tibetan poet Dondrup Gyel describes a version rendered into Latin.[38]

If in the mid-nineteenth century Buddhism had often been described as "gloomy" and "quietistic," the growing number of Western Buddhist followers began to view Milarepa as a symbol of religious optimism and active self-reliance. Readers found in his life story the appeal of an everyman hero, epic themes of sin and redemption, a Buddhist ecumenism free from religious dogma, and no small dose of literary panache. Milarepa towered as the "Socrates of Asia," the "Abraham Lincoln" of the Himalaya, a true Mahātma sheathed in the chaff of legend who yet possessed a kernel of historical truth.[39] The growing number of Buddhist devotees in the West came to see him as a foremost representative of the Tibetan tradition and its core Buddhist ideals, a position not far from the view of many Tibetans. But he was also made to serve as a sort of Tibetan ambassador to a global community of Tibetan sympathizers. Milarepa was thus written into two worlds. He was scripted to serve as a premier example of the Oriental mind, steeped in Tibetan tradition, founder of a major Buddhist sect (and by some accounts an entire hermetic movement), Tibet's most renowned enlightened master; he was, in short, "real Tibetan stuff." But he was also cast as a figure familiar to modern Western audiences, a child of enlightenment values, part poet, part scientist of mind, advocating the immediacy of a religious experience available to all.

The early translations reached a wide and varied audience, carrying Milarepa's life story into fairly mainstream cross-sections of European and American culture. The great twentieth-century Romanian sculptor Constantine Brancusi is said to have carried Bacot's translation of Milarepa's life with him at all times, quoting from it often.[40] According to his friends, the sculptor believed that he had in the yogin a personal—if unseen—protector. There were also rumors that he considered himself to be Milarepa's reincarnation. The first Tibetan teachers to reach America brought with them stories of the yogin and put their disciples into long meditation retreats in the tradition of Milarepa's own yogic practice. *The Life of Milarepa* continues to hold a privileged place on the syllabi of religious studies courses across the country, and the life story has been immortalized in several strip cartoons, numerous musical recordings, volumes of free verse, several novels, and a French theatrical production.[41] The response has not always been favorable, however: one modern Chinese critic writing under the pseudonym "The Fearless Proclaimer" published a polemical tract entitled *Smashing the Evil and Revealing the Proper*, deriding Milarepa as "the great demon king." He fearlessly proclaims:

> Belittling the Dharma, slighting the teachings, and holding the Sangha in contempt,
> Deriding the sutras, slandering the vinaya, his insane offenses multiply.
> He cheats others with his whispered transmission;
> With aberrant reckonings, he falls into the fiery pit.
>
> . . .
>
> Treacherous old villain he, a thief among the virtuous;
> The bad seed within Buddhism, is vile to the utmost.[42]

Still, *The Life of Milarepa* remains a captivating story for modern audiences. At least three directors have dramatized the yogin's life in film. The first, by Liliana Cavani in 1974, recounts the yogin's deeds in the form of narrative flashbacks set against a modern-day automobile accident. The life story was recently reimagined in two new feature-lenth films, both directed by Tibetan reincarnate lamas; the Seventeenth Karmapa, Orgyen Trinley Dorje, later dramatized the tale for the Tibetan stage.[43] In one of baseball's great hoaxes, renowned sports writer George Plimpton penned an article for *Sports Illustrated* describing the rookie player Sidd Finch, whose incredible fastball was traced to his early tutelage under "Tibet's great poet-saint Lama Milarepa."[44]

The 1950s brought increased critical reflection on the literary tradition of Milarepa's life. Early in the decade, Toni Schmid reproduced a series of nineteen biographical paintings depicting Milarepa's life, together with a brief analysis of the literature upon which they were based.[45] In 1959, J. W. de Jong published a critical edition of the *Life* based on four block-print texts.[46] It was, perhaps, with Gene Smith's seminal introduction to the biography of Tsangnyön Heruka a decade later that the academic study of Milarepa's biographical tradition began in earnest.[47] This work offered, for the first time, a glimpse into the religious, social, and political contexts in which Tsangnyön crafted his works; it also included what remains the most extensive discussion of the printing history of the *Life*.[48] Perhaps most important, Smith explicitly acknowledged the central role that earlier versions of the life story—especially that of the so-called *Twelve Great Disciples* (*Bu chen bcu gnyis*), discussed in chapter 3—played in Tsangnyön's literary efforts. The standard version's monolithic presence within the biographical tradition had begun to crack.

During the 1970s, French Tibetologist Ariane Macdonald-Spanian focused a seminar at the École pratique des Hautes Études in Paris on Milarepa's biographical tradition, and in 1982 she produced a brief but careful analysis of the life story.[49] Helmut Eimer later published a series of articles analyzing the various editions and printing history of The Hundred Thousand Songs.[50] The literature of Milarepa's life has been the subject of at least four doctoral theses and several extended critical studies. Charles van Tuyl's 1972 dissertation focused on the four earliest signed narrative fragments in the biographical tradition, based on Tsangnyön's record of them. In 1980, Paul Draghi completed a Ph.D. thesis on the themes found in the well-known "Hunter and the Deer" chapter from Milarepa's collected songs.[51] Victoria Urubshurow's 1984 dissertation examined the life story, again from Tsangnyön's version, as a storehouse of literary tropes and symbols informing the Tibetan Buddhist world.[52] In 1989, Francis Tiso completed a dissertation examining Milarepa's representation as a model Tibetan saint.[53] His was the first full-length study to explore and translate an early biographical representation and to question how that representation changed over time. In his 2000 dissertation, published in 2007, Peter Roberts discussed the biographical tradition of Milarepa's disciple Rechungpa, although he briefly surveyed many of the early texts studied here in detail.[54]

Dan Martin's 1982 study of Milarepa's early teachers provided one of the first historical treatments of the yogin's life story and for the first time translated selections from a version of the biography predating Tsangnyön Heruka's standard account.[55] An unpublished work by Hubert Decleer, completed in 1994, contains an extended section on the narrative traditions of Milarepa in Nepal based on the field work of several undergraduate students (of whom I was one in 1988), his own textual analysis, and partial translations of several episodes from early biographical works.[56] At the time of this writing, two Ph.D. theses have recently been completed on Tsangnyön Heruka's early life and the phenomenon of the mad saint in fifteenth-century Tibet.[57] In the last twenty years, a number of shorter articles have appeared referencing the early biographical tradition, although none has treated the tradition at length or in detail.[58]

A MODEL FOR STUDYING THE LIFE

Perhaps an appropriate model for the study of Buddhist biography, as it was for the writing of biography by Buddhist authors, is the life of the

Buddha. The history of scholarship on the Buddha's life story brings into high relief the larger concerns framing this book's account of Milarepa's biographical corpus. References to a Buddha-like figure appear in European literature early in the first millennium and were famously canonized in the Christian church through the story of Barlaam and Josaphat.[59] But the study of the Buddha and his life began in earnest in the West during the last quarter of the eighteenth century. At a time when Buddhist texts were not yet readily available in Europe, there was little ground for understanding the Buddha as a historical figure: a position that was to hold sway for more than half a century. Based upon tenuous etymological analysis, scholars such as Sir William Jones were already beginning to identify the figure of the Buddha with mythological personages such as the Greek god Mercury, the Scandinavian Woden, and in some cases, even Noah and Moses.

Approaching the first half of the nineteenth century, as Sanskrit and Pali texts were being discovered, translated, and published, the Buddha's life story was initially read as fabulous exaggeration or a pure invention of the Indian religious milieu. Scholars such as Émile Senart and Hendrik Kern promoted the theory of the Buddha as the central figure of a complex solar myth.[60] This was criticized in favor of a more positivist view by individuals such as Hermann Oldenberg and T. W. Rhys-Davids. These later scholars emphasized the Pāli texts of early Buddhist traditions in an attempt to reconstruct a historical founding figure, in the vein of Schweitzer's "quest for the historical Jesus." In their opinion, "the mythic elements . . . were considered to be a later addenda to the true historical memory, addenda which represented a degeneration of the tradition which it was the responsibility of critical scholarship to identify and discount."[61] The theories of Senart and Oldenberg are commonly used to illustrate the rift between contrasting versions of the Buddha's life story. As de Jong notes, "It has become customary to oppose Senart's mythological method to Oldenberg's rationalistic and euhemeristic method . . . in Senart's Buddha the human being is absent but in the one described by Oldenberg the god."[62] The pattern established here identified a dichotomy between the kernel of historical truth and the surrounding chaff of legend. The principal task of the scholar became the chore of peeling away layers of hagiographical fable and legend in search of the historical figure within.

In 1927, E. J. Thomas advanced a new approach to studying the Buddha's life story by attempting to determine the structures and relationships between various biographical sources, their narratives, and their roles within the wider tradition.[63] In the second half of the twentieth century, about the time that Milarepa's life story entered the Western academy, eminent Buddhist scholars such as Étienne Lamotte and André Bareau began to refine the study not so much of the historical Buddha as of the Buddha's biographical tradition. Lamotte especially argued for a gradual development and synthesis of fragmented biographical cycles originally found in early Buddhist literature of the *suttas* and the *vinaya*. In doing so, he criticized the notion, forwarded by Erich Frauwallner, that the Buddha's life story stemmed instead from a singular root narrative, the *Skandaka*, now lost. Lamotte's work was elaborated upon by individuals such as Bareau, Alfred Foucher, and more recently Frank Reynolds, to the point where "we may know very little about the 'Buddha of history,' but we know a great deal about the Buddha of story."[64] In this sense, as will be explored below, the pursuit of the Buddha's life story parallels the study of religious biography more generally, turning away from the quest for a historical root narrative and emphasizing instead the importance of biographical process.

This is in line with an observation by Frank Reynolds, in the prolegomenon to his study of the Buddha's life stories in India, that there is now

> widespread consensus that the most crucial problems which are amenable to future investigation cluster around the identification of the various levels or stages in the development of the biographical tradition, the question of the structure of the various biographical fragments and texts, and the role which these fragments and texts have played within the broader tradition.[65]

A similar case has been made in the study of founding Chan Buddhist figures in China, in which "all variants of a hagiographical topos should be first considered in a synchronic perspective, without trying to sort out the historical kernel from the shell of legend," and indeed "the very metaphor of shell and kernel, implicit in the work of most historians, should itself be questioned."[66]

This book is thus not a quest for the historical Milarepa. Despite the considerable uncertainty surrounding his dates, there is little doubt that such an individual once lived, even if—as with the Buddha—we know less about the Mila of history than the Mila of story. This is rather an extended analysis of Milarepa's biographical process as it unfolded over a period of some four centuries. It presents for the first time a study of an entire corpus of Tibetan writing about a single individual, tracing the lines of its textual production and dissemination. It demonstrates how these disparate texts were adopted and adapted to create a single canonical figure that would become universally accepted throughout the Himalayan region, and tries to understand how such a canonical portrait could influence the world of Tibetan Buddhism writ large.

METHODOLOGICAL APPROACHES TO THE LIFE

With the above discussion in mind, this book approaches the field of Tibetan life writing, and the life of Milarepa in particular, with three primary goals. First, it seeks to move away from traditional attempts to distill "fact" from "fiction" in early biographical literature by acknowledging that such stories have value for understanding religious, social, and literary history even if they tell us less about the text's purported subject than about its authors and readers. It further seeks to avoid conceiving of biography primarily as an inert mine of data—names, dates, lineage affiliations, and the like—to be excavated by scholars. Finally, it focuses on the formal literary qualities of a textual corpus while paying close attention to its production, dissemination, reception, and intertextual relationships. The first two goals follow broad trends undertaken in the field of hagiographical studies through the end of the twentieth century; here they address problems that have dogged at least some work on Tibetan biography. The third reflects an approach to religious life writing proposed by medievalist Patrick Geary as a corrective addressing the deficiencies in past avenues of research.[67]

The birth of modern scholarship on sacred biography is often ascribed to the Belgian Jesuit Hippolyte Delehaye. Although a member of the Bollandist community—tasked since the seventeenth century with compiling the *Acta Sanctorum*, an official catalogue of saints sanctioned by the Roman Catholic Church—he was among the first authors to adopt a critical approach to religious life writing. His *Les Légendes hagiographiques* (translated in English as *The Legends of the Saints*), published in 1905, advocated a sharp distinction between the literary forms of hagiography and historiography. For Delehaye, hagiographical writing constitutes a work of "religious character" aimed at the edification of a saint. Indeed, he notes, the term hagiography "must be confined to writings inspired by religious devotion to the saints and intended to increase that devotion."[68]

Most such works, in his view, borrowed standard tropes and motifs from other literature and were thus plagued by distortion, conflation, and corruption of the truth. They were, in short, little more than examples of Christian folklore. But some stories at least might have a kernel of historical truth buried beneath a shell of fabulous accretion and, like Oldenberg looking at the Buddha's life several decades earlier, he aimed to uncover those stories concealing the germ of fact—a category that, in the end, he seemed to find dishearteningly small. Yet Delehaye also suggested that the historian need not simply dismiss the works he feels are closer to legend than history. Hagiography is, by his definition, primarily meant to support the edification and cultic worship of the saints. By understanding the structures and functions of a story, readers can more clearly discern its author's purpose and agenda.

Scholars of medieval Christian hagiography may have long since ended the debate between "scientific free thinkers and pious defenders of the legends of the saints."[69] Yet as Rupert Snell has noted, scholars of South Asian literature have often dismissed traditional Indian biographies "out of hand as a tedious impediment to verifiable historiography."[70] This notion was shared by some pioneers of Tibetan literature, who understood biographical works as largely fabulous concoctions that could be mined for the occasional historical nugget. Tucci, for example, writes that "human events have nothing to do with these works," although careful examination "can find in these shadows allusions, hints, names, sometimes even dates, which . . . illuminate the dark and still uncertain horizon of Tibetan history."[71] Studies of Milarepa's biographical tradition have tended to reflect similar attitudes. Van Tuyl was concerned primarily with demonstrating that a "historical knowledge of the life and teachings of the religious genius [Milarepa] is possible."[72] Tiso made a similar claim, describing the commonly held view of Milarepa's biographical tradition as a "creative literary process" leading from a historically factual root narrative to a perfusion of fabulous and possibly spurious tales.[73]

Another potent example of such a bias is Michael Aris's 1989 *Hidden Treasures and Secret Lives*, which examines the autobiography of acclaimed Bhutanese teacher Pema Lingpa (1450–1521) and the so-called "secret" biography of the Sixth Dalai Lama (1683–1706/46).[74] Aris's work takes the historical project to its logical end, adopting the stories surrounding these figures as a "case study in the mystique of Lamaism" by debunking them altogether. Although he is keenly attuned to both linguistic and cultural contexts, his aim—again echoing Oldenberg—is to "reveal these saints as human beings rather than as gods."[75]

However, certain forms of Tibetan biography and autobiography, especially those designated as "outer biographies," are indispensable sources for reconstructing local histories. Scholars have long understood the importance of such works as repositories of historical data.[76] Biographical works lie at the heart of A. I. Vostrikov's pioneering survey, *Tibetan Historical Literature,* completed in the mid 1930s, and a granular understanding of Tibetan history would be nearly impossible without reference to them. But the scanning of Tibetan life writing for historical information has until recently tended to supersede a more careful exploration of a work's literary qualities, structures, and functions. To treat Tibetan biographical literature simply as a target for data mining, to the point of overlooking it as an important cultural formation in its own right, is to miss the literary forest for the positivist trees.[77]

In the century following Delehaye's landmark book, views on the partition between the writing of a saint's life and the recording of history have softened. The term "hagiography" was previously framed as historiography's Other, cast in the pejorative shadow of panegyric, but the critical study of medieval Christendom has largely backed away from attempts to separate historical fact from pious fiction.[78] One widely recognized transformational shift occurred in 1965, with the publication of Czeck historian František Graus's work on Merovingian saints, *Volk, Herrscher und Heiliger im Reich der Merowinger.*[79] Graus refocused the study of religious biography in two important ways. First, he foregrounded the importance of hagiography for the study of social history. Religious biography thus could serve not only as a window into medieval religious life but also as "a privileged source for the study of social values."[80] Perhaps more importantly, Graus also emphasized that the would-be historian must pay close attention to the formal properties of the hagiographic text, never forgetting its "essential literary nature."[81] Careful scrutiny thus becomes a prerequisite for the historical interrogation of religious biography. Yet, if hagiography forms a window into the past, it is by no means a transparent one.[82] A saint's life is shaped by the text's language, style, and structure, which in turn reflect the author's larger agendas and concerns. "If historians . . . must be formalists," Geary notes, so too "formalists . . . must be historians," capable of interpreting the literary features of the text within its social context.[83]

Since Graus's study, the field of hagiography studies has been dominated by voices that creatively explore the social worlds of saints, including Peter Brown, Caroline Walker Bynum, and Thomas Heffernan, among many others. Geary identifies four trends in the ensuing wave of publications: 1) a broad move from the study of saints to the study of society, recognizing biography as an important source for understanding social history; 2) a move from studying the individual to studying the collective, using the materials related to a constellation of saints in order to better foreground broad social ideals; 3) an emphasis on secondary texts, including collections of miracles, liturgies, hymns, martyrologies, and the like; and 4) with the "linguistic turn," a recognition of the critical problems of genre, rhetoric, and intertextuality. In short, the modern study of hagiography can be characterized as

> a focus away from the saints and toward the society in which they were sanctified; a focus shifted from *vitae* to other sorts of hagiographic texts; a tendency to study collectives and serial records; and a growing recognition that these texts are not transparent windows into the saints' lives, their society, or even the spirituality of their age.[84]

As life writing has moved to the forefront of scholarship on Tibetan religious literature, a series of recent publications illustrate many of the trends Geary outlines. Two studies of Tibetan autobiographies in particular exemplify the move toward examining the social worlds of saints. Janet Gyatso's pathbreaking *Apparitions of the Self* (1999) explores modes of self-presentation in the autobiography of eighteenth-century master Jigmé Lingpa (1729–98), focusing on ideal notions of the self expressed as forms of religious and social agency. Kurtis Schaeffer's *Himalayan Hermitess* (2004) likewise highlights the gendered ideals and social norms of localized Buddhist communities on the Tibeto-Nepalese border through the life of the Buddhist nun Orgyan Chokyi.[85] The move from individual to collective (Geary's second trend) has been made in Hildegard Diemberger's *When a Woman Becomes a Religious Dynasty* (2007), which examines the lives of the acclaimed female master Samding Dorjé Phakmo and the major religious institution formed by the lineage of her recognized incarnations.

Geary's third point, describing the trend to examine secondary forms of biographical writing, has broad implications for the study of Tibetan literature. As noted previously, life writing in Tibet takes a tremendous range of literary forms: principally biography and autobiography, but also accounts of previous lives (*skyes rabs*, *'khrungs rabs*), personal histories (*byung ba brjod pa*), receipt records (*thob yig, gsan yig*), and journals and daybooks (*nyin deb, nyin tho*). We may further expand this list to include ritual texts such as supplications (*gsol 'debs*), encomia and eulogies (*stod pa*), aspiration prayers (*smon lam*), and guru yoga practices (*bla ma'i rnal 'byor*), together with visual and dramatic narratives in the plastic and performing arts. This is a particularly rich area for future research, reflecting what I have elsewhere described as Tibet's biographical culture.[86] Much effort remains to more carefully examine the forms and functions of these kinds of biographical works.

In his final point, Geary turns to the critical discussion of genre, rhetoric, and intertextuality. This book addresses these topics in detail as it studies the constitution of Milarepa's biographical corpus, the process of creating the yogin's canonical portrait, the legitimating role of the madman's authorial voice, and the author's process of rewriting the corpus's own literary history. Geary, however, is describing a more reductionist approach, in which some medievalists have turned to "deconstructing hagiographic texts into their constituent literary and rhetorical echoes until little remains" save a "tissue of rhetorical topoi and textual borrowings, incapable of telling us anything."[87]

Geary maintains that such advances in the study of hagiography are important, but in some cases remain limited in scope. "Even as we have pursued the saints and their society," he argues, "we have too often lost sight of what a hagiographic text is, what an author is, and what the society—whose values an author is purportedly reflecting in his or her text—is."[88] He advocates a new approach to religious biography that echoes Thomas, Lamotte, and others writing about the Buddha's life, encouraging us to "consider the hagiographic tradition within which it was produced; the other texts copied, adapted, read, or composed by the hagiographer; and the specific circumstances that brought him or her to focus this tradition on a particular work."[89] He further suggests that a Life "stands at a threefold intersection of genre, total textual production, and historical circumstance. Without any one of the three it is not fully comprehensible."[90] Such a tack represents, in the words of Felice Lifshitz, a move "away from bobbing for data to reconstructing mentalities and, consequently, to move from searching for the original version of each saint's biography to studying all extant versions, each in its particular compositional context."[91]

This book aims to advance our understanding of Tibetan life writing by taking seriously Geary's approach. To that end, it conducts a broad survey of textual production—here imagined as Milarepa's biographical corpus—by not a single author, but a variety of writers working within Milarepa's biographical tradition spanning four hundred years. This body of literature allows me to avoid the shell/kernel problem by focusing instead on the biographical process of Milarepa's life story, tracking structural transformations of the genre of Tibetan biography as it developed within a changing set of historical, institutional, and doctrinal circumstances.

I adopt such an approach by formulating a metaphorical anatomy of the biographical corpus. Dissecting the corpus is not an exploratory maneuver, lancing off tumorlike accretions in search of an untainted historical persona within. It is rather a systemic approach to life writing that identifies broad structural similarities in versions across anatomical planes and maps their relationship to the body of literature as a whole. Examining the life stories of a figure such as Milarepa is no longer a matter of taking sides between the opposing factions of mytho-centrism and historical positivism. In the case of Milarepa, like that of the Buddha, the historical figure is distant enough and the biographical tradition complex enough to make searching for a historical figure divorced from the literary tradition an unenviable task. As Geary notes, the aim now is to "rediscover the meaning of hagiographic texts to their producers, the interrelationships among modes of hagiographic production and distribution, and the uses of texts."[92] Following his line of analysis, this study foregrounds the life of Milarepa's life story. If Milarepa the saint is to be found anywhere, it is not as a cold corpse lying beneath all the books, but embodied within the biographical corpus formed of the literature itself, a body of writing that authors transformed over time into a lifelike portrait.

One of the structural systems this study addresses as it dissects the various layers of Mila's biographical tradition is that of representation. A view that persists in discussions of hagiography asserts that the genre emphasizes the idealized image of a life over a life individually lived. This position holds that "the sacred biographer is not primarily concerned to provide a narrative portrait or 'likeness' of the subject. Establishing the mythical ideal—the biographical image—takes precedence over a simple chronicling of biographical facts."[93] Recent studies have begun to argue that authors of sacred biography were frequently driven to strike a balance between these extremes, a midpoint between Senart's approach that loses the human individual and Oldenberg's that loses the divine. "The sacred biographer," Heffernan argues, "sought to maintain a difficult balance between the narrative depiction of not quite a demigod . . . and a moral everyman. If this characterization . . . is weighted too far toward the supernatural, we lose the man, while if the exemplary is underemphasized, we end up without our saint."[94]

It has recently been demonstrated that authors of Tibetan life writing were indeed concerned with representations of individual lives.[95] The works of Milarepa's biographical tradition indicate a similar concern for representing the yogin as both exemplar and individual. As the life story matured, the relationship between these representations became increasingly complex, populating the story with myriad narratives describing details of an individual life, while framing the whole structurally and conceptually as an archetypical liberation tale. Ultimately the madman, Tsangnyön Heruka, exploits the tension between these two representations most effectively, forcefully rejecting the yogin's status as a miraculous emanation while structuring the biography after the Buddha's own life story in twelve acts. And the tension between the portrait of Milarepa as a struggling individual and the cotton-clad *repa* as an enlightened saint helped to animate the tradition.

In one sense, through the dissection of Milarepa's corpus, this book forms its own narrative: a biography of the yogin's life story, incorporating a birth and gradual development unfolding over a span of centuries. It tells the story of biographical transformations over time, the gradual embodiment of Milarepa's life story culminating in Tsangnyön Heruka's version that, in the eyes of many readers, presents an image both lifelike and enlivened. Yet this study, like all forms of life writing, maintains its own literary conceits. Just as founding figures of religious traditions rarely understood themselves as founders—a position more frequently projected upon them by subsequent devotees—the authors of early biographical works did not understand their texts as fragments that would later be integrated into a larger whole. The image of a biographical body comes into view with Tsangnyön Heruka's work, and through its lens, the body appears anatomically complete.

Tsangnyön Heruka's representation of Milarepa has formed the yogin's enduring image, in both Tibet and the West. But the madman has also dramatically reshaped the ways earlier versions of the yogin's life story are understood. "The fact is," Jorge Luis Borges writes, "each author creates his own precursors. His work modifies our conception of the past, as it will modify the future."[96] Early texts of Milarepa's biographical tradition may have been fragmentary, but they were not fragments until cast in the light of a fully formed corpus. To a large extent, it is the madman who has served to rewrite the yogin's past, by incorporating early texts of the tradition into his own work as the underlying anatomy of a larger biographical body. And in the face of Tsangnyön's creation, the early biographical tradition all but slipped out of sight.

PLAN OF THE BOOK

The anatomy of Milarepa's biographical corpus is examined here in five chapters. The principal subject matter is the works written in the period up to and including 1488, when the standard version of the Life was completed. Most of the texts considered have received relatively little attention in previous studies of the biographical tradition; numerous works have come to light only recently and are presented here for the first time. Where appropriate, the book also makes use of more historiographic forms of Tibetan literature in which brief biographies appear, such as religious histories (chos 'byung), annals (deb gter), and histories (lo rgyus). I have generally not addressed the yogin's biographical literature appearing subsequent to the standard version, except in several cases where works record significant discrepancies or add substantially to the discussion. Each chapter begins with an "orientations" section, which establishes the historical, political, and literary context for the discussion that follows. And each concludes with "reflections" that underline the main ideas and issues covered, while exploring some of their further implications.

Chapter 1 examines the earliest biographical fragments and narratives recording Milarepa's life. It describes a biographical birth that took place at the moment of the yogin's death and identifies the elements that would begin to form a rudimentary life story. The chapter opens by addressing a purported autobiographical voice associated mainly with the standard version of Tsangnyön Heruka, but also found in earlier works. It then describes the works attributed to two of Milarepa's earliest biographers, Ngendzong Repa and Gampopa, both close disciples of the yogin writing, so tradition holds, from their own personal experiences. The first examples of narrative fragments also address the relationship between life writing and the recording and transmission of specific doctrinal cycles of tantric instructions.

The chapter then examines Gampopa's version, which forms what is likely Milarepa's earliest complete life story spanning his birth, his deeds, and his death. Although primitive, this work established a basic format that would be adopted in almost every biographical portrait that followed. The chapter concludes with a discussion of what might be called a "rhetoric of orality." An assumption pervading many early studies of the biographical tradition is that the life story circulated only in oral form for nearly four centuries, until it was finally inscribed by Tsangnyön Heruka in his standard version. The presumed orality of Milarepa's early biographical tradition served to mute the extensive literary corpus that forms much of the present study.

Chapter 2 explores a form of life writing I have called "proto-Life/Songs" (proto-*rnam mgur*), signifying the basic literary structure that influenced the writing of Milarepa's life story for centuries to come. The spread of the yogin's teachings in the century or so following his death created a need for new forms of literature to authorize those transmissions within specific communities and institutions. Among these are the so-called "golden rosary collections" to which many of the proto-texts belong. For the first time, the life story formulates a skeletal structure consisting of a brief biographical narrative and song collection upon which more detailed accounts would eventually be hung—uniquely suited for inclusion within the brief space of golden rosary texts. The six works surveyed in this chapter span several centuries and are drawn from various sources, including the collected writings of influential Kagyu masters and independent publications.

Chapter 3 analyzes what were perhaps the most influential works in the formulation of the early corpus. These are what I have called the biographical compendia, and in them the representation of Milarepa's life takes on the finely grained, lifelike quality that would later appear in the standard version. The compendia stand as the mature versions of the proto-works appearing in the previous chapter; they combine structured and well-crafted biographical narratives from the early life with extensive song collections, and conclude with elaborate descriptions of the yogin's death.

The chapter first discusses the text known as *The Twelve Great Disciples* (*Bu chen bcu gnyis*), a work identified nearly four decades ago but until recently remained in relative obscurity. The chapter then moves to the mysterious tradition of extended biographical works known as *The Black Treasury* (*Mdzod nag ma*). These materials flowed directly from *The Twelve Great Disciples* and were closely connected to the influential Karma Kagyu hierarchs called the Karmapas—especially the illustrious Third Karmapa, Rangjung Dorjé (1284–1339). Until now, little was known about these works, but they are here shown to form the most extensive and complex records of stories and songs associated with Milarepa. These large biographical compendia offer an extraordinary window into the early biographical tradition, and indicate that both life and songs were fully established well before Tsangnyön Heruka began to formulate his version of the Life and Songs.

Chapter 4 examines the standard versions of Milarepa's Life and Songs in the context of the life of their author, Tsangnyön Heruka, during the late fifteenth century. It first surveys Tsangnyön's own early life and his role in defining a new form of Buddhist practice in Tibet—that of the religious madman, the *nyönpa* (*smyon pa*), from which his name derives. The chapter then turns to the influences and inspirations that led to his crafting Milarepa's life story. It discusses the traditional descriptions of his considerable activities in reimagining and recrafting the biographical texts as well as their execution, production, and distribution, including his use of woodblock printing, a technology that had only recently entered mainstream use in central Tibet, as well as his commissioning of related painted and ritual materials. In this light, Tsangnyön Heruka might be considered one of Tibet's first multimedia biographers. The chapter concludes by reflecting on Tsangnyön's contributions to the biographical tradition, including an examination of Milarepa's changing role as both miraculous emanation and ordinary human. In the end, we find that Tsangnyön has not so much rewritten Milarepa's life story as brought the biographical corpus to life.

Chapter 5 unpacks this process of vivification, discussing the ascendance of Tsangnyön Heruka's standard version of the life story, particularly the relationship to Milarepa that he himself maintained and that was later promulgated by his disciples. Past research has understood Tsangnyön as remaining somewhat agnostic about his own status as an incarnation; we find here strong evidence that he maintained a close relationship with the yogin throughout his life, and on several occasions explicitly claimed to be Milarepa's reembodiment. Tsangnyön's followers continued to actively promote this association after his death. The chapter concludes with a discussion of the changes this brings to the authorial voice of his work and explores the reasons for the ascendance and continued popularity of his literary works.

Following a chapter on conclusions and an epilogue, which reflects on the nature of an enlivened biography and the implications for its study, appendix 1 presents a translation of the earliest biography of Milarepa by his close disciple Gampopa. Appendix 2 provides translations of the colophons of the most important works in Milarepa's biographical tradition. Appendix 3 lists concordances for several of the extended biographical compendia, which allows for a close structural comparison of these works.

NOTES ON TERMS AND TRANSLATIONS

A few words on my own terminology are in order. In general, I use "life" to refer to the stories and deeds associated with Milarepa's biographical tradition, the yogin's life in its most quotidian sense as the content of his biography; "Life" serves as a synonym for biography or *vita*, so "the Life" may refer to any given biographical text. The terms *Life* and *Songs* (in italics), as well as "standard works" and "standard version," refer specifically to Tsangnyön Heruka's versions of *The Life of Milarepa* (Mi la ras pa'i rnam thar) and *The Hundred Thousand Songs of Milarepa* (Mi la ras pa'i mgur 'bum). I have also adopted a number of terms to describe forms of biographical writing pertinent to Milarepa's biographical tradition, including "proto-Life/Songs," "biographical compendium," and "biographical network." Their usage is described in subsequent chapters.

Tibetan proper names are rendered, with some modification, according to the phonetic system developed at the University of Virginia, and their correct transliterated Tibetan spellings are listed in the index. Transliterations for some technical terms are provided in the first instance when they may be helpful. Transliterations of Tibetan terms have been retained throughout the notes, which will be of greater interest to the specialist. Since many place names consist of compound toponyms, they have generally been transcribed as recorded in the text, and not unpacked (i.e., "Ngari Gungtang Mangyul [Mnga' ris gung thang mang yul]," not "Gungtang and Mangyul in Ngari").

In the translations, I have generally tried to find English equivalents for all Tibetan words, but occasionally have substituted Sanskrit renderings for certain technical terms such as saṃsāra and samādhi, especially in poetry when it suits the meter. I have maintained two Tibetan words in their original language: *jetsün* (rje btsun) and *repa* (ras pa). The latter economically avoids repeating the somewhat cumbersome "cotton-clad," especially in songs where Milarepa uses the term self-reflexively.

The term *jetsün*, a title of respect, translates the Sanskrit *bhaṭṭāraka*, and is defined in *The Great Tibetan Dictionary* as 1) "foremost, supreme," and 2) "someone described as a *lord* (jé) because he is like a helmsman among guides for others on the path to liberation, and as *venerable* (*tsün*) because he is utterly unsullied by the non-virtues of the three gates [of body, speech, and mind]."[97] Gene Smith has noted that "*rje btsun* was and still is applied to personages descended from respectable lineages, particularly those of Ldong, Stong, Bse, and Rmu, who have also taken religious vows."[98] The title is difficult to translate precisely and is often rendered as "Venerable Lord" in accordance with the definition above. Perhaps the closest and most poetic translation I have seen so far is "Majestic Lord," coined by Hubert Decleer. The title is found ubiquitously in references to the yogin, sometimes together with the name Milarepa (frequently in the abbreviated form Jetsün Mila), although it also appears on its own, in which case he is simply the Jetsün. I have therefore chosen to retain the term in its original Tibetan, treating it almost as part of his personal name. In some instances, the translations here are provisional, since their precise meaning was unclear even to my Tibetan informants.

As far as possible, dates for individuals and institutions are based on the electronic database of the Tibetan Buddhist Resource Center (TBRC) founded by E. Gene Smith.

A number of Tibetan materials were published or came to my attention too late to incorporate into this study. Zhijé Ripa's *Illuminating Lamp of Sun and Moon Beams* (*Rje btsun mid la ras pa'i rnam par thar pa nyi zla'i 'od zer sgron ma*) is now available in several published editions.[99] Dpal Brtsegs publishers have also released several collections of texts related to the life and works of both Milarepa and his guru, Marpa.[100] These should prove invaluable to future research on Milarepa's literary tradition.

1

EARLIEST SOURCES

A BIOGRAPHICAL BIRTH

ORIENTATIONS

Apropos of Biographical Anatomy

DAWN BREAKS on the morning after Milarepa's cremation, and his longtime follower Rechungpa wakes from a wondrous but disheartening dream: ḍākinī maidens were carrying off his master's mortal remains in the form of a radiant sphere of light. Anxious, he rouses his fellow disciples, and together they peer into the funerary cell, only to find the chamber empty. Neither ashes nor bones remain; gone too are the sacred pearl-like relics, causing even greater dismay. Celestial goddesses had swept clean the yogin's every physical trace, leaving nothing behind. Heartbroken, the assembly instead inherits his few worldly possessions: a cap, a walking staff, strips of his cotton robe, pieces of hard rock sugar. Such is the record of Milarepa's passing as told in the fifteenth-century standard version of his life story.

But in addition to these everyday items, Milarepa's disciples and patrons also kept stories of the yogin's life, his travels, his ascetic practices, and—perhaps most importantly—his songs. And although Mila's mortal remains had vanished from sight, his life would take shape once again through the gradual recording and reworking of these accounts. What might have first decomposed was eventually recomposed through the gradual codification of his biographical corpus. This emerged first as rudimentary outlines, a simple skeletal frame. Over time, the structure was modeled by subsequent literary works, adding depth and detail to its inner coil until finally—some four centuries later—a standard life story appeared, breathing life back into the biography. As the yogin's life came to an end, so his life story took birth.

This study is, in part, an exercise in literary archaeology, sifting through strata of textual fragments and narrative shards laid upon the bedrock of Milarepa's literary history. But it is equally an experiment in biographical anatomy, examining visceral layers of life writing that came to portray the yogin as a fully fleshed individual. It thus begins in this chapter with the deepest biographical stratum, the innermost layers that constitute Mila's biographical frame. These are the fragmentary records and notes written by two of the yogin's direct disciples, Ngendzong Repa and Gam- popa, with an additional reference to a work purportedly by Rechungpa.

In some cases these writings are referred to as a Life or biography (*rnam thar*), and they do fulfill the minimal requirements for such, as described in the introduction. Yet they are not fully formed life stories, at least as those are commonly understood. Ngendzong's work reviewed in this chapter contains great narrative detail, but lies removed from the yogin's larger spiritual career; Gampopa's text maintains a broad sense of biographic chronology (birth, activities, death), but achieves this through a series of largely ambiguous and disconnected vignettes. Both are sketches. They do, however, provide the core components of literary structure and narrative detail—the biographical frame—around which mature versions of the biography could be hung. Thus they mark an incipient form of life writing: a prototype for a combined life story and song collection, analyzed in the next chapter, which I have termed the "proto-Life/Songs" (proto-*rnam mgur*). These works first appeared in the context of abbreviated lineage records before serving as a model for more complete, more compelling, and perhaps more lifelike representations of the yogin's life and teachings.

As this chapter explores the early biographical fragments, it will also begin to address two other issues central to the tradition: the legitimation of biographical writing and the relationship between writing lives and promulgating Dharma. These early sources make explicit and repeated claims about their authenticity by stressing the close association of subject and biographer, teacher and disciple, absent from later versions. Ngendzong Repa is portrayed as an ideal archivist, endowed with perfect memory, and said to have verified his sketches directly with Milarepa on multiple occasions. Gampopa's text similarly stresses the direct transmission of its biographical portrait, recorded in the words of a witness to the subject's life.

Milarepa's biographical tradition, like his life itself, was closely tied to the spread of tantric instructions known as the aural transmissions (*snyan brgyud*), which became the seminal yogic practices of many early Kagyu practitioners. It is not surprising, therefore, that early representations of Milarepa's life developed in concert with literature documenting the aural transmission lineages. Even the *Blue Annals* (*Deb gter sngon po*), a late publication relative to Mila's biographical tradition, records the master's life not in the context of his guru's lineage (the so-called Marpa Kagyu) but specifically in terms of the promulgation of two aural transmission lines.[1] Authors of early biographical works were also important figures in the redaction and transmission of aural transmission texts; among them, Ngendzong Repa stands out most clearly.

Autobiography in Biography

Before turning to the writings of the yogin's disciples, however, we should first listen to a distinctly autobiographical voice rising through the biographical tradition, recording what are purported to be the words of Milarepa himself. Tibetan interest in self-authored life stories can be traced back at least to the time of Milarepa's own nascent biographical tradition, and to authors such as the twelfth-century master Lama Zhang, himself one of Mila's early biographers.[2] The genre of autobiography later flourished in Tibet, reaching a crescendo in the seventeenth century with the Fifth Dalai Lama's exhaustive multivolume memoir.[3]

The stories and songs of Milarepa's life are filled with first-person accounts; the standard version of his life story is rendered almost entirely as autobiographical narrative—a literary conceit that will be addressed in detail in chapters 4 and 5. Yet there is little evidence to suggest that Milarepa took any interest in recording his own life on paper. It appears he did not keep notes or diaries, and there is no reason to believe he requested his followers to do so.[5] Neither did he record his own songs as did, for example, the famed nineteenth-century master Zhapkar Tsokdruk Rangdrol (1781–1851) in his own magisterial autobiography.[6] As with the figure of the Buddha himself, every word ascribed to Mila has been mediated through one or more generations of disciples, authors, and scribes; there is little, if anything, we can claim to know about him directly.

Nevertheless, many of Milarepa's songs—in both the early biographies and the later versions—are distinctly self-reflexive. This stems, in part, from the style of verse for which he was famed: "songs of realization" (*mgur*) said to illuminate the personal experiences gained through sustained yogic meditation. These songs could describe a wide range of motivations and insights, from the meditator's dissatisfaction with worldly life and eventual renunciation to the hardships of solitary retreat and the blossoming of Buddhist awakening. One example, preserved in many early versions of the life story, describes Milarepa's overwhelming feeling of impermanence and renunciation upon finding his childhood home destroyed and his family broken:

Alas. Alas. Ay me. Ay me. How sad.
People invested in the things of life's round—
I think of them over and over; again and again I despair.
They engage and engage, and stir up from its depths so much torment.
They whirl and they whirl and are cast in the depths of life's round.[7]

Later he adds:

Alas. The things of life's round have no essence.
Ephemeral. Ephemeral. No essence.
Changing and changing. No essence.
Uncertain. Uncertain. No essence.[8]

Indeed, Milarepa's songs of realization are deeply personal records of both the context and the content of his spiritual career even as they are—in their written form—clearly the products of an outside author. And while the yogin's early biographies tell his life story by means of a third-person narrative, the songs of realization retain a deeply autobiographical flavor.

Some of his poetry likewise echoes Tibet's early epic tales of King Gesar, in which subjects narrate broad sweeps of their life, frequently introducing themselves with a stereotyped formula: "Do you know me? If you don't, I am so and so."[9] Milarepa repeatedly begins his verses with similar phrasing, as in this reply made to a passing merchant, recorded in Gampopa's early work:

Have you a clue who's before you now?
If you don't know who this is here now—
I am the yogin Mila.[10]

The corpus of Milarepa's poetry records numerous songs in which the yogin further recounts details of his life—the sins committed in his youth, the difficulties he underwent during his training—to illustrate the depth of his renunciation or the power of his devotion. One example occurs during his first encounter with future disciple Zhiwa Ö, affording an opportune moment for the autobiographical song that follows. The brash young man asks the yogin, "Where is your homeland and hermetic abode? Who is your lama? What did you do for studies? Which is your chosen deity? Where have you come from now?" In response, Mila reviews his vita in brief, here recorded in its earliest form from the compendium known as *The Twelve Great Disciples (Bu chen bcu gnyis):*[11]

Well then, now, my fine young man,
Inquisitive boy, listen to me here.
If you don't know who I am,
I am Milarepa.
I hail from the navel center Gungtang Mé.
I've studied in both Ü and Tsang.
From fatherly Gyertön and Ngakmi
Down to Rongtön Lhaga,
I've had some ten kind lamas.
I listened to their Dharma, the tantras making mind manifest,
I penetrated their views and intentions and came to understand them.
In particular, from Lhajé Nupchung
I received the wrathful mantra Zadong Marnak.
Though said to be accomplished in deed,
I yet held some small reservations about him.
It was said, in Lho Drowolung there lived a man
Possessing the blessings of Lord Nāropa and Maitrī,
Whose mind had met reality itself,
Whose body pierced the essence of interdependence.
Father Lotsāwa, whose fame had spread afar—
Just hearing his name set my hairs atingle.
I endured hardship on the road and arrived before him;
Merely seeing his face transformed my outlook.
He's certainly been my guru for lifetimes over,
Unrivaled Lord Lhodrakpa.
I possessed no material wealth
For the kind Jetsün,

So I reduced myself to dust [offering] service of body and mind.
I received the profound tantra of Hevajra,
And, in particular, Naro's path of means.
I received in full the four dreamlike empowerments
In the blessed glorious Cakrasaṃvara.
I was introduced to the Mahāmudrā Dharma.
I saw the essence of mind's genuine nature.
I realized the ground of reality itself, construct-free.
In general, I gathered nine great instructions
In the four streams of aural tantra.
I drew out the essence of the nine profound points.
For meditation I practiced wheels, channels, and drops
And mastered both mind and mental energies.
Thus am I a yogin of space:
Within, I've fully mixed the four gatherings;
Without, I've no fear of elements such as water.
My practice place is Gyalgi Tsibri.
This morning I came from Gungtang Tö;
It's uncertain where I'll go tonight.
Mine is such a yogic way of life.
This, young man, is contentment. Where'll you go to be happy?[12]

While it is difficult to gauge the degree to which songs such as these record the yogin's own words, examples are found among the earliest works of the biographical tradition. There is little reason to doubt that some captured at least the tenor of his poetry, if not its precise wording. Such self-sung biographies may have served as a model for Milarepa's close disciples recording their master's life story for the first time.

If the origins of Mila's autobiographical voice in the examples above remain somewhat opaque, later versions are murkier still, as the boundaries defining biography and autobiography are almost entirely breached. This is true most notably in Tsangnyön Heruka's standard version, where the biographer strategically adopts an autobiographical posture, claiming the subject's legitimating voice as his own. I will save a detailed exploration of this topic for chapters 4 and 5; here I will note just one example of how first-person narratives have been used to persuasively claim both authenticity and power for the text early on in the biographical tradition. In the days preceding Milarepa's death, according to the early compendia and later copied by Tsangnyön, the master responds in this way to his lay devotees' request that he visit their homelands one last time:

. . . .
In the land of Abhirati, may I meet
Those who've seen my face or heard my speech,
Remembered my life story (*rnam thar*),
Or those who've heard of it or of my name.

In the land of Abhirati, may I meet
Those who act and practice with my life (*rnam thar*) in mind,
Those who ask for, teach, or listen to it,
Read it, or pay it veneration,
And those who emulate my life's account (*rnam thar*).
. . . .
For those who practice an ascetic life
Lies merit beyond measure.
For those who push others to adopt that life
Lies gratitude beyond measure.
For those who hear my life story (*rnam thar*)
Lies blessing beyond measure.
Through these three immeasurable blessings
May they be liberated by merely hearing [my story], and then
Achieve their aims through its contemplation.[13]

In this passage, Milarepa's words are made to echo the author's own as he refers not so much to the life as lived event but to the Life as literary document. The yogin, and through him the author himself, argue for the liberative efficacy of Milarepa's life as a book to be read, an oral transmission to be requested, a narrative to be recollected, and a lifestyle to be emulated. The life story here becomes an authoritative locus of religious power for individuals who "ask for it, teach, or listen to it, read it, or pay it veneration," and the product is validated not through the author's proximity to the subject, but by the subject himself. Although Milarepa's life story would become the focus of a renewed cult under Tsangnyön Heruka's direction, the foundation for such activity appears to have been laid early on.[14] The author has adopted an autobiographical voice to "establish the text itself as a document worthy of reverence, as a relic."[15] And as such a relic, the corpus of Milarepa's biographical tradition has begun to fill the empty space left behind by the yogin's corporeal remains.

NGENDZONG REPA'S *STRAND OF PEARLS* AND *ROSARY OF NECTAR LIGHT*

Ngendzong the Compiler

The earliest literary sources for Milarepa's biographical tradition are those attributed to two of his closest disciples: Ngendzong Changchup Gyalpo[16] (b. late eleventh century), and Gampopa Sönam Rinchen (1079–1153). The former took an active interest in life writing and was responsible for recording a number of important Kagyu biographies.[17] He authored at least four chapters later incorporated into all of Milarepa's extensive biographies, and he may have played a central role in editing the first great biographical collection, commonly known as *The Twelve Great Disciples* (*Bu chen bcu gnyis*), examined in detail in chapter 3. It was Ngendzong who, for the first time, began the process of assembling fragments into the biography's skeletal structure.

Details of Ngendzong Changchup Gyalpo's life are recorded in a number of historical sources, including the *Blue Annals*, the *Religious History of Lhorong* (*Lho rong chos 'byung*), and an independent biography, which according to its colophon was "written by Lord Dampa Rechen and slightly improved by the yogin Götsangpa Gönpo Dorjé (1189–1258)."[18] His dates are not recorded, but sources agree he was born in the region of Chemlung in Latö Lho, likely in the late eleventh century, into the Ngendzong clan and a long family line of tantric practitioners.[19] By the age of eighteen, he had mastered the major Mahāyāna philosophical texts—and the five treatises of Maitreya, in particular—for which he earned the title *tönpa* (*ston pa*), or teacher. He also "received in full the initiations, explanations, and oral instructions of the aural transmissions from Lord Goyak."[20]

According to Ngendzong's biography, he first encounters his future guru when Milarepa arrives in Chemlüng begging for alms, accompanied by his disciple Seban Repa.[21] Ngendzong notes their yogic attire and humbly states that he too is a teacher of secret mantra. Milarepa responds with a song on the ultimate view, meditation, and action. Filled with devotion, Ngendzong offers the master his service, following him to the famed retreat site of Lapchi. This episode was later copied into Tsangnyön

Heruka's *Songs* with minor changes.[22] Ngendzong then spent seventeen years "inseparable from the lama, like the body and its shadow."[23]

Foremost, perhaps, among Ngendzong's qualities was his faculty of perfect memory. His biography opens with the verse:

> I respectfully bow down at the feet of the teacher Ngendzong:
> Learned sovereign who first perfected study,
> Accomplished sovereign who then perfected meditation,
> The one named Bo[dhi] [Ra]ja, scholar-adept who attained an indelible memory.[24]

It is not surprising, then, that Ngendzong should be credited as one of the earliest redactors of Milarepa's teaching and biography. With such mnemic ability, Ngendzong is reminiscent of Ānanda who, with perfect and total recall, is said to have recited the entire collection of sūtras at the first monastic council after the Buddha's death. Indeed, Ngendzong's biography continues: "He brought appearances under his power and then performed inconceivable enlightened activity in taming disciples. He attained an indelible memory and then compiled the sayings of the great Jetsün Milarepa, thereby benefiting beings."[25]

The compilations Ngendzong assembled were twofold: a systematization of Milarepa's instructions on the aural tantra (*snyan rgyud*, S. *karṇatantra*) lineages and a collection of narrative accounts recording Milarepa's activities and songs that were absorbed into the biographical tradition.

Ngendzong and the Aural Transmissions

The Tibetan term *nyengyü* (*snyan rgyud*, "aural tantra") and its homophone (spelled *snyan brgyud*, "aural transmission") are both closely linked to Milarepa's teaching tradition. The latter term—defined in the *Great Tibetan Dictionary* as "the pith instructions transmitted from ear to ear through a succession of masters"—is a general one, used in various contexts.[26] There is a well-known aural transmission of Tangtong Gyalpo (1361–1485) and a division of the Sakya Path and Fruition (*lam 'bras*) teachings into four aural transmissions (*snyan brgyud bzhi*). In the tradition following Milarepa, the aural transmission generally refers to specific instructions of the *nyengyü*, and within the biographical corpus, the image of instructions passing from mouth to ear came to symbolize the fundamental importance of the guru-disciple relationship.

The aural transmission (frequently referred to as the *Bde mchog snyan brgyud*, "the aural transmission of Saṃvara") originates with a root text, *Vajra Verses of the Aural Tantra* (*Karṇatantravajrapāda*, extant only in a Tibetan translation as *Snyan rgyud rdo rje tshig rkang*), said to derive from the primordial buddha Vajradhara, and later recorded by the Bengali adept Tilopa.[27] This text describes three main cycles: the transmission wish-fulfilling jewel (*brgyud pa yid bzhin nor bu*); the ripening path wish-fulfilling jewel (*smin lam yid bzhin nor bu*); and the liberating path wish-fulfilling jewel (*grol lam yid bzhin nor bu*).[28] The aural transmission also included a series of ancillary instructions that, according to traditional accounts, Tilopa received as a series of symbolic one-line verses from the formless ḍākinīs. These instructions and their later traditions thus became known as "the nine Dharma cycles of the formless ḍākinī aural tantra" (*lus med mkha' 'gro snyan rgyud chos skor dgu*) and are sometimes collectively referred to as the "aural tantra wish-fulfilling jewel" (*snyan rgyud yid bzhin nor bu*).[29]

Tilopa taught these instructions to the Bengali master Nāropa, who in turn passed them in part to the Tibetan translator Marpa, and in full to the Indian master Tiphupa. Marpa later transmitted four of the nine instruction cycles to Milarepa, who then famously sent his pupil Rechungpa to India in order to receive the remaining five from Tiphupa. Rechungpa returned to Tibet with the complete *nyengyü* instructions, and offered them to Milarepa. At least three of Mila's disciples (Ngendzong, Rechungpa, and Gampopa) received and transmitted these instructions in independent lines, which became known respectively as the *Ngendzong Nyengyü* (*Ngan rdzong snyan brgyud*), *Rechung Nyengyü* (*Ras chung snyan brgyud*), and *Dakpo Nyengyü* (*Dwags po snyan brgyud*).[30]

Even as Milarepa's first generation of spiritual descendants began to set down in writing the yogin's instructions and his life story, disagreements seem to have arisen over who possessed a complete transmission of the aural tantra lineage. According to the *Blue Annals*, Rechungpa returned from India and

offered the nine Dharma cycles to the lama [Mila], and the lama granted them to the teacher Ngamdzong. Ngamdzong then composed a variety of texts [on them], and the lineage that spread from them was called the "aural transmission of Saṃvara" (*bde mchog snyan brgyud*). The lineage that spread elsewhere from Rechungpa was known as the "aural transmission of Rechungpa" (*ras chung snyan brgyud*).[31]

Ngendzong's own biography is, unsurprisingly, more direct in singling him out as the legitimate holder of the lineage, stating that he received the aural transmission of Cakrasaṃvara together with its initiations, instructions, and *samaya* commitments. It then adds, "[Ngendzong] has said, 'In particular, this instruction of the wish-fulfilling gem aural tantra was not given to anyone other than me.'"[32] The text later notes,

> There is also the extraordinary Dharma not known to others, the instructions of the wish-fulfilling gem aural tantra: [Ngendzong] put them in annotated form from the speech of the great Jetsün Lord [Mila] without diminishing or exaggerating them. Thus, they became known as the aural tantra of Ngendzong.[33]

Ngendzong's Biographical Records

Ngendzong also played a central, though frequently overlooked, role in recording his guru's life story. Indeed, Ngendzong's writings are the earliest identifiable fragments in Milarepa's biographical tradition. Chapter 3 will examine the close relationship between Ngendzong's spread of the aural transmission and his likely involvement in helping to craft the yogin's earliest biographical compendium. For the moment, we will quickly survey Ngendzong's signed contributions to Milarepa's biographical tradition.

In the brief colophon to his version of the Collected Songs, Tsangnyön Heruka writes that Milarepa's songs were "retained with an indelible memory and recorded by his heart-son disciples."[34] Of the fifty-eight chapters comprising Tsangnyön's collection, however, only four have independent colophons identifying the author's name; Ngendzong appears in each one. They are found in all of the early biographical compendia and were retained in identical form by Tsangnyön for his standard work.[35]

Unusual in both linguistic style and content, these four chapters form a narrative miniseries describing Milarepa's encounters with the five Long Life Sisters (Tshe ring mched lnga).[36] The colophons to these chapters (presented in appendix 2 from their earliest forms in *The Twelve Great Disciples*) make clear that Ngendzong and his vajra brother Zhiwa Ö understood their main task to be preserving the transmission of their guru's tantric instructions. But though their role as biographers was secondary, the presence of these four accounts in every known biographical compendium demonstrates the blurred line between doctrinal record and transmission narrative.[37] Van Tuyl has described the quartet as "a secret manual for the most advanced mystics . . . never intended for general distribution."[38] A similar designation was applied to the entire work of *The Twelve Great Disciples* and emphasized by its authors/editors at the end of the text. The biographical document used to locate and legitimate a particular doctrinal system thus comes to embody the system itself.

Ngendzong notes the first chapter forms "an outpouring of 'skipping over' (*thod rgal*) experience" that should not be written down. "But," he continues,

> For fear that I might forget them,
> And in order to inspire and delight
> Future holders of the family line,
> I have written it according to the lama's speech.[39]

The practice of "skipping over" refers to a specific yogic technique associated with the Great Perfection (*rdzogs chen*) practices transmitted by Nyingma masters. The content was considered secret, to be revealed only to "great meditators who will appear in the future," lest they incite the *ḍākinīs*' displeasure, and it was only after requesting permission three times from Milarepa himself that Ngendzong was allowed to continue. The second chapter in this series, an account of the five sisters' inquiry about the nature of *bodhicitta*, was coauthored by Ngendzong and Zhiwa Ö, only after the latter conferred with the goddess Tseringma herself and consulted three times with their lama. The third chapter, instructions on the intermediate state (*bar do*), contains "songs of symbolic meaning" that were "recorded in writing with the power of indelible words by Ngendzong Tönpa Bodhirāja and Repa Zhiwa Ö, who requested them." The final chapter, describing Milarepa's practice of sexual yoga with the five goddesses as his consorts (*karmamudrā*), was likewise "recorded by the fortunate Ngendzong Bodhirāja and Repa Zhiwa Ö after presenting a maṇḍala offering and making supplications."

Indicative, perhaps, of the status these four chapters hold as both biographical narratives and records of tantric instructions is the colophon Tsangnyön appends to his version of the quartet:

> The instruction cycles of the long life [sisters] contain the command seal (*bka' rgya*) of the preceptor, the glorious Zhepa Dorjé; the secret seal (*gsang ba'i rgya*) of the petitioners, the five *ḍākinī* sisters; and the *samaya* seal (*dam tshig gi rgya*) of the two compilers, Ācārya Bodhirāja and Repa Zhiwa Ö.[40]

Three of these chapters were also absorbed from the biographical tradition directly into Ngendzong's aural transmission lineage, and later transcribed with commentary by the luminary scholar Jamgön Kongtrül Lodrö Tayé (1813–99) in his *Treasury of Oral Instructions* (*Gdams ngag mdzod*) under the title *Scripture of the Three Long Life Cycles: The Root Pith Instructions of the Glorious Cakrasaṃvara Aural Transmission According to Ngam rdzong* (*Dpal 'khor lo bde mchog ngam rdzong snyan brgyud kyi man ngag rtsa ba tshe ring skor gsum gyi gzhung*).[41]

GAMPOPA'S *LIVES OF LORD MARPA AND JETSÜN MILA*

A Life in Skeletal Form

For the earliest example of a *namtar* proper, we must turn to the work of Gampopa Sönam Rinchen, one of Mila's principal disciples and a leading figure in the rise of the nascent Kagyu religious institution. Gampopa trained as a doctor at an early age, so he is commonly referred to as Dakpo Lhajé (the physician from Dakpo), but renounced his career and received monastic ordination at the age of twenty-five, following the death of his wife. He initially studied under masters of the Kadam tradition and met Milarepa shortly before the yogin's death.[42] He later marked his teaching career by blending Kadam and Kagyu streams of instruction, developing dual systems of sūtra- and tantra-based Mahāmudrā, and promoting Milarepa's tradition of yogic practice within a monastic framework.

Gampopa's *Collected Works* open with two short biographical texts, emphasizing the direct line of his spiritual succession from early Kagyu masters and preserving what are perhaps the earliest known examples of Kagyu *namtar*. The first text records the lives of Tilopa and Nāropa; the second continues this lineage with accounts of Marpa and Milarepa. Both works are brief: their stories are sparsely woven around a skeletal frame, proceeding in jagged steps with little attention to literary styling or narrative flow.

It is unclear at present to what extent Gampopa's collected writings are entirely of his own creation. In a record of teachings received (*gsan yig*), sixteenth-century Drukpa Kagyu master Pema Karpo (1527–92) noted of Gampopa's *Collected Works*, "Since it appears that [texts] definitely written by others have been inserted here, I set [this matter] to the side as something to be investigated."[43] Changkya Rolpé Dorjé (1717–86), publisher of the first foreign-language translation of Milarepa's standard *Life* and

Songs (into Mongolian), makes a similar observation in reference to the writings of early Kagyu masters, noting that "there are numerous confused records in the collected sayings of these [masters], inserted by a host of informed and uninformed pupils, which do not appear trustworthy."[44] Regarding Gampopa's *Collected Works* in particular, David Jackson concludes, "at present one cannot accept for example even all that one finds in Gampopa's 'Collected Works' as coming from his hand, for much of it has obviously been transmitted through subsequent oral retelling or later editing."[45] It seems likely that this editorial work was, in part, accomplished by Sönam Lhundrup (1488–1552), Gampopa's distant relative and the sixteenth abbot of his monastic seat at Daklha Gampo, who played a leading role in compiling and publishing Gampopa's *Works*.[46]

Authorship of the Tilopa and Nāropa biographies is directly attributed to Gampopa in its title: *The Lives of Telo and Nāro Written by Lord Gampopa* (*Rje sgam po pas mdzas pa'i te lo nā ro'i rnam thar*). The biography of Milarepa contained in the next text (*The Lives of Lord Marpa and Jetsün Mila*, *Rje mar pa dang rje btsun mi la'i rnam thar*), however, is clearly *not* the work of Gampopa himself, but rather a transcription of his oral discourse, recorded in print at a later time by an unnamed disciple. The narrative is frequently punctuated by the Tibetan honorific words *rinpoche* (*rin po che*, a title meaning "precious") and *süng* (*gsung*, the honorific verb "to say or to teach"), usually referring to Gampopa and his discussion of Mila's life, as well as the word *zer* (nonhonorific "it is said"), indicating that other oral sources were also available at the time. The language of the Mila section, which occupies more than two thirds of the text, is often vague, its syntax ambiguous, giving the impression of hurriedly copied lecture notes.[47] This account clearly served as the basis for Lama Zhang's version, discussed in the next chapter, so it predates his death in 1193. Gampopa's work is the first study, however brief, of Milarepa's birth, activities, and death, drawn directly from sources present during the yogin's lifetime and recorded perhaps half a spiritual generation after his death. It occupies a unique position in the development of Milarepa's biographical tradition, situated at the junction between oral history and written record.

An Incipient Structure

The biographies inserted into the beginning of Gampopa's *Collected Works* generally anticipate the "golden rosary" (*gser 'phreng*) narratives, the collected lives of successive lineage masters, which became an important genre of literature within the Kagyu tradition and elsewhere. Perhaps more importantly, from the perspective of Milarepa's biographical tradition this text also establishes the basic structure and content for the proto-Life/Songs, prefiguring the great biographical compendia and, later, the standard versions of the *Life* and *Songs* themselves. Narratives informing the life story would ebb and flow as the biographical tradition matured, but the central platform for both life and songs were laid down with this work.

Although Gampopa's *Lives* is called a *namtar*, it preserves the basic framework of both Life and Songs exhibited in pre-Tsangnyön Heruka works, albeit in a somewhat crude and much condensed form. Prior to Tsangnyön's publication, most works in Mila's biographical tradition follow the same general tripartite outline: an account of his early life up to his practice of austerities (proto-Life part 1); a group of discrete narrative vignettes describing Mila's enlightened activities (proto-Songs); and a description of his final passing (proto-Life part 2). Tsangnyön Heruka was the first author/editor to divide the life story and collected songs into separate texts (a subject discussed at length in chapter 4), and Gampopa's proto-Songs serves as a model for the Collected Songs that would appear in the following centuries leading up to the standard version of the *Songs* itself.

Gampopa's *Lives*, translated in appendix 1, is the first text to demonstrate this tripartite biographical structure. It begins with a description of Milarepa's life from his birth to his practice of austerities and retreat at Drakar Taso, which can be divided into several narrative units:[48]

   I. early life
  II. sorcery
 III. early search for Dharma
 IV. training with Marpa and Ngoktön
  V. first retreat under Marpa
 VI. return to his homeland
 VII. practice of austerities

The text then begins the proto-Songs section portraying Mila's activities, his travels, and his interactions with patrons and disciples. The text describes the life story as documenting "the inestimable qualities [Mila] possessed," and as cataloguing "the qualities of his realization."[49] This may anticipate the structure of the later biographical compendia, which organized the song collections in thematic units according to specific "qualities" (*yon tan*) embodied by the yogin. Gampopa's work records fourteen discrete narrative units:

1. monastic dispute
2. Lapchi episode/"Song of Lapchi Gang"
3. journey to Nepal/"Song of the Staff"
4. death rites and horse offering
5. meeting three disciples
6. near-death episode
7. song of vultures at Drakmar Poto
8. invisible lama episode a
9. invisible lama episode b
10. falling off a cliff
11. crystal stūpa transformation
12. doubter/lion-riding/horn stūpa
13. snow falling/flying
14. encounter with Leksé/fasting

This section reveals a proto-Songs in its earliest form. Although the text does not record songs themselves, it does make reference to several *gur* (*mgur*) that would become famous in later versions, including the song of the Lapchi snow ranges and the "Song of the Staff." It also retains numerous narrative fragments that would find their way into subsequent collections. The text then concludes with a brief statement of Milarepa's death, forming the eighth and final section of the proto-Life.

A Skeletal Life Story

The story begins by describing Milarepa's early life with extraordinary brevity. His mother and paternal relatives, who figure so prominently in later versions, are not mentioned at all. Also lacking is any description of his father's death, an event that, in later accounts, sets in motion the entire arc of Milarepa's life story. The text instead implies that Mila's mother died early: "The spiritual son of those two [masters, Marpa and Ngoktön] was lama Milarepa. His family line was Mila of Gungtang. His name was Töpaga. Since [in their family] there were none but father and son, they were extremely poor."

Mila's practice of coercive magic is treated in a single sentence: "He traveled to Ü in search of sorcery, studied much sorcery, and then returned."

There is no description of the murder or hail casting that would motivate and inform his religious activities in later versions. The work proceeds by describing his early training in Buddhist practice.

He next received Dharma from the teacher Lhaga in Tsangrong. The teacher said, "You should be happy now. I possess the authentic Dharma of Great Completion, the apex of all vehicles, the quintessence of all pith instructions. Realize it by day, you're awakened by day; realize it by night, you're awakened by night."

Later, they learned that lama Marpa had arrived [in Lhodrak]. The teacher said, "We have been practicing this Dharma continuously, but it hasn't produced anything. It is said that the one called Marpa Lotsāwa who possesses instructions has arrived, so go there. I am unable to go because I am old and infirm. If I were able, I would go."

The description of Mila's subsequent training under Marpa and Ngoktön similarly lacks the most famous elements associated with the life story: the meeting with his guru disguised as a simple plowman, the trial of constructing towers, and his first meditation retreats. These are summarily glossed with the simple statement, attributed to Gampopa, that "there are many stories about that [period]." We also hear Gampopa's voice for the first time, crediting him as an eyewitness and principal source for the narrative:

When he heard of lama Marpa's fame, [Mila's] previous karmic dispositions were awakened. He went to see lama Marpa and then made the request: "I have no provisions at all; please provide me with both Dharma and material support."

"Both aren't possible, which do you want?" [replied the lama].

"I want Dharma," said [Mila], and the [lama] replied, "In that case, you will have to fetch water and the like."

Thereafter he was given the name Great Magician. From that day forth, he remained close [to the lama]. [Gampopa] has said that there are many stories about that [period]. Milarepa studied there with lama Marpa for five years and requested the instructions of the practice lineage. Thereafter, he studied with Ngok for one year. He cast a hailstorm upon Ngok's enemies and then served him. By appealing directly [to these teachers], no [instructions] were left out, and so later on he gained great faith toward lama Marpa. So [Gampopa] has said.

Gampopa's account presents an unvarnished portrait of his teacher who, as a young novice undertaking his first retreat, confuses ordinary lamp light for the profound illumination of meditation experience:

[Milarepa] then meditated in a cave with a butter lamp set upon his head. He opened his eyes right at daybreak and [saw] there was a brilliant light. Just after that experience he thought some good qualities of [meditation] had developed, but he had forgotten about the butter lamp. So [Gampopa] has said.[50]

Although this candid episode was elided from most subsequent versions, Tsangnyön Heruka later revives the account of Milarepa practicing with a lamp set upon his head as a sign of the yogin's steadfast determination.

Having completed his training with his guru, the yogin departs for his homeland, where he finds his childhood home in ruins, and begins his practice of meditation in earnest. The first part of the proto-Life concludes with a description of Milarepa surviving on nothing but cooked nettles; his body becomes "a mere head and bones draped with skin, with no flesh at all."

The proto-Songs then begin with a story of Milarepa's confrontation with a belligerent group of monks. Although later versions would edit out this particular episode, the biographical tradition would emphasize the contrast between the unsullied yogic path of the hermit and the monastic vocation largely depicted as misguided:

At one time, [the monks of] a minor religious center in Gungtang became jealous of the lama's great merit. Intending to disgrace [Milarepa], they invited him [to their center]. When he arrived, the monks said, "Since you are an accomplished master, you will serve as our venerable priest." They placed him inside the chapel and drew the lock. When they went outside, the lama was there. Not believing it was him, they looked inside and saw him inside too. The monks understood he was indeed an accomplished master, and they all begged for his forgiveness.

Another account describes the yogin's intention to visit Nepal, while also recording one of the text's few song fragments.

At another time, the lama set his mind on the Kathmandu Valley (Bal po), and the master and a group of disciples departed. Along the way, they met with numerous merchants.

The headman of the merchants grabbed the lama's staff and asked, "Who are you?"

The lama replied,

Have you a clue who's before you now?
If you don't know who this is here now—
I am the yogin Mila. . . .

and so forth, and he sang the "Song of the Staff." So [Gampopa] has said.

Then he reached the top of a pass with a view of the [populated] valley below. He said, "I will not go down to the valley, but will wander among the mountain peaks.

The retinue [of disciples] replied that if they wandered around a mountain peak for even ten years, they surely would not reach the end of it, and begged to go to the valley, but [Mila] did not give them permission.

Other stories are attributed to oral tradition, as with this enigmatic narrative fragment: "At another time, he turned himself into a crystal stūpa and then departed into space. So it is said."

The text concludes with only a cursory mention of the yogin's death, forming the second part of the proto-Life. Gampopa's work is one of only two biographies to maintain that Mila's corpse was cremated both at his longtime retreat at Drin in southern Tibet and at Mount Kailāsa in the west. It is also the original source for Mila's characterization as an emanated being (sprul pa'i gang zag), a tradition prominent in most early works that continued into the nineteenth century but struck from the standard version.

These, and many others, are the inestimable qualities [Mila] possessed. He was undistracted from samādhi. For him there was no difference between periods of resting in meditation and postmeditation. He was an emanated being who saw the truth of reality.

Later, when he passed away, his corpse was cremated at both Tisé and Drin. So [Gampopa] has said.

Gampopa's text surveyed here brings to light Milarepa's earliest biographical tradition. The stories, fragmented and frequently inconsistent, pay only the barest attention to details of plot development and narrative flow. But unlike the subsequent biographical compendia, this work was not intended to serve as the master's definitive portrait. Although Gampopa never appears explicitly as an heir to Milarepa's spiritual tradition, the text is one of several biographical works inserted as a prelude to the other materials in his *Collected Works*. Together with parallel biographies of early Kagyu founders, it serves to document an authentic source and unbroken lineage for the instructions that follow. Many biographies addressed in the next chapter serve a similar function.

Yet Gampopa's *Lives* marks an important point of transformation in Milarepa's life story, a liminal period in which stories of the yogin were first transcribed but still bore marks of their roots in the oral tradition. Its voice records, in the terms of Albert Lord's famous study, a nascent oral literature in which "a fixed text was established. Proteus was photographed, and no matter what other forms he might appear [in] in the future, this would become the shape that was changed, this would be the original."[51] Although the text comprises a series of disparate and fragmented narratives, the life story took shape in skeletal form, fixing a profile that would underlie nearly all future representations of Milarepa's life.

"RECHUNGPA'S" AURAL TRANSMISSION BIOGRAPHY

The collection of texts and manuals (*yig cha*) pertaining to the *Cakrasaṃvara Ḍākinī Aural Transmission* (*Bde mchog mkha' 'gro snyan rgyud*), compiled by the sixteenth-century lama Changchup Zangpo, includes a series of biographies recording the lives of lineage holders of the aural tantra transmissions.[52] In an unusual move, authorship of each life story is attributed to the subject's principal disciple (in the context of the aural transmission lineage), so that the biographies of Tilopa and Nāropa are written by Marpa, Marpa's by Milarepa, and Mila's by Rechungpa. This is no doubt a pious fiction; Roberts calls it "a fanciful attribution of authorship."[53] It is clear, through an analysis of both structure and content, that these biographies predate Changchup Zangpo's compilation of them; yet it is equally clear that they postdate their purported authors.

Milarepa's biography in this collection, though attributed to his disciple Rechungpa, illustrates a middle period of development of the proto-Life/Songs, significantly more complex than Gampopa's *Lives* but not as comprehensive as those to come, analyzed in the next chapter. It follows what became a standard division of the yogin's life into two sets of qualities: hardships undertaken, connected with his familial lineage; and experiences, connected with his meditation.[54] The second section is further subdivided into seven sections. This is far less elaborate than the standard seventeen found in the later compendia, and here reflects the main purpose of the biography, which is to document the lineage history of the aural transmissions. There is little attempt to portray Milarepa's complete life by means of a fully developed narrative, although it does record excerpts of several songs (including the famous "Song of Essencelessness"), each of which concludes with the statement that the entire song may be found in the Collected Songs. As this biography appears to predate Tsangnyön Heruka's standard work, the reference to a collected songs (mgur 'bum) likely points to the first such collection, The Twelve Great Disciples.

Although these biographies may not be as early as first suspected, they are still of interest, demonstrating an important function of namtar, which is to record the transmission of the aural tantra from guru's mouth to disciple's ear. The life story is not merely a support for the aural transmissions but an integral part of the transmission itself, documenting the authority of the transmissions that follow and inspiring the reader to practice them. This is made clear in the outline to Changchup Zangpo's nyengyü collection, written several centuries earlier by the scholar-adept Zhang Lotsāwa Drupa Pelzang (d. 1237).[55] Here the corpus of texts is first divided into root and commentarial works; the latter are again divided into outer, inner, and secret collections. The texts of the outer division are headed by the statement, "the appearance of the unbroken teachings of the tantra [is made clear through] the succession of sacred biographies from the wisdom ḍākinīs down to the root lama."[56] Lives of the masters are thus not supplementary to the aural transmission curriculum but preliminaries (sngon 'gro) for them. These biographies constitute the first part of the aural transmission, "the transmission wish-fulfilling jewel" (brgyud pa yid bzhin nor bu). More mature biographical works such as The Twelve Great Disciples later make this point explicitly.

Tsangnyön Heruka, a contemporary of Changchup Zangpo, elaborates on the role biography plays in the aural transmission tradition, here in a passage from his own textbook of the Cakrasaṃvara Ḍākinī Aural Transmission:

> If a student neither hears nor reads about the qualities in the life stories of the gurus, [even though] he receives and engages in the teachings, he will not attain the state of ripening and liberation. Therefore, in order that confidence in the lineage and the instructions, as well as a recognition of their authenticity, arise, and in order that the special qualities of

students arise effortlessly in their mind streams through the blessings of the lineage, I will describe, roughly and in brief, the life stories of the gurus of the lineage.[57]

Chapter 3 will explore how this relationship was maintained even by the later compendia.

REFLECTIONS

The steady trickle of work published on Milarepa's biographical tradition during the past three decades has produced two competing views of the life story. First, at least since E. Gene Smith's pioneering introduction to the life of Tsangnyön Heruka, it has generally been understood that the fifteenth-century standard version was a product of literary accretion, predicated upon a rich tradition of early biographical literature including texts such as *The Twelve Great Disciples*. In the decade following Smith's introduction, a number of early Mila biographies were reprinted in India. Lhalungpa later noted several important works in his 1977 English translation of the *Life*, most notably *The Twelve Great Disciples*.

The second view, seemingly irreconcilable with the first, adopts what might be called a "rhetoric of orality," asserting that the songs and stories associated with Milarepa's life were transcribed and disseminated in written form *only* after centuries of oral transmission. This of course refers to Tsangnyön Heruka's standard version, produced four centuries after Milarepa's death, and testifies to the profound impact that work has had on our understanding of the biographical tradition. So dominant is Tsangnyön's representation of the life story that it has eclipsed and effectively silenced an extensive literary tradition spanning hundreds of years.

This is not to say that Milarepa's life was not passed along and handed down as part of an oral tradition; it most certainly was. The songs so central to his career emerged from a genre of recited poetry cultivated as an oral practice. As we have seen, Gampopa's biography appears to have originated in the form of notes transcribed from lectures he taught; chapter 2 provides additional evidence for such activities. Even today, contemporary Kagyu teachers continue to pass on Milarepa's life and songs as part of a living oral tradition.] modern day

Nevertheless, scholars and translators of the past few decades have repeatedly adopted a rhetoric of orality in describing the story of Milarepa's life. The Nālandā Translation Committee's elegant 1980 translation of a famed Kagyu song collection describes an account of his life that "differs factually" from the standard version, having "developed from changes that occurred as the songs were passed from disciple to disciple."[58] In her 1984 dissertation, Victoria Urubshurow asserts that "the textual formulation of [Milarepa's] life story and a compilation of his songs were rendered into block print in the fifteenth century after some four hundred years of oral transmission."[59] Francis Tiso echoes this claim in his 1989 dissertation:

> I am led to suspect that the Mila corpus was for a very long time an oral tradition handed on by the story-tellers who did not memorize. Rather, these poets were creative the way a bard is creative and only in the late fifteenth century were the oral tales collected and organized by a literary genius into a coherent but highly redacted romance.[60]

More recently, in the introduction to his masterful translation of Milarepa songs, Brian Cutillo posits "three hundred years before the oral versions were transcribed."[61]

Such presumptions are perhaps due to Milarepa's fame as a founding figure of the so-called Oral Transmission school (Bka' brgyud) or his promulgation of a doctrinal system known as aural transmissions. These traditions emphasize the direct, oral communication of practical meditation instructions, yogic insight, and even songs of realization between teacher and disciple. But as we shall see in chapter 4, Tsangnyön's own hagiographers adopted a similar rhetoric of orality, underscoring the role he played in gathering together strands of an oral tradition while deemphasizing what will be shown to be his overwhelming dependence on existing literary works.

Tsangnyön Heruka's disciple Lhatsun Rinchen Namgyal (1473–1557), founder of the monastic seat at Milarepa's famed meditation site Drakar Taso, published his own collection of Milarepa songs, clearly emphasizing the oral tradition in its title: *Some Miscellaneous Oral Traditions Including Jetsün Milarepa's Six Vajra Songs* (*Rje btsun mi la ras pa'i rdo rje mgur drug sogs gsung rgyun thor bu 'ga'*). Although this text awaits more detailed study, it is evident that he too relied on materials that had long since been written down.[62]

In all fairness, scholars have previously had limited access to works of the early biographical tradition. Yet, as the sources examined throughout this study demonstrate, biographers recorded the life story early on, and they recorded it frequently. The first biographical sketches appeared through the work of close disciples, most probably while the yogin was still alive; this is at least what the sources themselves maintain. The colophons to Ngendzong Repa's quartet of biographical chapters repeatedly assert that the disciple counterchecked his information with Milarepa himself—much to the guru's chagrin—and then discussed it with at least one of his vajra brothers before committing the stories to writing. Gampopa's text likewise retains the voice of eyewitness testimony, in which narrative accounts were perhaps first written in personal diary form or memorized before their dictation and eventual transcription.

Tsangnyön Heruka did not craft his masterful portrait upon the blank literary canvas of a purely oral tradition. He inherited an extensive and mature literary tradition of life writing that served as his principal source and primary model. But the rhetoric of orality effectively hid his sources from view, as if lifting the ink from their pages and disguising them as voices from the distant past. The literature of the biographical corpus took birth with Milarepa's empty cremation cell, when the works described here first coalesced. These life stories are transitional, capturing the moment following Milarepa's death in which authors began to transform an oral tradition into a new literary form. The texts were unpolished, fragmentary, and unstable. But they formed the core around which the image of Milarepa would take shape.

2

PROTO-LIVES

FORMATIONS OF A SKELETAL BIOGRAPHY

ORIENTATIONS

The Early Spread of Milarepa's Life Story

MILAREPA'S EARLIEST biography, established by the yogin's own disciples, had achieved a life of its own within a single generation as students of his direct pupils began to adapt, expand, and promulgate accounts of his religious career. By the mid-twelfth century, within decades of the yogin's death, the biography was already being taught publicly in lecture halls by luminaries such as Pakmodrupa Dorjé Gyalpo (1110–70), who had himself studied with Gampopa. The *Blue Annals* records an account of one Kunden (1148–1217, also known as Kunden Repa), younger brother of Pakmodrupa's disciple Gyaltsa Rinchengön (1118–95), who visited the master's seat: "When he reached Pakmodru carrying provisions for his older brother [Gyaltsa], he found Jetsün Mila's life story (*rnam thar*) being taught. He thought, 'I should act like [Mila],' and nodded his head three times there in the religious assembly."[1]

We do not know what form the life story took in the context of teaching lectures such as this. Perhaps Pakmodrupa received an oral account of Milarepa's deeds from his guru like the one recorded in *Lives of Lord Marpa and Jetsün Mila*, described in the previous chapter. Yet Pakmodrupa's narrative inspired young Kunden to publicly declare his intention to follow Mila's yogic path of the cotton-clad *repa*. It is not unreasonable, then, to conclude that oral accounts of the master's life far more detailed than those documented in Gampopa's early work circulated among spiritual communities of his followers. These accounts would quickly solidify into a skeletal frame that served to structure the nascent biographical tradition.

A Time of Change and Changing Lives

The late twelfth and early thirteenth centuries saw great transformation and development among the communities of Milarepa's followers that came to be known as the Kagyu, the tradition of "oral transmission." Charismatic disciples such as Gampopa and Pakmodrupa inspired a proliferation of new guru-disciple lineages, instruction transmissions, and teaching institutions, resulting in the eventual recognition of "four great and eight minor Kagyu branches" (bka' brgyud che bzhi chung brgyad). According to traditional sources, teachers of two subsects, the Drigung and the Drukpa, dispatched thousands of meditators to Milarepa's retreat sites throughout western Tibet, especially Mount Kailāsa.[2] A popular Tibetan saying boasts: half of the people are Drukpa; half of the Drukpas are beggars; half of the beggars are saints. By the last quarter of the twelfth century, at least six major teaching centers for these Kagyu subsects had been established in central Tibet.[3]

As Kagyu religious communities grew and centers for their teaching and meditation expanded, there was an increased need for literature that would support their activities. New monasteries required study curricula, which in turn necessitated textbooks describing new doctrinal systems of philosophical exegeses and practical application. It has recently been suggested that the spread of new doctrinal cycles during this period contributed to an "enormous upsurge in interest" in the writing of religious history—historical perspective providing a powerful form of legitimation.[4] The accretion of life writing, adding significantly to the earliest biographical stratum of Milarepa's life story, likely served much the same purpose. From a traditional perspective, sacred biography offers both inspiration and roadmap for the neophyte embarking upon the yogin's path. But like the writing of history, hagiography supports the religious authority of a founding figure together with his or her claim to holding and transmitting an authentic, incontrovertible lineage. As discussed in chapter 1, Ngendzong Repa's activities as both biographer (of his guru's life) and anthologizer (of his guru's aural transmission instructions) are an early example of these parallel processes at work. Production of Milarepa's biographical material and the dissemination of his lineage accelerated in the century following his death. If the Kagyu Zeitgeist did not directly entail a new stratum of biographical materials, it at least fertilized the soil in which such narratives matured.

Indeed, a new form of biographical literature began to appear at this time: collected biographies, recording lives of individuals within a single teaching or abbatial lineage. These texts, called "golden rosaries" (*gser 'phreng*), perhaps drawn originally from devotional supplications, evoke images of lives linked by the thread of transmission, read as if telling beads on a prayer string.[5] They were not intended to be fully formed hagiographies of individual personalities, but rather to document the transmission of instructions through an authentic lineage down to the time of writing. They were pared down to essentials, covering enough material to plausibly assert that each member had received instruction from a genuine master of the lineage, perfected it in study and practice, and transmitted it to worthy disciples, while remaining brief enough to allow space for a dozen or more individual lives. Some golden rosary texts are found among a teacher's collected writings, as is the case with Gampopa's *Works*, where they introduce and contextualize both author and literary corpus; others were produced as discrete biographical works, meant to serve as independent support for a master-disciple lineage. The present chapter draws upon examples from both types of literature.

A New Biographical Model: The Proto-Life/Songs

Milarepa's early biographical tradition adopted a model that fit well with the rise of golden rosary literature. Authors needed to represent the yogin's life story (*rnam thar*) while also preserving the contexts for, and content of, his principal teachings: songs of realization (*mgur*).[6] The structure of works discussed in this chapter, which I have termed proto-Life/Songs (proto-*rnam mgur*), satisfied this requirement by offering a template for abbreviated Life and Songs that also allowed substantial variation of content, style, and other details of metastructure. These templates were particularly useful in golden rosary texts, since much narrative content—including fragmentary oral material and discrete literary segments culled from various sources—could be conveyed economically, in a relatively small space.

It is widely recognized that the Tibetan tradition of spiritual songs, songs of realization known as *gur* (*mgur, nyams mgur*), was deeply influenced by Indian vernacular song styles such as *dohā*, *vajragīti*, and *caryāgīti*.[7] When Tibetans began traveling to India on pilgrimage in search of tantric texts and lineages between the tenth and twelfth centuries, as did Milarepa's guru, Marpa, they came into contact with communities of tantric adepts (*siddha*) and the song traditions they promulgated. The Tibetan genre of *gur* was originally considered either a synonym for or a subdivision of *lu* (*glu*), Tibet's oldest poetic form, attested in Dunhuang documents and other early sources.[8] *Lu* rose to prominence during the royal dynastic period, when it served primarily as a political mechanism for expressing exuberance at having overcome obstacles and accomplished one's aims (on the battlefield, presumably). As Tibetan translators began returning to their homeland with Indian *dohās* and other song forms, they quickly adapted both local style (adding a Tibetan melody [*dbyangs* or *'debs*]) and content (by adopting local metaphors and symbolism) to fit within the framework of *gur*.[9] This term thus came to refer to songs with predominantly religious content: either the direct, personal experience of realization and awakening or the expression of practical instructions for such. Some explicitly religious *gur* date from the time of Padmasambhava (ca. eighth century), who is credited in some accounts with originating the tradition.[10] As a fully formed genre, however, they primarily date from the time of Milarepa. These types of song were apparently his preferred vehicle for teaching, and Tibet's earliest spiritual song collections were produced, at least in part, by his immediate disciples and followers.

The Tibetan term *namgur* (*rnam mgur*, "life and songs," here rendered as Life/Songs) is an abbreviation for the words *namtar* (*rnam thar*) or "biography" and *gurbum* (*mgur 'bum*), literally "one hundred thousand songs," here rendered "collected songs."[11] As will be discussed in the next chapter, it became standard practice in Tibet to record what we now think of as Milarepa's Life and Songs in a single text. Although these works almost universally use the word "biography" (*rnam thar*) in their titles, they are, in effect, a combination of biography and song collection: that is, a *namgur*. This is true for most works in the tradition—the proto-works as well as the larger compendia—up to the time of the standard version, whose architect, Tsangnyön Heruka, published the *Life* and *Songs* as independent works for the first time.[12] This chapter will describe the evolution of proto-works into a skeletal structure around which later versions of the life were molded.

.I use the term "proto" in "proto-Life/Songs" in two slightly different ways. The first is diachronic, indicating that these texts display an early stage of development in the biographical tradition, specifically locating them as precursors to the larger, more mature compendia discussed in chapter 3. I also intend an atemporal usage in reference to texts that retain the structure of proto-works even though they postdate, and were influenced by, the compendia. In this sense, the term refers to the condensed and often truncated structure of the proto-texts regardless of when they were actually produced.

The proto-Life/Songs structure follows the pattern established by Gampopa: a brief biographical outline (the proto-Life) is used to introduce and conclude a series of abbreviated anecdotes recording songs or song fragments (the proto-Songs). The Life's opening acts generally extend through Milarepa's practice of austerities and long retreats in and around Drakar Taso. Following an extended middle section comprising the rudimentary song collection, the proto-Life concludes with a description of the yogin's final passing.

The middle portion is composed of proto-Songs episodes, some transcribing Milarepa's songs of realization in full, others preserving only fragments; occasionally, nothing but a title is retained. The earliest works refer to very few songs at all, recording instead narrative fragments from the oral tradition. This may seem counterintuitive but is immaterial to the model. The proto-Songs episodes take the same place as their mature cousins (between the early life and the death), adopt the same form (discrete, often dislocated narrative units), and serve much the same function (to record isolated incidents in the yogin's spiritual career during the middle part of his life). And as the underlying proto-Songs structure would be adopted in all of Mila's biographical works surveyed in this study, many proto-Songs fragments would be absorbed into the mature Songs episodes recorded in the compendia.

Six Proto-Life/Songs Narratives

We can now turn to the development of the proto-Life/Songs texts and to the spread of such narrative accounts during the century or so following Milarepa's death. The six works surveyed in this chapter comprise much of the biographical tradition's earliest literary corpus and indicate a movement from the "oral texts" to more structured written narratives.

The first work examined here, Lama Zhang's *Life of Lama Milarepa*, closely follows Gampopa's model. The second and third biographies, *Life of Jetsün Milarepa* by Dönmo Ripa and *Life of Milarepa* by Sangyé Bum, likely joined Lama Zhang's work as early models for the larger compendia. The fourth text, Gyaltangpa's *King of Jetsüns*, introduces a new format but retains the same general structure as other early works while adding much narrative content that would later come to be associated with the standard life. *The Kagyu Rosary*, the fifth text, reflects influence flowing in the opposite direction: the larger compendia shaped the structure of Mila's representation within the format of an abbreviated proto-Life/Songs text. Later authors continued to use the abbreviated format of the proto-model long after the more mature biographies were disseminated, including the second Zhamar's *Cloud Bank of Blessings*, the sixth text discussed at the end of this chapter.

Proto-Structural Topoi

As noted in the introduction, critics of sacred biography (beginning with Victorian scholars of the nineteenth century) have viewed such works as "leitmotifs for a benighted, mass-indulged credulity," the term "hagiography" itself used as a pejorative "epithet for the unreliable" pitted against historical truth.[13] Moreover, it was frequently argued that sacred biography, especially in Asian contexts, represents its subject not as a life individually lived (believed to be a wholly Western/European concern) but as an ideal model conforming "to a pattern of holiness or right conduct that has already been established by the religious tradition."[14] Chapter 1 questioned this notion, arguing that even the earliest strata of biographical materials (based on oral sources witness to the subject himself) showed parallel concern for the biographical subject as both exemplar and individual: Gampopa established the basic structural arc of the life of liberation, and Ngendzong recorded detailed narrative accounts, preserving the type of information associated with individual lives. Here I argue that texts of this stratum continued to address these two issues of representation, eventually uniting them in a way that best suited the compact medium of golden rosary biographies.

How did Milarepa's biographers balance these competing concerns? One answer, adopting Heffernan's view of medieval European hagiography, is style, the persuasive skill medieval rhetoricians called *elocutio*.[15] To unpack this notion, the following chapters will explore two categories frequently identified in discussions of narrative. The first includes the macro structures of biographical narrative, what is commonly referred to as "discourse." This has been described as the development of plot, serving as "the outline or armature of the story, that which supports and organizes the rest," but also as "the dynamic shaping force of the narrative discourse."[16] It points to the basic structures of narrative as well as to the ways they are arranged to achieve a specific type of story, in this case a complete liberation, a *namtar*, juxtaposing events of the subject's life with those of the Buddha. The earliest Lives gave little attention to these elements, but as the tradition matured they gradually employed discursive structures both as the story's frame and as a shaping force to propel the narrative from beginning to end. Tsangnyön Heruka would exploit these most fully in his standard account, contributing to its rise as the yogin's definitive representation.

The second category of analysis focuses on the content of discrete episodes, generally referred to as "story." This comprises the narrative components that make a life story the story of a life, and that allowed biographers to represent an increasingly complex individual even within the framework of an ideal model. Authors gradually fleshed out the narrative fragments of the earliest works, creating more coherent constituent parts (the early life, training, practice of hardships, death) and a more compelling story overall. The narratives of Milarepa's biographical tradition populated the Life with an increasingly dense layer of detail. Some, such as the elaborate descriptions of his status as a miraculous emanation, served a clear didactic purpose from their earliest appearance. Others, such as the famous trial of the towers, accumulated symbolic importance only as the story developed over time. But Milarepa's biographical tradition also recorded much narrative information that served no clear didactic purpose at all. These countless quotidian details serve to illustrate an individual and individuated life, even within a frame of an exemplary model.[17]

The nexus of oral and literary sources available to authors for their representations of the master in this period is far from transparent, and the chronology for the production of the proto-Life/Songs remains uncertain. This is true particularly of the four middle texts examined in this chapter, which may have been composed in close succession. Rather than attempting a genealogy for every narrative element appearing below (tempting though that might be), I will focus instead on the broader formation of the life story, emphasizing implicit structural similarities that underlay the texts even as the explicit structure of the Life and Songs became progressively more complex. I try to highlight particular innovations each work offered the biographical tradition; some were accepted into the standard version, others were left on the editing floor. It should become clear, even from such a brief survey, that this early period of biographical formation was unstable and volatile, very much in a state of becoming.

Textual Lacunae

Several important works were written during the same period as those analyzed here but have not yet come to light. The catalogue of the Drepung archives lists a number of previously unattested works pertaining to Milarepa's life, one of which may well constitute the earliest known biography of the yogin, written—unusually—by his own teacher, Ngoktön Chödor.[18] In his historical study of Milarepa's life, *An Illuminating Lamp of Sun and Moon Beams*, the fourteenth-century author Zhijé Ripa further notes,

> In general, I have seen some one hundred and twenty-seven attempts at the biography of Mila Rechen. In particular, I have made [my version] taking as a basis the accounts of (1) Lord Khyungtsangpa Jñānaguru, and (2) the Dharma Lord Zhang Lotsāwa Drupa Pelzang, who is unmistaken regarding the objects of knowledge of the five sciences.[19]

Zhijé Ripa repeatedly refers to these two masters throughout his study. The first, Khyungtsangpa Yeshé Lama (1115–76), is counted among Rechungpa's closest disciples.[20] The *Blue Annals* (completed 1478) records Mila's life based, in part, upon Khyungtsangpa's account, indicating the latter was still considered an authoritative work even a century after Zhijé Ripa's remark (written 1373) and a mere decade prior to the publication of Mila's standard *Life* and *Songs* (in 1488).[21] Zhang Lotsāwa, discussed in the previous chapter, was Khyungtsangpa's spiritual grandson (*yang slob*). Although it is not known precisely how, or in what form, they presented Milarepa's life, both masters were also instrumental in the early codification and promulgation of the aural transmissions.

For reasons of space, brief biographical accounts recorded in religious histories (*chos 'byung*), such as the *Blue Annals* and the *Religious History of Lhorong* (completed 1451), are excluded from the survey in this chapter, although they are discussed in reference to other accounts.

LAMA ZHANG'S *LIFE OF LAMA MILAREPA*

The first biographical treatment of Milarepa's life following those of his direct disciples is in the *Collected Works* of Lama Zhang Yudrakpa Tsöndru

Drakpa (1123–93), founder of the Tselpa Kagyu tradition.[22] This work, *The Life of Lama Milarepa* (*Bla ma mi la ras pa'i rnam thar*, LMN), is found among thirteen biographies in a section on "Lives and Deeds [of Lineage Gurus] as taught by Zhang Yudrakpa" (*Zhang g.yu brag pa'i gsung mdzad pa rnam thar gyi skor*). The lineage preserved in this collection extends first up to Gampopa and then to five of Lama Zhang's teachers, including Dakpo Gomtsul Tsultrim Nyingpo (1116–69), Gampopa's nephew and senior disciple. This work thus appeared around the time Pakmodrupa was also promulgating the life story, a single generation after Gampopa's version of the biography, to which it is closely related.

Lama Zhang relies heavily upon his spiritual grandfather's work, Gampopa's *Lives of Lord Marpa and Jetsün Mila*, preserving much of its proto-Life/Songs structure and content. The minor changes that do appear indicate some disparity among oral accounts of Mila's life circulating at the time. The text also removes the ubiquitous attributions "so Gampopa has said," thereby shifting the life story one step away from the oral tradition toward a more strictly literary form. Yet this transformation was not inevitable; in the biography of his guru Vairocanavajra, for example, Lama Zhang frequently uses the Tibetan words *süng* (*gsung*, honorific "to teach," "to say") and *ké* (*skad*, "it is said") in reference to his master's direct speech and to other oral traditions, precisely as Gampopa had done.[23] In the context of his own guru's biography, Lama Zhang sought the authorial (and authorizing) voice of direct attribution to the oral tradition. The life story of Milarepa, however, had already been transcribed by Gampopa and his disciples, suggesting that it was no longer necessary to directly attribute quotations since the story had previously been established as authentic. The nascent literary tradition provided an authority to which Lama Zhang could defer.

The work begins with a brief overview of Mila's early life up to his practice of austerities, following Gampopa's *Lives* with some variation and loss of detail.[24] For example, Lama Zhang elides the deprecating account in which Milarepa confuses light from the butter lamp for meditation experience.[25] When the yogin finally departs the populated valley for strict solitary meditation, Lama Zhang makes no mention of the famed retreat site at Drakar Taso, stating simply that he "remained a long time in the mountains of Mangyul."[26] But he does incorporate several important additions, underscoring Mila's sense of determination and highlighting the start of his spiritual career as a hermit and meditator. The first describes Mila's resolution to overcome adversity in meditation:

He meditated in mountain retreat for nine years but experienced no *samādhi*, and he then became severely depressed. He resolved, "I shall remain in a single isolated place and, though this body of mine may wither and die right here, I shall not stir from this seat until *samādhi* is born."[27]

Milarepa's vow not to move from his seat until he developed some sign of realization was later absorbed into the biographical narratives of the larger compendia such as *The Twelve Great Disciples* version in the next chapter, where this promise transforms into an eightfold vow.

After nine months of intensive practice, Mila's meditation produces some yogic warmth, a sign of spiritual progress, at which time he is visited by his sister and aunt:

"Aunt," said Mila, "I have now experienced yogic warmth."
"What is this so-called warmth?" replied both [aunt and sister].
"This so-called warmth means I no longer need clothing," Mila replied.
"How happy we are," they said, "that our brother has become an accomplished master," and they celebrated.[28]
Then in a short time, bliss-warmth and nonconceptuality blazed forth in an explosive manner. A coemergent realization of the genuine nature vividly arose and he thought, "Up to now, I've taken mistaken appearances to be real and have been deceived." He summoned his sister and aunt, saying that he had a spectacle to show them.
The two of them arrived and he sat there naked, exposing his genitals. "Our relative has gone crazy," they said, and they wept.[29]

At this point, Milarepa sings the "song of six examples[30] and seven meanings," which inspires the sister and aunt to develop great faith. He initially refuses their request to cover his body with clothing, but they offer him a bolt of cotton cloth (*re*), and thereafter "he ever had a cotton robe wrapped around his naked body and hung over his shoulders; he lived without [a concept] of purity, filth, or shame."[31] Here, for the first time, we find written documentation of Milarepa's transformation from ordinary individual to cotton-clad adept that earned him the name *repa* (literally "cotton-clad"). A life dedicated to meditation was, in his relatives' eyes, something to be celebrated, but the yogin's transgressive behavior was a sign of insanity. The local residents reacted with similar skepticism:

A group of people from the region and a group of locals gave gifts to three or four beautiful young maidens dressed in ornaments. The girls then led [Mila] to an isolated dell and pleasured the lama's penis. At first it grew aroused. But then it became smaller and smaller, until it finally retracted out of sight. Then all the locals and officials developed great faith and were amazed.[32]

Neither of these two episodes turns up in later texts. The former, however, seems to form the basis for the famous account in which sister and aunt reproach Mila for his nakedness, to which the yogin responds with a song of freedom from shame.[33] The latter episode was excised from the biographical tradition altogether, although echoes remain in Tsangnyön's version, where Mila encounters a number of bejeweled young maidens.[34]

Lama Zhang's *Life* then begins a series of proto-Songs episodes, largely reproducing the content and arrangement in Gampopa's earlier work, with minor variations. Like its model, this section of fourteen brief stories lacks cohesion. The stories appear to record fragments from the oral tradition, like chips from a Tibetan wood shop, devoid of a larger narrative context.

The text lacks a clear record of Milarepa's death and makes no mention of his cremation at either Drin or Tisé. Lama Zhang, however, transforms Gampopa's concluding words into verse, once again emphasizing Mila's status as an emanation:

Such were his limitless excellent [qualities]:
Undistracted from *samādhi*,
Lacking meditation and postmeditation,
Seeing the truth of reality,
An emanated being—so it is taught.[35]

Only in the final few words of the concluding verse does Lama Zhang directly refer to the oral tradition from which his text (and its main source) clearly draws. For the most part, he has deemphasized the orality of the text's origins (by removing references to Gampopa's direct speech) while maintaining Gampopa's rudimentary structure.

Little effort is given to representing a full or fully fleshed life story. Rather, the writings of Gampopa and Lama Zhang serve principally as introductions to their authors' *Collected Works*. They document links in the chain of a transmission lineage extending back to authoritative sources meant to support and legitimate the body of teachings that follow. In this context, the transmission line, not the individuals who constitute it, is of paramount importance. There is little indication that a fuller presentation of the yogin's spiritual career is required, beyond the assertion that he was an "emanated being" who "saw the truth of reality," and thus a fully qualified master of the lineage. During the next half century, however, this began to change.

DÖNMO RIPA'S *LIFE OF JETSÜN MILA*

The next datable proto-Life/Songs text is found in a collection of Kagyu biographies compiled by Dorjé Dzé Ö, a Drigung master active during the mid-fourteenth century.[36] Although his compilation appears to date from that time, all but the final few biographies were written perhaps a century earlier by one Dönmo Ripa (b. 1203) around 1245.[37] These life stories are described as having been dictated by Dönmo Ripa's guru, known as Ritrö Wangchuk (1181–1225), who was himself a spiritual grandson (*yang slob*) of Pakmodrupa; this would place the biography of Milarepa only four teacher-student generations from the yogin himself.[38] The text of Mila's biography, titled *The Life of Jetsün Mila* (*Rje btsun mid la'i rnam thar*, JMN), appears largely based on Gampopa's early work, as might be expected in a lineage stemming directly from Gampopa, but also draws upon Lama Zhang's version in at least one instance.[39]

Moreover, Dönmo Ripa's account adds both content and polish to Milarepa's life story, including new biographical data and employing, for the first time, a formal narrative structure. This is the first proto-Life/Songs text to weave the earliest strata of biographical materials (including those of Gampopa and Zhang) into a fully formed and cohesive story. It is also the first work to define its contents as both biography (*rnam thar*) and historical record (*lo rgyus*), perhaps implying a correspondence between, if not a conflation of, these two literary genres.[40] It was a well-known and influential text among Kagyu authors, and later an important source for major works by the Second Zhamar and Zhijé Ripa.

The biographies recorded in Dorjé Dzé Ö's collection, up to that of Milarepa, are explicitly structured around thematic divisions. The Buddha's life, for example, follows the so-called "twelve great deeds." Marpa's biography is structured around three "qualities" (*yon tan*) evident in his life story: the qualities of prophecies received; the qualities of his practicing austerities in relation to his family line; and the qualities of his experience in relation to *samādhi*.[41] Milarepa's life story instead divides what it calls the "biography or historical records" into four chronological parts: an account of his life up to the time he met Lord Marpa; the way he met Lord Marpa, rendered him service, and then received Dharma and instructions; the way he attained Dharma and instructions and then practiced them as service to the lama, thereby achieving ordinary and extraordinary qualities; and the way he nurtured worthy disciples.[42] Stories of the Life are no longer fragmented and displaced, but rather explicitly plotted around the central themes of renunciation, devotion, meditation, liberation, and transmission.

Part 1 follows the general template established by Gampopa and Lama Zhang, with several noteworthy variations: Mila has a second sibling named Tepchung; his father does not die; he does not train in magic; the father (not the mother) inspires him to seek out Dharma. At this point, however, the text descends into layers of detail far deeper than its predecessors; of particular interest is the description of Mila's early Dharma training, which conflicts with the Gampopa/Lama Zhang narrative, and much of which was not recorded in the standard biography. Young Mila leaves his homeland for the central regions of Tibet,[43] where he encounters a series of five teachers:

> From Lhajé Yeshé Zung in Rukulung he requested the comprehensive [instructions] on the Lord of Death (*gshin rje*) and the wrathful mantra of the guardian of the teachings, Red-Black Faced Za (*gza' gdong dmar nag*). Practicing these for eight years, signs [of accomplishment] appeared. Then he went to Nyangtö Koré and received [instructions] on magical display (*sgyu 'phrul*) from Bami Bodhirāja. From Gyertön Wangé in Nyangtö Gyenkar he received Great Completion [instructions]. From Dretön Wangé in Yupuk of Rong he also received Great Completion [instructions]. Then he went to Yamdrokdo and received [Great Completion instructions on] texts of the mental class (*mdo sems phyogs*) from Marpa Jungé.[44]

This passage is the source for several later accounts, including Zhijé Ripa's biographical survey, Pema Karpo's religious history, and the supplement (*kha skong*) to Situ Paṇchen's history. Here it indicates a deepening interest in recording details of Milarepa's early spiritual career. The first section concludes with Mila's departure for southern Tibet, where he meets his destined guru, Marpa.

Part 2 documents Mila's training with Marpa and lays the foundation for many famous stories stemming from this period of Milarepa's training:

he makes an offering of a copper kettle to Marpa; he goes begging in the countryside for barley; and for the first time he carries out construction projects for his guru. The series of towers he built—so central to later versions—are not explicitly mentioned; rather, he is described as hauling giant boulders, and for each stone moved, he is granted a single session of Dharma instruction. He later receives instructions from Marpa's disciple Ngoktön, at which point he is described for the first time as casting hailstorms. Mila has now been trained and is described as ready to commence his life as an itinerant yogin.

Part 3 records an extensive series of narratives that make up the proto-Songs section of the text. Its first pages repeat Gampopa's account in which Mila mistakes the light of a butter lamp for the illumination of meditation experience. After six years and eleven months with Marpa, he is inspired by a dream to go "south, in the direction of Nepal," and thus returns to his homeland. He meets both mother and sister but finds his father long dead; giving away his house and possessions, he then sets out on the yogin's path.

If the proto-Life in this work shows signs of developing narrative depth and complexity, the proto-Songs follows suit, nearly tripling the number of individual stories. Although the boundary between one narrative unit and the next is frequently blurred, it is possible to count some thirty-three discrete episodes.

Many narratives newly added here would later become famous in the standard version: Mila's meeting with his disciple Rechungpa, an extensive encounter with Tashi Tseringma, a visit with a ḍākinī in pigeon form. These may reflect stories that had spread among Drigung meditators following—in some cases literally—in Milarepa's footsteps.[45] Yet the work is firmly rooted in the existing literary tradition. Details of locations and interlocutors frequently differ, but all of the earlier proto-Songs episodes from Gampopa and Lama Zhang lie embedded within this text in their original order; the latter third of the proto-Songs is almost entirely dedicated to preserving those early anecdotes.

The section then ends with a brief statement, following Gampopa and Lama Zhang, about the yogin's death and cremation at both Tisé and Drin. For the first time, however, the author records the date of the yogin's passing: a bird year at the age of eighty-two. The text also repeats earlier claims that Milarepa appeared as an emanated being, adding the statement that he departed not in a single form, but manifesting several bodies: "It is also taught that, at that time, from among his three physical manifestations in the shared perception [of ordinary people], one departed as Tashi Tse-ringma's personal master, and another went to India."[46]

The text's fourth and concluding section briefly lists the recipients of Milarepa's Dharma transmission—recording, again for the first time, a list of nineteen principal disciples divided into several categories: four heart sons (*thugs sras*), eight close sons (*nye ba'i sras*), six sons born during his old age (*sku bsgres kar 'khrungs pa'i thugs zin gyi sras drug*), and his lineage-holding son (*rgyud pa 'dzin pa'i sras*), Gampopa. This system of classifying the yogin's followers would become a standard feature of nearly all Mila-repa's later biographies.

The orality of Mila's biographical tradition has often been taken for granted; yet, as was demonstrated in chapter 1, the yogin's life story (or at least its outline) was first presumably transcribed toward the end of his life and shortly thereafter. Dönmo Ripa's *Life of Jetsün Milarepa* aug-ments those original sources with new material, adding another layer of biographical narrative; tighter structure and richer content combine in a more coherent portrait of the master's life as both exemplar and individ-ual. This is perhaps unsurprising for an independent compilation entitled *Great Biographies of the Kagyu*, whose polemical focus was directed inward, toward legitimating the lineage and its individuals, as opposed to the col-lected writings of its author (as was the case with Gampopa's and Lama Zhang's accounts). It had absorbed the existing literary tradition while creating it anew.

SANGYÉ BUM'S *LIFE OF MILAREPA*

Another undated work may have appeared around the same time as Donmo Ripa's biography. Titled simply *The Life of Milarepa* (*Mi la ras pa'i rnam thar*, MNT), this text appears in a four-volume golden rosary collec-tion of Drukpa Kagyu biographies that record the transmission lineage of Ralung monastery, founded in 1180 by Tsangpa Gyaré Yeshé Dorjé (1161–1211) in western Tibet.[47] The Ralung transmission line, which formed the so-called "middle Drukpa" (*bar 'brug pa*) tradition, was eventually established in Bhutan through the activities of individuals such as Pajo Drugom Zhikpo (b. twelfth century) and later Zhapdrung Ngawang Nam-gyal (1594–1651), the eighteenth abbot of Ralung, who fled to the region and established a new, unified state.

The compilation was reproduced from a set of late eighteenth-century Bhutanese wood blocks.[48] However, the short biography of Milarepa therein was likely written in the mid-thirteenth century by one Sangyé Bum (b. twelfth century). The text itself is unsigned, but the preceding life story of Nāropa concludes with the statement that Sangyé Bum compiled the work based on five existing *namtars*.[49] The Twelfth Jé Khenpo Kunga Gyatso (served 1769–71) repeats this attribution in his introduction to the compilation.[50] *The Life of Milarepa* echoes the claim that the text was based upon five existing *namtars*. It is therefore not unreasonable to likewise attribute this record of Milarepa's life to Sangyé Bum.

Sangyé Bum served as the fifth abbot (1214–31) of Tsel Gungtang monastery, the institution established by Lama Zhang in 1175.[51] In 1242 Sangyé Bum founded the adjacent meditation college known as the Eastern Residence (*sgom sde gzims khang shar ma*).[52] He was later recognized as the preincarnation of the influential seventeenth-century master (and teacher of the Great Fifth Dalai Lama) Zurchen Chöying Rangdrol (1604–69). If Sangyé Bum wrote his *Life of Milarepa* during the latter part of his abbacy or shortly after his retirement, it might have been produced sometime between 1225 and 1250.

Sangyé Bum's *Life of Milarepa* broadly agrees with other golden rosary accounts from this early period. As in Gampopa's text and the *Kagyu Rosary* (discussed below), many passages conclude with the Tibetan word *ké* (*skad*, "so it is said"), implying that the account belongs to a living oral tradition. The life story is divided into two sections: the biographical account in which he relied on his lama and practiced austerities (*bla ma rten cing dka' ba spyad pa'i rnam thar*); and the biographical account of how experience and realization came forth (*nyams su myong ba rtogs pa skyes tshul gyi rnam thar*).[53] After a brief discussion of family ancestry, the father dies while Milarepa is a child. Unnamed relatives then steal the young boy's patrimony, and his mother sends him to study magic in order to exact revenge. After training with several teachers, he is sent to Ngami Changchup Gyaltsen (called Bami Bodhirāja in Donmo Ripa's text). After eight months of magical practices, the teacher exclaims, "My protector appeared carrying the heads and entrails of many Gungtang people, so the magic has worked."[54] A traveling merchant then brings word that a terrible plague struck Milarepa's homeland of Tsa in Gungtang, killing some forty people. He further reports that locals believe the plague was cast by Milarepa himself. Eventually Mila repents his misdeeds, meets his guru, Marpa, and carries out his religious training.

The second section records a variety of narratives from the yogin's later life, describing his retreats, attracting disciples, and performing miracles, and concludes with a brief but evocative narration of his death. These stories include many of the proto-Songs episodes of Lama Zhang and Dönmo Ripa, but Sangyé Bum further records a number of extended songs in their entirety. In at least one instance he also advises the reader to consult an extended Collected Songs (*mgur 'bum nam rgyas pa*) for clarification, although he does not specify a particular text.[55] Unlike other proto-works, the section lacks subheadings, and there is little structural organization evident in the many narrative threads.

Sangye Bum's text diverges from other early golden rosary accounts in one important way: the author makes no mention of Milarepa's status as a miraculous emanation. Accounts of magic and miracles abound, but the text nowhere asserts that the yogin was anything but an ordinary human capable of extraordinary effort in practice. He is said to have died at the age of seventy-three, a detail found only in Gyaltangpa's work (discussed next) and for which Sangyé Bum may have served as a source.

GYALTANGPA'S *KING OF JETSÜNS*

Sometime in the early second half of the thirteenth century—a few decades, perhaps, after Dorjé Dzé Ö's and Sangyé Bum's contributions—another golden rosary compilation appeared, evocatively titled *The Garland Biographies of Golden Mountain* (*Gser ri'i phreng ba'i rnam thar*), by Gyaltangpa Dechen Dorjé (ca. thirteenth century).[56] Gyaltangpa was a disciple of the renowned Drukpa master Götsangpa Gönpo Dorjé (1189–1258). As expected, then, this work documents the lives of teachers in the author's Drukpa Kagyu lineage, twelve in total, from the Bengali adept Tilopa to the author's guru Götsangpa, and prefaces these with a "biography" of the lineage descending from Gampopa itself (the *Dpal ldan dwags po bka' brgyud pa'i rnam par thar pa*). Individual lives take the unusual stylistic form of root verses of praise (*stod pa*) and prose autocommentaries.

The yogin's life story, titled *The Biography of Milarepa, King of Jetsüns* (*Rje btsun gyi rgyal po mi la ras pa'i rnam thar*, JGM), encompasses twenty-six verses and commentary chapters.[57] While this format differs significantly from previous accounts, it shares their underlying narrative structure, beginning with the early life (proto-Life part 1) followed by a series of proto-Songs episodes, and concluding with a brief description of his final passing (proto-Life part 2). This follows, in broad strokes, the outline of biographies extending back to Gampopa's original text:

[proto-Life part 1]
verses 1–7: early life
verse 8: sorcery
verse 9: early search for Dharma
verses 10–13: training with Marpa and Ngoktön
verses 14–15: return to his homeland
verses 16–17: practice of austerities
[proto-Songs]
verses 18–25: proto-Songs episodes
[proto-Life part 2]
verse 26: final passing

The early proto-Life sections introduce many new narrative elements into the biographical tradition while creating a storyline more fluid, and a tone far more dramatic, than in previous works. The text begins, in the first verse, with a clear declaration of Milarepa's status as an extraordinary being:

> Jetsün lama Milarepa, Lord,
> Supreme emanation body who tamed beings according to their needs,
> Assumed an ordinary form and through diverse austerities
> Gained countless qualities—to you I bow down with devotion.[58]

He is, the commentary adds, "but an emanation of the Buddha," an assertion then supported with citations from both sūtra and tantra.[59] The narrative proper begins with Milarepa himself made to announce his miraculous status:

> The lama said, "I am an emanation of the one called Ārya Nāgārjunagarbha, who was prophesied by the Buddha and appeared as an emanation of the Buddha himself." Thus Milarepa, king of Jetsüns, was truly Nāgārjunagarbha, an emanation of the Buddha. He also [said,] "In the perception of ordinary individuals, I have now emanated in an ordinary body, and have appeared for the benefit of ordinary people."[60]

This of course stands in direct contrast to Tsangnyön's standard version, where Milarepa explicitly rebukes his disciples for viewing him as an emanation of a buddha—an event discussed further in chapter 4. Mila's conception is then foretold in his mother's dreams, and miraculous signs accompany his birth. The yogin's representation as an emanation is no longer appended, somewhat perfunctorily, to the end of the life story; rather, it becomes a pivotal theme for the entire Life to follow. Even prior to birth he is styled an extraordinary being, his life a skillful performance enacted for the benefit of others.

Gyaltangpa, like Dönmo Ripa before him, adds new detail to the story of Mila's early life and training, much of which would later appear in his standard biography. Themes of calculated revenge are for the first time plotted out in detail: his family is dispossessed of its wealth by disparaging relatives; the mother dispatches young Mila to exact revenge through the practice of sorcery; he murders twenty-five members of his uncle's family through magical means; he casts hailstorms to stave off repercussions from enraged villagers.

Likewise, subsequent verses emphasize themes of repentance, mortification, and purification: Mila seeks out Dharma, eventually meeting his destined guru, Marpa; he perseveres through the trial of constructing a nine-storied tower (only one is mentioned); he secretly approaches Marpa's disciple Ngok for instruction. As he returns to his guru's home, Mila's hardships are explicitly described—for the first time in the biographical tradition—as a technique for purifying the misdeeds of his youth, skillfully meted out by Marpa. Verse 12 reads,

Accompanied by master [Ngok], he went to Marpa.
Karmic obscurations spent, he became master of all Dharma teachings,
A worthy vessel for instructions.
To the Jetsün once foretold, I bow down with praise.[61]

Upon Mila's completion of the tower, as he stands before his guru in what will become a moment of reckoning for many years of hardship and pain, the commentary continues,

"This is most excellent," said Marpa. "This past year I did not impart Dharma to Mila and I showed little kindness. His mindstream was filled with unimaginable negativities, and, in order to purify them, I forced him to till the earth, construct a tower, and so forth.

"In general, Mila, you are an individual who is a worthy vessel and a suitable recipient for instructions. Your preliminary practices of purifying negativities are thoroughly completed. Now I can give the instructions of the actual practice."[62]

Mila then returns to his homeland, embarking on his yogic career.

The text continues, in verses 18–25, with the proto-Songs. These progress in an uneven fashion, some stories receiving great attention, others sketched only in profile. The account of Mila's visit to Lapchi, for example, is extended through two entire verses; his stay in the forest of Sengé Ling, the meeting with his aunt, and conversion of the Tsheringma sisters are narrated in one verse each. The remaining seven episodes are grouped together, spread across the following two verses. The penultimate verse serves as a more general synopsis, first mapping the landscape in which Milarepa stayed and then cataloguing a list of disciples he attracted.[63] In terms of both structure and function, this verse resembles chapter 11 of the standard version, for which it may have served as a model.

The text concludes with a verse describing Mila's death, once again casting him in the Buddha's image as one "who possesses the six qualities."[64] This correspondence becomes clearer in the commentary, where the yogin himself states, "During the present year, this illusory physical heap shall act out the play of impermanence."[65] At the age of seventy-three Mila pledges that he will pass from suffering in a manner that benefits beings, just as the Buddha had done long before. The text unfolds the drama of his death as it once again records the core narrative tradition that would serve as a basis for all later versions: he is poisoned through the machinations of a jealous Bonpo priest and succumbs to illness;[66] he submits his final testament; he passes away amid miraculous signs; and his body is cremated, famously relinquishing no corporeal relics. The yogin is described as following the path of the Buddha's own complete perfected awakening (mngon par rdzogs par sangs rgyas pa). He leaves behind no physical remains, yet it is foretold that his emanation bodies (sprul pa'i sku, nirmāṇakāya) will endure in the world for the benefit of suffering beings.

On a micro level, King of Jetsüns may be understood as forming a biographical stream distinct from other works in the early stratum. The author added significant detail to the life story, some of which cut across the grain of earlier representations and would eventually be absorbed into the dominant traditions of the compendia and, later, the standard version. Yet, as noted above, Gyaltangpa also retains the larger structure implicit in other works of this type; his text's division into discrete verses and verse commentaries does not diminish its underlying proto-Life/ Songs format. And like Dönmo Ripa, he reflects a growing concern with a more formalized expression of the yogin's life as a story of complete liberation.

THE KAGYU ROSARY OF WISH-FULFILLING JEWELS

Another significant moment in the evolution of Milarepa's biographical tradition, and further evidence that the mid-thirteenth century saw a flurry of creative approaches to writing sacred lives, is found in a second collection of Drigung Kagyu biographies known as *The Kagyu Rosary of Wish-fulfilling Jewels* (Bka' brgyud yid bzhin nor bu yi 'phreng ba, KGW). Milarepa's life story, untitled and with no attributed author, is one of nine biographies preserved in the collection. Though originally thought to have been written by the famed adept Orgyan Rinchen Pel (1229/30–1309), the final biography has recently been identified as the work of another Orgyanpa, author of the final biography and nephew of its subject, Gardampa Chödingpa (1180–1240).[67] As a result, a date for the entire collection's completion has tentatively been pushed back one sixty-year cycle to circa 1244, and is likely contemporary with the works of Dönmo Ripa and Sangyé Bum discussed above.

This work has preserved one of the period's most extensive and structurally complex proto-Life/Songs representations of Milarepa's life. Its author uses a terse writing style and frequently marks episodes with the phrase "so it is said" (skad, gsungs), implying that stories were still being recorded from oral tradition. Many narratives, however, appear ambiguous or confused, making sense only if understood as hurried abbreviations of much longer accounts. Indeed, much of the material appears to originate in the earliest biographical compendium, known as *The Twelve Great Disciples*, for which it may have served as a sort of précis.

Mila's biography in *The Kagyu Rosary* is divided under two main headings, documenting first his early life and training and then his later spiritual career. The latter part is subdivided into seventeen sections, each titled for a specific "quality" (yon tan) of the yogin's mastery or realization. These sections are, in turn, composed of individual episodes: largely narrative fragments and partial songs drawn from the larger compendia. This structure will be examined in detail in the next chapter. Here, I will merely note that, for the first time, a proto-Life/Songs text adopts the complex narrative structure that would become standard in all of the larger compendia.

The text begins with an explicit assertion of Mila's status as an emanation of a fully enlightened buddha, more in line with the larger compendia than with the previous proto-Life/Songs texts: "Vajradhara emanated as Akṣobhya; Akṣobhya emanated as Mañju[śrīmitra]; having emanated in that form, he then displayed the need for diligence in practice [as Milarepa]."[68] The early life generally follows the presentation in the later compendia, with some variation of detail drawn from other sources: Mila's father dies while he is young, the family wealth is seized by relatives, the mother sends young Mila to exact revenge through sorcery. The proto-Life of part 1 concludes with his training under Marpa and departure for his homeland in Mangyul.

Part 2 is headed by the subtitle "qualities of his experience, connected with his *samādhi*," which begins the series of proto-Songs by enumerating seventeen distinct qualities, each serving as a subheading for one or more discrete narrative episodes. These follow the titles used in *The Twelve Great Disciples* and the later compendia discussed in the next chapter, with only minor changes in their arrangement. In other early works, the proto-Song episodes were recorded with little apparent emphasis on chronology or narrative flow. Here, likely drawing on the compendia as a model, Milarepa's spiritual career is explicitly structured from the first chapter, in which he embarks upon the yogin's path ("the quality of understanding saṃsāra as having no essence") to the last, prior to his passing away ("the quality of his recognizing Mahāmudrā").

ZHAMAR KHACHÖ WANGPO'S *CLOUD BANK OF BLESSINGS*

The last of Milarepa's biographies, surveyed only briefly here, is a relatively late text poetically titled *Cloud Bank of Blessings* (*Byin rlabs kyi sprin phung*), composed by Khachö Wangpo (1350–1405), second of the Karma Kagyu Zhamar ("red crown") hierarchs. The text is preserved in a golden rosary collection, the first two volumes of Khachö Wangpo's (incomplete) *Collected Works*.[69] Although it maintains the general Life/Songs structure of other works in this stratum, its genealogy is more complex than most. Entire passages of its proto-Life are copied directly from the larger compendia, although it lacks the complex structural divisions of those later sources. Its proto-Songs section is the most extensive of all six texts discussed here, due at least in part to its relatively late production. In some instances, these episodes draw extended quotations from Dönmo Ripa's *Biography* and the *Kagyu Rosary*. Other narratives seem to have been added from the later compendia. And unlike earlier versions, nearly every episode records songs or song fragments, apparently drawn from the larger, unabridged works. The text is thus a blending of early and later sources, providing evidence that the proto-Life/Songs format maintained its cachet even after more extensive biographies began to circulate.

The second Zhamar's work begins with a quotation from the compendia, recognizing Milarepa's miraculous status:

> The great Jetsün Milarepa himself, sovereign lord among victors without exception who perfectly accomplished the secrets of the Vajrayāna, emanation of the great being of the Ārya land Mañjuśrīmitra, without rivals of any sort in the snowy region to the north. . . .[70]

At this point, however, the text diverges, eliding from this passage the compendia's major structural division into two headings and seventeen qualities. The early life story generally follows the compendia, with many details drawn directly from the tradition of *The Black Treasury*. The next chapter will demonstrate that the Second Zhamar was part of a lineage that transmitted *The Black Treasury* but was bound by certain restrictions from disseminating it openly. This work, *Cloud Bank of Blessings*, seems to have allowed him to incorporate materials from *The Black Treasury* tradition without transgressing his vows.

Zhamar's proto-Songs, comprised of some forty-five discrete episodes, reflects its sourcing from both early and later works. Episodes 3 and 5, for example, are styled directly after Dönmo Ripa's *Biography*. Episodes 5 and 16 (referring to Milarepa's interaction with unruly villagers and with the king of Bhaktapur) are united in the compendia, but here follow the *Kagyu Rosary*'s somewhat enigmatic separation. Other stories, such as the yogin's meeting with the doctor Yangé in episode 17, are drawn directly from the compendia. Many accounts show signs of editorial revision: early fragments, retained in the works of Gampopa, Lama Zhang, and Dönmo Ripa, have been absorbed into other narrative episodes and are no longer evident as independent stories.

The text concludes with the second part of the proto-Life, narrating an account of Milarepa's death at the age of eighty-four. Of particular interest is this statement summarizing the master's life:

> Thus the great Jetsün lama was in actuality a Bhagavan Lord of the Family. However, in order to guide trainees in snowy Tibet through various means, he first acted in a worldly manner, honoring his mother and carrying out her instructions in full. Then, he attended an authentic lama, sacrificing his life with no [concern for it] whatsoever, in the manner of Sudhana

and the great being Nāropāda. Then, so that the oral tradition of the practice lineage would not degenerate for future generations of disciples, he wandered from mountain retreat to mountain retreat without concern for food or clothing and put only practice at the center his life. Then, in order to completely fulfill the prophesied intentions of the Kagyu elders, he imparted in full the practical guidance on oral instructions to worthy disciples, yogins, and yoginīs.[71]

This brief passage classifies the events of Milarepa's life in a manner absent from the biographical narratives themselves: early life; training; practice; transmission. These categories match those enumerated in the explicit structural divisions of an earlier proto-Life/Songs work, Dönmo Ripa's *Life*, described above. In this case, however, the structure has been transformed into narrative itself, form serving as content. And if these four narrative plot points seem to describe the content of sacred biography in general, they also came to define the contours of Milarepa's life as they would be mapped for centuries to come: as an enlightened being, he chooses to appear in the world in order to benefit beings; his early life is directed specifically by the intervention of his mother; his training follows not only that of Sudhana, the protagonist of the *Gaṇḍavyūha Sūtra* famed for meeting with fifty-three spiritual masters, but also the earlier gurus of his own Kagyu lineage; his practice requires the endurance of great austerities as he wanders among mountain retreats; and his transmission fulfills activities foretold by the teachers of his lineage, teaching new generations of yogin practitioners.

REFLECTIONS

The century or so following Milarepa's death provided fertile ground for the representation of the yogin's life. Indeed, many of the works surveyed in this chapter may have been composed within a few decades of one another: Donmo Ripa's in about 1245, Sangyé Bum's between 1225 and 1250, the *Kagyu Rosary* in about 1244, and Gyalthanpa's between 1258 and 1266. This period is set amid the so-called "latter diffusion" of Buddhism (*phyi dar*) in Tibet, following what is traditionally described as a "dark period" of religious and social unrest, and recently characterized as both a "Tibetan renaissance" and a "rebirth of Tibetan culture."[72] The diffusion was also an infusion, in which "Tibetans used the evolving literature and practices of later esoteric Buddhism as iconic forms and points of reference to reconstruct institutions, found monasteries, and reorganize the political realities of . . . Central Tibet."[73] This was, according to Tibetan histories, a period in which the shattered was made whole again, when "Tibetans knit together their fragmented culture by using the textual and ritual tools provided by Buddhist religious systems of Indian tantric Buddhism."[74]

If Milarepa's nascent biographical tradition took birth and began to coalesce within this socioreligious milieu, it also reflects the period's concerns. Golden rosary biography collections began to appear, providing tangible links between Indian tantric adepts and the religious vitae of Tibetan masters who, like Milarepa, promulgated their doctrinal transmissions. Moreover, the very terms used to describe Tibet's latter diffusion are equally germane to Mila's early biographical stratum, a stage during which biographers gradually bound together fragmented stories into a skeletal frame using the tools of narrative discourse provided by the dominant biographical works of the time (i.e., golden rosary texts).[75] These proto-Lives and proto-Songs were narrative collections supplying foundation and model for later works; they served (and continued to serve) ends both didactic and polemical, but were largely overshadowed by the comprehensive Lives they in turn helped to generate.

The earliest texts of this type—those of Lama Zhang and, by extension, his source, Gampopa—are rudimentary expressions of a life with little explicit structure or plotting, certainly nothing on the order of a "dynamic force shaping narrative discourse." The constitutive stories occasionally illustrate candid moments (the neophyte mistaking lamplight for inner realization or the yogin exposing his naked body to his sister and mother), but they too are mostly undeveloped and disconnected narrative fragments: Mila simply "traveled to Ü in search of sorcery, studied much sorcery, and then returned"; he later "turned himself into a crystal stūpa and then departed into space." Gampopa mentions the yogin's death in a single brief sentence; Lama Zhang foregoes even this reference. Since the arc of liberation is both swift and shallow, these works are of modest didactic value; their representations maintain their polemical effect primarily as constituents in the golden rosary of lives that authenticates the collected works they preface. And yet, these texts established prototypes for both Life and Songs, the format implicit in all subsequent vitae.

Later works of this period (preserved in the independent collected biographies of Dönmo Ripa, Sangyé Bum, Gyaltangpa, and the later *Kagyu*

Rosary and *Cloud Bank of Blessings*) would build on these foundations, augmenting the proto-Life/Songs configuration with new literary structure and a sharpened emphasis on narrative detail. Authors actively promoted Mila's status as exemplar, a miraculous emanation whose birth, life, and death paralleled those of great masters of the past. Biographical texts were structured accordingly, dividing the life into dramatic sequences, improving narrative flow. Entire songs of realization appeared together with their framing tales, some augmented and re-edited from the earliest fragments, others added from previously undocumented sources; for the first time, the broad sweep of Milarepa's later spiritual career was brought into focus, together with the record of his yogic success.

The life writing in this stratum matured but did not achieve (and perhaps never aspired to achieve) the fine polish of biographical grain in the later compendia or the standard version centuries later. And the details of the life story were still very much in flux; retellings were often similar but seldom consistent. Even in their most mature form, proto-works primarily served to promote the legitimacy of transmission, passing from mouth to ear, from teacher to student. Portraiture of individual lives was of less concern than the integrity of the rosary itself. Once again, however, these priorities would transform with the advent of the larger biographical compendia, repositories of Milarepa's great biographical narratives, to which this study now turns.

BIOGRAPHICAL COMPENDIA

LIVES MADE FLESH

ORIENTATIONS

Biographical Compendia

AFTER THE proto-works addressed in the previous chapter began to assemble the underlying framework for Milarepa's representation, the yogin's portrait came into sharper focus with the advent of a new, more comprehensive form of life writing: the biographical compendium. This chapter will introduce and analyze two related forms of compendia in Milarepa's biographical tradition, each of which predates the standard version by Tsangnyön Heruka. The first, informally known as *The Twelve Great Disciples*, is perhaps the earliest extensive record of the yogin's life, composed by his close followers. The second, a series of related works collectively known as *The Black Treasury*, expands the earlier compendium to what would become the yogin's most extensive biography. The name *Black Treasury* refers to the temple in southern Tibet where the work was originally archived, but the text's designation as a treasury also reflects its status as an exhaustive compilation of stories about Milarepa's activities. Both collections have gained wide circulation and popularity in Tibet. And as autonomous and mature biographies, they mark a significant evolution both in the structuring of Tibetan life writing and in the representation of the yogin's life.

The term "compendium," used to describe these works, may at first seem counterintuitive; the first definition from the *Shorter Oxford English Dictionary* ("a work presenting in brief the essential points of a subject") even appears contradictory. In the present context, however, I use the word in its other sense, referring to "an assortment, a varied collection," since the compendia portray their subject using a far richer palette than previous writings. I also use the term to indicate that these are the first works to explicitly encompass two forms of biographical literature: liberation narrative and song collection. The word has yet one further connotation, echoing the Tibetan term it frequently translates: *kuntu* (*kun btus*), literally "collection of everything." These biographical writings claim, to use the traditional Buddhist formulation, not only to reflect the life in all its variety but also to record its full extent. Structure and content are married in the promotion of an individual life and in presenting the life story as a vehicle for emulating an exemplary figure and ultimately for liberation itself.

The following discussion will begin by examining the structure and content of *The Twelve Great Disciples*, which served as a model for nearly all of the later extensive works. Frequent quotations from the text illustrate the innovations of structure and content this new format introduced to the biographical tradition. The chapter then turns to the subsequent but closely related *Black Treasury* tradition, noting its continuities with the early compendium and its contributions to the later standard version.

It is unclear exactly how widespread these compendia were in Tibet, although nearly a dozen unique manuscripts have recently come to light, many of which are richly illustrated with scenes of the yogin's life. Wood blocks for at least one print edition of *The Twelve Great Disciples* are known to have been produced, suggesting an interest in expanded distribution. Such works likely first developed and spread among Kagyu communities looking to Milarepa as a founding figure, specifically those committed to the aural transmissions. The Tibetan historian Pema Karpo later made reference to *The Twelve Great Disciples*; the Eighth Karmapa excerpted sections from the text's early life in his *Ocean of Kagyu Songs*; and Tenzin Chökyi Lodrö (1868–1906), the thirty-fourth Drigung Kagyu hierarch, quotes from *The Black Treasury*. But the compendia also gained cachet across the wider Tibetan Buddhist world, capturing the attention of exegetes and historians from diverse religious affiliations long after Tsangnyön Heruka's standard version began to dominate the Tibetan literary landscape.

Lives and Songs: Biographical Forms

The century following Milarepa's death saw a flurry of religious activity among the lineages that became known as the Marpa Kagyu, the oral transmission stemming from the yogin's guru, Marpa. As these lineages began to institutionalize and spread, eventually forming the so-called four major and eight minor Kagyu subsects, there was a growing need to represent their founders not merely as beads in a golden rosary, but as autonomous figures and authoritative sources for their tradition.[1] A host of extended biographical writings began to appear around this time: a biographical "itinerary" of the Bengali master Atisha (982–1054) by his disciple Dromtön Gyalwé Jungné (1005–64), the life of Ra Lotwāwa Dorjé Drak (1016–1198) in some three hundred folios by his grand-disciple Yeshé Sengé (b. twelfth century), and Nyangrel Nyimé Özer's (1136–1204) revealed biography of Padmasambhava.[2]

Milarepa's biographical compendia fit squarely within this milieu, both quantifying and qualifying earlier works of the tradition. The two discussed in this chapter wrapped layer upon layer of biographical detail around the proto-works' skeletal armature—new thematic elements, plot points, and narrative structure—modeling the corpus as with sinews, muscles, and flesh. The result is a finely grained biographical portrait, more sophisticated than anything previously attempted. Building on the discussion in chapter 2, this chapter argues that the parallel concerns of Milarepa's biographical tradition—his representation as both individual and exemplary figure—were advanced through the simultaneous development of new biographical forms: the Life and the Collected Songs.

Authors of the biographical compendia drew upon emerging types of life writing implicit within the early golden rosary texts, developing the proto-Life/Songs into more explicit biographical forms. The so-called *Twelve Great Disciples*, earliest of Milarepa's extensive biographies, combined—perhaps for the first time—extended narrative sections and major song compilations to fashion the Life and Collected Songs as structurally autonomous but thematically integrated elements within a single text. These works are uniformly titled biographies (*rnam thar*), yet each encompasses both biographical forms while bringing the division of Life and Songs into progressively sharper focus.

Unlike the earliest proto-Lives, constructed from terse, frequently disconnected narrative fragments, the compendia present life stories both detailed and formally structured. Each of these biographical accounts records Milarepa's life as a series of chronological narratives, advanced through the judicious use of plotting and thematic development and framed by a series of explicit structural markers tracking the evolution of the yogin's mundane and spiritual "qualities" (*yon tan*). These versions thus conform to the normative view that lives occur over time, and that biographical writing best represents them through a progression of inter-related stories, describing events unfolding chronologically. The compendia emphasize continuities in Milarepa's early life, forming a unified narrative unit spanning his troubled youth, vilification by his paternal relatives, and his retribution by magic and murder, through his apprenticeship under Marpa, his practice of austerities, and eventual awakening in mountain retreat. They also add significantly to the representation of Milarepa's death. The concluding sections, frequently ignored in the early proto-works, describe the elaborate drama of his parting instructions, final passing, and cremation, amid a display of miraculous appearances. The Lives thus seamlessly track Milarepa's life, from his worldly birth to the distribution of his remains.

The Songs display an even greater level of development. Where the proto-Songs generally record only the barest of song fragments, the compendia preserve entire exchanges between guru and disciple in verse, composed of multiple songs; where the proto-Songs lack coherent narrative framing, the compendia incorporate dozens of song cycles, each forming a discrete narrative unit. As the Songs began to manifest as a unique literary genre, they also became a new form of life writing. Few would dispute the fact that the Collected Songs are biographical in nature, but the means through which they represent a life are of a different order. Rather than the strict narrative chronology common to biographical writing, the Songs might be better understood as forming biographical networks: a structure of narrative units contributing to the overall representation of a life, yet without any specific chronological relationship.[3]

As a biographical network, the Songs offer a panoramic view of the yogin's teaching career, situated between Milarepa's early life and his death, but do little to advance a sense of temporal movement between individual chapters.[4] This is somewhat mitigated by the structure framing the Songs around a series of seventeen section headings, each describing a particular quality of Milarepa's yogic realization. Yet even these lack any underlying temporal relationship. While each cycle describes a story occurring in time, taken as a whole the Songs are primarily static, in contrast to the Life that passes through time. The Songs record many episodes of Milarepa's life without telling a unified or ultimately coherent story. The underlying portability of individual episodes, as nodes in its biographical network, would later be reinforced by Tsangnyön Heruka, who significantly redacted the Songs, cutting fragments from one cycle only to append them to another elsewhere in the text. Throughout the development of the biographical tradition, authors have emphasized the songs themselves over any given relationship among them, and they could be reformulated and rearranged without losing their general biographical sense.

The compendia also increasingly show Milarepa's life story in a miraculous light, emphasizing his role as enlightened emanation and revealing his life to be a performance staged for the benefit of ordinary beings. Mila's characterization as an exemplary figure gradually builds in the presentation of the Life, culminating in the standard version, which explicitly models the biography in the form of the Buddha's twelve deeds. But it is the Collected Songs, not the Life, that can perhaps best be understood as setting the pattern for Mila's mature teaching career through a network of interrelated but synchronic narrative cycles. Each individual song cycle defines Milarepa's roles as both yogin and teacher, and those roles were translated into the Tibetan Buddhist cultural milieu, much as his songs of realization rendered Indian forms into the Tibetan vernacular. The standard version would later present the Songs as a commentary, a means of illuminating the pattern of his life as exemplar and teacher. But as a teacher, Milarepa remains, above all, a uniquely Tibetan individual who could be claimed as the master of the snowy land.

THE TWELVE GREAT DISCIPLES: LIFE OF THE GLORIOUS ZHEPÉ DORJÉ

Editions and Manuscripts

During a visit in 1948 to Milarepa's famed retreat known as Whiterock Horse-tooth (Brag dkar rta so) near the Nepalese border, Dezhung Rinpoche—recognized as one of his generation's preeminent scholars—saw a xylograph edition of a text he called *The Twelve Great Disciples* (*Bu chen bcu gnyis*), which he referred to as "the earliest version of the biography and collected songs of Mi-la ras-pa, and repeatedly mentioned . . . as *the* necessary source for definitive research on Mi-la ras-pa's life."[5] Dezhung Rinpoche then introduced this work, said to have been compiled by an inner circle of Milarepa's closest disciples, to Western researchers over the next few decades. E. Gene Smith briefly referred to the text in his introduction to the *Life of Tsangnyön Heruka*, asserting its role as an early source for Milarepa's standard biography.[6] In the introduction to his English translation of *The Life of Milarepa*, Lobsang Lhalungpa likewise mentions "a notable version [of the Life] compiled by the twelve Great Disciples," citing Smith's work.[7] More recently, in the early 1990s Cyrus Stearns played the role of modern treasure revealer, "recovering" an edition of a text he identified as *The Twelve Great Disciples* and briefly introduced it in an unpublished survey for the Newark Museum; Francis Tiso made note of it several years later, and Peter Roberts used it as a source to study the narrative traditions of Milarepa's disciple Rechungpa.[8] Several pages of the manuscript have previously appeared in print.[9]

An early compendium of Milarepa's Life and Collected Songs has thus been acknowledged (though largely unstudied) in Western academic circles for more than four decades; rare as it was, however, this "earliest version" and "necessary source" was not at all unknown in Tibet. It likely served Tsangnyön Heruka in his crafting of the standard *Life* and *Songs*. But it also formed the basis for a stream of early compendia collectively known as *The Black Treasury*, attributed to the editorial hand of the Third Karmapa, Rangjung Dorjé (1284–1339), more than a century and a half prior to the standard version. The Drukpa Kagyu hierarch Pema Karpo mentions the text in his record of received teachings (*gsan yig*), noting a "Life and Collected Songs of Jetsün [Milarepa] arranged by Ngamdzongpa and the twelve cotton-clad yogins (*ras pa*)," a work he takes to be an authentic representation (*tshad mar byed pa*) and one generally in accord with the standard version by Tsangnyön Heruka.[10] Pema Karpo's contemporary Mikyö Dorjé, the Eighth Karmapa, preserved extensive passages from this version of the Life in his *Ocean of Kagyu Songs*, a collection traditionally recited each year by hundreds, if not thousands of monks. As we shall see, at least one block-print edition of the compendium was produced before the end of the sixteenth century, facilitating its wider dissemination, while manuscripts of the text were being copied at least as late as the seventeenth century in eastern Tibet. If it was a rarity, the biographical work known as *The Twelve Great Disciples* had also been absorbed deeply into Milarepa's biographical tradition.

The Twelve Great Disciples exists in several known editions, only three of which are currently accessible for study: the Stockholm edition, a xylograph held in the Museum of Ethnography in Stockholm, Sweden;[11] the Oxford edition, a manuscript held in the collection of Oxford University's Bodleian Library;[12] and the Newark edition, an illuminated manuscript held in the archives of the Newark Museum, Newark, NJ.[13] At least four other editions of this text are known. The newly published catalogue of the Drepung monastery archives lists a printed (*dbu can*) manuscript titled *Life of the Glorious Zhepé Dorjé* (*Dpal bzhad pa'i rdo rje'i rnam thar*), arranged by the twelve cotton-clad disciples (*ras pa bu chen bcu gnyis kyis bkod pa*) in 210 folios.[14] Zhepé Dorjé is the secret initiation name given to Milarepa by his guru, Marpa, and this title and attribution agree with the colophons of the Oxford and Newark editions. Other editions said to exist include block prints from Gonkar Chödé and the Tsé Podrang, as well as a manuscript from Drungtö monastery in Nyarong, Kham.[15]

The first of these, the Stockholm edition, bears the cover title *The Great Life and Collected Teachings of Jetsün Mila the Great Repa, Arranged by the Twelve Accomplished Cotton-Clad Yogins* (*Rje btsun mid la ras chen gyi rnam thar bka' 'bum chen mo grub thob ras pa bcu gnyis kyis bsgrigs pa*).[16] This may identify the work as the one referenced by Pema Karpo (and later seen by Dezhung Rinpoche), so it may have been completed prior to his death in 1592. The printer's colophon states: "The great cotton-clad Guṇamati of Gangtö, a yogin of Dakpo in the east, completed [this work] in the isolated place of Shambu Gangkar."[17] Thus, although Dezhung Rinpoche saw this text in the library of Drakar Taso, the print seems to have originated in the region of the famed sacred mountain Shambu/Shampo in central Tibet.[18]

The editions from Oxford and Newark (the focus of this study), are closely related and generally agree in both structure and content. Their points of divergence, however, are also of interest. Both manuscripts retain spelling corruptions: *rgyud* for *brgyud*, *bsha' ma* for *gsha' ma*, *'gur* for *mgur*, etc., the last of which may represent an early spelling, as it is adopted in many early works. They also vary between the early version of the name *Mid la* and the more common *Mi la*. Both likewise confuse genitive for instrumental cases (i.e., *gi* for *gis*) and vice versa, although they regularly disagree in their use of these particles. Occasionally, the two editions record different words or phrases; in almost every instance the Newark edition agrees with Tsangnyön Heruka's standard version, most likely indicating its late date and influence from that work, while the Oxford edition preserves an alternate account. The Oxford edition also retains passages and several chapters elided from the Newark manuscript.[19] Since editions tend toward standardization, and since the Oxford text shows no influence from Tsangnyön's work, it is plausible that the Oxford manuscript predates both the Newark edition and the standard version and was perhaps inscribed sometime prior to the late fifteenth century.

The Newark manuscript can be ascribed a *terminus a quo* no earlier than the late seventeenth century. Near the beginning of the chapter recounting Mila's first encounter with his divine female disciples known as the five Long Life Sisters (Tshe ring mched lnga), an illustration depicts the Geluk founder Tsongkhapa (1357–1419), portrayed in his usual form as a Buddhist monk in the gesture of teaching Dharma. The end of that chapter is marked by another Geluk figure seated next to the yogin, draped in the robes of a fully ordained monk and a scholar's hat, his right hand raised to his ear in a gesture of singing, clearly copying Milarepa's iconography. This figure, also identified by inscription, is Kalden Gyatso (1607–77), the famed scholar and adept of Amdo in eastern Tibet, renowned—as was Milarepa—for his hermetic lifestyle and his songs of realization.[20]

Kalden Gyatso recognized his older half-brother and teacher Chöpa Rinpoche (b. 1580) as an incarnation of Milarepa, but he also identified himself with Mila, modeling both his life and his songs after those of the great yogin.[21] It seems that Kalden Gyatso's followers maintained this association: his visual representations are ubiquitously fashioned after Milarepa's singing posture, as in the Newark illustration.[22] Kalden Gyatso founded a hermitage and active retreat center (sgrub sde) called Tashikyil (not to be confused with the famous monastic center Labrang Tashikyil), where he spent much of his later life.[23] It may have been there that his disciples commissioned the Newark manuscript, sometime after the Amdo master's death at the end of the seventeenth century.[24]

The history of this manuscript thus illustrates that the earliest autonomous version of Milarepa's Life and Songs, found in The Twelve Great Disciples, maintained its relevance long after the standard version appeared. In this fully fleshed life story and extensive song catalogue, disciples of a Geluk scholar could find precedent for their guru's activity as yogin and poet. And perhaps more importantly, the representation of Milarepa as a miraculous incarnation, redacted out of the standard version, allowed the possibility of a direct equivalence between an eleventh-century mendicant and the seventeenth-century monk, a correspondence read in the songs of realization and depicted visually on the manuscript folio.[25]

The Name and Date

Like the many biographical works surveyed in preceding chapters, these texts are called Lives (rnam thar); the Newark edition is titled The Profound Life of the Great Jetsün Milarepa (Rje btsun chen po mid la ras pa'i rnam thar zab mo).[26] For the first time, however, the split between Life and Songs implicit within the proto-model is incorporated explicitly into the narrative structure. This is evident in the title of the Stockholm edition, described as both Life and Collected Teachings (*rnam thar bka' 'bum*). The colophons to these works are even clearer, describing the narrative as "the Life of Glorious Zhepé Dorjé, together with a song-outline."[27]

This version of the Life and Songs was never formally titled *The Twelve Great Disciples*; that name derives instead from the work's attribution to Milarepa's inner circle of students. The colophon begins by stating, "For the benefit of fortunate meditators, this Life has been set down in words by the twelve great cotton-clad disciples, such as Ngendzong Tönpa Bodhirāja."[28] Chapter 1 described the role Ngendzong Repa played in codifying the aural transmissions and recording the life of his guru through four signed biographical episodes. Here, Ngendzong is identified as leading in the compilation and production of the yogin's first extensive biographical treatment.

It is unclear to what degree Ngendzong and his colleagues actually recorded this tradition on paper, although that is obviously the meaning this line intends to convey.[29] Textual composition was frequently a complex process wherein works could be dictated by the author to a disciple acting as scribe, by whom the text was then edited and revised; occasionally, this process could extend over generations, as seems to have been the case with Gampopa's *Collected Works*.[30] Thus the words of *The Twelve Great Disciples* may indeed have sprung from Milarepa's followers, even if they were transcribed in their present form at a somewhat later date. From the tradition's point of view, at least, this would do little to harm the integrity of the narrative or the authenticity of its origin. The biographical compendium that came to be known as *The Twelve Great Disciples* may thus have been recorded as early as Ngendzong's death in the mid-twelfth century. Perhaps Ngendzong's disciple Dampa Rechen, author of his guru's biography, had a hand in its production.[31] Either of these possibilities would situate the text approximately one hundred years before those of Dönmo Ripa and Gyaltangpa; while the compendium is more comprehensive in scope and structural development, each of the latter authors displays a concern for narrative structure not incompatible with *The Twelve Great Disciples*.[32] Other biographical elements, such as the categorization of disciples, closely parallel one another.

It is also possible that Götsangpa Gönpo Dorje (1189–1258) oversaw a reworking of the text, much as he reedited Dampa Rechen's biography of Ngendzong; this would instead push the appearance of *The Twelve Great Disciples* into the first half of the thirteenth century. Orgyanpa's proto-Life/Songs version of 1244 sets a *terminus ad quem* for this version, since it appears to rely directly on *The Twelve Great Disciples* for its narrative structure.[33] This earliest compendium of Milarepa's Life and Songs thus likely emerged within a century of the yogin's death, between the mid-twelfth and mid-thirteenth centuries, offering a new, if parallel model for life writing contemporary with the proto-works.

Life as Aural Transmission

The authors of *The Twelve Great Disciples* offered a new framework for representing Milarepa's life. Before addressing their innovations of structure and content, it will be helpful to understand what claims they made regarding the text itself. As discussed in chapter 1, the distinction between biographical narrative and tantric doctrine was initially blurred; the proto-Life/Songs served as legitimating introductions to an author's collected works and as preliminary texts for the aural transmission curricula. In particular, Ngendzong's colophon to his first signed narrative fragment refers to the episode as a direct expression of meditative realization, sealed by his guru's command, and meant only for followers endowed with "authentic experience of the practical instructions."[34]

The final colophon to *The Twelve Great Disciples*, replicated in all known editions, clearly derives from Ngendzong's first contribution mentioned above, transferring the identification of life writing and doctrinal transmission from a single chapter to the text as a whole. After recording the text's purported authors and classifying Milarepa's disciples, the colophon concludes by equating Life and Songs in their entirety with the transmission of tantric instructions. The biographical project is not merely a descriptive account of an individual's complete liberation (*rnam thar*), it becomes the vehicle for liberation itself. In the metaphor of tantric practice, the result is taken as the path.

The *Twelve Great Disciples* colophon ends:

This transmission wish-fulfilling jewel
Of the Cakrasaṃvara aural tantra
Has been put into writing according to the lama's words
For fear it might be forgotten by those of inferior minds,
For future holders of the family line.
I pray for patience of the lama and *ḍākinī*s.
Except for individuals of future generations, supports [for the teachings],

Who delight in initiation, blessing, *gaṇacakra* feasts,
And making offerings to hero and heroine protectors,
This is sealed by the lord guru's command.
If you transgress this command
The *ḍākinīs* will show great displeasure.
Therefore I ask, don't spread these words, keep them secret.
The transmission wish-fulfilling jewel. *Ḍaki samaya*.[35]

The text is characterized here not as a public Dharma teaching but as a tantric instruction requiring initiation, propitiation of Dharma protectors, pure *samaya* vows, and above all, secrecy. It is likewise not a general teaching, but rather is identified with a specific stage of aural transmission doctrine. The first and last lines of verse refer to the Life and Songs as "the transmission wish-fulfilling jewel" (*brgyud pa yid bzhin nor bu*) of the Cakrasaṃvara aural tantra.[36] As described in chapter 1, this is the first of three divisions of the aural transmission curriculum, the preliminary stages in part devoted to the lives of lineage holders. Thus, even though the biographical narrative has matured from proto-form into an autonomous work spanning both comprehensive Life and Songs compendia, its association with the aural transmission curriculum remains intact, serving as a central marker for the text's identification.

The Life and Songs

Like all of the biographical compendia, *The Twelve Great Disciples* is thematically structured around the description of Milarepa's qualities (*yon tan*). The text's introductory paragraph emphasizes Mila's exalted status as an emanated being, echoing claims in the proto-texts, before dividing the yogin's life into two parts:

> The great Jetsün Milarepa himself—sovereign lord among victors without exception, who perfectly accomplished the secrets of the Vajrayāna, manifestation of the great being of the Ārya Land, Mañjuśrīmitra himself, without rivals of any sort in the snow-covered region to the north—possessed two qualities: the qualities of hardships he faced, which are related to his family; and the qualities of his experience, which are related to his meditation.[37]

Part 1 briefly describes Mila's early home life, his search for Dharma, and training under his guru, Marpa. Part 2 is divided into seventeen discrete sections, named for the qualities of meditative experience developed during his later spiritual career; these are, in turn, composed of one to five or more chapters, each of which records a collection of songs within a narrative frame.

The "qualities of hardships" and "qualities of experience" underscore what would become *the* two principal themes associated with Milarepa's biographical tradition: the hardships he faced as a child, as a disciple, and as an ascetic; and the depth of his awakening, which in later accounts would be described as taking place in one body during a single lifetime. This division roughly maps the earlier proto-structure, organizing the text into Life and Songs. It is, however, an imperfect mapping, since what the text refers to as the "early life" (*snga ma*) includes—somewhat unintuitively—part 1 and the first two divisions of part 2; these are respectively called the early, middle, and latter stages of the early life (*snga ma'i gong ma, snga ma bar ma, snga ma 'og ma*). The last of these chapters refers to the "three chapters on the early life" (*snga ma skor gsum*). As in the proto-model, the yogin's death is recorded in the text's final chapter, concluding the larger narrative structure.

The earliest proto-texts formed a loose skeletal framework for Milarepa's biographical tradition. *The Twelve Great Disciples* provides a far richer physiognomy, fleshing out these bare bones with the qualities that would come to represent both individual and exemplar. The text's dialogue is frequently rough and uneven, its poetry unpolished, but even within its new framework, the Life incorporates a set of narrative units found in the earliest proto-work by Gampopa: childhood, sorcery, early search for Dharma, training under Marpa and Ngok, first retreats under Marpa, return to homeland, practice of austerities. And the text develops thematic elements and plot points that drive the narrative away from its fragmented antecedents toward a story that is both cohesive and compelling, and that would form a template for the standard Life several centuries later. To illustrate how far *The Twelve Great Disciples* has evolved from the proto-models, and to show how thoroughly Tsangnyön Heruka relied on the compendia for his own work, the following discussion will draw upon extended citations from part 1 of the early life and the final chapter recounting his death, as well as a brief overview of the Songs in part 2.

The Life begins with a few sentences briefly summarizing Milarepa's family background: he was born in Gungtang to the Khyungpo clan and given the name Töpaga, "delightful to hear." A sister followed several years later. But with broad strokes and terse dialogue, the narrative quickly sets in place dramatic elements that would direct his life's trajectory, establishing what would become the received history of Milarepa's early life:

> When the Jetsün turned seven years old, his father died. His paternal relatives conferred with one another and then seized [his family's] fields, their house, and all their possessions.
>
> The mother responded, "Since these two children are of your own flesh and blood, give them at least enough so they won't starve."
>
> "Hah hah," said [the relatives]. "Perhaps we should kill you then, mother and children," and sent them away in fear.
>
> At that time, the son studied letters with a Nyingma teacher while the mother was reduced to begging. One day, mother and son met at a [family] member's wedding. "They are the ones who have done this to us, mother and son," said the mother, and she wept.[38]

The mother then incites her son to exact revenge through magical means. After a period of training, Mila uses sorcery to murder his paternal family, sparing only the aunt. The text emphasizes Milarepa's youthful determination, although the mother is also implicated in the crime, an element that would later be edited out of the standard version:

> The Bönpo then taught magic to both his son and Töpaga, and put them in retreat. Due to Mila's great perseverance, he accomplished in three months what should have taken three years. He gave an acacia-wood magic dagger in his possession to two [runners] who were endowed with the ability of fleet-footedness and said, "I am sending you to race, measure by measure, up the pass to my paternal relatives' manor, and to place this in the hands of my mother."
>
> Overcome with anger [and dagger in hand], the mother made many striking gestures at the house. A servant girl saw a scorpion, nearly [the size of a] grown ox, rip out the house's pillars. Again, the mother made many striking gestures with the dagger toward the house, where Mila's uncle was hosting his son's wedding. Those outside [the family] were separated [from the house]; those inside [the family] were not separated and, with its pillars destroyed, the house collapsed. Twenty-five men and women died; the aunt alone was spared.[39]

Milarepa then casts hailstorms, devastating the countryside, and barely escapes with his life when a village mob tracks him down. As the karmic weight of his actions becomes too great to bear, Mila seeks atonement through Buddhist practice. His first (and in this version, only) early teacher, Rongtön Lhaga, informs him,

> It is fortunate that you have come. I possess an unmistaken instruction, a Dharma that abruptly awakens great sinners called Great Perfection (*rdzogs chen*). . . . If one hears it in the morning, one reaches buddhahood by morning; if one hears it at night, one reaches buddhahood by night.[40]

Once again, Mila is portrayed as exerting uncommon diligence, meditating "all day and all night without even a moment's distraction," so that even his teacher "shrank away in fear." Yet Mila's intensive practice yields no results and—in a sharp rebuke of the Nyingma tradition of practice—the teacher is forced to admit, "While the view of this Great Perfection of mine is lofty as the sky, its meditation is not embraced by experience. Although the many black methods in its conduct are appealing, I myself have no cause for confidence in it."[41]

Mila is then inspired to meet the translator Marpa, with whom, the text describes, he forged a connection during previous lives. His journey in search of this principal guru figures prominently, adding dramatic weight to the story while providing a brief comic aside:

> He placed a volume of Great Perfection atop the provisions and then set off. At a riverbank, he removed his shoes and absent-mindedly placed them on top of the text [upon his back], and then continued on. Along the way he encountered a number of children, who asked him, "Why are you carrying your shoes on top of a religious text?"
>
> Ashamed, he replied, "I am a simpleton come from far away."
>
> "Where are you going?" they asked.
>
> "I'm going to seek an audience with Lhodrak Marpa to ask him for Dharma. Do you know where he lives?"
>
> [Most] replied that they did not. But one cried, "I know him!"
>
> [The others] laughed and said, "Who is he then?"
>
> "He's the one we call Uncle Lodrö." With that, [Mila] went off on the path advised by the children.[42]

He then has the following encounter in the fields near Marpa's home; the old man, of course, is the guru himself, coming to greet his new disciple in disguise.

He came upon an old mantrika with graying hair, plowing a field of dark red-colored earth. [Mila] asked him, "Where does Marpa live?"

"There's no chance he'll meet with you. What's your business?"

"I'm going to ask him for Dharma."

"Oh, really? The likes of you isn't one to get Dharma. It's difficult because you need many offerings."

"Well then, how can I find out where he lives?" asked [Mila].

"Nobody but me knows where he resides. You turn over the remainder of my field; I'll have a look and come back." He then drew a line on the ground, said to furrow up to there, and went off.

By evening [Mila] had finished. [The mantrika returned and] said, "Now, make a meal with your own barley flour and I will offer you drink. Since you are an energetic worker, furrow my field, and as a wage I will give you a nugget of gold; use that as a gift and you should receive an audience." Then he departed.

[Mila] worked on the field for a month in anticipation of his fee. One day a messenger unexpectedly arrived who said, "If you want to meet the lama, come now."

[Mila] said, "I am waiting for the mantrika to come with the nugget of gold to use for my gift, so I haven't had a chance to meet with the lama."

[The messenger responded,] "If you want to meet him, go ahead." And they departed.[43]

Mila's training under Marpa fills the remainder of this chapter and lays the groundwork for what would later come to define the guru-disciple relationship in Tibet, emphasizing the central traits of steadfast devotion and unwavering perseverance. Marpa famously greets his new disciple disguised as a roughshod plowman and quickly displays a formidable temper as spiritual master. He assigns his new disciple the trial of constructing four towers, which, unlike Dönmo Ripa's description, is an exhausting and utterly thankless task in which Mila "hauled stones day and night without being granted Dharma until, exhausted, he was on the verge of collapse."

As Milarepa stands on the brink of utter despair, the narrative poignantly describes his flight from Marpa's home, illustrating a moment of deep pathos: he sits in the snowy wilderness, conflicted, confused, but his sense of determination ultimately prevails.

That evening he sat beside a rock cliff; later snow fell as he slept, piling up a full three feet. [When he woke,] he searched for firewood and hearthstones to prepare a meal, and spent a good while idling about. Full after finishing his meal, his mind began to race: "I am alone. I have just enough roasted barley flour. But after making a meal this morning there is only this much left. My previous work was half for the lama, half service for my food. The lama has not accepted me. But when I was tired, the lady filled my stomach with food and seasoning, and when parched, she set out drink till I was drunk. She is very kind. I don't have any clear destination at all. And the lama does have instructions of the sort [I'm after]." With these emotional thoughts, he set out through the snow and returned.[44]

He finds solace in the kindness of his guru's wife, who acts as his champion and later devises a scheme for him to sneak away and study with one of Marpa's senior disciples. This interrupts Mila's principal task of constructing towers. Here the narrative introduces a plot point that—once again—influences the way Milarepa's later life would be interpreted. Had Mila completed his work on the final tower, the text notes, "he would have been liberated [merely] through hearing [Dharma]. The towers would likely have purified Mila's negativities and obscurations." As in some proto-versions of the Life, Milarepa's trial of the towers is understood as the skillful means for expiating his earlier sins. In this case, however, the purification is incomplete, and this becomes the underlying rationale for his subsequent period of ascetic meditation and the difficulties it would entail. This interpretative shift is stated explicitly when Marpa asserts, "Had you and the lady, in your naiveté, not curtailed the natural turn of events in the construction of my towers, things would be easier [for you in the future]. Now you shall require great perseverance in Dharma, and [realization] will come over time."

The end of part 1, describing Mila's final days with his guru prior to leaving for his homeland, also records a number of extended songs that would become an integral part of the standard version. At the time of his first initiation, Mila offers a copper kettle to Marpa, who interprets the gift as an omen of his disciple's bright future:[45]

The very best of offerings, this is excellent indeed.
Since nothing could make this kettle better, you're a worthy one yourself.
Since it has four handles, you'll pervade the four directions.
Since its ring is sweet, you'll find great renown.
Since the outside couldn't be better, your commitments will be pure.

Since the inside is red, *ḍākinīs* will gather.
Since it's made from excellent materials, your lineage will grow better
and better.[46]

Framed as prophecy, these lines foreshadow Milarepa's spiritual career, described in the next section of the text. As the moment of his departure approaches, guru and disciple trade a series of long, heartfelt songs, recorded for the first time and retained in all subsequent versions. Mila pleads, "You know of this beggar's happiness and sorrow; / Grant blessings that I maintain a life of mountain retreat," and in response, Marpa famously sings, "In the rock caves of uninhabited places / Lies a market to barter life's round for transcendence."

Part 1 concludes with a song—again, recorded for the first time— that would come to encapsulate Milarepa's role in the burgeoning lineage known as the Kagyu: the so-called "song of four pillars," describing Marpa's prophetic dream about four great disciples and their chief contributions to the lineage. Of Milarepa's role, Marpa sings,[47]

I dreamt north of the sun a great pillar was raised.
I dreamt high on the pillar a vulture alighted.
I dreamt the vulture's plume fanned open wide.
I dreamt its aerie was built in a crag.
I dreamt a chick was born unto the bird.
I dreamt fledglings filled the sky.
This dream of the north is not ill-fated—what a wonderful dream it is.[48]

He then interprets the dream thus:

The pillar raised to the north of the sun
Is you, Milarepa of Gungtang.
That a vulture alighted high on the pillar
Means your character is like that of a vulture.
That the vulture's plume fanned open wide
Means you understand the lama's instructions.
That its nest was built in a crag
Is a sign your life force will be firmer than rock.
That a chick was born unto the bird
Is a sign that an unrivaled one will arrive.
That fledglings filled the sky

Is a sign that the Kagyu teachings shall flourish.
Such a wonderful dream of the north is excellent indeed.[49]

The song emphasizes Milarepa's determination and fortitude, with his life-force "firmer than rock"; it also identifies him with the source of a new religious tradition, the Kagyu, both founder and parent to fledglings who will ensure its promulgation. As the curtain closes on Milarepa's early life and the qualities of the hardships he endured, the stage is already being prepared for the details of his spiritual career.

Part 2, the collected songs enumerating the "qualities of Mila's realization," is divided into seventeen sections, the names of which typically refer to a song or story they record. Each section is, in turn, divided into a number of discrete cycles, with the total greatly outnumbering those recorded in the proto-works.[50] As mentioned earlier, the first two sections ("the quality of saṃsāra having no essence" and "the quality of dreams arising as signs") complete the record of Mila's early life with one cycle each.[51] Of the following sections, several include cycles related to a single theme, individual, or location. Sections 3 ("the quality of radiating bliss-warmth") and 4 ("the quality of freedom from longing for food and clothing"), for example, record five cycles frequently associated in the proto-works with the initial phase of Milarepa's spiritual career. Sections 6 ("the quality of realization arising as the path") and 11 ("the quality of the god of gods") recount six cycles that occur during his journeys to Nepal. Section 17 ("the quality of being introducing to Mahāmudrā") recounts four cycles on Mila's encounters with the Long Life Sisters, as well as several stories of his senior disciples, Rechungpa and Gampopa. The remaining sections generally lack any overarching organizational principles of either chronology or praxis. They instead form a biographical network of discrete events, illustrating and exemplifying Milarepa's spiritual career while recording the content of his instructions.

The Twelve Great Disciples concludes with another major contribution to Milarepa's Life: his death. The earliest proto-texts contain only the briefest mention of Mila's passing; Gyaltangpa's later work sketches a broad outline for the narrative, making general reference to the Buddha's final days. But *The Twelve Great Disciples* elevates the narrative of Milarepa's death to the level of high drama, introducing many new songs and expanding central plot points that would form the basis for later compendia and the standard version. And it is the account in this early compendium that fully fleshes out the yogin's final days, shaping the narrative into a model death with obvious parallels to that of the Buddha, while retaining a strong sense of Mila as a unique individual.

The chapter opens with the yogin foretelling his own demise when, to his disciples, he sings:

> The blossom of this yogin's body
> Shall by the frost of death's workings
> Be ruined. The time for it to pass on
> I have seen, and all kinds of visions will appear.[52]

And it will be no ordinary passing; Mila describes the drama that will soon unfold:

> For my twelve disciples there will be twelve visions of me: six pure and six impure; altogether twelve pure and impure forms will appear. Only pure gods, vīras, and ḍākinīs will see my pure form, seated on a bejeweled lion throne in the sky accompanied by umbrellas, victory banners, flags, and the sound of music brought by mother goddesses and ḍākinīs. It is possible that the disciples and accomplished masters, each individually, will also see this.[53]

The disciples are at first concerned with the mundane ritual aspects of their guru's death; Seban Repa asks, "When the lama passes, what should we do for the weekly rites, the rituals, a stūpa monument, memorial services, and so forth?" In a series of verses, the yogin admonishes them against such thinking, emphasizing instead the practice of Dharma free from fixation on external material trappings:

> . . . .
> Without conduct in accord with Dharma
> What use is it to perform rituals?

> . . . .
> Without sacred outlook rising in your mind,
> What use is it to construct stūpas?

> . . . .
> Without offering prayers from your heart,
> What use is it to offer memorials?

. . . .
Without taking heed of my instructions,
What use is it to make offerings to my corpse?

. . . .
Without having faith while I'm alive,
What use is it to view my corpse?[54]

This exchange highlights the opposing concerns of guru and disciples, contrasting the outer veneration of physical remains and the inner practice of meditation. Such a disparity is best exemplified by the ensuing conflict over Mila's corporeal relics, an event that would come to identify the entire death narrative.[55] Milarepa's death, like his life, forges a unique identity set within the frame of an exemplary being.

He bequeaths his few meager possessions (hat, walking staff, strips of his robe) to his foremost disciples, noting, "These are of no great value, but it is possible that they will bring about accomplishment. I do have one nugget of gold that I have hidden in a crack in the wall at the back of my meditation hut. Distribute the gold." When a patron goes to investigate, she finds only a small bit of rock sugar and a knife wrapped in cloth. An accompanying note instructs that the sugar and cloth be distributed and that they will supply everyone without being exhausted. The note famously concludes: "Those individuals who said Milarepa has gold, stuff their mouths with shit!" And his disciples laugh even in their grief.

The yogin is poisoned through the scheming of a jealous Bönpo priest; yet, when the latter dies through the punishment of ḍākinī goddesses and falls to the lowest hell realm of Avīci, Mila sings a song to purify his negativities. If Milarepa's ensuing sickness echoes the account of the Buddha's final illness—with a bowl of curds taking the place of the Buddha's famous last meal of "pig's delight"—his poisoning at the hands of a jealous priest of the indigenous Tibetan religion likewise resembles the Buddha's attempted murder at the hands of his jealous cousin Devadatta.[56] Finally, against a backdrop of miraculous signs, the stage is set for Mila's death. In a hare year, at the age of eighty-eight, he states, "I will not meet anyone for seven days, after which I will have something to say." The text continues,

On the fifth day [the disciples] slowly peered in on him and [found that] the lama had passed away. They watched him for a further six days of unbearable waiting, during which time the body shrank until it was just one measure of grain (*zan bre*) in size, made of insubstantial light. As all the *repas* gazed upon the corpse, some said Heruka was present; some said Avalokiteśvara was present; some said there was a light; some said there was a stūpa; some said it was in flames; some said it was in water; some said it was in stone; some said it was in the midst of a whirlwind; some said it was gold; some said it was a vase; some said it was a handbell. They did not agree [on what they saw], and at the end of the seventh day they touched the body, after which its complexion diminished.[57]

It is perhaps the status of Milarepa's physical remains that most clearly defines the contribution of *The Twelve Great Disciples* to the biographical tradition. Of the early proto-works, only Gyaltangpa's addressed the issue of relics, noting merely, "*Vīras* and *ḍākinīs* spirited away the corporeal remains without leaving so much as a fingernail [for human disciples] to take."[58] Beginning with *The Twelve Great Disciples*, however, relics become a central concern for the followers of Milarepa, much as they were for those of the Buddha.

As the yogin's body continues to shrink, his disciples wonder if anything will remain for their own veneration. Seban Repa worries, "In seven days, the corpse will vanish altogether," and the gathering contemplate their future without a "religious support for prostrations." A group of patrons and local chiefs arrive, stirring up a quarrel with the disciples about the guru's cremation, again recalling the Buddha's death, after which the various assembled royal patrons refuse to share the relics among themselves, pushing them to the brink of war. In this case, it is not the Brahmin Droṇa who defuses the situation, but rather a young boy who miraculously appears and scolds the gathering: "You fools from the land of humans, here / Bickering over Milarepa's body." The Buddha's body refused to ignite until the arrival of his disciple Mahākāśyapa; here, ḍākinī goddesses themselves declare that Mila's body has no need for ordinary flames, singing: "Since this person ever meditated on / Tummo's divine fire, his own mind, / What use is karmic fire?"[59]

For months, the cremation chamber is surrounded by miraculous signs described in minute detail, creating a magnificent scene of splendor and majesty:

The sky was filled with garlands of all types of flowers, pearls, interlaced garland strands, and a palette of color spots in white, red, blue, dark blue, green, and yellow. An unimaginable rain of flowers descended from the heavens—white, red, yellow, blue, greenish red, dark blue, multicolored, and so forth—like a flurry of snowflakes or tufts of wool. Upon each flower was a canopy of five-colored rainbow light and a maṇḍala equal to the complexion of a lotus. They swirled and spun, and when they reached the heads of [ordinary] people, they rose back up and vanished.[60]

Finally the yogin's body is engulfed in a spontaneous blaze, from which issues a physical relic:

A pearl relic from [Milarepa's] heart about the size of a swallow's egg and bathed in light appeared above the funerary chamber; light shone from its upper portion. The *repa*s clamored, "It's mine, it's mine," and the commotion caused [the relic] to split into two parts. One had a lotus and sun seat. The other revealed a crystal stūpa, a full arm-span in height, in which the bodies of the thousand and two buddhas vividly appeared. A small form of the Jetsün, twelve finger-spans in height, emanated upon the lotus and sun.[61]

In this miraculous form, Milarepa once again rebukes the assembly in verse:

Within a small reality body sphere
Is a relic the size of a hen's egg—
A religious support for all living creatures.
If you act like it's yours, it will vanish.
How could it last in a mundane environ?
But if you perform supplications,
Its compassion will never diminish;
Such is the general pledge of *ḍākinī*s.[62]

As a *ḍākinī* drapes the orb in a white silk scarf and prepares to take it away, Milarepa's disciple Zhiwa Ö earnestly prays to retrieve the relic, concluding his song by saying, "The stūpa that's held in the *ḍākinī*'s hands / Give it to your children disciples, I beg."[63] In what will be Milarepa's final reply, he sings,

This stūpa in the care of mother goddesses and *ḍākinī*s
Is the pure land of the three times buddhas,

The assembly hall of gods and goddesses,
The Jetsün lama's meditation cell.

In the pure land of the eastern quarter,
A place where a host of *ḍākinīs* gather,
In that pure land of Abhirati
The Bhagavan Buddha, Cakrasaṃvara,
Avalokiteśvara, and protector Tārā are assembled.
In that place of perfect bliss
A host of *ḍākinīs* wait to greet me.

You should make prayers from the bottom of your heart
And shed tears without artifice.
This unfabricated gift is most excellent,
Strewn with flowers of keen discrimination,
Bathed with the ablution vase of enlightened mind,
Protected well with faith unwavering.
To receive the initiation of nondual wisdom
Place your head underneath this [stūpa].[64]

With this, "the *ḍākinīs* carried [the crystal stūpa] up off the ground, lightly touched it to the heads of the great *repa* disciples, and then carried it off into the sky."

INTO *THE BLACK TREASURY*: THE LIFE OF *MILA DORJÉ GYALTSEN*, AND OTHERS

From Compendium to Compendia: The Making of *The Black Treasury*

As we have seen, in contrast to the early golden rosary versions of Milarepa's life, the biographical compendia began to display a growing concern with representing the yogin as an autonomous, founding member of the Kagyu tradition. They did so, in part, by employing new literary structures and rhetorical strategies, but also through the sheer accumulation of biographical detail. And the most extensive version of Milarepa's life story is also among the most mysterious: a work attributed to the editorial hand of the Third Karmapa, Rangjung Dorjé (1284–1339), and long known only by the ambiguous title *The Black Treasury*. New sources that have come to light only in the past few years finally allow us to crack open the treasury and bring its contents into view.

As a general title, *The Black Treasury* does not indicate a single text or even multiple editions of a single text. Rather, the name refers to a broad collection of biographical compendia sharing common (if not always identical) sources, structures, and content. In this sense *The Black Treasury* seems to have been understood as a container into which all known material about Milarepa's life and career might be locked away. But the tradition of *The Black Treasury* is also closely associated with the line of Karmapas, Kagyu hierarchs famous for their iconic black crowns, for which reason the name might equally be rendered "the treasury of the black." It is now clear that the name refers to a specific chapel—or perhaps a single room in a chapel—in southern Tibet associated with the Karmapas wherein an early version of *The Black Treasury* was preserved.

The tradition itself identifies the principal source for *The Black Treasury* as the work of Milarepa's own disciples—that is, the earliest compendium known as *The Twelve Great Disciples*. A series of Kagyu masters transmitted the text through a sharply restricted lineage, not unlike the system used for esoteric meditation instructions.[65] A brief unsigned history found in several *Black Treasury* colophons records the work's genesis and its gradual transmission. It is therefore worth citing here at length:

> In the female water-ox year (1133) when the Jetsün was eighty-two—after the *repa* disciples led by Ngamdzong Repa and Repa Zhiwa Ö had repeatedly asked to assemble his biography and collected songs—the Jetsün said, "I will consider its propitiousness." He covered his head with his robe and sat still for a moment. Then he promised to do as they had requested, saying, "You should go to the places where I previously meditated. I have written bits and pieces on tree bark and leaves. Tseringma knows much of it, and much is already clear to Ngamdzong Repa and the rest of you."
>
> The *repas* then gathered stories from all directions. Before offering a ritual feast, they asked Tashi Tseringma. The Jetsün himself then supplemented [the details] that the senior *repa* disciples had heard and added those that were missing. After the biography was arranged, the Jetsün gave its oral transmission and said, "Hold on to this dearly. In a year or two, when I die, everyone will have an auspicious connection of faith and devotion in my teachings." Then he offered prayers of aspiration and good fortune.[66]

Here, the text augments claims in *The Twelve Great Disciples* that Milarepa himself collaborated with the senior pupils in the writing of his biography.

The completed work was first entrusted to Rechungpa and then copied by the First Karmapa, who brought it to the Karma Kagyu tradition's primary seat at Tsurpu monastery. The colophon next describes the line through which the text was disseminated, as a so-called *chikgyu* (*gcig brgyud*) or "individual-transmission mandate" passed to a single Karma Kagyu lineage holder each generation, in the manner of a secret Dharma instruction. Transmission holders included many of the early Karmapas themselves, as the line passed from the First Karmapa, Dusum Khyenpa, to Sangyé Rechen Paldrak (1148–1218); Pomdrakpa Sonam Dorjé (1170–1249); the Second Karmapa, Karma Pakshi (1204–83); Orgyanpa Rinchen Pal (1229/30–1309); the Third Karmapa, Rangjung Dorjé, Yungtönpa Dorjé Pal (b. 1284–1365); the Fourth Karmapa, Rolpé Dorjé (1340–83); the Second Zhamar, Kachö Wangpo (1350–1402); Kazhi Rigpé Raltri[67] (d.u.); the Sixth Karmapa, Tongwa Donden (1416–53); Drung Rinchen Dorjé (d.u.); and finally Rasmri Bhadra (d.u.).

The history concludes with a description that succinctly explains the title *Black Treasury*.

> Rangjung Dorjé took this text and deposited it in the Black Treasury of Tsé Lhagang in Kongpo. Later when the Dharma Lord Tongwa Donden was invited by Nangso Kunga Gyaltsen, he withdrew this version of the collected songs from the Black Treasury. . . . Then, using it as a model, the faithful made many copies and the text spread far and wide.[68]

Here the Third Karmapa, Rangjung Dorjé, is credited with stashing the text within the actual Black Treasury; all versions of *The Black Treasury* identify him as one of its principal editors. But once the treasury had been opened and the restriction of the individual transmission line was loosened, copies of the text began to proliferate and spread, leading to the great variety of manuscripts witnessed today.

The name Tsé Lhagang refers to the contemporary administrative center Menling Dzong in the southern Tibetan region of Kongpo, as well as its neighboring mountain.[69] The locale once housed a renowned library, established by the First Karmapa, Dusum Khyenpa, and promoted by subsequent Karmapa hierarchs up to the tenth. It is said to have housed a collection rivaling that of the Karmapa's seat at Tsurphu, although it was destroyed in the wake of the Cultural Revolution.[70] At present, there are scant historical data about this location.[71] However, the Katok Situ Chökyi Gyatso (1880–1925) recorded the following note in his diaries regarding his visit to Kongpo in 1920:

I traveled down [from Gyamda in Kongpo], and at the confluence of the Nyang and Lang rivers—the Nyang River coming from Nyangpo, the Lang River from Langpo, in the directions of the Bhutan pass ('Brug la) and Draksum [Lake]—is found the Karmapa's black treasury (*karma pa'i mdzod nag*) atop the Namsé monastery on a small hill.[72]

Chökyi Gyatso's entry attests that the Black Treasury at Tsé Lhagang was intact at least into the early twentieth century. Other objects in Tibet from this repository, including statues and coins, continue to be known as *dzönagma* (*mdzod nag ma*), "[from] the black treasury."[73] Thus the title *The Black Treasury* often appears as an informal appellation, serving to designate sectarian affiliation, recording the work's direct connection to the Karmapas and the Karma Kagyu tradition and thus to the direct heirs to Milarepa's tradition. The title was later appended more formally to the variety of works copied from the original text.

Opening *The Black Treasury*: Versions, Authors, Sources

At present, seven unique manuscripts have been identified as versions of *The Black Treasury*.[74] Their earliest and common source may be understood as some form of *The Twelve Great Disciples*; all extant *Black Treasury* texts follow the basic structure of that early work, and several copy its colophon verbatim. Authors and editors of later versions of *The Black Treasury* also drew upon a wide range of other materials, incorporating narrative elements and songs from new sources that significantly expanded the text. The result is a body of literature that became increasingly complex over time. A complete historical evaluation of the various *Black Treasury* texts, including a formal stemmatic analysis, will require further examination of the materials, but it is possible to draw some general conclusions about their sources and their possible relationships.

Of the seven known versions of *The Black Treasury*, five can be broadly categorized into earlier and later strata according to their structure and sources; two require further analysis.[75]

Early Stratum
1. DNM-Lhasa: a manuscript housed in the Drepung Archives in Lhasa.
2. DNM-RD: recently published in the collected works of the Third Karmapa, Rangjung Dorjé.

Later Stratum

3. DNM-I: a two-volume edition published in India in 1977.
4. DNM-S: an unpublished manuscript in the collection of E. Gene Smith, fundamentally identical to DNM-I.
5. DNM-D: recently published as part of an extensive collection of Drigung Kagyu works.

Before turning to the major contributions of *The Black Treasury* to the biographical tradition, it will be useful to first present a brief analysis of these individual works, their sources, and possible chronology.

1. DNM-LHASA VERSION: This text, perhaps the earliest known version of *The Black Treasury*, lacks a cover title page, although the final scribal dedication refers to the text as "the Life of Jetsün Zhepa Dorjé" (*rje btsun bzhad pa rdo rje'i rnam par thar pa*).[76] The narrative concludes with a statement that it was recorded by Milarepa's twelve senior disciples led by Ngendzong Repa, a sentence copied directly from *The Twelve Great Disciples*.[77] Indeed, the entire text follows *The Twelve Great Disciples* very closely. It incorporates verbatim the entire early Life, most of the Songs, much of the death episode, and the final colophon—attesting to its position as an early formulation of *The Black Treasury*—although its divergences from *The Twelve Great Disciples* are of interest and bear further scrutiny.[78] The final colophon then accounts for its additional material in a brief and somewhat ambiguous statement:

> The Dharma Lord Mipham Gonpo has said, "The great Jetsün Mila's collected songs seem to be limitless in number, but most fall within the some one hundred compilations I have seen. Since it was written by Lord Rangjung Dorjé himself, he taught it as a valid source, and then this volume came to be universally known as a finely executed compilation of his personal research."[79]

These few sentences were subsequently copied into the larger colophon of later editions. Their phrasing and honorific language suggest that the text was not written by the Karmapa himself, but rather by a scribe in the Karmapa's lineage, perhaps under the hierarch's personal direction. Rangjung Dorjé died in 1339, so that date should set a *terminus ad quem* for the work, although it may have only circulated some decades later, perhaps a century after *The Twelve Great Disciples*.

It is unclear what materials would have been included in the "some one hundred compilations" noted here, although this statement attests to the proliferation of narrative traditions by the early fourteenth century. It is the first example of an author quantifying the existing biographical tradition as a means of legitimating his own composition, a practice seen in many later works.

2. DNM-RD VERSION: This version of *The Black Treasury*, recently published with that name in its title, appears to be largely based on the Lhasa version or a common source.[80] Its structure and content are strikingly similar to the Lhasa version, although it combines certain chapters and adds close to a dozen new song cycles. It also inserts an additional, eighteenth section just prior to the narrative of Milarepa's death. And like the Lhasa edition, it claims to have been written by Milarepa's twelve senior disciples and incorporates most of the original colophon found in *The Twelve Great Disciples*. It includes the Lhasa manuscript's description of "some one hundred compilations" and its reference to the third Karmapa, with minor clarifications of grammar. According to its scribal colophon, the manuscript was produced by the scribe of the Fourth Zhamar, Chödrak Yeshé (1453–1524).[81] Thus the text may be an example of a *Black Treasury* version produced shortly after the individual-transmission mandate was lifted, and perhaps within decades of Tsangnyön Heruka's own work on the standard edition.

3–4. DNM-I, DNM-S VERSIONS: These two manuscripts, nearly identical apart from brief introductory and scribal materials, are independent copies of the same version. They are also far more extensive than the preceding works, demonstrating a later period of development that took place once *The Black Treasury* began to circulate. The India edition was published in India in 1978.[82] The Smith edition is an unpublished, and previously unstudied, manuscript in the collection of E. Gene Smith.[83] Both versions refer to the text as *The Collected Songs of Lord Zhepé Dorjé, Powerful Lord Among Yogins, A Compilation Embellished with Historical Anecdotes* (*Rje rnal 'byor gyi dbang phyug dpal bzhad pa'i rdo rje'i 'gur 'tshogs tshad phyogs gcig du bsgrig pa lo rgyus kyis spras pa*).[84] Both works also include the poetic title *A River of Blessings Relieving the Tormenting Heat of the Mental Afflictions* (*Byin brlabs kyi chu rgyun gyis nyon mongs pa'i tsha gdung sel bar byed pa*).

The source colophon in this version is a complex amalgamation, made more confusing by the way it has copied, with minor changes, the authorial statement of the Lhasa version presented above. Although it does not name an author, it identifies three distinct literary sources:

This compilation of the great Jetsün Milarepa's biography, vajra songs, and spiritual songs [has three sources]: (1) the Dharma Lord Karmapa said, "Most of [the songs] are present within the some one hundred compilations of the great Jetsün's collected songs I have seen. Then, the Dharma Lord Rangjung Dorjé wrote the most excellent *Black Treasury*, personally researched and based upon authoritative sources; (2) [a text] said to be a compilation of seventeen different collected songs excellently completed in the Gungtang Pelkyi Tsuklakhang; (3) [a text] said to be a compilation [made] having seen one hundred and twenty-seven different biographies of the Jetsün. These [versions] have been compiled and supplemented with as many of the Jetsün's song collections as could be found. Through the merit of completing this well, may the precious teachings of the Practice Lineage flourish and expand in every direction and during all periods, and may it endure for a long time.[85]

The DNM-I/S version derives its structure and much of its content from the previous Lhasa version (and through it, *The Twelve Great Disciples*), whose colophon is incorporated as the first source here. The second source, a compilation of seventeen Collected Songs, remains unidentified, although its place of composition, Gungtang Pelkyi Tsuklakhang, can be recognized as the monastery near Lhasa established by Lama Zhang in 1187 as a seat for his Tselpa Kagyu tradition.[86] Its author was likely a member of this lineage, perhaps an abbot or prominent monk at that religious center, after the fashion of Sangyé Bum described in chapter 2. The third source must refer to the biography written by Zhijé Ripa.

Based upon these data, it is possible to propose a tentative dating for this version of the Life and Songs. Its time of origin is marked by Zhijé Ripa's work, completed in 1373. The compendium shows no evidence of being influenced by Tsangnyön Heruka's standard version, completed in 1488, and so likely predates it. Moreover, its song cycle on the Nepalese hunter Khyira Gönpo Dorjé seems to have served as the source for the abbreviated account recorded in the *Religious History of Lho Rong*, written between 1446 and 1451.[87] This suggests a date of composition between the last quarter of the fourteenth and the mid-fifteenth century.

5. DNM-D VERSION: This version, recently published in two different editions, appears to be largely based on the DNM-I/S version or a common source. The colophon describing its sources is largely a gloss on the DNM-I/S manuscripts, with much clearer grammar eliminating many of the passage's ambiguities.

Life and Songs in *The Black Treasury*

In terms of sheer volume, the later stratum of *Black Treasury* texts, represented in the following survey by the DNM-I/S version, formed the culmination of Milarepa's biographical tradition. With extensive sections covering Mila's early years, his spiritual career, and his death, including some seventy-five individual song cycles, this work easily surpasses even the standard version in its comprehensive attention to details of the yogin's life. It is the most inclusive work in Mila's early biographical tradition, and also the most syncretic. It preserves the core structure and narrative traditions established by the earlier compendia, copying much of those texts verbatim. But it is also embellished by a flood of new narrative accounts, stories that further flesh out and model the figure of Milarepa even as they continue to recast his life as a fabulous and extraordinary display.

Indeed, this work, more than any other in the tradition, garners its legitimacy on the basis of sheer inclusivity, emphasized by the hundreds of sources enumerated in the author's colophon. References to "some one hundred compilations of the Jetsün's Collected Songs," "seventeen different Collected Songs," and "one hundred twenty-seven biographies" may border on pious hyperbole, but they do underscore the richness and depth of Mila's biographical tradition in the century leading up to Tsangnyön Heruka's standard version. Authors unable to assert direct knowledge of the yogin's life could maintain their authority by deferring to an established biographical tradition ostensibly leading back to the subject himself.

As the product of this great proliferation of life writing, the DNM-I/S version of *The Black Treasury* remains composite, a mélange of authorial voices. The majority of its stories, drawn from the earlier compendia, were later copied by Tsangnyön Heruka to form what would become the canonical biography. Yet their narrative tempo occasionally stumbles, disrupted by the introduction of an alternate account written in a lighter, more casual style. Some additions gloss the preceding storyline, clarifying an event's underlying rationale; others serve to emphasize a plot point that will direct (or redirect) Milarepa's spiritual career. Nearly all of the major additions to the narrative reflect the yogin's extraordinary status through the lens of quotidian detail. But many episodes are also treated with skepticism, concluding with the Tibetan marker *ké* (*skad*), "so it is said," and were lost on the cutting room floor when later struck from the standard version. The result is compelling drama that serves as a narrative clearinghouse for stories otherwise lost to the tradition, but it is not yet the finely styled and seamless narrative portrait that would emerge through Tsangnyön Heruka's skillful editorial work.

The Black Treasury maintains the fundamental structure of the earlier compendia: two main parts define the Life and Songs, the latter subdivided into eighteen sections and numerous discrete song cycles. Part 1 emphasizes the early life as an autonomous unit by the addition of a concluding colophon, anticipating Tsangnyön Heruka's separation of the Life and Songs.[88] Part 2 likewise adds an eighteenth and final section, further marking the death as an extraordinary event in its own right. Significant details are added to the stories of Mila's youth and training, which, unlike earlier accounts, resonate with portent and presage, hinting at the great figure he will become. This work begins with an explicit identification of Milarepa as an emanation of the figure Mañjuśrīmitra, copied directly from the earlier compendia. At every turn thereafter, the reader is reminded that the young boy, the sorcerer, the seeker is not an ordinary individual but an enlightened emanation, acting out a role in order to demonstrate the path to liberation.

After Mila's birth, for example, the text reports an alternate account of his naming. One early proto-work states simply, "The boy was called Goyak."[89] In this case, however, the event takes on a deeper symbolic meaning:

> The father said, "As he is the good beginning (mgo yag) of my entire male line, I will call him Goyak (Good Beginning)." The mother said, "This son will become a Dharma practitioner, and as he is the good beginning of a Dharma line, I will call him Goyak."[90]

The mother here is made an instrument of prophecy foreshadowing her son's promising future. Describing his more common name, the early work by Dönmo Ripa writes, "Mila was given the worldly name Töpaga."[91] The two previous compendia state simply, "The great Jetsün's name was Töpaga." The Black Treasury, however, offers the following explanation:

> When the villagers held a celebration, he would beg and sing little insignificant songs such as he knew. On occasion he also took care of the local cattle and goats. Around that time he sang:

This rope slingshot I hold in my hand
Is a meditation belt to wear.
Whatever I wear upon my back
Is but a simple cotton robe.

He sang countless songs like this that pleased the mind. He was extremely skilled in composing songs and stories and the like. He also knew many tales, and he told them in his home and the spinning courtyards, to the delight of all. He was then given the name Mila Töpaga (Delightful to Hear).[92]

Milarepa's childhood name identifies his skill in song, an attribute that would come to define his spiritual career.[93] But in this case, even a simple country song forms a prophetic statement, transforming a child's humble shepherding gear into the attributes of a yogin.[94]

Events of Mila's childhood, his practice of sorcery, and early Buddhist apprenticeship unfold according to the general plan of the earlier compendia. His initial encounter with Marpa, however, is given additional weight, transformed from the fairly straightforward plot element in *The Twelve Great Disciples* into a preliminary Dharma transmission that serves to predict his future spiritual attainment. The first sentence here is drawn from *The Twelve Great Disciples* tradition, after which appears the addition from *The Black Treasury*.

Once more he set out on the path described by the children. He reached that place and encountered a fat, old mantrika with a long rosary of rakṣa beads hanging from his long neck who was tilling a field. With some trepidation, [Mila] went forward and said he had something to ask. "It's said that someone called Marpa Lotsāwa lives around here. I would like to request an audience with him," he said.

The great lama Lotsāwa drew a line on the ground and said, "Furrow up to here and I will go get word." Then he recited this verse:

The lama's authentic instructions
Gather the channel constituents into the central channel.
If the unworkable [ground] of the afflictions is loosened up,
The fruit will quickly ripen.

Mila did not understand at all, [but] the lama was pleased with the furrowing he had done up until then and said, "Here is a yogin whose karma has arrived."

Again, [Mila] asked for a message [from the lama] and, again, [the man-trika] drew a line in the ground and said, "Furrow up to here and I will send a message." And again, he recited this verse:

Through blessings of the tantric lama
Mind itself abides in its relaxed natural state.
If, through mindfulness, the unworkable [ground] is loosened up,
The harvest's fruit quickly ripens.

It is said that Mila thought, "The old priest has paid [for my work] with talk." The lama then brought forth a large vessel brimming with beer from a hollow in the ground. First the great lama drank a large swallow. It is said that he gave the remainder to Töpaga, and as Mila was tired, he drank his fill. Then, once again, the great lama recited this verse:

In reality the beer is great bliss.
If this secret, the great genuine truth,
Loosens up the genuine unworkable [ground],
The harvest's fruit will ripen.

It is said that Mila thought, "This is Dharma put into words, but I've become drunk on the old priest's beer and haven't noticed what was being said."

It is said that during this period Lord Marpa was giving Mila Töpaga Dharma meditation instruction on Mahāmudrā for those of highest and moderate capacity, although [Mila] did not understand it. Moreover, regarding the activities of [plowing up to] the two lines: one was a sign of the toil of service, the other was a sign of the toil of afflictions in medita-tion.[95] His subsequent drinking beer to his fill was a sign of the sudden arising of accomplishment, experience, and realization.

Then the great lama said to Töpaga, "Now yogin, you stay here and I will go get word." The old priest placed a mare and a woven basket in Töpaga's care and went off to his home. Mila remained in that place until a call came from the lady, "Now come!" and she led him to their home.[96]

In this episode, Mila is presented as only marginally aware of the Dharma instruction he receives in the form of esoteric verses on the path and fruition of Mahāmudrā. Nevertheless, his actions are described—in the author's voice—as a reflection of the yogin's impending career.[97] Later, after completing his religious training, Marpa addresses the symbolic referent of Mila's beer drinking directly, predicting "that [Mila] would attain supreme accomplishment in a single lifetime."[98] The theme of enlightenment in one lifetime—seated comfortably, if somewhat incongruously, alongside his status as an already enlightened buddha—would assume a central position in Milarepa's standard biography, discussed in the next chapter.

Mila's apprenticeship with Marpa also concludes with prophecy: one evening while he is in retreat, a ḍākinī goddess appears in a dream, encouraging him to return to his homeland. Tsangnyön Heruka would later adopt this as the central rationale for Mila's departure. Before guru and disciple separate, the text recounts the famous "dream of four pillars," now attributed to Mila, as it would be in the standard version. The early life concludes with two descriptions of the departure; one follows *The Twelve Great Disciples*, the other (marked by the notation "also, according to one biography") describes a variant narrative that adds a final visit with Ngoktön; this too would be incorporated into the standard version of the life.

Unlike the previous compendia, part 1 of *The Black Treasury* extends through Milarepa's practice of austerities, his first extensive meditation retreats at locations such as Drakar Taso, and his subsequent attainment of yogic realization:

> One evening, yogic warmth flared up and, unable to remain seated, he went up to the summit of the glacier. When he arrived, the five sense pleasures descended like rain and he attained the final accomplishments, both ordinary and supreme.[99]

The early life, demarcated by both its structural framing and its narrative content, is thus emphasized as an autonomous biographical unit extending from Mila's birth through his awakening. Part 1 further encapsulates the representation of Milarepa's early years with a concluding summation, emphasizing its central themes and narrative tropes:

> Thus Lord Milarepa himself was equal to and no different from all the buddhas of the three times, imperturbable in the state of great bliss. However, he arrived as an ordinary person, taking the guise of someone to be trained during this age of strife. In the beginning, he served the lama by means of undertaking numerous hardships, and then he received the aural tantras and precious instructions. In the middle, he practiced asceticism and

meditation without any distortion and carried out the benefit of beings. In the end, he displayed the means for transcending suffering.

Up to this point was the complete cycle on his perseverance in practicing hardships. It is the cycle about the early part of his life.[100]

The second section, constituting the Collected Songs, also reveals signs of major editorial revision, following the structural model of previous compendia while adding significant new narrative content to further widen the ambit of Milarepa's spiritual career. The text enumerates eighteen "qualities" characterizing the yogin's later life and forming a structural frame for the collected songs. These have been expanded and reorganized to incorporate seventy-two song cycles (including twelve absent in the earlier compendia), creating the single most comprehensive portrait of Mila's later life, surpassing even that of the standard version. Newly added, for example, is the cycle describing Milarepa's journey to Mount Kailāsa in western Tibet, which later became one of the best-known stories in the biography's standard version.[101] New chapters also describe the yogin's female disciples, Paldar Bum and Salé Ö. Some editorial revisions divide a single chapter of the earlier compendia (*brin gi lha grong gi skor*) into two autonomous song cycles (*jo bo bon ri'i skor* and *brin gi lha grong gi skor*). Others expand a brief record, as is the case with DNM-Lhasa's alternate version of hunter-disciple Khyira Gönpo Dorjé's conversion, which is significantly enlarged into a full-length song cycle of its own. One chapter, "the cycle of miscellaneous stories" (*lo rgyus yod med 'thor bu'i skor*), preserves a collection of disparate songs with little narrative framing, supporting the author's claim that the text is "supplemented with as many of the Jetsün's song collections as could be found."[102]

The text's concluding section further defines Milarepa's death as a core narrative of the biographical tradition. Structurally, it is an autonomous section within part 2, the eighteenth quality of the yogin's life, "displaying the achievement of the unified vajra body in a single lifetime and its dissolution into the rainbow body" (*tshe gcig gis zung 'jug rdo rje'i sku 'grub cing 'ja' lus su yal ba'i tshul bstan pa'i yon tan*). As it did with other aspects of his life, the text records two variant narrative traditions of Milarepa's death. The latter cites *The Twelve Great Disciples*, while the former roughly follows DNM-Lhasa, including its emphasis on Rechungpa and his central role during the cremation, and further elaborates the miraculous visions appearing around the cremation pyre. Of particular interest is an account of Milarepa's relics that, although brief, deviates significantly from the standard version. Rechungpa has reached the site of his guru's cremation and stands among the other disciples and patrons as the pyre spontaneously bursts into flame. "Extraordinary *samādhi* arose in the minds of the *repa* disciples," the text records.

> In particular, lama Rechungpa saw innumerable pure visions. At that point, the sound of the lama's voice resounded from a window in the cremation chamber and said, "A bit of corporeal relics the size of a pea appeared at the center of my forehead, and the divine physician Lady Tsheringma has carried it away as a devotional support. Pour half of the funerary ashes into the Yeru Tsangpo [river], half into the Bongchu, and all sentient beings encompassed by the rivers will be freed from negative rebirths."[103]

This episode contrasts with what would become the standard account in several ways. The ambiguous location of Milarepa's cremation may echo the dispute over possession of the yogin's corpse, appearing first in *The Twelve Great Disciples* tradition and more prominently in the standard version.[104] More importantly, however, this episode preserves the first, and perhaps only, account in which a portion of the yogin's corporeal relics remains under the care of his human disciples. According to the standard narrative of events—formulated first in *The Twelve Great Disciples* and *The Black Treasury* and later emphasized by Tsangnyön Heruka—the disciples were chastised for their fixation on the material trappings of Mila's death. The yogin himself characterized desire for physical remains as a distraction from yogic discipline, and *ḍākinī* goddesses swept away the mass of relics, leaving behind little more than a collection of personal effects to augment his legacy of stories and song. In an inversion of a common explanation of relics forming a presence in the teacher's absence, within his standard biographical tradition, the potency and presence of Milarepa's relics stem primarily from their absence.[105]

In *The Black Treasury*, the principal portion of relics is also carried away, this time by Mila's divine consort Tseringma. Milarepa himself then commands his disciples not to enshrine the remaining ashes within a reliquary, but to part with that which they desire most by dispersing them into the river. In more than six hundred folio sides, this text fleshed out the yogin's life in detail more finely grained than any preceding it, yet through this act the yogin's corporeal remains dissolved back to the Tibetan landscape from which he sprang, encompassing both the land

and its inhabitants. In the end, Tibet's iconic yogin has become, like the text itself, a river of blessings.[106]

REFLECTIONS

Authors of the earliest proto-works in Milarepa's biographical tradition paid slight, although growing, attention to the yogin's representation and the literary constituents—narrative, structural, thematic—of the life story. This began to change with the advent of new autonomous biographies, which, like many forms of life writing, attended specifically to the crafting of both story and discourse, "overtly, through stylistic and rhetorical means, and covertly, through theme, structure, and interpretation."[107]

This chapter has outlined the development of such a new model for representing Milarepa's life story: the biographical compendium, which for the first time presented a detailed and comprehensive account of the yogin's life in concert with the content of his teaching career. The compendia addressed here generally follow the format implicit within the proto-works, but explicitly record two distinct biographical forms—Life and Songs—within a coherent and integrated literary framework. The biography, no longer a fragmented character sketch, now spans Mila's early life, awakening, and death through a richly detailed and plot-driven narrative, grounded by its own sense of causal logic. The Songs have likewise been transformed from a disconnected series of discrete vignettes into a comprehensive biographical network of song cycles, linking a multitude of narratives in song and prose that collectively record the yogin's spiritual career.

The combination of fully articulated Life and Songs allowed biographers to frame the yogin's life story as an exemplary model, in line with the earliest assertion of his status as miraculous emanation, while recording a life both individuated and uniquely Tibetan. Ultimately, the mediation of tensions between these two positions, exploited most effectively by Tsangnyön Heruka in his standard version, helped transform the biographical tradition from mere framework into embodied presence.

These innovations were, in part, predicated upon the reinforcement of early literary structures and the introduction of new ones, around which additional narrative detail could be organized. The compendia elaborated upon the basic model of the proto-Life/Songs, explicitly defining the life story through division into an early period of hardships and a later period of meditation experience; a series of seventeen qualities then organized the network of song cycles. This 2/17 structure, attested first in *The Twelve Great Disciples*, came to define the life in the tradition of *The Black Treasury*. Later versions further refined this system by adding an eighteenth quality, effectively highlighting the yogin's death as a critical event in itself.

The compendia repeated the claim, ubiquitously found throughout the proto-works, that Milarepa was a miraculous emanation, an assertion that appears clearly at the beginning of all three works. Their authors further emphasize the yogin's extraordinary status by framing the life through the continued use of prophecy, introduced by both mother and guru as well as authorial narrator at regular intervals throughout the life story. The text also presents episodes in comparison to the Buddha's own exemplary life, a trope most visible in the account of Milarepa's death. Yet the death is equally cast in the mold of the great Indian adepts who show little concern for the outer rituals of religious tradition. Where the Buddha famously discourses at length on details of his funerary arrangements, Milarepa forcefully scorns such activities altogether; where the Buddha's corporeal relics are enshrined for public worship, the yogin's remains are swept off to the heavenly realms or cast into the sea.

While the compendia portrayed Milarepa as an exemplary model, they also translated the story into a Tibetan idiom, depicted it as a life individually lived. New layers of narrative detail flesh out the sketches first presented in the proto-works, presenting a portrait that retains the fine lines of a full life, its obstacles, ambiguities, fallibilities, and of course its triumphs. The expanded Songs characterizes the life story as fundamentally embedded within the Tibetan landscape: as the verses describe and document the innumerable places where Milarepa lived and meditated. But the translation of model liberation tale into unique Tibetan life is perhaps best encapsulated by the later versions of *The Black Treasury*, in which the description of Milarepa's awakening has replaced the Buddha's own seat of enlightenment under the bodhi tree with summits of high mountain glaciers; the fabled location on the Gangetic plain has been transformed into the snowy land, a native metonym for Tibet itself.

As we shall see in the next chapter, Tsangnyön Heruka drew inspiration and borrowed freely from these works; nearly every aspect of his *Life* and *Songs* was anticipated in the compendia. He adopted much of the narrative content from the earlier traditions of *The Twelve Great Disciples* and retained the plotting and pacing of *The Black Treasury*, further refining its structural division of Life and Songs. But even as the compendia were eclipsed by Tsangnyön Heruka's innovations, they did not disappear entirely from Tibet's literary landscape. They retained a unique status as "alternative" sources for the Life and Songs, drawing the attention of scholars and meditators with a wide range of sectarian affiliations. The standard version's status would ultimately rest not so much on its content, which stemmed almost entirely from earlier works, but on the reworking of its literary form and the mastery of its narrative representation.

A NEW STANDARD

TSANGNYÖN HERUKA'S *LIFE* AND *SONGS OF MILAREPA*

ORIENTATIONS

A Singular Life Amid Uncertain Times

THE LATE fifteenth century was a defining moment for Milarepa's life, even though he had been dead for almost four centuries. It was a period of both civil unrest and religious expansion in central Tibet. As the Yuan imperial court declined and eventually fell in 1368, political influence likewise began to wane within the Tibetan Sakya institution that had effectively ruled Tibet since the Mongol installation of Sakya Paṇḍita (1182–1251) in 1249. This coincided with the ascent to power of Changchup Gyaltsen (1302–64) between 1350 and 1354, beginning a century of political rule under the influential Phakmodru hegemony.[1] That period of relative calm would be shattered in the last quarter of the fifteenth century, when war broke out between the far western kingdom of Gugé and the central Tibetan region of Latö Lho in 1472.[2] Instability increased with the rise in 1477 of the Rinpung family in the western Tibetan province of Tsang; patrons of the Kagyu Karmapa hierarchs, they waged a bitter civil war against the predominantly Geluk supporters of Ü province and Lhasa.[3] In the midst of partisan attacks and retaliatory clashes, one Rinpung prince, Donyö Dorjé (1462/3–1512), was an influential patron for the author who would recast the figure of Milarepa for centuries to come: Tsangnyön Heruka.

If Tsangnyön Heruka's world was consumed by regional and sectarian conflict, it was also "an age of fervent religious reform and doctrinal systematization."[4] During the fourteenth century, great Tibetan intellectuals, such as Butön Rinchendrup (1290–1364) and Longchenpa (1308–64), began to synthesize new systems of Buddhist literature and practice. The decades leading up to Tsangnyön Heruka's birth were marked by the activities of renowned individuals such as the Sakya scholars Rongtön Mawé Sengé (1347–1449), who established the famed central Tibetan monastery of Nalanda, and his disciples Gorampa Sönam Sengé (1429–89) and Shākya Chokden (1428–1507). This was also the time of Tsongkhapa (1357–1419), the brilliant scholar who regrounded teachings of the earlier Kadam sect within a system of strict monasticism and rigorous philosophical study. Together with his disciples, he established Lhasa's three great seats of monastic learning—Ganden (1409), Drepung (1416), and Sera (1419)—that would serve as a platform for the nascent Gelukpa tradition they inspired.

In the midst of this activity, variously referred to in Western literature as a Tibetan reformation or renaissance, Tsangnyön Heruka promoted his own vision of religious reform as part of a tradition of unconventional figures known as *nyönpa* (*smyon pa*), or religious madmen.[5] As the antithesis of the scholar-monk, the mad yogins were not unlike Indian tantric adepts of the *siddha* tradition, adopting lives of transgressive and antinomian behavior. For the faithful, their outrageous behavior signaled their yogic realization and lack of attachment to society's trappings, especially the Byzantine world of Buddhist monasticism. Yet, as Gene Smith points out, Tsangnyön's activities were not simply a reaction against Tibet's growing monastic institutions; the religious madman, rather, "represents an attempt to re-dedicate the Kagyupa sects to old truths and insights that were being forgotten." It was a movement, however symbolic, away from the rising tide of corporate religion back to the solitary, itinerant yogin, an ideal upon which the Kagyu tradition was founded and an image embodied in the figure of Milarepa.

This chapter will examine Tsangnyön Heruka's literary activity, understanding him as not only participating in Milarepa's biographical tradition but also reframing the yogin's portrait, in part by reinventing the genre of life writing. Although I frequently refer to his version of Milarepa's life story as the "standard" account, that word could well be replaced with "canonical," pointing to the text's role as both the benchmark for and the measure of the yogin's life.[6] As a canonical account, the standard life story not only becomes the "text of record" but further "acts to terminate unsanctioned oral tradition and coalesces the myth-making powers of the community around its paradigms."[7] This would have profound implications for the fundamental transformation in Milarepa's representation from miraculous emanation to ordinary being. Some aspects of the yogin's biography were subject to reformulation, as, for example, was the topography associated with his life. Yet Tsangnyön's account set the standard that has dominated up to the present day. Whereas the previous biographical tradition had presented the yogin's detailed physiognomy in the mode of *Gray's Anatomy*, Tsangnyön's version captured the life like a Chuck Close portrait.

Writer of the Life

Tsangnyön Heruka's life began as did those of many other great religious figures in his time.[8] The second of three brothers, he was ordained as a novice monk at age seven; inspired by a vision at fourteen, he met the teacher who would become his principal guru, Shara Rabjam Sangyé Sengé (1427–70).[9] From this master he received the core doctrinal and ritual instructions of the Kagyu tradition, including the practical instructions of the six yogas of Nāropa based upon notes (*zin bris*) written by Milarepa himself.[10] Soon thereafter, Tsangnyön is described as having achieved the power of yogic heat marked by the ability to wear nothing but a simple cotton robe, thus earning the status of *repa* in Milarepa's tradition.[11] He later received the various aural transmission lineages of Rechungpa, Ngendzong, and Gampopa, described as the "essence or the root of all the profound Dharma instructions of the precious Kagyu."[12]

At age seventeen, he began a four-year period of study at the monastic institute of Palkhor Chödé of Gyantse.[13] Overcome with a feeling of renunciation and resolving to carry out the instructions of his guru, he gave away his robes and possessions and, as a young man of twenty-one, departed for the renowned mountain wilderness retreat of Tsāri.[14] During this period of intense meditation, Tsangnyön renounced his monastic vows and adopted the unconventional activity of a mad yogin for which he became famous:

> Upon his naked body he rubbed human ashes, daubs of blood, and smears of grease; he wore a necklace of intestines from a human corpse and with them made ornaments for his hands and feet. He cut off the fingers and toes, tied them together with thread, and bound them into his hair. He wore fine ornaments of bone that someone offered him. Sometimes he laughed, sometimes he cried, and he made a point of carrying out all manner of outrageous behavior in the marketplace. Thus, although the people

of Tsari[15] were uncivilized and quite wild, his abilities overwhelmed them and his compassion brought them under his control. As a consequence, they became extremely devoted. In agreement, they all gave him the name Tsangpa Nyönpa, "Madman of Tsang," and in every direction he became as famous as the sun and moon.[16]

He continued, and further escalated, this kind of transgressive behavior. On one occasion he disrupted a gathering at a full moon service by eating the ritual offerings, taking out his erect penis (referred to as his "vajra"), and grunting as he chased the women. He then retracted his penis, leaving nothing but a hole ringed with hair, and ran after the men shouting, "Fuck me!"[17]

In this way the young *repa* earned the name by which he is best known: Tsangpa Nyönpa, contracted to Tsangnyön: the Madman of Tsang. He later received the epithets Traktüng Gyalpo (*khrag thung rgyal po*, "King Blood Drinker") and Tsāriwa Rupé Gyenchen (*tsā ri ba rus pa'i rgyan can*, "Man of Tsāri Dressed in Bone Ornaments").[18] The former incorporates the Tibetan translation for the term *heruka* (*khrag thung*), from which the second part of his name stems; he would use the latter sobriquet to sign many of his literary works, including the *Life* and *Songs* of Milarepa.

Tsangnyön Heruka was twenty-four years old when he completed three years of intense yogic practice in Tsāri, and he spent the remainder of his life literally following in Milarepa's footsteps as he wandered along Tibet's southern borderlands, inhabiting the yogin's favored meditation caves and wilderness retreats. He developed close personal ties with numerous political leaders of western Tibet, including the Rinpung prince Donyö Dorjé, the royal family of Gungtang—Tri Namgyal Dé (b. 15th c.) and his sons Norbu Dé (1450–85) and Samdrup Dé (1459–1505)—and the rulers of Mustang. On one occasion, he helped broker peace negotiations between the warring factions of Gugé and Mustang.[19] These individuals would serve as benefactors for Tsangnyön's literary activities, and would be among the first to receive copies of the newly completed Mila corpus.

Tsangnyön Heruka undertook three trips to Nepal, the last of which he used to sponsor major renovations of the famed *mahācaitya* monument of Swayambhū.[20] He composed a broad range of ritual and commentarial texts dedicated to the tradition of the aural transmissions.[21] But it is his biographical writings for which he is best remembered. In addition to his works on Milarepa, Tsangnyön completed an extensive biography and song collection of Mila's guru Marpa, fostering what has been called "a whole school of Kagyupa biographical works."[22]

Writing of the Texts

Tsangnyön Heruka's own biographies emphasize his activities in reformulating Milarepa's Life and Songs. Illuminating though they may be, these accounts of biographical production should be read with caution. It was in the interests of biographers like Ngödrup Pelbar, Lhatsun, and Götsang Repa—as it had been for other authors in Mila's biographical tradition, including Tsangnyön himself—to portray the actions of their guru as the awakened activity of a buddha, miraculous and visionary. Their description of Tsangnyön's efforts to produce Milarepa's life story forms a metanarrative emphasizing the legitimacy of a literary creation (Mila's Life as text) through the authority of its creator (Tsangnyön's life as author). Representations of this relationship between author and authored, the hagiography of the hagiographer, have been almost entirely ignored in discussions of Milarepa's biographical tradition; chapter 5 will address this further. For the moment, we turn to the biographical record itself.

The circumstances under which Tsangnyön Heruka first developed the intention to reformulate Milarepa's life story are recorded in some detail. Returning from Mount Kailāsa in far western Tibet, he stops in Gungtang, near the border with Nepal, where he is received by the king and his family. After visiting several of Milarepa's meditation sites near the royal castle of Dzongka, he makes a pilgrimage to the small village where the yogin was born. He was perhaps thirty-two at the time.[23]

> Then [Tsangnyön Heruka] went to Kyi Ngatsa, the birthplace of Jetsün Mila, where he encountered a chapel called the Small Red Temple,[24] which was later constructed on the original site of the ruins of Lord Mila's uncle's house, and which housed a blessed statue of Jetsün Mila. At that time, the strong-willed, powerful, and wealthy caretaker said, "Venerable Lord Rinpoché, please compose a biographical prayer for Lord Mila."
>
> The Lord [Tsangnyön] replied, "You examine a butter lamp [for signs]. If they are favorable, I will write one."[25]

The caretaker fills a small offering lamp, meant to burn for half a day, which miraculously remains lit for three consecutive days. This, of course, was taken as an auspicious sign: "Lord [Tsangnyön Heruka] was delighted and then composed a praise of the life of Jetsün Zhepa Dorjé from the point of view of twelve deeds."[26]

Two points in this brief passage are worthy of note. First, Tsangnyön's composition—his earliest version of Milarepa's life—is not a full literary biography but a short work of praise, an encomium (*bstod pa*) likely written in verse form. This episode also describes Tsangnyön's intention to reframe the yogin's life through the narrative trope of twelve deeds. Although not stated explicitly, this refers to the presentation of the Buddha's life as encompassing a series of eight or twelve great acts (from his descent from Tuṣita heaven to his final passing into *parinirvāṇa*), a tradition promulgated in Pāla India through artistic motifs in stelae and pilgrimage tokens, with their related pilgrimage traditions. The Buddha's life in twelve acts was later incorporated into Tibetan literature as a favored biographical trope.[27] Tsangnyön Heruka here follows what had become a well-established literary tradition, and this composition would influence his later crafting of the standard Life.

Milarepa's *Life* and *Songs* were afforded a prominent place within Tsangnyön's own life story; all three biographers devote a separate chapter to their creation. The following description, cited at length, begins with Lhatsun's account, which greatly amplifies the miraculous context in which Tsangnyön Heruka's activities occur. The following verse introduces the scene:

> While staying at Dröpuk, Nāro Paṇchen
> Revealed himself directly, commanding you,
> "Write Zhepa Dorjé's Life," and Tseringma
> Said she'd complete this activity; to you I bow down.[28]

The chapter then begins with an elaborate description of Tsangnyön Heruka's visionary encounter with the Bengali adept Nāropa, forefather of the Kagyu tradition and guru to Milarepa's own master, Marpa. The narrative, here excerpted in full, begins in Dröpuk (Belly Cave), one of Milarepa's retreat sites near the Tibetan border with Nepal.

At one time, [Tsangnyön] remained in retreat for a month at Dröpuk in Nyanam, abiding in the river-flow absorption of reality just as it is. At that time, in a vision that was a mixture of dream and luminosity, the glorious Nāropa appeared with an enormous body whose attitude was just as he had heard described previously. He had an amazing body of enormous size, even larger than if it were seen in a dream. His naked form, resplendent and bathed in light, was beautified by the six kinds of bone ornaments. He was seated upon a mat of fine blue brocade draped over a white snow lion, his two hands in the gesture of teaching Dharma and his two legs in the posture of royal ease. He was surrounded by a retinue of innumerable gods and humans and sat there teaching Dharma.

[Tsangnyön] offered prostrations and a maṇḍala, and made a prayer request for the six yogas, so [Nāropa] spoke forth in Sanskrit with a beautiful voice. Without understanding a syllable of it, [Tsangnyön] again offered prostrations and a maṇḍala, and made supplications. In response [Nāropa] gave one line of vajra verse in a mixture of Indian and Tibetan languages, after which he said,

> In the gloomy darkness of the north
> Is the one called Töpaga
> Like the sun rising upon the snows.
> That individual . . .

and at that point [Nāropa] said many things in Sanskrit, which [Tsangnyön] did not understand, so he sat there looking back and forth at everything. There was an Indian dressed in the garb of a paṇḍita who could translate Indian and Tibetan languages. He said, "In the Indian language [Nāropa] said, 'Arrange the collected songs (*mgur 'bum*), which lays out in successive order a biography (*rnam thar*) of Jetsün Milarepa from his birth to his awakening, and carve the blocks. By distributing the printing, a prayer to Milarepa will reach wherever the Buddha's teachings have spread.'"

The accomplished master [Tsangnyön] said, "I don't have patrons for [an endeavor] like that."

Jetsün Nāropa said something in the Indian language and pointed toward Lowo Gungtang, glancing up in that direction.

The translator said, "[Nāropa] said he indicated that [people in] those [regions] will be your benefactors."

"But I don't have arrangements for carvers, scribes, and the like," said [Tsangnyön].

Again [Nāropa] pointed his finger at five women seated side by side. The five women rose and said, "We would wholeheartedly like to carry out these activities," and then [Nāropa] sang forth songs in Sanskrit.

[Tsangnyön] had the pleasing thought that he had seen the face of Lord Panchen Nāropa, heard his Dharma, and received his prophetic command, at which point the vision of Panchen Nāropa and the others dissolved, and he remained in a state of luminosity free of appearances.[29]

In this account, it is Kagyu forefather Nāropa himself who, through the medium of a visionary translator, inspires Tsangnyön's literary career. As Nāropa famously predicted Milarepa's arrival to Marpa, a prophecy partly quoted in this exchange, he likewise commands Tsangnyön's production of the yogin's *Life* and *Songs*.[30] Support for the project is promised in the form of both human patronage by local benefactors and divine intervention by Milarepa's own heavenly disciples. Dawn breaks, and Tsangnyön resolves to begin in this way, here quoting from Götsang Repa's text:

The Lord [Tsangnyön Heruka] thought, "At present in this snowy land there exist numerous biographies and collected songs of Jetsün Zhepa Dorjé. However, the [transmission of] his extraordinary biography has been interrupted. I should rectify this, teach the profound and vast Dharma and instructions to my worthy disciples, and then bring them to liberation; indeed, that is what [such a work] does. All agree on the need to accumulate merit. Yet from the king, too busy for the proper activity of authentic Dharma, ministers, and important leaders full of arrogance, to the majority of common people, all are proud of their Dharma activity; and even if they have time to practice and do so, they don't know how to practice the profound key points. Rather than stirring up bubbles of technical jargon, [such a biography] would be a wish-fulfilling gem, an exceptional means for leading them to buddhahood in one lifetime. It would thus awaken the inner potential for virtue in arrogant *geshe*s who are on the verge of becoming non-Buddhists.

If this biography of Jetsün Zhepa Dorjé were available to be seen, for those attached to sense pleasures and their own lives it would become a support for enduring the hardships of ascetic practice. For those who take pleasure in distraction, it would become a support for practicing one-pointedly. For those who doubt the possibility of attaining buddhahood in one lifetime or say they have no time for meditation on the profound, it would serve as a perfect example of those very things. They would have confidence in the authentic Dharma of definitive meaning, and the most capable individuals would be liberated in their lifetime or in the intermediate state at the moment of death. People of intermediate ability, even though they have no personal experience, would develop faith and devotion in experienced individuals and provide them material support. They could make pure aspirations, enter retreat, and based upon practice in future lifetimes they would reach liberation. Even the least capable would abandon perverted views and engender exceptional faith and then develop certainty that they would reach the limits of life's round. Once this printing is finished it will benefit limitless beings."[31]

This passage presents Tsangnyön's rationale for producing yet another version of Milarepa's Life and Songs, couched in the traditional language of a Buddhist author whose intention is to "benefit limitless beings." The "numerous biographies and collected songs" refer, no doubt, to the compendia discussed in the previous chapter. I will, however, temporarily set aside Tsangnyön's intriguing statement that the "extraordinary biography has been interrupted" and return to it in the next chapter to examine what such a biography might entail.

The passage defines a prospective audience far greater than for *The Twelve Great Disciples* or *The Black Treasury*, which concluded with strict commands of secrecy. Here, the texts are addressed to people of all social strata and every level of ability, from kings and ministers to the common man. Singled out are the "arrogant *geshes*," marginally Buddhist, merely "stirring up bubbles of technical jargon," who would become favored antagonists under Tsangnyön's pen.[32] Milarepa's Life and Songs are for the first time intended—and actively promoted—as works for a popular readership, their subject a moral everyman capable of reaching across social and sectarian lines.

Tsangnyön's research and production of the texts is described, not unlike Milarepa's own life story, as requiring great dedication and personal sacrifice. Lhatsun's account continues,

> The previous evening's prophecy was excellent, and as the next morning was the eighth day, complete with the favorable astrological conditions, [Tsangnyön] began to compose the introductory expression of worship. It appears that texts of the Life and Songs were, for the most part, very widespread and therefore easy to seek out. Although some scattered sayings were extremely difficult to gather, he dispatched monks to look for each of the songs. He sought them out, with immeasurable difficulty, in Ngari, Ü, Tsang, all the way to Dak[po] and Kong[po], and made use of his material possessions without hesitation. He sent an assistant wood-block cutter to search in every direction for scribes and printers, and then arrived at Shelpuk[33] (Crystal Cave), where he had the biography carved in an excellent manner.[34]

Lhatsun, like Ngödrup Pelbar before him, refers to Milarepa's early biographical tradition as being widespread and readily accessible, the reference to both Life and Songs clearly pointing to the compendia. Götsang Repa, however, conveniently drops any reference to the early works as easy to find, emphasizing Tsangnyön's personal hardship in seeking early traces of the Life "with immeasurable difficulty," across western, central, and southern Tibet. Götsang Repa further underscores Tsangnyön's dedication to a project of enormous scope and the miraculous support for his activities:

> By autumn the wood printing blocks were prepared and [Tsangnyön Heruka] next thought about the necessary printing materials. He collected offerings and begged for donations. That spring he gathered all his disciples at Shelpuk and began carving the wood blocks, which he carried out without holding back any of his wealth or possessions. Around this time he fell extremely ill, partly from his begging activity and partly due to obstacles created by harmful spirits. He then carried out a retreat at Drakmar.[35] One morning at dawn he dreamed that the five Long Life Sisters said, "We will carry out the enlightened service of completing activities of the Kagyu teachings such as this printing, so don't concern yourself with it," and then he awoke. All of his disciples offered prayers and performed ceremonies of long life, through the power of which [Tsangnyön] quickly recovered and then moved to Shelpuk.[36]

If the challenges involved with such a printing project exacted a toll on Tsangnyön himself, they are described as pushing his disciples to the brink of mutiny, exacerbated by the region's civil unrest.

> A few disciples said, "Whatever wealth we had previously has been exhausted,[37] on top of which Latö Lho is still in the midst of great upheaval. It is indeed uncertain that this printing will be completed, so it should be postponed. Then, if instead the master and we disciples were to stay practicing meditation, [at least] the lot of us would emerge realized masters. Therefore it would be good to postpone [this project]."
>
> In response Lord [Tsangnyön] said, "The five ladies gave their promise, so it will certainly be completed. You all shut up!" He scolded them in this way and then said, "This is not the time to put it off," and they did not delay the project.
>
> The situation in Latö Lho was extremely unpleasant, but in accordance with the Jetsün's own commandments, there was little harm done. He became the focus of worship and the protector and refuge for all, and with

this status he took control over the printing work of a few monks [who had previously dissented]. The master and disciples went out to collect offerings in Gungtang, the nomad lands, and so forth, and then, having returned with a great deal of capital, they completed the printing in two years.[38]

According to the *Life* itself, Tsangnyön finished writing the work on the eighth day of the eighth lunar month of the year called *phur bu*, the earth-monkey year, equivalent to 1488.[39] The printed texts were consecrated thereafter.[40]

In carrying out this project, Tsangnyön was availing himself of printing technology relatively new to central Tibet. Tibetan-language woodblock printing began on the cultural margins. The earliest known printed Tibetan book was made in 1153 in Khara Khoto; other Tibetan works were printed in China during the centuries that followed.[41] The first extensive xylographic edition of Tibetan literature—the Kangyur, or collected translations in more than one hundred volumes of canonical scriptures attributed to the Buddha— was produced in Peking in 1411, sponsored by the Ming Emperor Yongle and the Fifth Karmapa, whose Kagyu lineage stemmed directly from Milarepa. But large-scale printing projects did not begin in central Tibet until the early fifteenth century.[42]

The half-century following Tsangnyön's efforts witnessed a flurry of new xylographic editions of *The Life of Milarepa*, produced at Ron Ösal Puk (1538), Lendé Lang Puk (1540), and Drakar Taso (1555), all located in southern Tibet. Another block printing was prepared prior to 1541, perhaps in the border region of Nyenam, by one Sönam Lodrö.[43] This rapid succession of reprint editions seems to indicate two points about Tsangnyön Heruka's wood blocks. First, they were used frequently enough during their first fifty years that they needed replacing. Perhaps more importantly, there was enough demand for printed versions of Milarepa's life to sustain at least four unique editions prepared in the same geographic region within a decade or so of one another.

This trend would continue. During the next four centuries, wood blocks for Tsangnyön Heruka's *Life* and *Songs* would be carved, and new editions published, in the great printing houses of Drakar Taso, Pungtang in Bhutan, Derge in eastern Tibet, Peking, and Lhasa.[44] Chökyi Wangchuk, the historian from Drakar Taso, bore witness to this profusion in the early nineteenth century, noting that he personally saw editions from Ronkyi Ösal Puk, Tashilhünpo, Bhutan, Derge, and Yershong Chödé in Amdo, in addition to the set at Drakar Taso, and that "it is certain that there are others as well."[45] By the mid-twentieth century, at least nineteen separate editions had been printed throughout the Tibetan Buddhist cultural world.[46] Tsangnyön Heruka's goal was not only to reshape the life story but also to redefine the entire biographical tradition, creating a canonical standard. Ultimately, the support of such institutions would ensure its reproduction, and its continual reintroduction to future generations of readers.[47]

With his new version of the *Life* and *Songs* complete, Tsangnyön Heruka proved equally shrewd in its promotion and distribution, commencing what may have been one of Tibet's first concerted multimedia approaches to life writing. To ensure its wide distribution, Tsangnyön transported blocks to Dröpuk, where he "made many prints and some three or four times distributed them through Ü and Tsang. He sent many copies of the *Songs* together with the *Life* throughout Ngari, Lho, Chang, and so forth."[48] He then sent copies of the texts to all the officials in Tsāri as well.[49] Among the most important recipients was the Fourth Zhamar incarnation, Chödrak Yeshé (1453–1524). To this powerful Kagyu lama, Tsangnyön "sent a letter together with all of the printed items: the *Life* and *Songs*, a devotional petition (*gsol 'debs*), and a guru worship ritual (*bla ma mchod pa*)."[50] The latter works formed a corpus of supporting materials emphasizing Milarepa not only as a literary subject but also as the focus of ritual biography, raising the profile of Tsangnyön's literary endeavors by solidifying the yogin's growing devotional cult.

Praises (*bstod pa*) and petitions (*gsol 'debs*) were an important part of Milarepa's biographical tradition stemming back at least to the proto-work by Gyaltangpa, whose root verses comprise just such a praise. The half-century prior to the completion of Tsangnyön's standard works saw the composition of several well-known praises by Zhangzhung Chöwang Drakpa (1404–69) and Namkha Samdrup Gyaltsen (active fifteenth century).[51] The latter's work, written in 1448, was frequently published together with Milarepa's *Life* and *Songs* in later editions of the standard version, and such works continued to proliferate in the centuries that followed.

Tsangnyön Heruka's multimedia approach to life writing is perhaps best illustrated by his use of visual materials to promulgate a standardized version of the life story. These efforts are worthy of a separate detailed study; I will mention them only briefly here.[52] The power of images in Asian and Buddhist artistic traditions, as a locus of the subject's consecrated presence and as a product of social agency whose identity is fashioned through the interaction of a community of viewers, has been well attested.[53] In the context of Mila's biographical tradition, however, illustrated lives served yet another function. Printed texts offered Tsangnyön's standard version access to elite teaching institutions and an educated social class; visual narratives of Milarepa's *Life and Songs* expanded the audience to include more general, nonliterate communities, in line with his stated authorial intentions cited above.

Paintings depicting the Buddha's life appeared in Tibet at least as early as the late thirteenth to early fourteenth centuries.[54] Among the earliest known visual biographies of a Tibetan master is a work depicting the life of Butön Rinchendrup, perhaps based on the two-volume life story written by his disciple Rinchen Namgyal (1318–88).[55] Tsangnyön Heruka's activities serve as another early and influential example of visual biography, employed specifically for the promulgation of his new literary works. With the printing blocks half completed, Tsangnyön Heruka and his disciple Sönam Drupa collaborated to lay out three biographical scroll paintings (*thang kha*) following Tsangnyön's new version of the Life.[56]

Later, after the new prints had begun to disseminate, the powerful benefactor Donyö Dorjé invited Tsangnyön Heruka to his Rinpung estate, where he requested a copy of the "biographical painting with the deeds of the Lord of Yogins, based on [Tsangnyön's version of] Lord Mila's Life."[57] Tsangnyön agreed before returning to the center of his activities in Latö Lho. Götsang Repa then records,

> [Tsangnyön] thought, "Paintings of Lord Mila's life story following his biography such as this were previously unknown in Tibet. Since they were not common, this is the version that will flourish and become widespread." He sent a biographical painting to Tö—Guntang, Lowo, and so forth—and they became plentiful. Keeping one for himself, he had them spread in great numbers throughout Latö Lho. It was his wish that, in accordance with Donyö Dorjé's request and [his own] promise, they spread throughout Mé, including Ü and Tsang. To his heart disciple, Sönam Drupa, he commanded, "Son, make [another] such biographical painting," and he said, "You should distribute prints of it in Ü, Tsang, Tsari, and so forth, and benefit beings."[58]

No copy of Tsangnyön Heruka's original painting is known to have survived. In line with his own wishes, however, subsequent visual depictions of Mila's life story, beginning with a series fashioned by his disciple Lhatsün Rinchen Namgyal, followed his version of the *Life* and *Songs*.[59]

ARCHITECTURE OF A NEW LIFE

New Approaches to an Old Story

Few would disagree that Tsangnyön Heruka had crafted a powerful new form of biographical literature, rooted in the tradition but unlike anything that had come before. No longer the mere flesh-and-blood representation of an individual's life, for its readers the life story had come to embody, with crystalline clarity, the underlying truths of the Buddhist path, evocative, inspiring, transformational. Tsangnyön's *Life* and *Songs* are thus frequently described as triggering moments of both great emotion and profound spiritual awakening—a trope that came to embellish many Tibetan memoirs.

The famed scholar and statesman Tenzin Peljor (b. 1760), known as Doring Paṇḍita, recorded his poignant response to Milarepa's life story. Witnessing the ravages of the Nepalese Gorkha army during its border dispute with Tibet, in which local inhabitants were "squeezed like sesame seeds," he was struck by a deep feeling of impermanence. In that state of mind, he writes,

> One day I saw the Azure Queen snow mountain (Gangs mthon mthing rgyal mo), palace of the five heavenly physician Long Life Sisters.[60] This caused me to recollect the life and deeds of the precious protector of beings, the great *repa* Mila. Choking with tears, I immediately composed a prayer summarizing the meaning of the great Jetsün's *Life* and *Songs*, together with a commentary in eighty-seven verses. As much as I knew how, I aspired to remain inseparably under his care in all of my lifetimes.[61]

The Fourth Khamtrul incarnation, Tenzin Chökyi Nyima, Doring's contemporary, describes his own emotional epiphany at the age of eighteen (in 1747), directly inspired by Tsangnyön's literary creation: "Then, for a few days I borrowed and read a copy of Lord Mila's *Life* and *Songs* arranged by Tsang[nyön]. Although I had previously read it many times in my studies as a child, on this occasion a feeling arose such as I had never had."[62] He describes how the story's essential meaning aroused feelings of detachment leading to a spontaneous and powerful sense of world-weariness and renunciation.[63]

Early European and American scholars of Tibet likewise discovered in Tsangnyön's works a unique example of biographical literature. Writing in the late 1940s, Giuseppe Tucci found Tibetan biographies in general to be particularly vexing, compelling the historian to "go through hundreds of pages to find a point of reference, an allusion, an important piece of information," in contrast to Mila's life story, which he described as one of the few "noble masterpieces breathing a fresh, serene and robust poetic spirit."[64] Some thirty years later, R. A. Stein also noticed that Tsangnyön's rendition of the *Life* and *Songs*, in addition to his biography of Marpa, stood apart from other examples of Tibetan life writing:

> Now these two biographies, which are exceptionally famous and well-loved among Tibetans, are distinguished from many other, quite boring and pedantic, works by their near colloquial language, their lively style, and above all the interest they take in countless details of real life. It is just this communion of the "mad" saints with popular sources of inspiration that made them the greatest creators of Tibetan literature.[65]

Russian scholar A. I. Vostrokov summed this up, noting that Tsangnyön's works on Milarepa and Marpa "can be (rather must be) regarded not so much as biographies in the proper sense of the word as literary works."[66] Indeed, Mila's life has been hailed as "one of the great masterpieces of Tibetan and world literature."[67]

The strict partitioning of biography from literature more generally is not a traditional Tibetan distinction, but rather stems from Western categories of literary study. Yet a brief discussion of modern views of biographical writing will offer a useful perspective to better understand the ascendance of Tsangnyön's new *Life* and *Songs*. If narrative, as Roland Barthes famously remarked, "is international, transhistorical, transcultural . . . simply there, like life itself," modern readers would likely agree that the world (or a life in it) does not "present itself to perception in the form of well-made stories, with central subjects, proper beginnings, middles, and ends."[68] Life writing entails more than the accumulation of biographical data; it requires narrative structure, thematic development, plotting, and pacing—that is, the elements of fiction. The power of Tsangnyön Heruka's works comes at least in part from the fictionalizing of his subject. "Fictional" in this context refers not to a story's falsity,

but to its "forming, shaping and molding elements: the crafting of narrative."[69] And it is "the fictive power of 'story' [that ultimately] provides
us with a coherent vision of a life."[70] Earlier versions of the life began to
construct cohesive stories from the raw data of biographical detail; the
compendia, in particular, shaped finely wrought models of the individual
life in exemplary form. But it is Tsangnyön Heruka's fiction—his "crafting
of narrative"—that has most powerfully captured the enduring truths of
Milarepa's life.

Biography, since the European enlightenment, has been frequently
viewed as the cousin of history and therefore the antithesis of hagiography, a repository of factual details meant to establish the authenticity of
a life. One contemporary genre of life writing, heir to this tradition, has
emphasized the sheer accumulation of information drawn from rapidly
swelling archival sources.[71] Some such works, however, are "in danger of
suffocating from the collected mass of material, becoming lost in minor
details, adhering too strictly to chronology and failing to separate what is
important from the trivial."[72]

Beginning in the mid-nineteenth century, a new form of biography
emerged, a "counter-tradition attempting to free the biographer from
the compendious life for the shaped, interpretative life where perspective, dimension and a point of view control the material."[73] At the heart
of this new form was the notion of the "creative fact": a "fertile fact, the
fact that suggests and engenders."[74] The creative fact allowed authors to
remain faithful to the content of a life story while granting them license
to emphasize form over the rote accumulation of biographical minutia,
creating a work of both "truth and pleasure."[75]

Thus it seems that Tsangnyön's concerns as a biographer were to an
extent in line with some modern formulations of life writing. The effec-
tiveness of his depiction of Milarepa's life story largely stems from the fictionalization of his writing, its representation of a "shaped, interpretive
life." His raw materials come almost entirely from the early biographical
tradition. But in his hands these factual details are stretched and bent,
rearranged, intensified, and at times glossed over altogether, forming creative facts Nadel calls "authorized fictions":

> the alteration of facts into new forms which, despite their original or
> inventive presentation, do not lose their authenticity. Such transforma-
> tions, caused by the pressures of language and the act of composition,
> alter the shape but not the legitimacy of fact.[76]

The most effective (and affective) biographies "re-invent rather than re-construct," and Tsangnyön's reinventions would likely be translated into Buddhist terms as *upaya*, skillful means.[77] If, as the tradition holds, Tsangnyön's intention was to restore an "extraordinary version" of the life aimed at a broad audience for the purpose of illustrating in definitive terms the path to liberation, new forms of life writing could be viewed as skillful activity, even in their apparent contradiction of earlier tradition. Vostrikov's suggestion to view *The Life of Milarepa* broadly as a work of literature rather than strictly as religious biography seems to have been on the mark: Tsangnyön Heruka's *Life* and *Songs* represent a break with previous biographical works despite their grounding in the early tradition. And in formulating a new kind of biography, they retain the fictive power of literature, for both the Western scholar and the Tibetan devotee.

New Lives, New Songs

As part of his conceptual plan for a new version of Milarepa's life story, Tsangnyön divided the *Life* and *Songs* into separate texts.[78] Freed from the complex narrative structure of the collected songs, the biography could, for the first time, be read from birth and training to liberation and final passing as a coherent and integrated story. That Tsangnyön intended the *Life* to be read in this way, as a continuous narrative encapsulating the Buddhist path, is evident from his chosen title: *Life of the Great Powerful Lord of Yogins Jetsün Milarepa, Demonstrating the Path of Liberation and Omniscience* (*Rnal 'byor gyi dbang phyug chen po rje btsun mi la ras pa'i rnam thar thar pa dang thams cad mkhyen pa'i lam ston*).[79]

While the narrative core of the life story draws significantly from earlier biographical works, Tsangnyön considerably elevates the status of his creation, representing it in the form of canonical scripture. The *Life* begins with the traditional frame of Buddhist sūtras, opening with the formula, "Thus did I hear at one time," evoking Ānanda's own perfect recitation of the Buddha's teachings during the first Buddhist council. It continues the sūtra model, setting the narrative stage with the yogin, just prior to his death, dwelling at Dröpuk surrounded by a host of human and nonhuman disciples. Here, Rechungpa is cast in the role of Śāriputra, who, through miraculous intervention, becomes the agent inspiring his guru's exposition, which in this case is a detailed accounting of his own life. Chapter 5 will return to this scene; here, this conceit reveals what is perhaps Tsangnyön Heruka's foremost innovation: the reformulation of biography as autobiography, in which the story is narrated by Milarepa himself.[80] The shift in authorial voice from third to first person had clear implications for how the life story was authorized, and for the relationships among the author, his subject, and its representation, topics analyzed in further detail in the next chapter. As an ostensibly autobiographical narrative, the story of Milarepa's life garnered an immediacy that masked nearly four centuries of repetition and revision.

As noted earlier, Tsangnyön also reframed Milarepa's life story in terms of twelve deeds, again elevating the subject's status by modeling it after representations of the Buddha's own life. Rechungpa introduces his request for Milarepa to describe his life with the leading statement, "Lama, precious Jetsün, the buddhas who passed away long ago taught their inconceivable life stories of twelve deeds and so forth for the benefit of beings."[81] His implication is that Milarepa should formulate the story of his own life in the same manner. This allows Tsangnyön to structure the *Life* as he did his work of praise years earlier. But this structure also echoes the biographical compendia, dividing its "twelve marvelous and amazing deeds" into three "ordinary worldly deeds" during the early part of his life and nine subsequent "deeds of supreme peace and nirvāṇa."[82] The framework of twelve deeds is a general conceit, bearing little relationship to the actions commonly attributed to the Buddha. It does, however, establish at least a categorical equivalence to the Buddha's life. Perhaps more importantly, a brief introductory statement summarizes each of the twelve chapters, forming a biographical outline in broad strokes that could be easily memorized and repeated. (See the table.) This practice would later be copied in works such as the autobiography of Zhapkar Tsokdruk Rangdrol.[83]

Comparison of the 12 deeds of Milarepa to the 12 deeds of the Buddha

MILAREPA	THE BUDDHA
1. Birth, together with the reason his paternal family was named Mila and the origins of his ancestral lineage.	1. Descent from Tuṣita
2. During his youth, with his father dead, his nearest relatives rose up as enemies and, bereft of both inner and outer possessions, he experienced the truth of suffering in its entirety.	2. Entrance into the womb of his mother

3. Encouraged by his mother's command, he accomplished the activity of wrathful intervention and then annihilated his enemies.	3. Birth
4. On account of his world-weariness and renunciation, he sought out a qualified guru.	4. Youthful skill in sport and play
5. He met his guru and, submitting to his every command, he purified evil deeds and obscurations, excluding none, through insufferable and exhausting hardships.	5. Enjoying life with a harem
6. He was accepted by his guru with affection and received the ripening and liberating instructions.	6. Renunciation
7. As he meditated on reality in the guru's presence, the sprouts of experience and realization emerged.	7. Austerities
8. He mastered the general instructions and then, compelled by symbolic acts within a dream, he obtained tantric instructions and departed from the lama.	8. Going to the Bodhi tree
9. He vowed to practice, having been reminded once again of the essencelessness of saṃsāra.	9. Subduing Māra
10. In order to practice the guru's teachings, he renounced his present life and meditated undistracted in the mountains with perseverance and through severe austerity.	10. Attaining complete enlightenment
11. By meditating in that manner, he perfected his experience and realization, and through the results of his practice he benefited both the teachings and sentient beings.	11. Turning the wheel of Dharma
12. He completed the activities of an enlightened being and, in order to compel beings to practice Dharma, he dissolved his form body into the sphere of reality.	12. Passing into *parinirvāṇa*

With the life story elevated to a place of prominence, Tsangnyön recast the *Songs* in a supporting role, its position identified by the new title he used: *The Collected Songs Expanding on the Life of Jetsün Milarepa* (*Rje btsun mi la ras pa'i rnam thar rgyas par phye ba mgur 'bum*). This work is, in Döndrup Gyel's terms, a supplement (*kha skong*) to, or a commentary ('*grel bshad*) on, the *Life* as a whole, thus emphasizing its function as a biographical network situated outside (or at least beside) the biography's largely chronological narrative.[84] But as a commentary on the life story, the *Songs* specifically glosses the biography's penultimate section, the brief eleventh chapter (eighth of the "supreme deeds") surveying Mila's meditation sites and disciples. It is from this point in the compendia that Tsangnyön extracted the collected songs, and chapter 11—the deed of benefiting the teachings and sentient beings—is clearly intended as a general marker for Milarepa's mature teaching career. The chapter concludes by noting, "These [activities] are taught at great length in the chapters of the *Collected Songs*."[85] Tsangnyön clarifies his intentions in his letter to the Fourth Zhamar, in which he refers to the *Songs* as "the *Collected Songs* that expand upon the eighth of the supreme deeds from the *Life* of Jetsün Zhepa Dorjé."[86] The *Songs* itself concludes with a similar note, stating that the work has elaborated upon the eighth deed of benefiting the teachings and sentient beings from Milarepa's *Life*.[87]

Tsangnyön further simplified the collection's organizational structure, replacing the compendia's somewhat cumbersome division into seventeen sections with a tripartite thematic arrangement: 1) "the cycles of binding under oath nonhumans who inflicted harm" (1–8); 2) "the cycles of accepting the great heart disciples who were worthy trainees" (9–41); and 3) "various assorted cycles" (42–58). This framework emphasizes the text as a record of Mila's mature teaching career, his subjugation of nonhuman spirits and the landscape they inhabit, and his conversion of human disciples who would promulgate the Kagyu tradition. As in the compendia, the new collection is a biographical network of song cycles documenting the yogin's collected teachings, but here it further illuminates his character as Buddhist master and teacher in relation to a specific period of his life. The division of diachronic *Life* and synchronic *Songs* is not unlike the interplay of *praxeis* and *ethos* that came to dominate Greek, Latin, and some later medieval European biography, in which *praxeis* "summed up [the life] in a chronological manner," and then *ethos* presented "a somewhat rigorous and interpretive discussion of character."[88]

Although Tsangnyön published *Life* and *Songs* as independent texts, it is in their union that the record of Milarepa's life is most fully revealed. "If one studies Milarepa's *Life* without the *Songs*," Döndrup Gyel concludes, "one is unable to gain a deep understanding; and likewise, if one doesn't know about the *Life* while reading Milarepa's *Songs*, one is unable to understand the background for the stories of the songs."[89]

It is difficult to precisely define Tsangnyön Heruka's role in the formulation of Milarepa's life story. In one sense, he served as editor for a literary tradition that was, by his time, both extensive and well established. His main contribution in this regard was re-dressing a portrait that had already been sculpted in great detail. He standardized spellings and glossed grammatical obscurities; streamlined alternative storylines (as recorded, for example, in *The Black Treasury* texts); rearranged songs and narrative threads to heighten the story's dramatic weight and tension; and further emphasized the relationship between life and landscape. From the vast corpus of competing narrative traditions, he crafted a polished and coherent picture of the yogin's life.

But Tsangnyön's editorial work ultimately remains greater than the sum of its parts, elevating him to the level of author who successfully reimagined and then re-presented the yogin, yielding a story received as a work of both truth and pleasure. This is perhaps Tsangnyön's greatest achievement: the fictionalization of biography, creating a form of life writing that encompasses evidentiary documentation, didactic resource, and even the programmatic legitimation of lineage, but is not constrained by them. Earlier traditions produced a lifelike portrait, but Tsangnyön Heruka ultimately brought it to life.

The *Songs* likewise illustrate Tsangnyön Heruka's awareness of the "danger of suffocating from the collected mass of material" and his determination to "separate what is important from the trivial" and make a more streamlined narrative, in line with Nadel's observations above. The seventy-three song cycles of *The Black Treasury* are here reduced to just fifty-eight.[90] In some cases, song cycles fell on the proverbial editing room floor, elided from the text altogether. In others, sections of prose narrative or the songs themselves were cut and spliced elsewhere in the text, appended to an existing cycle. Tsangnyön at times used this technique to create a new chronology, as for example in the chapters on the conversion of hunter Khyira Gönpo Dorjé and Mila's invitation from the King of Bhaktapur, two famous episodes from the standard version commonly depicted together in sculpture and on canvas. Tsangnyön here made explicit the collection's status as a narrative network. The songs themselves were considered most important; their context was frequently of secondary concern. As examples of Nadel's "authorial fiction," the recombination of narrative fragments to form new episodes could be viewed as a Buddhist illustration of *upāya*, or skillful means, performed in the name of crafting a more elegant—and ultimately more effective—narrative.

THE QUESTION OF MILAREPA'S INCARNATION

Early (and Late) Incarnation Traditions

One significant—and, as we shall see, strategic—change Tsangnyön made in his representation of Milarepa's life was to shift the yogin's status from miraculous emanation to ordinary human. Tsangnyön did not originate the description of the yogin's liberation in one lifetime and one body (*tshe gcig lus gcig*); this appears in the late *Black Treasury* works and Zhijé Ripa's *Illuminating Lamp* before them. But he was the first—and perhaps the only—author to categorically deny the yogin's status as a previously awakened buddha, contradicting numerous works in the biographical tradition, including most of his principal sources.

Nearly every author prior to Tsangnyön, and some following him as well, equated Milarepa with enlightened masters of the past, doubly legitimating his position as Kagyu founder and Buddhist teacher. This occurred first through his ordinary lineage of human gurus and the transmission of his religious instruction, and second by an extraordinary means similar to what has been termed "the Buddha lineage"—positioning him as merely the latest successor in a line of enlightened beings, manifesting in order to demonstrate the path and teach Dharma.[91] How, then, was Milarepa's life predicated upon his status as miraculous emanation, and what was Tsangnyön's rationale for fundamentally altering that representation?

The assertion of Milarepa's miraculous status first appears in the earliest proto-works of the biographical tradition by Gampopa and Lama Zhang, whose concluding remarks refer to the yogin as "an emanated being who saw the truth of reality." Zhijé Ripa cites early Drigung Kagyu claims (made perhaps by the twelfth-century Drigung founder Jikten Gönpo himself, or his immediate followers) that Milarepa was an emanation of Nāgārjunagarbha; as noted in chapter 2:

Some people, including the Drigungpa of Lama Kyura Rinpoché, say that Jetsün Milarepa was born as master Ārya Nāgārjunagarbha, a physical birth of the Bhagavan Amoghasiddhi, but Lord Khyungtsangpa and Zhang Lotsāwa don't clarify the matter."[92]

Milarepa's identification as an emanation of a specific figure thus seems to have appeared within a century following his death. As we have seen, Gyaltangpa further emphasized this claim by having Milarepa *himself* declare, "I am an emanation of the one called Ārya Nāgārjunagarbha, who was prophesied by the Buddha and appeared as an emanation of the Buddha himself."[93]

Far more common in the biographical tradition, however, was Milarepa's association with the Indian adept Mañjuśrīmitra (Tib. 'Jam dpal bshes gnyen), a name first encountered in *The Twelve Great Disciples*. As noted previously, all of the biographical compendia begin by identifying Milarepa with Mañjuśrīmitra, as do the shorter works by Orgyanpa and the Fourth Zhamar. The fifteenth-century historian Gö Lotsāwa (1392–1481) recognizes this claim, noting that "great accomplished beings have said that this great Jetsün was Ācārya Mañjuśrīmitra."[94] The tradition was well enough established that a famous praise to Milarepa used its name: the *'Jam dpal bzhes gnyen ma*.[95] Authors continued to describe the yogin's miraculous status as an emanation of this Indian adept long after the publication of Tsangnyön's standard version, as indicated by the writings of Karma Chakmé (1613–78) and Chökyi Wangchuk, noted below.[96]

Mañjuśrīmitra was an important founding figure in the Nyingma lineage, believed to have been active during the mid-eighth century. He is most closely associated with the scriptural tradition of Atiyoga, particularly the "mental class" (*sems sde*) instructions of Great Perfection (*rdzogs chen*); one of the eighteen mental class texts, *Gold Refined from Ore* (*Rdo la gser zhun*), is attributed to him.[97] He was, by some accounts, especially concerned with the *Litany of Names of Mañjuśrī* (*Mañjuśrīnāmasaṃgīti*) and attempted to make it "the center of an entire Vajrayāna system of practice."[98] Mañjuśrīmitra is traditionally believed to have received the mental class instructions from the legendary Indian figure Garap Dorjé and in turn passed them to his disciples Śrī Siṃha and Buddhajñānapāda.

While Milarepa's identification with Mañjuśrīmitra—and through him, the mental class instructions—extends back to the origins of his biographical tradition, the underlying rationale for this correspondence remains complicated and murky. His biographies agree that, prior to training under Marpa, Milarepa studied with one or more Nyingma masters of the early translation (*snga 'gyur*) traditions. But it is with Mila's magic teacher that the first clue is revealed. Dudjom Rinpoché's encyclopedic history of the Nyingma school records this note:

> When the venerable Milarepa first received the mental class (*sems sde*) of the Great Perfection from Nup Khulungpa he could not be equipoised in awareness itself. . . . Finally, on the basis of the venerable Marpa . . . he attained accomplishment on the path of Great Perfection.[99]

Nup Khulung is known, under various permutations of the name, in nearly every version of Mila's life story as his principal magic instructor, from whom he received the wrathful practice resulting in the murder of his paternal family. He is, however, most frequently associated not with the mental class traditions but with the transmission of the Mahāyoga class *Guhyagarbha tantra*.[100]

Among Mila's other early Dharma instructors is an individual called Marpa Jungné Yeshé of Yamdrok Langbudo. Although these accounts record slight variations in his name, the early texts agree that he taught Mila the Dosem Chok (Mdo sems phyogs), an alternate name for the mental class instructions.[101] Little is known about Marpa Jungé Yeshé, but it is possible that he may be identified with Marpa Dopa Chökyi Wangchuk, an influential contemporary of Milarepa who studied under Mila's guru Marpa Chökyi Lodrö (in addition to sharing his family name).[102] Marpa Dopa was known for his role in transmitting cycles of the *Cakrasaṃvara tantra*, but he also studied under the Nyingma luminary Rongzom Chökyi Zangpo (eleventh century), and it is possible that he received the mental class instructions from him.[103]

Kagyu authors seem to have woven this relationship between Milarepa and Mañjuśrīmitra into the narratives of their own lineage histories. The First Karmapa, Düsum Khyenpa, was perhaps among the first Kagyu leaders to draw a connection between Milarepa and Mañjuśrīmitra, in a statement recorded by the acclaimed historian Pawo Tsuklak Trengwa (1504–64). The Karmapa identified his disciple Tsangsowa as having formerly taken birth as a king of Kalingka (in India), at which time he is said to have relied upon Milarepa, who was then Jampel Shenyen (Mañjuśrīmitra), and Gampopa, who was Sangyé Yeshé Zhap (Buddhajñānapāda).[104] The Karmapa's remark thus asserts the guru-disciple relationship between Milarepa and

Gampopa even in former lifetimes. It is perhaps on this basis that the correspondence began within Karma Kagyu circles.

Chökyi Wangchuk's history of Drakar Taso records a similar correspondence. The author begins by making the general assertion, "Chief among all those [masters of India, Nepal, and Tibet] is the great Jetsün Mila, emanation of the *mahācārya* Mañjuśrīmitra, Jampel Shenyen."[105] This by-now shopworn statement is followed, however, by a number of scriptural citations in the form of revealed treasures (*gter ma*), meant to support the yogin's miraculous identification:

It says in *Questions and Answers at Khari* (*Mkha' ri'i zhus lan*):
The Great Master (Padmasambhava) said to the Dharma king Tri Songdetsen,
Mahārāja, many translators and scholars will appear and many translators will come from Tibet. In particular, the emanation of Kṛṣṇa[ācārya] called Drokmi and the emanation of Ḍombi Heruka called Marpa Lotsāwa will spread study, teaching, and meditation. The emanation of my guru Mañjuśrīmitra, known as Mila, will come to spread meditative concentration. . . .
It says in the treasure revealed by Letro Lingpa, *Silver Mirror: Prophecy of Mahākaruṇika, Spontaneous Liberation from the Lower Realms* (*Thugs che chen po ngan song rang grol gyi lung bstan dngul dkar me long*):[106]
At that time, the emanation of Śrī Siṃha,
Marpa Lhodrak, will appear in the direction of Lhodrak
And establish the wellspring of accomplished masters in Tibet.
Then, the emanation of Mañjuśrīmitra
Named Mila will become famed throughout India and Tibet.
. . . And there are quotations from sources including the *Luminous Expanse Innermost Essence of the Ḍākinīs* (*Klong gsal mkha' 'gro snying thig*), numerous as a mountain range (*ri rnyil?*), but I am fearful of putting them into words here. In this way, [Milarepa's] emanation as Mañjuśrīmitra is generally known in Tibet; he is renowned accordingly throughout India and Tibet.[107]

The date of the initial treasure text identified here, *Questions and Answers at Khari*, is uncertain. Nevertheless, the first quotation identifies Padmasambhava himself as making a connection between Mañjuśrīmitra and Milarepa, and providing an early prophecy of the yogin's future appearance. The second quotation records yet another instance of a guru-disciple relationship translated, in the form of revealed prophecy, back into the subjects' previous lives. In this case, however, the roles are reversed, with Marpa (Śrī Siṃha) appearing as the disciple of Milarepa (Mañjuśrīmitra). Chökyi Wangchuk further amplifies these relationships within the Kagyu transmission history by inserting identical citations into the life stories of Marpa and Milarepa, as part of a golden garland collection of Drukpa Kagyu biographies he wrote four years later (in 1820).[108]

The Mañjuśrīmitra/Milarepa emanation line was personally adopted at about the same time by another acclaimed Tibetan master: Zhapkar Tsokdruk Rangdrol (1781–1851). Zhapkar consciously cast himself in Milarepa's mold, a century after Kalden Gyatso's activities in Amdo, described in chapter 3. He spent much of his life emulating Milarepa's virtuosic yogic practice, staying for extended periods in the yogin's retreat locations of Lapchi and Gungtang, and continuing his tradition of teaching through spontaneous song. In response to a patron's query about his past lives, Zhapkar replied (here in the third person) with some eight examples, beginning,

> At the time of the Buddha he was Avalokiteshvara,
> In the land of India he was Manjushrimitra,
> . . . .
> In the Kagyu Tradition he was Milarepa.[109]

Zhapkar's activities in Lapchi further convinced his followers that he was Milarepa's incarnation. Perhaps unsurprisingly, his principal teacher was likewise recognized as an emanation of Mila's guru, Marpa.[110] The core elements of Milarepa's life—his renunciation, resolute practice, and above all his devotion to the guru—had been well-enough established that he could be held up and claimed by early Kagyu lineage holders, Geluk monks, and eighteenth-century charismatic masters as an exemplary model of a hermit.

If Zhijé Ripa was somewhat agnostic about Milarepa's status as a miraculous emanation of a previously enlightened figure, he had no trouble describing him as manifesting both in pure realms and in physical form after his death. "At present," Zhijé Ripa wrote in 1373,

> [Milarepa] is a bodhisattva *mahāsattva* in the Dharma palace of Akaniṣṭha. He took the name Kunga Lodrö and in the *dharmakāya*, unsullied and endowed with realization, he attained the pure ground of wisdom, where

he abides, listening to the authentic Dharma before the sixth Bhagavan Buddha Mahāvajradhara. This is clearly indicated in the prophecies of former masters such as the *saṃbhogakāya* formless [*ḍākinīs*], Telopa, and Nāropa, in the affirmations of the great father Jetsün Lhodrak Marpa, in the extraordinary teachings of the Great Jetsün Mila Rechen himself, and in the teachings of his great disciples such as the supreme heart son Rechung Dorjé Drak, and particularly in the teachings of Lord Khyungt- sangpa Jñānaguru and the Dharma lord who is undeluded regarding the objects of knowledge of the five sciences, Zhang Lotsāwa. It is also clearly indicated in the [writings] of the succession of lives of glorious Pakmo- drupa Dorjé Gyalpo.

His *saṃbhogakāya* and *nirmāṇakāya* forms are incomprehensible, but at present there are *nirmāṇakāya* who hold the [transmission] of the wish- fulfilling gem aural tantras of the *saṃbhogakāya* formless *ḍākinīs* and those individuals who maintain, without error, the six yogas of Nāropa are *nirmāṇakāyas* of guru Mila Rechen.[111]

Milarepa is here described postmortem as having attained a place in the pure realm of Akaniṣṭha. Yet he is also said to manifest in untold forms, both physical and miraculous. Indeed, all those who follow perfectly in his tradition, practicing the core yogic instructions of the lineage, are considered to appear as the yogin's emanation bodies.

These traditions continued well into the nineteenth and twentieth centuries when, for example, the Kagyu polymath Kongtrul Lodrö Tayé described Milarepa as manifesting innumerable emanations, including Mañjuśrīmitra.[112] The preface to a recently published biography of Nam- kha Gyaltsen, Tsangnyön's contemporary and author of the famed Mila encomium, identifies the subject as Milarepa's mind incarnation (*thugs sprul*).[113] Perhaps most interestingly, famed Geluk scholar Pabongka Dechen Nyingpo (1878–1941) described Milarepa as the reincarnation of eleventh-century Kadampa *geshe* Chaktrichok, thereby bringing the yogin into the circle of founding figures for the later Geluk tradition.[114]

The Drakar Taso incarnation Chökyi Wangchuk records an astonishing list of early Kagyu masters considered to be miraculous emanations of Milarepa:

In an ultimate sense, he was completely enlightened in one lifetime and one body and then sent forth a manifold display of manifestations per- vading space. Here in Tibet, he is famed for having revealed a series of manifestations with identical qualities, including Drigung Kyopa Rinchen Pel, Loré Darma Wangchuk, and Götsangpa Gönpo Dorjé.[115]

He concludes this list by identifying a final individual considered to have appeared as the yogin's emanation: "later on, at this place [i.e., Drakar Taso], the accomplished master Tsangnyönpa," that is, Tsangnyön Heruka.[116] Clearly, this would have a considerable impact on how Tsangnyön presented, and his Tibetan audience received, the standard version of Milarepa's life story, repercussions that will be examined in the next chapter.

Rebirth as an Ordinary Individual

Milarepa's status as a miraculous emanation had become an integral part of his biographical tradition, but Tsangnyön did not merely strike it from the life story, he actively repudiated it. At the end of the tenth chapter of the *Life*, prior to the *Songs* summary and the yogin's death, the storyline reaches its dramatic peak; the following pages are as much a "moral to the story" as can be found anywhere in the text. As the action breaks away from Mila's narration of his life story, it turns to the disciples seated around him, in awe of the tale they have just heard. Overwhelmed by the virtuosic example set by his guru, Zhiwa Ö states, "When we think about [your] actions, it seems we are only pretending to practice Dharma. . . . What can we do?"[117]

Disciple Ngendzong is moved even further, and poignantly delivers the following plea:

> It seems that the precious Jetsün is himself the great Vajradhara manifesting in human form and that he has displayed these actions for the benefit of sentient beings. Otherwise, it is certain that he is a great being of immeasurable fortune. . . . If we ordinary people cannot even comprehend the manner in which the Jetsün practiced austerities for the sake of Dharma, the deeds he undertook with devotion while living with his lama and so forth, who could actually emulate them? . . . That is why it is certain the Jetsün was, from the start, either a buddha or a bodhisattva. . . . I beg the Jetsün to tell us whether he is an emanation of Vajradhara or a bodhisattva.[118]

The story has reached a decisive moment; its dialogue turns inward, self-reflective, clarifying how the biographical subject, and the life story itself, should ultimately be understood. The voice of Ngendzong—architect of Milarepa's earliest extensive life story—echoes, under Tsangnyön's pen, the tenor of four centuries of biographical tradition.

To this, Milarepa replies with what may be the most crucial passage of the text, spoken by the yogin to his disciples and, through him, by Tsangnyön to his reading audience:

> I have no idea whose incarnation I am. . . . Although this belief that I am an emanation comes from your pure perception of me, there is no greater misunderstanding of Dharma. This is because you do not recognize the greatness of perfectly practicing pure Dharma.
>
> In general, the greatness of genuine Dharma is such that even an ordinary person who carried out terrible sinful deeds such as I did in the early part of my life can eventually gain conviction in the law of cause and effect. If he is then able to renounce this life and meditate without his three gates becoming distracted, he can reach a state not far from attaining buddhahood. In particular, if you are able to follow a properly qualified lama; if you can then receive the initiations and oral instructions that introduce one to nakedly perceiving—without obscurations and conventional thought—the essential points and heart-instructions of the short path of Secret Mantra; and if you can meditate on them, there is no doubt that you shall gain buddhahood in this life. . . . To suggest . . . that such an individual is an emanation of a buddha or a bodhisattva is a sign that you lack conviction in the short path of Secret Mantra.[119]

This passage can only be read as an ironic jab thrown across some four centuries, aimed at the individual responsible for promoting Milarepa's miraculous status. No longer an emanated being, the yogin has become an ordinary human whose proximity to enlightenment is due solely to the intensity of his own practice. Both life and life story have become living metaphors for the Buddhist path. Viewing him as an emanation may be a sign of devotion, but ultimately serves as an impediment to spiritual progress, tantamount to the root mental affliction of wrong view.

Tsangnyön Heruka's motivations for this fundamental change to Milarepa's biographical tradition were manifold. In part, they stem from a desire to return the Kagyu tradition to its core values, rooted in the early tradition of yogic meditation and retreat. This was perhaps best exemplified by the trope of liberation in one lifetime and one body that first appeared in the biographical tradition a century earlier and was adopted by Tsangnyön as a central unifying theme. But the new biography was, above all, a crafted work of literature. Tsangnyön no doubt understood the tension between Mila's representation as an ordinary human set within the structural framework of an exemplary life, and employed that tension to propel forward the reading of the text.

Tibet during the eleventh and twelfth centuries, the period in which Milarepa and his immediate followers lived, had not yet developed the elaborate system of recognized incarnate teachers—*tulku* (*sprul sku*), literally "emanation bodies"—for which its system of Buddhism would became famous. The Karmapas are traditionally described as forming the first such incarnation line, with their lineage extending back to Milarepa's grand-disciple Düsum Khyenpa (1110–93) and his recognized reembodiment, Karma Pakshi (1204–83).

By the late fifteenth century, Tibet's religious landscape had changed significantly. Although the institution of the Dalai Lama was still a century off, the Karmapas had risen as powerful religious and political leaders and other Kagyu communities likewise amassed power and prestige under the guidance of charismatic leaders. The communities frequently coalesced around a particular familial line, such as the Pakmodrupa's Lang clan, which together with the recognized reincarnations, formed what has been called a stratum of "hereditary religious nobility."[120] And if Tsangnyön Heruka's adoption of the madman's lifestyle was, in part, "a reaction against the great prestige and wealth of the hereditary [and incarnation] lineages" in an attempt to "re-kindle the incandescent spirituality of the early yogis," his representation of Milarepa served much the same purpose.[121] It is, therefore, not without irony that in describing the biographical tradition that began with the standard *Life* and *Songs*, Smith notes, "Tsangnyön and his students glorified their gurus by proclaiming them incarnations of the Indian and Tibetan yogis who had practiced and passed on the Kagyupa teachings."[122]

Although Tsangnyön eschewed describing Milarepa as an emanation, his biography of Marpa preserves the tradition of viewing him as the Indian adept Ḍombi Heruka and an emanation of the tantric deity Hevajra. And as we shall see in the next chapter, Tsangnyön quietly promoted himself, with the active support of disciples, as maintaining a close connection with Milarepa, in some instances identifying himself as the yogin's reincarnation. It is therefore not surprising that Tsangnyön emphasized Milarepa's liberation in one lifetime and one body; he made this claim regarding his own yogic practice, and included the trope as part of his intention to compose the life story.[123]

REFLECTIONS

As a follower of Milarepa's tradition, Tsangnyön Heruka carried the mantle of the yogin's lifestyle as his own. He spent years undertaking solitary retreat practice in isolated and fearsome locations, eventually earning the status of a cotton-clad *repa*. He later wandered among the caves and hermitages along Tibet's southern borderlands in which Milarepa meditated, and encouraged his disciples to do the same. At one point, in a prophetic statement inserted into the *Life*, Tsangnyön explicitly referred to his own role as one of Milarepa's "spiritual descendents."[124] The following chapter will examine in detail how the relationship between Mila the yogin and Tsangnyön the madman was promoted in Tsangnyön's own biographical tradition.

But as a standard bearer for Milarepa's yogic tradition, Tsangnyön also moved beyond the role of a world-weary mendicant, taking on many activities the yogin himself had shunned. Four hundred years after Milarepa's death, Tibet's religious and political landscape had transformed considerably, and while Tsangnyön Heruka had adopted the persona and conduct of a mad yogin, he also proved a shrewd agent in a time of significant religious and social change. Tsangnyön forged alliances with the Rinpung prince Donyö Dorjé and other powerful rulers of southern and western Tibet, who would later support his literary activities. He fostered peace negotiations between warring principalities in the south and west. He accepted an invitation from the Nepalese King Ratnamalla to undertake a major renovation of the Swayambhū *mahācaitya* in 1504.[125] Tsangnyön also received from Donyö Dorjé possession of Milarepa's hermitage known as Omchung near Drin in the Rongshar valley, where he established a retreat center that remained active long after his death.[126]

Tsangnyön's role as innovator is also reflected in his literary activities, most notably in his crafting of Milarepa's life story. As we have seen, Tsangnyön based his *Life* and *Songs* almost entirely upon works already present in the biographical tradition. But he reimagined and re-presented them in a form that was, in Milarepa's tradition at least, groundbreaking. With the Lives of Marpa and Milarepa, Smith has noted, Tsangnyön inspired a new tradition of biographical literature in Tibet, focusing on the great yogin masters of the early Kagyu lineage. This tradition was continued by his close disciples, Lhatsun Rinchen Namgyal and Götsang Repa, among others.[127] Under Rinchen Namgyal's stewardship, the monastery of Drakar Taso became an important site of literary production and printing in southern and central Tibet.[128]

In one sense, the *Life* and *Songs* can be understood as forming part of Tsangnyön Heruka's larger conceptual project, the first in a series of related literary works. Though the madman was a follower of Milarepa's yogic lifestyle, his principal religious affiliation—insofar as he maintained one—was not to any of the influential Kagyu institutions, but to the traditions of the aural transmissions themselves.[129] Shortly after finishing the blocks for the *Life* and *Songs*, he began compiling a massive collection of instructions from the aural transmissions, along with his version of Marpa's life story. The preliminary portion of Zhang Lotsāwa's aural transmission curriculum was devoted to the life stories of its lineage holders. At least some early works in Mila's biographical tradition, *The Twelve Great Disciples* in particular, were explicitly defined as constituting this preliminary section. In the broader context of his literary oeuvre, Tsangnyön's biographical writings might be understood as the preliminaries to his grand record of the aural transmission traditions, establishing authentic and authorized accounts of the lives of their two principal Tibetan founders, Marpa and Milarepa.

Beyond this programmatic aspect of his work, Tsangnyön also brought a number of important rhetorical, structural, and hermeneutic innovations to the *Life* and *Songs* that dramatically altered the biographical tradition and its representation of Milarepa and his life. These did not so much replace the biographical corpus as re-present its existing detail with new clarity. Rhetorically, Tsangnyön directed his works to a far wider audience than previously attempted. Early texts such as *The Twelve Great Disciples* were first intended for a carefully circumscribed community of readers (including those specifically initiated into the traditions of the aural transmissions). Tsangnyön, however, envisioned a biographical narrative that would appeal to all levels of Tibetan society, from the religious and political elite, to the meditator in retreat, to the uneducated and largely illiterate population of the Tibetan countryside. For his readers, Tsangnyön emphasized the elements of form and style, such as plotting and narrative pacing, serving to fictionalize the life story in a manner previously unseen in the tradition. But he equally addressed a nonliterate audience, distributing paintings depicting Milarepa's life in visual narratives that would later be used by itinerant storytellers, the so-called Maṇipa, who taught such stories publicly as they wandered from village to village.

Structural changes likewise broadened the appeal of Tsangnyön's works. Tsangnyön separated the *Life* and *Songs*, creating a smoother and more manageable biographical narrative that could be read easily from birth to final passing. He reorganized the *Songs*, streamlining the somewhat cumbersome division into seventeen sections found in the early compendia. In their place, he incorporated three sections, thematically arranged to emphasize the major activities of Mila's later life: taming demons and training disciples. The *Songs* became a commentary on the *Life*, providing context for better understanding the mature period of Milarepa's teaching career. It also lent itself to being read in small pieces, allowing the reader to choose individual stories pertinent to a particular situation, not unlike the great Indian collections of *jātaka* and *avadāna* tales.

As will be addressed in further detail in the next chapter, he also shifted the life story's perspective from the third person to a first-person narrator, transforming biography into autobiography. The story was no longer recorded by an author hundreds of years after the fact but was apparently told by the subject himself. Yet even as Milarepa's own voice seemed to rise to the surface, describing a life actually lived, Tsangnyön explicitly framed the *Life* by invoking the paradigmatic liberation tale of the Buddha's own life in twelve acts.

Tsangnyön's shift in interpreting the life story may have made the most indelible impression on the biographical corpus. For more than three centuries, Milarepa was understood as a miraculous being: first an unnamed emanation, later the reimbodiment of an Indian *siddha*, prophesied by Padmasambhava himself. Tsangnyön's repudiation of this view was in part perhaps a commentary on the degree of power and prestige that the institutionalized incarnation traditions had garnered. But the figure of Milarepa as an ordinary human also demonstrated the possibility of religious practice, yogic insight, even liberation in a single lifetime for all individuals. In this way, the story reaffirmed that ultimately, one's progress on the path is due entirely to the effort applied during one's own life. As Tsangnyön says, through Milarepa's voice,

> It is possible for every ordinary or common person with perseverance to do as I have done: First, develop devotion for the lama. Next, persevere in meditation on the oral instructions. Finally, persevere in nurturing your

experience and realization. . . . Have conviction in the law of cause and effect. From the life stories of previous masters, contemplate the cause and effect of actions, the faults of life's round, the difficulty of attaining a human rebirth endowed with leisure and opportunity, and the uncertainty of the time of death. Apply yourself to the practice of Secret Mantra.[130]

These words form a condensed instruction encompassing the entire Buddhist path: reflecting on the lives of past masters; engaging in the preliminary practices of the "four thoughts that turn the mind" (*blo ldog rnam bzhi*) by reflecting on the cause and effect of karma, the faults of saṃsāra, the preciousness of human rebirth, and the uncertainty of death; and eventually taking up the swift path of the Vajrayāna. Here, these practices and their resultant "spontaneous awakening" are advocated for all individuals, regardless of their status or standing. No longer did Milarepa's life story merely describe the life of a single individual or the founding of an isolated religious institution. It presented an overview of the path from birth to liberation that could be adopted by the faithful across Tibet's religious landscape and appealed to practitioners of diverse sectarian affiliations. The biographical corpus had coalesced over the centuries, forming an ever more lifelike portrait; Milarepa now stood as both an exemplar of Buddhist practice and a Tibetan individual of great humanity.

5

THE YOGIN AND THE MADMAN

A LIFE BROUGHT TO LIFE

ORIENTATIONS

Biography as Autobiographical Voice

BY THE middle of 1507 Tsangnyön Heruka was dead, his passing marked by weeks of rituals and miraculous appearances.[1] In his absence, close disciples began the process of recording his life anew. As with Milarepa's life story, it was only after the master's death that the tradition of his life (and his Life) could take birth. As we have seen, Tsangnyön's activities in crafting Milarepa's *Life* and *Songs* form a significant part of his own life story, and his biographers devoted extensive sections to their description. There is evidence that Tsangnyön Heruka's disciples planned to print Milarepa's biography and collected songs together with the madman's own life and songs as a four-volume set.[2]

This chapter turns to representations of Tsangnyön Heruka and his role as the literary and perhaps literal voice of Milarepa's life story, the authorial seal authenticating the yogin's living image. What were the reasons underlying Tsangnyön Heruka's dominance in the landscape of Milarepa's life story? How did the author's perspective affect the crafting of his biographical subject and influence its reading? How were these actions defined through the language he used in Milarepa's Life, and later recorded in his own biographies? The relationship between Milarepa and Tsangnyön Heruka was intimate—so close that the boundaries between biographical author and subject, the crafting of a Life and the telling of one's own life story, were effectively broken down.

When Tsangnyön Heruka concluded the biography, he affixed to it neither his ordination names nor the title conferred upon him by the faithful of Tsāri, Madman of Tsang (Tsangnyön). He used instead a moniker evoking the inspired antinomianism of Indian tantric adepts who were the sources for his spiritual lineage: "He Dressed in Bone Ornaments, the yogin who wanders charnel grounds" (dur khrod nyul ba'i rnal 'byor pa rus pa'i rgyan can). It appears that Tibetans (at least the religious virtuosi, scholars, and historians among them) could easily identify Tsangnyön as the author of his two works. This is hardly surprising given the effort he exerted in promoting his literary productions.

Western audiences had a rather more difficult time of it. In his Tibetan-English dictionary, Jäschke referred to the Life as "Milarepa's autobiography," as did Das two decades later; this was due, no doubt, to Tsangnyön's transformation of the text from third-person to first-person narrative.[3] Bacot, however, states that the life story was written in the twelfth century by Milarepa's disciple Rechungpa, describing it as an autobiography dictated by the subject himself and recorded as an eyewitness account.[4] Once again, this supposition was predicated on Tsangnyön's framing tale, discussed below, in which Rechungpa inspires the entire account by urging his guru to speak.

Evans-Wentz maintained this attribution, noting that "our version [of the Life] is by Rechung, the second of disciples," and later, in reference to Tsangnyön's literary pseudonym, "From this place name it appears that the History was either written or completed while Rechung was on Pilgrimage to Lapchi-Kang . . . or else while he was in hermitage there."[5] He begins the biography's opening verses with the title "Introduction (from the Tibetan) by Rechung, Disciple of Milarepa."[6] More surprisingly, the translator Kazi Dawa-Samdup also refers to the story as having been written "more than eight hundred years ago," pointing to Rechungpa's supposed hand in its creation. Even Tucci refers to the "mgur 'bum by Ras c'uṅ, Milaraspa's favorite pupil."[7] De Jong, however, was more circumspect, noting only that the author's pseudonym in the colophon (dur khrod nyul ba'i rus pa'i rgyan can) also appears in the biography of Marpa.[8] It was not until Chang's English translation of the Songs, published in 1962 with a supporting letter from Herbert Guenther, that both works were "established to be by Saṅ.Rgyas.rGyal.mtshan, the 'Insane Yogi from Gtsaṅ,' who bears many different names."[9] Seven years later, Gene Smith's survey of Tsangnyön's own biography offered definitive proof of the text's origin at the hands of the mad yogin.[10]

The confusion over who authored the *Life* and *Songs*—largely a problem among non-Tibetan commentators—was understandable. Although the life story is clearly titled a biography (*rnam thar*) as opposed to a self-written life (*rang rnam*), it takes the structural form of an autobiography narrated primarily in the first person. As noted in the previous chapter, Tsangnyön Heruka's switch to a first-person voice made for compelling literature, but it also invested the text with a layer of authenticity, as if capturing the life of the subject himself in his own words. This was an unprecedented move within Milarepa's biographical tradition.

Yet the correspondence of author and subject lies deeper still; the first-person narrative was not merely a literary conceit, but underscored a direct relationship between Milarepa and Tsangnyön Heruka initiated by the author himself and later promoted by his disciples. If Tsangnyön Heruka's *Life of Milarepa* is *bios* shaped as *autobios*, it may also be understood as an autobiographical voice set within a biographical frame. This creates an utter conflation of self and other, one that is less Defoe's Caruso than Stein's Alice B. Toklas. It is in this sense—with the yogin's *Life* a vehicle for the madman's self-reflection, and the madman's identification with the yogin serving to authorize the *Life*—that the underlying mechanism of the biographical act may be understood. And through this act, a biographical corpus four hundred years in the making was effectively brought to life.

An Extraordinary Life

Tsangnyön Heruka's own life stories credit him with the traditional Buddhist motivation for crafting his version of Milarepa's life story: spreading the Buddha's teachings and thereby benefiting innumerable beings. Biographer Götsang Repa, however, records another incentive, first mentioned in chapter 4: inspired with the intention to create Milarepa's Life anew, Tsangnyön is described as having the following thought: "At present in this snowy land there exist numerous biographies and collected songs of Jetsün Zhepa Dorjé. However, the [transmission of] his *extraordinary biography* has been interrupted." To what work or works might Götsang Repa, the only biographer to record this particular phrase, be referring when he specifies Milarepa's extraordinary biography (*thun mong ma yin pa'i rnam thar*)? Perhaps more importantly, what about such a work would distinguish it from other forms of life writing?

One published reference to Tsangnyön's statement seems to have missed the mark. Introducing his English translation of the *Life*, Lhalungpa cites this passage in the following way: "The Revered One (Tsang Nyon) thought that even though many editions of the autobiography and collected songs did exist, I must revive this uncommon version *based on the oral tradition.*"[11] Although Götsang Repa's work indeed mentions an "uncommon (or extraordinary) version" that had been interrupted, it nowhere specifies that this version stems from an oral tradition. Lhalungpa, it seems, has himself succumbed to the rhetoric of orality: the notion that Tsangnyön Heruka's main achievement was recapturing a biographical tradition that, for four centuries, circulated primarily in oral form.

Neither does the "extraordinary biography" stem from previously unknown or undocumented literary sources. Tsangnyön's reported searches for rare and undocumented biographical narratives (described as a difficult undertaking only in the last of his three biographies) may have turned up some miscellaneous, previously unattested fragments. For the most part, however, this was a rhetorical device; his efforts in terms of literary content were largely editorial. Tsangnyön predicated nearly the entire text of his *Life* and *Songs* upon the proto-texts and compendia surveyed above, and the stories from those works could in no way be described as "interrupted."

Although the extraordinary biography refers neither to previous oral tradition nor to some unknown literary work, contemporary Tibetan poet and critic Döndrup Gyel describes it in the following way. The yogin's close disciples composed biographical bits and pieces (*thor bu*) based upon what they saw and heard, but after four hundred years the extraordinary biography had become interrupted, cut off. Those parts that were not cut off and lost were mixed with various kinds of misinformation so that they became untrustworthy and ineffective. For this reason, Döndrup Gyel argues,

> Tsangnyön edited together into a single work all of the biographical fragments he saw and heard. In order to restore what had degenerated and further develop what had not degenerated, he made pure the impure elements that had proliferated, he made true the untrue parts that had been infiltrated by misinformation.[12]

Döndrup Gyel likely wrote this without direct knowledge of the vast corpus of early literature in Milarepa's biographical tradition, particularly the compendia upon which Tsangnyön based his works. But if his description wanders astray in its history of the *Life*'s production, it aptly describes how the final version, the extraordinary biography, came to be viewed: pure and precise in its representation, reclaiming a "true account" of the yogin's life from a variety of exaggerated or misreported claims.[13] This work appeared to capture Mila's life in the flesh, as if reaching back in time, touching the source directly.

In these terms, Döndrup Gyel's claim is particularly relevant. His description of Tsangnyön's work concerns not the content of the text so much as the means by which it was authorized. And the process of making "pure the impure" and making "true the untrue" refers less to editorial technique than to the specific claims that Tsangnyön Heruka, and later his followers, could make about his relationship to his subject. The madman's "extraordinary biography" of Milarepa does not merely consist of some other version or combination of versions pieced together in a more compelling manner. Rather, it reflects Tsangnyön's direct knowledge of the life, not as an author working from secondary sources generations after the fact or even as a direct witness to events, but as the biographical subject himself. The fame Tsangnyön received upon finishing the *Life* and *Songs* earned him status as Milarepa's incarnation, which he advocated and his followers promoted. This in turn bolstered the legitimacy of his literary works, lending credibility to his authorial voice. Thus, as we shall see, the madman's biography of the yogin can be read, in part, as his own autobiography, an autobiographical biography, a life within a life.

Autobiographical Biography

The contemporary study of autobiography has become increasingly aware of an autobiographical presence within biographical literature, in which the author's voice may serve as a form of rhetorical support for the shortcomings, manipulations, and natural lacunae inherent in any written life story. That voice may be distant, declared "off stage" through the use of language, emplotment, and literary structure. It might also take a more central role, appearing instead before the curtain, directly in the narrative itself. The writing of biography is to some degree a self-reflexive process through which the author defines the subject in terms of his own position, a practice that has been described as "the biographer's secret."[14]

In extreme cases, the authorial voice might encroach upon the subject itself, as in A. J. A. Symon's classic biography of Baron Corvo, pseudonym for the mysterious nineteenth-century British novelist Frederick Rolfe. This life story, subtitled "an experiment in biography," has been described as a "remarkable self-portrait, a study of the obsession and sympathy that inspires the biographer's art."[15] As a biographer, Symon "does not impinge on the story of his subject; he becomes it."[16] And as the subject of his own biographical reflection, Symon casts himself alongside his protagonist, creating an autobiographical locus within a biographical frame.

Heffernan describes a similar phenomenon manifesting in medieval European hagiography, in which "the biographer's persona becomes part of the narrative fabric" forming what he calls "autobiographical biography."[17] He is commenting on Walter Daniel's famed twelfth-century biography of Aelred, third abbot of the Cistercian abbey at Rievaulx. In particular, he focuses on Walter's moving description of Aelred's final words before his death, a scene in which Walter himself plays a substantial role. Heffernan notes,

> The single most crucial effect that this complex narrative can have on the reader's imagination concerns the degree to which the text can claim authenticity for itself. Through the use of his first-person narration and the dramatized persona, the biographer confronts his audience with his own personal testimony.[18]

That confrontation serves to support the story's claim as a legitimate representation of the subject's life. To doubt the text is to question the reliability of the narrator, a response "not leveled lightly at works of biography."[19]

We have already seen this illustrated in the texts of the previous chapters. In the earliest of Milarepa's biographical writings by Gampopa and Ngendzong Repa, the authors' relationship to their subject is historical; their writings bear direct witness to the events recorded. While Gampopa's voice permeates the text, Ngendzong remains in the background, evident mainly through his editorial efforts and the autonarratives of his colophons. Whether or not the authors actually saw or heard the events they describe—or, for that matter, whether or not they wrote them—is immaterial; it is the purported relationship that strengthens their authorial voice. And as the distance from Milarepa as a biographical subject grew, many authors remained in the wings, maintaining a link with their subject through references to a rapidly swelling corpus of biographical writing. Zhijé Ripa stands as a rare exception.[20]

Tsangnyön Heruka presents a very different case. The relationships between biographer and biographical subject described above, and observed in Milarepa's early Lives, are largely dialogical, voices in conversation. An author may interject his or her presence into the story, confronting the audience with personal testimony, but a divide between author and subject endures; the *autos* of the autobiographical biography remains a distinct voice, segregated from the subject itself. Tsangnyön Heruka would radically change that relationship.

Certainly, Tsangnyön's skill as editor and literary stylist left a profound imprint on the biographical tradition. As described in the preceding chapter, it was in part his ability to fictionalize the life story through the crafting of narrative that led to the work's success. But Tsangnyön and his followers professed a different sort of relationship between the madman (as author) and the yogin (as biographical subject), one in which Tsangnyön was cast as Milarepa himself. Tsangnyön's process of making "true the untrue" and making "pure the impure" might thus be understood as writing himself into the story, not as a competing subject but literally as the subject himself. From this ultimate vantage point of biographical authority, Milarepa's first-person narration becomes Tsangnyön's own voice, unimpeachable and in a sense unmediated, as if speaking out directly to readers across a span of four centuries.

TSANGNYÖN HERUKA'S LIFE WITH MILAREPA

Visionary Encounters

Ever since Gene Smith introduced Tsangnyön Heruka's biography to scholars in 1969, the prevailing view of the madman has been that he demurred in the face of recognition as a miraculous emanation. "To him," Smith writes, "emulating the lives of the great masters of the past was more important than the incarnation lineage to which a teacher belonged."[21] Smith translates a passage, frequently cited, from the biography to illustrate this point: when a disciple "announced that he dreamt that Tsangnyön was the incarnation of Tilopa, Tsangnyön replied: 'That may indeed be your vision. I am indeed one who upholds the tradition of Tilopa. I have no idea whether I am an incarnation or not.'"[22] As previously noted, Tsangnyön did turn to the examples of the great yogins of the early Kagyu lineage for inspiration; his biographical project was at least in part predicated upon a desire to reemphasize their traditions.

Tsangnyön Heruka clearly modeled his life after Milarepa's. He adopted the yogin's cotton-clad lifestyle, wandered among his mountain retreats, meditated in his caves. On closer examination, Tsangnyön's own bio-graphical tradition reveals that he maintained a particularly intimate relationship with Milarepa throughout his life, and that his religious career was punctuated by visionary encounters with the yogin. On more than one occasion, he admitted that he was in fact Milarepa's incarnation. At times he did so obliquely, as if in a kind of code, but at others, he made a direct and unmistakable connection. Tsangnyön's followers maintained and actively promoted this view, elevating the status of both their own guru and his major literary enterprise.

Lhatsun Rinchen Namgyal's biography records many of Tsangnyön's early visionary encounters with Milarepa. He writes that even as a two-year-old toddler, Tsangnyön spontaneously made prayers to the early masters of the Kagyu lineage, including Milarepa, Rechungpa, and Pak-modrupa.[23] At age twenty-six, Tsangnyön traveled to Milarepa's retreat site Drakmar Chonglung in Drin, where he is described for the first time as meeting the yogin in a vision: "While [Tsangnyön was] abiding evenly in a state of river-flow *samādhi* for one month, Milarepa would sometimes teach his life story; sometimes he would give compassionate advice, sometimes he would teach Dharma, and sometimes he would display miracles."[24] From Milarepa himself, Tsangnyön receives not only Dharma teachings and advice but also a direct transmission of the life story. Perhaps a decade before he completed the *Life* and *Songs*, Tsangnyön is described as hearing it from the biographical source.

During this period, Tsangnyön traveled to another of Milarepa's medi-tation sites, Poto Namkha Dzong, where he is described as having a trans-formative vision, couched in the symbolic activity of tantric practice. While resting in meditation, he is visited by the five Long Life Sisters, the Tsering Chenga, who figure prominently in the earliest fragments of Milarepa's life story. They appear with large pendant breasts and swollen vaginas from which trickle the five types of nectar. As they stand there before him with palms pressed together, he places a drop of spittle on each of their vaginas. After remaining in *samādhi* for some days, he then has a visionary encounter with Milarepa, here referred to as Zhepa Dorjé:

> Several days passed, and from within a state that was a mixture of dream and clear light, Jetsun Zhepa Dorjé appeared amid a sky filled with rainbow light, his body incredibly radiant, holding in his hand a crystal *kapāla* filled with nectar. He said, "The symbolic acts of last night are called the initia-tion revealing the secret name. Have confidence that the secret initiation

unraveling knots of the channels and the knowledge-wisdom initiation bringing the pervading wind under control were granted simultaneously. Thus wisdom will arise in your five channel wheels—you'll become such a person." He poured nectar from the *kapāla* into my [Tsangnyön's][25] mouth, and I experienced its taste on my tongue. Accordingly, with an uncontaminated bliss extending to all the tips of the hairs on his body, he slipped into a state of intoxicated *samādhi*.[26]

At dawn the next morning, the five Long Life Sisters return, and he receives each in turn as a consort, after which each imparts a different set of instructions. As a result, the knots of his five channel wheels unravel, and at each one of those places in succession the deities Guhyasamāja, Mahāmāyā, Hevajra, Cakrasaṃvara, Kālacakra—the body, speech, mind, qualities, and activities—as well as the five bodies and five wisdoms all manifest.

Sometime later, on his way to the religious center of Langkor near Dingri, Tsangnyön has a vision of the Indian yogin Padampa Sangyé (who once taught in the region), together with Milarepa and his disciples Rechungpa and Ngendzong Repa.[27] That summer, he travels to Lapchi, one of Milarepa's favored retreat locations, and "while staying there, in order to accomplish the benefit of others, he gilded the footprint of Lord Mila. The earth quaked three times and the letters *oṃ āḥ hūṃ* rose forth upon Mila's footprint."[28] The author of this passage, Tsangnyön's disciple, then records that the footprint can still be seen and serves as an object of offerings by pilgrims. This footprint would later serve as an important clue in Tsangnyön's admission to being an emanation of Milarepa, described below. All of these activities are said to have taken place before Tsangnyön's thirtieth year, prior to his composing the praise to Milarepa modeled after the Buddha's twelve deeds.

Sometime before the age of thirty-four, Tsangnyön spends two months in a retreat location called Ösal Puk. While residing there, he has yet another visionary encounter with Milarepa:

One morning at dawn, in a very clear state of *samādhi*, [Tsangnyön] had a vision of Jetsün Zhepa Dorjé himself, completely luminous within a canopy of rainbow light in the sky, ablaze in brilliant light. His right hand [made a gesture of] teaching Dharma; his left hand rested in meditation holding a *kapāla* filled with nectar. His legs were crossed in half-vajra posture, and he was seated on a cushion of rainbow light like a thousand-petal lotus.

With devotion and immeasurably fervent longing, [Tsangnyön] made many prostrations and requested blessings. Lord [Mi la] gently stroked his head many times with his right hand and said, "You have two names: formerly Dewa Kyong and now Tutop Wangchuk," and then he dissolved into rainbow light.[29]

Up to this point, Tsangnyön's biographies have described the madman's close relationship with the yogin during his early years. His monumental project of preparing Milarepa's *Life* and *Songs* would further emphasize that relationship in the minds of the general public, Tsangnyön's followers, and Tsangnyön himself. The madman's biography describes an episode in which one Lodrö Tashi, who later became one of Tsangnyön's close disciples, was stricken by a black pox (*'brum nag*). Afflicted with this terminal illness, he decides to undertake an intensive meditation retreat. While making preparations, he is informed by a merchant that "these days in Latö Lho the Powerful Lord of Yogins Tsangnyönpa, an emanation of Lord Mila, is printing the *Life* and *Collected Songs* of Lord Mila."[30] Lodrö Tashi's body quivers with faith at the mere sound of Tsangnyön's name, and he later meets the master, who is indeed in the middle of preparing the prints. In this case, Tsangnyön is not only described explicitly as Milarepa's emanation (*sprul pa*) but also afforded the epithet by which Mila is most frequently known: Powerful Lord of Yogins (*rnal 'byor gyi dbang phyug*).

Shortly after this incident, the madman's biography describes another encounter set against the backdrop of Tsangnyön's literary efforts, just as the wood blocks were being completed:

Then the prints were carried to Nyanang Dröpuk. Different faithful patrons, such as Depa Tsadawa, rendered whatever service was needed. They prayed that the printing estates would continually produce clear and bright reproductions while at the same time clarifying the precious teachings and serving as a source for the joy and happiness of beings without exception. At that time everyone paid excellent respect to the master [Tsangnyön] and his disciples. In particular, the great lama of Nyanang Gönsar, Ngawang Drakpa, offered a ritual feast together with offerings. Afterward he said, "Venerable Precious Lord, wherever one looks at your activities, you ought to be an emanation of a buddha or bodhisattva. People say you are an incarnation of Jetsun Rechungpa or Ngendzong Tönpa or some other person, but there is no consensus. Of the different things people are saying, which is it? Whose incarnation are you? Please tell us which of the exceptional masters who appear in the life story of Jetsün Mila are you?"

The Lord [Tsangnyön] replied, "By looking at the footprint at Lapchi Rechung Puk, you'll know whose incarnation I am; which exceptional master will become clear after I die."[31]

In an exact parallel to the culminating point in chapter 10 of *The Life of Milarepa*, Tsangnyön Heruka's disciples ask their master to reveal his identity as a miraculous emanation. Yet unlike the yogin, who reprimands his followers, the madman encourages his students' pious view. The footprint he describes is, of course, none other than Milarepa's imprint he had gilded some years earlier.[32] He has admitted, if somewhat obliquely, that he is indeed the yogin reborn.

Tsangnyön's edition of the yogin's *Life* and *Songs* earned him the praise of many powerful individuals within the Kagyu lineage, including the Seventh Karmapa, Chödrak Gyatso (1454–1506).[33] He was also visited by a group of religious masters who further reinforced this relationship between Mila and Tsangnyön, as recorded in the following encounter:

At that time, some masters, including the nephew of the precious incarnation Zhamar Red Crown Holder called Minyakpa[34] and Tsari Rabjampa, heard of the Lord [Tsangnyön Heruka]'s renown and, feeling an attraction, went to visit him. They were accepted with initiations and instructions. One morning at the break of dawn, during meditation, Pönpo Minyakpa dreamt that five beautiful maidens dressed in cotton robes and many ornaments appeared and inquired, "Will you request the great *repa* Mila teach Dharma?"

"Of course I will ask him. Where is he staying?" he replied.

"He is sitting on a white flat boulder," they said.

He left accompanied by the maidens, and found the Precious Lord [Tsangnyön Heruka] seated upon a boulder with his legs loosely crossed, adorned with bone ornaments and accoutrements from the charnel ground, touching the earth with his left hand and preaching Dharma with his right. [Minyakpa] thought, "This is the precious father [Tsangnyön Heruka]; where is Milarepa?"

The maidens said, "This is Milarepa right there. You haven't recognized him. Now request Dharma," and they prostrated themselves. The nephew [Minyakpa] likewise offered prostrations and sat on the ground. He was given many provisional and definitive Dharma teachings, and his mind was eased. When he awoke from the dream, a fervent longing arose within him with a sense of devotion he had never felt before. He decided with firm conviction that Jetsün Mila had actually been present.[35]

Tsangnyön was described as having maintained a close relationship to Milarepa throughout his life, and was viewed as the yogin's incarnation. He is said to have described this most clearly on his deathbed. In his final instructions to followers just before passing away, he proclaims (here recorded in his earliest biography by Ngödrup Pelbar): "Monks and disciples, together with my patrons, you have directly met Milarepa himself during the degenerate age, and so you have good karma and excellent fortune. Moreover, look at Mila's life (*rnam thar*) and equate your life with practice."[36] During these final moments, Tsangnyön turns to the figure of Milarepa, presenting himself as the yogin incarnate, returned to the world for the benefit of beings during a period of degeneration and decline.

For the most part, Tsangnyön seems to have remained aloof from the tradition of recognizing incarnations, at least insofar as his own status was concerned; he appears to have had little trouble receiving praise and support from the great incarnations of his day. On the question of his own role as an incarnation of Tilopa, he publicly demurred (although did not categorically deny it), and his initial claim to being Mila's incarnation was offered in the form of a riddle. His presentation of Milarepa as an ordinary human, however, attacked the model of recognized incarnations insofar as such a view impeded practice by making the final goal of liberation appear out of reach to common individuals. Only during his last moments among close disciples, in what amounted to his final testament, did Tsangnyön explicitly admit his position as Mila's incarnation.

It seems, therefore, that Tsangnyön's views were flexible, changing according to context. When it might have appeared unseemly to proclaim an exalted status within a public teaching forum, he responded with a noncommittal "I have no idea." At another public event, celebrating the consecration of the blocks for Mila's biography, Tsangnyön again responded with only the coy suggestion that he was the yogin's reembodiment. At the moment of his death, however, his claim to being Mila's incarnation could be viewed as a final skillful act engendering inspiration and devotion among his disciples; it would also serve as a starting point for those followers in formulating hagiographical accounts of their own guru. But in denying Milarepa the status of an incarnation in the context of the biography, Tsangnyön emphasized not so much the religious politics of his times as the themes underlying the life story, meant to inspire a broad audience.

Later Traditions

It is difficult to know the degree to which Tsangnyön Heruka was actually viewed as Milarepa's incarnation during his lifetime. But if the mad saint did achieve such a status due to his promotion of the yogin's biography, his followers actively endorsed it. The matter of Milarepa's miraculous incarnation, so adamantly elided from the yogin's biographical tradition by Tsangnyön, ironically came to play a central part of the madman's own life story. Indeed, the stories recounted above were all recorded under his disciples' direction, as Tsangnyön Heruka's part in Milarepa's life story took on an importance second only to that of the yogin himself. After Tsangnyön's death, his followers clearly represented him as an incarnation, frequently but not exclusively Milarepa. In the concluding verses of his biography, Lhatsün Rinchen Namgyal describes the madman as an emanation (*rnam sprul*) of Tilopa.[37] Two centuries later, in his biography of famed eighteenth-century teacher Changkya Rolpé Dorjé, who was responsible for the production of the Mongolian version of Milarepa's *Life* and *Songs*, Tukan Lozang Chökyi Nyima (1737–1802) counted among the master's previous incarnations both Mila's guru Marpa and Tsangnyön Heruka.[38]

As noted, however, Tsangnyön Heruka's early biography uses the madman's own words to explicitly recognize his status as Milarepa's incarnation. Later biographies followed suit, incorporating this correspondence into the early narrative. Even in his introductory matter, before the biographical narrative begins, Götsang Repa describes how, in one life and one body, Milarepa manifested "the high state of Vajradhara" and then continued to work for the benefit of beings.[39] He then states that "the Lord of Conquerors possessing an emanation body, Powerful Lord of Yogins called Tsangnyön Heruka, Rupé Gyanchen" appeared in the northern direction during the age of degeneration and strife.[40] Götsang Repa repeats this account in his first chapter of the biography, titled "The manner in which [Tsangnyön] displayed his emanation body taking birth in the human realm and awakening his virtuous karmic fortune" (*sprul sku mi yul du bstams shing rnam dkar gyi las 'phro sad tshul stan pa'i le'u*). Here, the author explicitly begins his account of Tsangnyön's birth with the life of Milarepa, describing how the yogin descended from a pure land to the human world, taking the form of an emanation body:

> The Powerful Lord of Yogins, Glorious Jetsün Zhepa Dorjé himself, carried out most amazing activities through which he traversed the thirteen levels of the Vajra Holder in a single lifetime. Yet, through the power of his immeasurable kindness and his aspiration prayers, he took a body that tamed disciples each in their own way. Thus he pervaded all the vast buddha realms and benefited beings to the limits of existence. Then following upon that, in this the last five hundred years of the age of the increasing five degenerations, here in the realm of the northern quarter, light rays of wisdom and love radiated from the spontaneously present pure land of Akaniṣṭha, and the great emanation body [Tsangnyön Heruka] took birth in his mother's womb.[41]

Several centuries later, in a quotation referred to previously, the historian Chökyi Wangchuk includes Tsangnyön Heruka as the last member of Milarepa's incarnation line:

> Here in Tibet, [Milarepa] is famed for having revealed a series of manifestations with identical qualities, including Drigung Kyopa Rinchenpel, Loré Darma Wangchuk, Götsangpa Gönpo Dorjé, and later on, at this place [i.e., Drakar Taso] the accomplished master Tsangnyönpa."[42]

He later repeats Tsangnyön's final message given on the verge of his death: "Monks and disciples, together with my patrons, rejoice that you have directly met Milarepa during the degenerate age." Wangchuk then concludes, "Due to this, the lineage of his disciples accepted him as asserting that he was an emanation of the Jetsün himself."[43] In the twentieth and twenty-first centuries too, followers of Milarepa's tradition have maintained this relationship between the yogin and the madman. In a commentary on the Collected Songs, preeminent Kagyu scholar and lineage holder Khenchen Thrangu Rinpoché has referred to Tsangnyön Heruka as "an emanation of Milarepa."[44]

A LIFE BROUGHT TO LIFE

Virtually all of Milarepa's early biographies open with a humble description of the yogin's origins, including perhaps a simple record of his birthplace and his family lineage.[45] Gampopa begins, "[Milarepa's] family line was Mila of Gungtang. His name was Töpaga. Since [in his family] there were none but father and son, they were extremely poor." *The Twelve Great Disciples* offers a slightly more extended beginning: "The region of his birth was Gungtang. His clan was Khyungpo. His father was called Mila Sherab Gyaltsen, his mother Nyangtsa Kargyen. They had a son and a daughter, and the great Jetsün's name was Töpaga." Tsangnyön, however, introduces his version with an extensive narrative frame that opens in the following way:

> E ma ho. Thus did I hear. At one time the Powerful Lord of Yogins, the great Heruka himself, greatly renowned as Jetsün Mila Zhepa Dorjé, was residing in the sacred place called Dröpa Puk in the region of Nyanam, turning the wheel of the Mahāyāna Dharma seated in the midst of his heartdisciple yogins, bodhisattvas abiding on the *bhūmis*, including Rechungpa Dorjé Drak, Repa Zhiwa Ö, Ngendzong Repa, Seban Repa, Khyira Repa, Drigom Repa, Lengom Repa, Repa Sangyé Kyap, Shengom Repa, Dampa Gyakpuwa, Tönpa Śākyaguṇa; his fortunate male and female lay disciples such as Leksé Bum and Shendormo; rainbow body *ḍākinīs* such as the five Long Life Sisters; and also gods of completely pure lineage, together with an assembly of human yogins and yoginīs.[46]

The text begins with the exclamation *e ma ho*, a Tibetan expression suggesting wonder and amazement, found in both tantric liturgies and songs of realization. The scene that unfolds, however, clearly evokes the literature of the Indian Buddhist sūtras. The passage begins with the formula "thus did I hear," repeating the words (in their Sanskrit rendering, *evaṃ mayā śrutam*) attributed to Ānanda and intended to reflect his perfect recitation from memory of the Buddha's teachings at the first monastic council.[47] In the context of the early Pāli *suttas*, the later Mahāyāna sūtras, and their many translations into other languages, these words are meant to describe the text as an eyewitness record and thus project upon it an authority reserved for the canonical word of the Buddha (*buddhavacana*).

In the commentarial literature of the *Prajñāpāramitā*, the words "thus did I hear" have been glossed as the scriptural "opening" (*gleng slong*, S. *upodghāta*).[48] The remainder of the passage, beginning with "at one time," forms the text's "setting" (*gleng bzhi*, S. *nidāna*) that describes where the discourse was given and who was in attendance. Traditional commentaries have defined the setting's function in this way:

Now, one might ask, "When, from whom, where, and with whom did you hear this precious sūtra?" In order to indicate that one is a reliable person, one sets forth the setting (*nidāna*)—the place, the time, the teacher, the marvelous retinue that [together] are the cause of [the sūtra] being taught—saying, "At one time."[49]

Many sūtras establish the elements of the setting with a statement such as, "At one time the Bhagavan was abiding at Vulture Peak in Rājagṛha with a great assembly of monks and a great assembly of bodhisattvas." In the passage above, Tsangnyön adapts this format to suit his own dramatis personae: the place is identified as Dröpa Puk, "Belly Cave," while the teacher, Milarepa, is discoursing on the Mahāyāna doctrine to the marvelous retinue consisting of his close disciples and a host of human and nonhuman devotees. Later in the episode, Rechungpa is inspired, first by a miraculous dream and then by the five divine Long Life Sisters themselves, to request that Milarepa recount his life story. In this case, the disciple is cast in the role often played by Śāriputra in the Mahāyāna sūtras: the agent eliciting his guru's exposition. The yogin then proceeds to narrate the deeds of his life that constitute the main body of the text.

Buddhist commentarial literature has further discussed the identification of the "I" in "thus did I hear." This individual is described as the *saṃgītikartṛ*, the "rapporteur," referring to his activities ranging from "the marker of the Buddha's word, to the leader of its public recitation, to the convener of a council to determine its content, that is from speaker, to reciter, to redactor."[50] In Tibetan, he is the *bka' sdud pa po*, literally "the gatherer of the Buddha's word," the speaker, reciter, and redactor of the Buddha's authentic speech (*buddhavacana*). In the sūtras, this individual is frequently, although not always, identified as Ānanda, and his identification (or not) as rapporteur carried deep implications about how, when, and for whom such teachings were given, especially in the context of later Mahāyāna works.[51]

As noted at the beginning of this chapter, many who first read the *Life* outside Tibet understood the speaker of "thus did I hear" to be the yogin's close disciple Rechungpa, leading them to attribute the entire biography to him. But the rapporteur's voice may be equally understood as belonging to Tsangnyön Heruka, the author equated inside Tibet with gathering and preserving not the Buddha's word (*sangs rgyas kyi bka'*) but Milarepa's collected words (*Mi la ras pa'i bka' 'bum*). In the view of commentators such as Haribhadra in the quotation cited above, the "opening" identifies the rapporteur's eyewitness experience of the teaching, while the "setting" functions primarily to authorize him as a "reliable person" and a valid source. As Brough has noted, the words "at one time" (*dus gcig na*, S. *ekaṃ samayaṃ*) "are particularly apt for recalling what is within the personal experience of the speaker," and thus stand in sharp contrast to the fairy-tale preamble "once upon a time" that locates action in the distant past.[52] But what does it mean that Tsangnyön himself can state "thus did I hear"—a phrase meant to imply his status as an eyewitness—about the words of an individual who lived some four centuries earlier?

Unlike the Mahāyāna writers who were forced to adopt complex strategies of interpretation and legitimation to defend their works as *buddhavacana* long after the Buddha's demise, Tsangnyön and his biographers took a fairly straightforward approach. Tsangnyön concludes his colophon to the *Life* by stating, "Although I have seen many biographies of the Jetsün, I, Rupé Gyanchen, the yogin who wanders in charnel grounds, put this into writing perfectly and completely . . . just as it was recounted by an extraordinary master (*thun mong ma yin pa'i slob dpon*)."[53] Tsangnyön was indeed described as having received, at age twenty-six, the direct transmission of Milarepa's life story through a visionary encounter with the yogin. From the perspective of Tsangnyön's own biographical tradition, at least, he not only read early accounts of Milarepa's life story but also *heard* it directly from the guru's own mouth. Yet the madman's direct experience of the yogin's life was described as extending deeper still: as the yogin's re-embodiment, he *lived* it himself.

Tsangnyön may thus have written his account with himself as the "I" of the *Life*'s "thus did I hear."[54] The content of what he heard—designated "thus"—would refer to the "extraordinary biography," a version of the life story extraordinary not so much in its content but in the means through which it was authorized. The tradition could claim that Tsangnyön formulated his "extraordinary biography" in two ways: first, through its transmission by an "extraordinary master," in this case Mila himself; and also through the author's direct knowledge of the life, as an incarnation of the biographical subject. This establishes two distinct but interrelated literary frames within the text. The inner frame shapes the principal life story as an autobiographical reflection, a description of Milarepa's deeds as narrated by the yogin, beginning with an account of his early life in chapter 1 (following the introduction) and extending through the first half of chapter 11. Here the autonarration concludes, marking the outer frame with the author's statement, "Up to this point I have recorded the Jetsün's own sayings just as they were. I shall expand a little on this summarized description, taught by the Jetsün himself, of the deeds that will benefit the teachings and sentient beings through the results of his practice."

The text's outer frame—including the opening, setting, and subsequent narrative, as well as the description of Milarepa's death—suggests that the story is told through the voice of Tsangnyön as author and rapporteur, long after the yogin's passing. Yet the inner and outer frames are closely related, and it is the text's introduction that defines the relationship between the two. By opening with "thus did I hear," Tsangnyön Heruka is not merely mimicking the standard literary conceit of scriptural legitimation; he is locating his own position(s) vis-à-vis the text. As biographer, the madman can claim to record the life as a witness to the yogin's own words; as biographical subject, he speaks as the agent of the life itself, bringing it into being.

REFLECTIONS

Stepping back from the examination table, we might pause to take stock of the biographical corpus. The features visible, as it were, to the naked eye are those embodied by Tsangnyön Heruka's version. And it is this form—presenting an ordinary human who long endured the hardships of religious practice, set within the frame of the Buddha's extraordinary deeds—that has come to define the yogin's life most completely. Tradition holds that Tsangnyön crafted a narrative free from the taints of omission and exaggeration. In a strange inversion of the preoccupation with genealogies, origins, and earliest sources (common in both Tibet and the West), a relatively late version is believed to capture the life story in its most perfect and authentic form.

But as we have seen, there were numerous other versions that might also have assumed such a position. Why, for example, was the standard portrait not embodied in the account first crafted and authorized by Milarepa's twelve great disciples? Or *The Black Treasury* that constituted the tradition's most extensive compendium? Each of these texts remained present within the biographical tradition and continued to be reproduced long after the *Life* and *Songs* had been completed. Yet each was superseded by the form of Milarepa's life story modeled in Tsangnyön Heruka's works.

Reasons for the preeminence of Tsangnyön's work were manifold. First, in his hands, the final form of the biographical corpus was molded upon the existing framework of earlier narrative and structural traditions. Tsangnyön added his own innovations, fictionalizing the story by first establishing the *Life* as an autonomous text, then improving its literary styling through more effective plotting and pacing, stronger thematic development, and more uniform language. For the first time, Tsangnyön repudiated the yogin's status as an incarnation, presenting him instead as an ordinary human, albeit one endowed with superhuman perseverance. At the same time, he reformulated the narrative to parallel the Buddha's life in twelve great acts, heightening the tension between exemplar and individual to propel the story forward. He also conscientiously targeted an audience far broader than ever before. Authors had previously confined their works to fairly circumscribed contexts (the introduction to Collected Works or groups of aural transmission initiates, for example). Tsangnyön imagined his biographical tradition reaching political elites, religious virtuosi, and ordinary individuals alike.

The second reason for the success of the *Life* follows from this: namely, that Tsangnyön and his followers ensured the reproduction and distribution of his version through the use of mass and multiple media. Tsangnyön's original blocks were completed shortly after 1488, and in the decades following the madman's death, printing houses in southern Tibet carved multiple new sets of blocks for the *Life* and *Songs*, culminating in the edition from Drakar Taso in 1555. The wood blocks continued to multiply, especially during the eighteenth century, as printing estates throughout central and eastern Tibet, China, and Bhutan all together produced some nineteen unique editions. Tsangnyön further expanded the biographical tradition, promoting a wider cult of Milarepa by releasing the two works together with new prayers of supplication and guru devotion, and by commissioning a series of paintings committing the life story to visual media for the first time.

Third, Tsangnyön ensured the completion and distribution of these works by winning support from the region's religious and political leaders. The madman was received in courts across southern and western Tibet, and local rulers eventually helped underwrite his extensive literary projects. He likewise earned the praise of key figures within the Kagyu corporate structure, including the Seventh Karmapa and Fourth Zhamarpa; this guaranteed the life story's acceptance within the broader Kagyu tradition. Tsangnyön freely distributed his works, and these individuals were among the primary recipients of the newly published *Life* and *Songs*. Such access to the great religious institutions of the time provided Tsangnyön the opportunity to form a new canonical standard, promote its traditions, and ensure its continued reproduction for future generations.

Another factor contributing to the predominance of Tsangnyön's *Life* is a reaction, primarily among readers, that stresses its reliance on oral tradition, a phenomenon I have described as a rhetoric of orality. The madman himself acknowledges in his colophon to the *Life* that he had seen early accounts of the life story. But subsequent versions of Tsangnyön's own biography (culminating in Götsang Repa's account) emphasize the difficulty he faced in finding stories of the yogin's life. This seems to have supported the impression that many narratives recorded in the *Life* previously circulated in exclusively oral form—which is not borne out by an examination of the texts. This emphasis on orality in Milarepa's biographical tradition has effectively silenced nearly four centuries of early literature, as successive generations of readers relied almost exclusively on Tsangnyön's version of the *Life* and *Songs*.

Tsangnyön Heruka's works transformed the biographical corpus into what would become Milarepa's most recognized form. But the madman's intimate relationship with the yogin, a tradition preserved well into the nineteenth century, was also a defining feature in accounts of his own life story. Consequently writing from the position of ultimate authority—as the biographical subject himself—he also took a story that had been made lifelike and effectively gave it life. The process appears to follow a pattern laid out during the ritual consecration of an image of the Buddha. At first, the new statue is considered a mere likeness, a hollow shell that serves as the physical support (*rten*) for the Buddha's abiding essence, which must be ceremonially invited. After the statue is filled with relics, scrolls of mantras, *dhāraṇīs*, and other substances, the officiating master then calls forth the Buddha's numinous essence to abide within the image. At this point, tradition holds, the statue is no longer a mere representation but rather an embodiment of the Buddha's active presence, a living image equal to the teacher himself. Likewise, it was as if Tsangnyön was able to take the corpus as a kind of religious support and, through his authorial voice reaching back across the centuries, consecrate it with the yogin's living presence. We might wonder if, four hundred years after Milarepa's corporeal remains vanished from his cremation chamber, the yogin's followers finally gained the relics they had so keenly desired.

6

CONCLUSIONS

T HIS BOOK has explored the life of Tibet's most extensive and best-known biographical tradition, set against a shifting religious, political, and social terrain. The central challenge has been to broaden the way Milarepa's story, and Tibetan life writing more generally, have been studied. To that end, it has questioned how lives are recorded and transmitted, how their structures and functions transform over time, and how their changing forms affect the reading of their content. It described the literary practices that gradually shaped Milarepa's portrait as authors reimagined and rewrote the story. By examining an extended collection of literature that coalesced over a period of nearly four hundred years, the book has also addressed the process of canon formation, highlighting the means through which a series of divergent representations converged in a single undisputed standard. Finally, it parsed the authorial exploits that elevated this new standard to its preeminent position, effectively silencing centuries of other literary production.

This investigation of Milarepa's biographical tradition has three broad methodological goals: to turn away from the kernel/shell paradigm that characterized some early studies of religious biography and has continued to dog readings of the yogin's life story; to move beyond the rote mining of Tibetan biography for historical data; and in turn to pay closer attention to the literary qualities of the corpus, its production, dissemination, reception, and intertextual relationships. I have closely followed an approach advocated by Patrick Geary as a response to the field of European hagiographic studies, especially Geary's suggestion to probe such literature by concentrating on the "threefold intersection of genre, total textual production, and historical circumstance."

The corpus of Milarepa's biographical tradition, which encompasses an enormous body of texts and a diversity of literary forms and functions, is well suited for such analysis. Over the course of dozens, if not hundreds of discrete texts, we find early narrative fragments, notes from eyewitness accounts, selections from serial biographies, transmission and lineage lists, partial song collections, historical records, encyclopedic compendia of prose and poetry, and of course the madman's singular masterpiece. This array of literature has allowed me to avoid the shell/kernel problem by focusing instead on the biographical process of Milarepa's life story, parsing structural transformations of the genre of Tibetan biography within its various historical, institutional, and doctrinal circumstances.

The critical study of hagiography may have sprung largely from sources in European Christendom. But scholars working on the Buddhist traditions of Asia, and on Tibet and the Himalaya in particular, have likewise made significant contributions to our understanding of religious life writing. Thomas, Lamotte, Bareau, Foucher, Reynolds, and others sought to make sense of the Buddha's biographical process by addressing the issues of genre, textual production, and historical context. By closely examining the corpus of Buddha life materials—described by Lamotte as "a skein of inter-woven legends"—they sought to identify stages of literary development, to analyze the structures and interrelationships of biographical forms, and to understand the functions and influences of the texts within their own traditions.[1] A similar strategy for Tibetan literary studies has been advocated and demonstrated by E. Gene Smith, arguably the most influential scholar of Tibetan Studies in the twentieth century. His approach has been recently summarized as "Smith's Rules for the History of Tibetan Literature":

Know the breadth and depth of Tibetan history.
Read single works for depth.
Read collected works for breadth.

Collect all available works on a topic.
List all unavailable works on that topic.
Find those unavailable works.
Make those works available.

Collect, describe, and compare all editions of a given work.
Know which edition you are reading and why.
Know the material context of the text.
Know the social context of the work.

Know the author's biography.

Know the author's teachers, students, friends, and enemies' biographies.

Know the author's collected works.

Know the author's teachers, students, friends, and enemies' collected works.

Do not trust the text to be that of the author.

Trust the text to reveal something interesting about the content.

Trust the work to reveal something interesting about the author.

Rely on the context to discern what is interesting about the author.

Study the breadth of Tibetan tradition.

Study the depth of Tibetan history.

Read single works with breadth.

Read collected works with depth.[2]

This study has undertaken the far less ambitious task of studying the breadth of Milarepa's biographical tradition while also studying its depth: reading its single works with breadth and the entire corpus with depth. As far as possible, I have collected all available editions, described them, and compared them. Although it has not been possible to know the students, friends, and enemies of every author included here, I have largely trusted the texts to reveal something interesting about their contents, and the works to reveal something interesting about the authors.

First examining the earliest biographical fragments recording Milarepa's life, I described a biographical birth that occurred at the moment of the yogin's death and identified the elements that began to form a rudimentary life story. The signed compositions of Ngendzong Repa, Mila's disciple praised for his perfect memory, are afforded the legitimacy of eyewitness accounts, written "according to the lama's speech." Gampopa's work is likewise styled as a direct record of his teacher's words drawn, perhaps, from his own hastily drafted notes. His efforts to institutionalize the Kagyu tradition are reflected in his text: a sketchy and fragmented narrative, yet one that establishes for the first time a record of the yogin's life as part of a lineage extending back to the great *siddhas* of India.

The writings of these early disciples also blurred the boundary between biographical narrative and doctrinal record. Ngendzong Repa and Gampopa, together with their vajra brother Rechungpa, laid claim to the yogin's esoteric aural transmissions. Their *vitae* portray Milarepa as a valid source—he was, in Ngendzong's words, "an emanated being who saw the truth of reality." But Ngendzong Repa also undertook the task of preserving tantric instructions themselves, and his biographical writing became an important vehicle for this project. He described the content of his quartet as secret teachings, to be revealed only to "great meditators who will appear in the future." When he was finally permitted to write them down, he included them as chapters in Milarepa's collected songs. But they were likewise absorbed from the biographical tradition directly into Ngendzong's aural transmission lineage. The literature of some later tantric curricula make clear that Milarepa's life story, and the lives of other Kagyu founders, are not merely supports for the aural transmissions but rather integral parts of the transmission itself, attesting to the instructions' authority and inspiring the reader to practice them. The nineteenth-century luminary Jamgön Kontrul Lodrö Thayé would later incorporate these narratives into his renowned *Treasury of Oral Instructions* (*Gdams ngag mdzod*) under the title *The Root Pith Instructions of the Glorious Cakrasaṃvara Aural Transmission According to Ngendzong*. The close relationship between biographical writing and the aural transmissions would become even more explicit in the extended compendia that soon appeared.

This examination of Milarepa's earliest biographical sources revealed what I have called a "rhetoric of orality"—an assumption implicit in many studies of the tradition that the life story circulated for some four hundred years as an exclusively oral tradition before the madman Tsangnyön Heruka put it in writing. Both Tibetan writers and Western scholars of Tibet have fallen prey to this rhetoric, due in part, perhaps, to Milarepa's identification as a founder of the Kagyu or "oral transmission" sect of Tibetan Buddhism—predicated largely upon the madman's story. But the rhetoric of orality is also a confirmation of the canonical standard's power to silence its precursors and thereby "modify our conception of the past." The yogin's life story was recorded early, perhaps while he was still alive. It was also written often; by the late fourteenth century Zhijé Ripa claimed to have seen 127 different versions. Tsangnyön Heruka did not craft his masterful portrait upon the blank literary canvas of a purely oral tradition. Rather, he inherited an extensive and mature literary tradition of life writing that would serve as his principal source and primary model. But the rhetoric of orality effectively hid his sources from view, as if lifting the ink from their pages and disguising them as voices from the distant past.

The period following Milarepa's death provided the opportunity for new representations of the yogin's life reflecting the evolving practices, institutions, and related literature that coalesced during the "later diffusion" of Buddhism in Tibet. Chapter 2 described such works as proto-Life/Songs, an incipient form of life writing that combined basic biographical narratives with the general outline of a song collection. Such a template allowed for a significant variation of content, style, and metastructure while maintaining the integrity of Milarepa's life. It kept a record of the yogin's encounters with disciples, whom he frequently taught through poetic verse, even though few songs appear in full. This format allowed a good deal of narrative content—including fragmentary oral material and discrete literary segments culled from various sources—to be conveyed economically, and was thus well suited for use in the collected biographies of the golden rosary texts. And such texts began to proliferate in order to record tangible lineages connecting the Indian tantric adepts, early Tibetan founders such as Marpa and Milarepa, and later teachers of the tradition.

Texts of this type did not achieve the fine literary qualities exhibited in the extended works, but the realistic portraiture of individual lives was of less concern than the integrity of the rosary itself. The early proto-texts examined here, those of Lama Zhang, Dönmo Ripa, Sangyé Bum, and Gyaltangpa, illustrate a nascent stage of narrative development and served as precursors to the more mature compendia that would follow. But later texts by Orgyanpa and Zhamar Khachö Wangpo can also be considered "proto" in the sense that they retain the format of the early works even though they postdate and were influenced by the compendia.

These biographical compendia were among the most influential works in Milarepa's early biographical corpus. Mature formulations of the proto-Life/Songs structure, they reinforced basic elements found in the early proto-texts but for the first time combined detailed accounts of Milarepa's early life and death (the biography) with his verse instructions (the collected songs). The narrative is no longer a fragmented sketch. Instead, it forms a seamless exposition of the yogin's childhood, spiritual training, awakening, and final passing through a rich, plot-driven narrative, grounded in its own sense of causal logic. The collected songs have been likewise transformed from a series of discrete vignettes into a comprehensive network of song cycles that record the yogin's mature teaching career.

The first of the compendia, *The Twelve Great Disciples*, claims authorship by Milarepa's close disciples and served as a model for all of the extended texts that followed. Although the story has matured from proto-form into an autonomous work spanning both Life and Songs, its association with the aural transmission curriculum remains intact. The authors explicitly identify their work as the "transmission wish-fulfilling jewel of the Cakrasaṃvara aural tantra," first of three divisions in the aural transmission curricula. The biographical project does not merely describe Milarepa's complete liberation, it serves as a vehicle for liberation itself. *The Twelve Great Disciples* directly influenced the series of narratives that came to be known as *The Black Treasury*. These works shared common sources, structures, and content and became increasingly complex in both content and style. *The Black Treasury* thus seems to have served as a storehouse into which all known material about Milarepa's life and career could be locked away. The compendia displayed a growing concern for representing the yogin as an autonomous, founding member of the Kagyu tradition. Indeed, *The Black Treasury* texts were originally passed on through an "individual-transmission mandate" and thereby given to a single Karma Kagyu lineage holder each generation, in the manner of a secret tantric instruction.

The compendia increasingly drape Milarepa's life story in a miraculous light, emphasizing his role as an enlightened emanation and revealing his life to be a performance staged for the benefit of ordinary beings. Yet by combining a fully developed life story and a comprehensive song collection, authors of the compendia were able to frame the biography as an exemplary model while also presenting a life both individuated and uniquely Tibetan. While these texts praise Milarepa as an enlightened being, they also record a life fully lived, with all its obstacles, ambiguities, fallibilities, and triumphs. The Collected Songs catalogue the innumerable places Milarepa lived, taught, and meditated, and thus characterize the life story as deeply embedded within the Tibetan landscape. The compendia were the most detailed records of Milarepa's life, and Tsangnyön Heruka certainly relied heavily on them; nearly every story in the standard version originates in an earlier collection. But even as the compendia were eclipsed by the madman's standard version, they maintained a unique status as "alternative" sources for the Life and Songs, and drew the attention of historians and scholars from the yogin's tradition.

Chapter 4 discussed Tsangnyön Heruka's central role in transforming Milarepa's biographical tradition. The madman's world was marked

by regional conflict, doctrinal reform, and religious institutionaliza-
tion. Tsangnyön's own trajectory as a holy madman led him away from
powerful monastic centers to life as a solitary itinerant yogin, an ideal
upon which the Kagyu tradition—and Milarepa's enduring image—were
founded. Tsangnyön's role in the yogin's biographical tradition was complex and multifaceted: he served as author and editor, production and
distribution supervisor, benefactor and advocate. Ultimately the madman
not only reimagined the yogin's image but also reinvented the genre of
life writing and helped establish a new tradition of biography, continued
by his disciples.

Tsangnyön reframed his representation of Milarepa's life through a
series of rhetorical, structural, and hermeneutic innovations foreground-
ing the text's high literary qualities. He standardized spellings and glossed
obscure points of grammar. He struck alternate storylines (recorded in
the compendia) and rearranged songs and framing tales for consistency.
He published the *Life* and *Songs* as separate texts so the life story could,
for the first time, be read seamlessly, proceeding from birth and childhood to Milarepa's trials and retreats, inner realization, and final passing.
The last chapter, recounting the yogin's death, unfolds as an elaborate
and emotional drama staged on a grand scale. Tsangnyön likewise reorganized the *Songs*, replacing what had been an elaborate division into seventeen sections with a simplified tripartite arrangement to emphasize the
major activities associated with Milarepa's later life: taming demons and
training disciples. The *Songs* came to serve as a commentary on the *Life*
that allowed the reader to better understand Milarepa's mature teaching
career.

Tsangnyön also adapted the principal storyline to emphasize a series
of central Buddhist themes in line with his tradition's own priorities:
purification of karma, the primacy of guru devotion, perseverance in
meditation, and the transformative power of yogic practice. To that end,
the madman novelized the story through the use of "authorized fictions"—elements that sacrificed consistency with the earlier tradition in
the service of shaping a more coherent and compelling narrative. Tsangnyön forcefully repudiated Milarepa's status as a miraculous emanation,
thereby emphasizing the centrality of personal practice. He recast the
yogin as an ordinary—and unmistakably Tibetan—human whose liberation was solely predicated upon the intensity of his own efforts. At
the same time, the madman framed the entire biography in terms of
Śākyamuni's twelve great deeds. The result is the story of a buddha who

was born not in India but the Himalayan landscape, a wholly Tibetan buddha who became enlightened through instructions from his Tibetan master and who taught with a Tibetan voice to a largely Tibetan audience.

Finally, and perhaps most radically, the madman shifted the story's perspective from third to first person, effectively creating a fictionalized autobiography. The story no longer stands as a record hundreds of years distant from its subject's death but is narrated by the subject himself. Chapter 5 unpacked Tsangnyön Heruka's transformation into both the literary and the literal voice of Milarepa, which effectively brought the life story to life.

There were numerous reasons for the ascendance of Tsangnyön Heruka's text. He was able to build upon the extant biographical corpus, incorporating its existing framework while composing the *Life* and *Songs* as independent and autonomous works. The biography forms a seamless narrative while the collected songs serve as a kind of commentary "expanding" on the life story. He added his own innovations to *The Life of Milarepa*, improving its literary style through more effective plotting and pacing, focused thematic development, and a uniform language.

Tsangnyön also disseminated his new version through the use of mass and multiple-media. With support from the region's religious and political leaders, he produced the first xylographic edition of Milarepa's life and distributed it together with new prayers of supplication and guru devotion, in addition to a series of biographical paintings. Such activities earned the praise of key figures within the Kagyu religious hierarchy, who in turn ensured the life story's acceptance within the broader Kagyu tradition. Such access to the great religious institutions of the time offered Tsangnyön the opportunity to create a new canonical standard, promote its traditions, and ensure its continued reproduction for future generations.

The reception of Tsangnyön's version reflects his stated motivation to produce a text that reached all levels of Tibetan society. Rhetorically, Tsangnyön directed his works to a far wider audience than previously attempted. The early biographical compendia were intended for a closely guarded community of readers: those initiated into the esoteric traditions of the aural transmissions. The madman instead addresses his compositions to "the king, too busy for the proper activity of authentic Dharma, ministers, and important leaders full of arrogance, to the majority of common people." Thus for the first time, Milarepa's life story is actively promoted as a work for popular consumption, written in such a way as to illustrate the basic truths of the Buddhist path and to appeal to readers across sectarian lines. And the tale was indeed powerful. A trope common in many Tibetan memoirs describes how reading Tsangnyön's *Life of Milarepa* triggers moments of great emotion, often accompanied by tears, and profound spiritual awakening.

The most significant transformation, however, was Tsangnyön Heruka's change in narrative voice from the third to first person, which positioned him as his own biographical subject. The first-person narrative was not merely a literary conceit but rather underscored a direct relationship between the yogin and the madman first prompted by the author himself and later promoted by his disciples. Tsangnyön's life was punctuated by visionary encounters with Milarepa and even an oral transmission of his life story directly from the yogin himself. But on his deathbed, Tsangnyön announced that he was in fact the yogin's reembodiment by informing his disciples and patrons that they had "directly met Milarepa himself." The madman's biography of the yogin can thus be read, in part, as his own life story, an autobiographical biography. Tsangnyön makes clear that *The Life of Milarepa* is an "extraordinary biography" that derives its legitimacy from the author's direct relationship to his subject. Writing from the position of ultimate authority, he took a story that had been made lifelike and effectively brought it to life in the manner of a traditional consecration. And by including a framing tale that begins "Thus did I hear. At one time," he has recorded not only a life story but a new Buddhist discourse, a Tibetan sūtra taught by Tibet's own buddha.

EPILOGUE

MILA COMES ALIVE!

"WRITING THE life of the historical Gautama," Étienne Lamotte noted in his *Histoire du Bouddhisme Indien*, "is 'a hopeless enterprise.'"[1] Like Antoine Roquentin, pursuing his own biographical subject in Sartre's *Nausia*, we can empathize with Lamotte's lament. Despite the fact that he is commonly referred to as "the historical Buddha," there is little we can claim to know directly about the Śākya prince, be it the details of his life or the content of his teaching. In a similar way, Milarepa left no record of his life, and slicing open the flesh of Tsangnyön's lifelike image, we uncover a corpus of bewildering complexity, an organic network incorporating dozens, if not hundreds of biographical works.

There is little apparent consensus among them regarding even the basic facts of the yogin's life: he appeared in the world as a miraculous emanation, he was born an ordinary human; his mother died in his youth, he was raised with only his mother and sister; he avenged his mother through magic, he studied nothing but Buddhist teachings; he exhausted his body building towers, he never lifted a finger in construction. Details of the places he traveled, the individuals he trained as disciples, and the songs he sang are likewise disputed. This is not to argue that such a thing as the historical Milarepa might not one day be exhumed; indeed, an analysis (by means of a Milarepa Seminar, perhaps) sorting and comparing all the narrative threads of each version of the life story might yield such a result. It would be understandable, though, if the practitioner of such an operation, having peeled away the flesh and pulled apart the eviscerated sinews and bones from the life story's corpus, felt as if the body had vanished and, like Roquentin, was cast into a profound state of nausea.

Few Tibetan readers concerned themselves with how Milarepa's biographical corpus developed. Among those who did, there was no clear consensus on how the disparity of versions should be read, or rectified. A century before Tsangnyön published his *Life*, Zhijé Ripa attempted to clarify what he believed were mistakes and misunderstandings in previous versions of the life story. Writing just a decade prior to Tsangnyön's works, Gö Lotsāwa likewise notes, "Up to this point I have written [Mila's life story] in some detail since I have seen many spurious accounts; I believe this [account of mine] is more or less correct."[2] Writing in the sixteenth century, however, Pema Karpo is reported to have described Padmasambhava's biographical tradition in this way:

> Someone like Guru Pemajungné possessed the miraculous feats of miracles with the power to transform an instant into an eon and an eon into an instant. Thus within an oceanlike number of biographies, there are apparent contradictions, including some that say he was born by miraculous means and others that say he was born from a human womb. One cannot be certain and so should accept as correct each and every one of these explanations, whatever they may be.[3]

Indeed, even after the standard version of Milarepa's life was published at the close of the fifteenth century, authors freely drew from the biographical tradition broadly defined, many deferring to Tsangnyön's master works, but others relying upon earlier, competing versions.

To add a final anatomical metaphor, the principal aim of this book has been a kind of extended autopsy on the corpus that Tsangnyön crafted, a body that he made although, or perhaps because, Mila left behind no corporeal relics. An autopsy is not routinely performed at the time of death, but rather only in the event of some unnatural occurrence: an untimely death, an accident, a murder. Some abnormality must have turned up within the biographical corpus. What is unnatural about Tsangnyön's biography is precisely that it appears so natural, so real. It seems so close to its subject, to the point of *being* its subject. Yet it is a work composed centuries after the subject's death. What seems wrong, then, is that this late work, so mediated, could appear so immediate as to cast centuries of biographical traditions into obscurity. The purpose of this book has been not only to bring those forgotten traditions back into the light but also to understand why a work so late could seem so early, how a work so far removed from its subject could claim the place of origin.

In obscuring much of the earlier biographical tradition and claiming to be a faithful representation of Milarepa, Tsangnyön Heruka's version appears as a kind of apotheosis, the natural culmination of a life that began at the moment of the yogin's death. As this biographical postmortem has peered inside the corpus, sorting through the various layers forming the life, we have found that the account of Milarepa's life was not so teleologically framed. Early authors did not view their works as parts contributing to a larger whole; the final product was not waiting to be written, in order to perfectly mirror the yogin's life. Rather, in hindsight, with Tsangnyön's production in the foreground, the biography of the biography, the story of Mila's life story, comes into focus. Tsangnyön created a work that appears lifelike, seamless, and complete, but is constructed from many parts. In this sense, he resembles another madman of sorts, Shelley's Victor Frankenstein, the "modern Prometheus" who knit together his own patchwork of anatomical bits and pieces, which he then sparked into life.

To call this project a dissection, an autopsy, or postmortem might be a little misleading, however, since the body is not really dead. Instead, this study might be thought of as a kind of biographical MRI, a detailed and multilayered analysis of a living being, for the Mila corpus embodied in Tsangnyön's work certainly lives on.

Milarepa did indeed live, and he remains a presence for the multitude of individuals who read his life story, see it performed, or bow their heads to its presentation on a temple wall. He is continually born anew for modern-day meditators who invoke the yogin's presence through prayer, in the consecration of statues and paintings calling the master's essence from the pure realm in which he is thought to reside, and perhaps in any of the practitioners who follow in his footsteps and sit in his caves. Milarepa's life now serves as a component of children's Tibetan-language textbooks in contemporary Tibet, sanctioned by the Chinese authorities. For centuries after his death, authors have reimagined and rewritten versions of the yogin's life story; those stories form the corpus of narratives that embody his life both as an individual who traversed the Buddhist path to enlightenment and as an exemplar of how that might be accomplished.

If Lamotte was correct that formulating the Life of the historical Buddha is a hopeless endeavor, authors from Milarepa's biographical tradition—from Ngendzong to Tsangnyön Heruka—have shown that there is hope still of writing a Life that is inspired, revelatory, magisterial. The narrator of Kazantzakis's fictional *Zorba the Greek* (published six years prior to Lamotte's opus) carries just such a burden as he wrestles with his manuscript on the life of the Buddha. One evening, walking alone on the Cretan sands, he suddenly notes, "I was plunged into a burning atmosphere; I could feel a burning from both my temples." Returning to his hut, with Zorba sleeping in the corner, he sits at his writing desk:

I wrote quickly, I was in a hurry. *Buddha* was completely ready within me and I could see it issuing from my brain like a blue ribbon covered with symbols. It was coming forth rapidly, and I tried desperately to keep up with it. I wrote; everything had become simple, very simple. I was not writing, I was copying. A whole world was appearing before me composed of compassion, renunciation and air. Buddha's mansions, the women in the harem, the golden coach, the three fateful encounters—with the old man, with the sick man, with death; the flight, the ascetic life, the deliverance, the proclaiming of salvation. The earth was covered with yellow flowers; beggars and kings donned saffron robes; the stones, the trees and the flesh became lighter. Souls became vapor, the vapor became spirit, the spirit became nothing. . . . My fingers were beginning to ache, but I would not, I could not stop. The vision was passing swiftly and vanishing; I had to keep up with it.

In the morning Zorba found me asleep, with my head on the manuscript.[4]

ABBREVIATIONS

BA	*Deb gter sngon po.* See 'Gos Lotsāwa.
BC	*Bu chen bcu gnyis.* See Ngan rdzongs ston pa Byang chub rgyal po.
BCN	*Bu chen bcu gnyis,* Newark edition.
BCO	*Bu chen bcu gnyis,* Oxford edition.
C	*The Hundred Thousand Songs of Milarepa.* See Chang 1962.
DJ	*Mi la ras pa'i rnam thar: Texte Tibétain de la vie de Milarépa.* See de Jong 1959.
DK	*'Bras spungs dkar chag.* See Dpal brtsegs bod yig dpe rnying zhib 'jug khang 2004.
DKT	*Dung dkar tshig mdzod.* See Blo bzang 'phrin las 2002.
DNM	*Mdzod nag ma.*
DNM-D	*Mdzod nag ma,* 'Bri gung edition, published as *Mi la'i gsung mgur mdzod nag ma* (Khren tu'u: si khron mi rigs dpe skrun khang, 2008), 2 vols.
DNM-I	*Mdzod nag ma,* India edition, published as *Rnal 'byor gyi dbang phyug mi la bzhad pa rdo rje'i gsung mgur ma mdzod nag ma zhes pa ka rma pa rang byung rdo rjes phyog gcig* (Dalhousie: Damchoe Sangpo, 1978), 2 vols.
DNM-Lhasa	*Mdzod nag ma,* Lhasa edition.
DNM-RD	*Mdzod nag ma,* Rang byung rdo rje edition, published as *Rnal 'byor gyi dbang phyug mi la bzhad pa rdo rje'i gsung mgur mdzod nag ma zhes pa karma pa rang byung rdo rjes phyogs gcig tu bkod pa.* In *Karma pa rang byung rdo rje'i gsung 'bum* (Zi ling: Mtshur phu mkhan po lo yag bkra shis, 2006), vol. ga.
DNM-S	*Mdzod nag ma,* Smith edition.
L	*The Life of Milarepa.* See Lhalungpa 1977.
LRC	*Lho rong chos 'byung.* See Tshe dbang rgyal.
MD	*Gang can mkhas grub rim byon ming mdzod.* See Grags pa 'byung gnas, et al. 1992.
NG	*Rnal 'byor gyi dbang phyug chen po mi la ras pa'i rnam mgur.* See Gtsang smyon Heruka, NG.

Q	*Life of Milarepa.* See Quintman 2010.
RA	*Deb gter dmar po.* See 'Tshal pa Kun dga' rdo rje.
SM	*Brda dkrol gser gyi me long.* See Nga dbang tshul khrims 1996.
Toh.	Sde dge edition of the Tibetan Canon. *A Complete Catalogue of the Tibetan Buddhist Canons.* See Ui, et al. 1934.
TTC	*Bod rgya tshig mdzod chen mo,* 2nd ed.

APPENDIX 1

THE LIFE OF JETSÜN MILA BY GAMPOPA

Earliest complete presentation of Milarepa's life.[1]

THE SPIRITUAL son of the two [masters Marpa and Ngoktön] was lama Milarepa. His family line was Mila of Gungtang. His name was Töpaga. Since [in their family] there were none but father and son, they were extremely poor.

He traveled to Ü in search of black magic, learned much magic, and then returned.

He next received Dharma from the teacher Lhaga in Tsangrong. The teacher said, "You should be happy now. I possess the authentic Dharma of Great Completion, the apex of all vehicles, the quintessence of all pith instructions. Realize it by day, you're awakened by day; realize it by night, you're awakened by night."

Later, they discovered that lama Marpa had arrived [in Lhodrak]. The teacher said, "We have been practicing this Dharma continuously, but it hasn't produced anything. It is said that the one named Marpa Lotsāwa who possesses instructions has arrived, so go there. I am unable to go because I am old and infirm. If I were able, I would go."

When he heard of lama Marpa's greatness, [Mila's] previous karmic dispositions were awakened. He went to see lama Marpa and then made the request: "I have no provisions at all. Please provide me with both Dharma and material support."

"Both aren't possible, which do you want?" [replied the lama].

"I want Dharma," said [Mila], and the [lama] replied, "In that case, you will have to fetch water and the like."

Thereafter he was given the name Great Magician. From that day forth, he remained by the lama's side. [Gampopa] has said that there are many stories about that [period]. Milarepa studied there with lama Marpa for five years and requested the instructions of the practice lineage. Thereafter, he studied with Ngok for one year. He cast a hailstorm upon Ngok's enemies and then served him. By appealing directly [to these teachers], no [instructions] were left out, and so later on he gained great faith in lama Marpa. So [Gampopa] has said.

[Milarepa] then meditated in a cave with a butter lamp set upon his head. He opened his eyes right at daybreak and [saw] there was a brilliant light. Just after that experience he thought some good qualities [of meditation] had developed, but he had forgotten about the butter lamp. So [Gampopa] has said.

[Milarepa] wished to depart for his homeland, but the lama did not grant [permission] to go. [Mila] requested again and again, and the lama [eventually] granted [permission].

By the time he arrived in Gungtang, many years had passed since his father[2] died. Weeds had sprouted on the roof of his former house and the doors had all fallen into disarray. Sleeping there, he became extremely depressed. The next day he offered his house and fields to the mantrika who had formerly been his teacher. After that, he went to a secluded spot on the outskirts of the village and meditated without leaving his seat. So [Gampopa] has said.

The lama had no provisions and used nettles for food, so he turned green. His cooking pot, bowl, and ladle also turned green. His sister and aunt showed up carrying beer made from fifteen handfuls of barley. All three of them drank, so it didn't go far. One day the sister and aunt said, "Why has our brother gone astray and come to this?" and then they wept. At that point, the lama looked at [his] body [and saw] that he'd become merely a skull and bones draped with skin, and no flesh at all. His legs were little more than boney appendages. [Gampopa] has said he didn't know what [Mila] was like before that.

Then he went to the mountains. At the time of the autumn harvest, he ascended a pass with a view of the region where a harvest was ready to be reaped. There were cattle and sheep all filled with playful energy, and he felt a desire to go there. When he went, he was provided with much curd and butter. So [Gampopa] has said. He stayed there for two or three days, which filled him with world-weariness, and then returned to the mountain and meditated for a long period of time. His clothes lasted three years, and then he told his sister he needn't wear clothes [at all]. The sister said, "My brother has become an accomplished master," and was pleased.

At another time when his provisions were depleted, he went down to seek [supplies] in the region. There was a crowd of beggars at the gate of a person performing a ritual, and he sat among them. At their head, a group of mantrikas carried on a Dharma conversation. Someone said, "Many years have passed since the yogin Mila went to meditate. Now he has become an accomplished master."

"We should see this amazing man in the flesh. If we look, will we find him?" said another.

Someone said, "He's right here today."

"Whatever else he has done, he has meditated in the mountains," another person said, "so I will recognize him."

"Now then, which one is he?"

[Someone] grabbed the lama and said, "This is he."

"I will make him my resident priest," the person said.

[Mila] became displeased since this was not consistent [with his practice]. [So Gampopa] has said.

As they spoke back and forth, [Mila] escaped and immediately fled to his mountain hermitage. He went a day's distance away and, without ever returning to the region, he remained for a long time in the mountains of Mangyul Gungtang, at the place called Drakar Taso.

At one time, [the monks of] a minor religious center in Gungtang became jealous of the lama's great merit. Intending to disgrace [Milarepa], they invited him [to their center]. When he arrived, the monks said, "Since you are an accomplished master, you will serve as our resident priest." They placed him inside the chapel and drew the lock. When they went outside, the lama was there. Not believing it was him, they looked inside and saw him inside too. The monks understood he was indeed an accomplished master, and they all begged his forgiveness.

Then he went to the mountains of Nyenam and Mangyul. At yet another time, he served as the priest for a childless elderly couple. [They supplied him with offerings, and so,] carrying six measures of parched flour, a container of butter, and a carcass of meat, he went to Lapchi Gang. It snowed the entire winter. All the people of the region berated the elderly couple [for sending Mila off]. The elderly couple looked in the lama's direction and did nothing but cry.

The following spring, the snow melted a little and [the couple] wondered if there was a chance the lama had remained alive and not passed away. They provided three men with parched flour provisions and snowshoes and then sent them off in search [of the lama]. The three men reached a pass where the snow had melted and called out. The lama thought, "There's no chance that any humans have come; it must be an animal." But it sounded more and more like human voices, and he sent up a smoke signal. [The search party] saw smoke rising and when they reached it, the lama was resting there. About a third of his parched flour and about half of his butter remained, which he gave to the three men. After resting for three days, they returned home. Along the way, snow froze the three men, but they slept beside the lama and were warmed. So it is said.

When he arrived in the region, the villagers offered prostrations and inquired about his health. At that time the lama sang the song of Lapchi Gang. So [Gampopa] has said.

At another time, the lama set his mind on the Kathmandu Valley (Bal po), and the master and a group of disciples departed. Along the way, they met with numerous merchants.

The headman of the merchants grabbed the lama's staff and asked, "Who are you?"

The lama replied,

Have you a clue who's before you now?
If you don't know who this is here now—
I am the yogin Mila. . . .

and so forth, and he sang the "Song of the Staff." So [Gampopa] has said.

Then he reached the top of a pass with a view of the [populated] valley below. He said, "I will not go down to the valley, but will wander among the mountain peaks."

The retinue [of disciples] replied that if they wandered around a mountain peak for even ten years, they surely would not reach the end of it, and begged to go to the valley, but [Mila] did not give them permission.

After the yogin Mila had retreated up into the mountains, a much beloved man in Latö died. [The man's son acting as patron] led many people in a search [for Mila] to perform the religious ceremony. [The patron] found him and then invited [the yogin] to his homeland. Everyone gathered there made numerous offerings. The patron offered a horse admired throughout the region of Latö. The lama said, "You should take away all the offerings you have made. I won't keep them." So they each took some of [the offerings]. When [Milarepa] would not accept the patron's horse either, the patron said, "My father has just now died," and wept. The lama replied, "In that case, I shall take the leather bridle[?] affixed to the horse."

[Gampopa] has told the story of how, from there, [Mila] went to Tashi Tsering. While he resided there, the three great masters of Latö—Geshé Ngasukpa, Dringtön Pakpa, and Josey Chöpa—searched for the lama. They found him and then invited him to their region and paid him reverence.

Then the lama announced he would die, but his retinue [of disciples] would not let him pass away. Later he was stricken with a pain in his head. As he was on the verge of dying from it, the downward-moving wind reversed and ascended to the top of his head [as if to depart from his crown]; he ceased breathing through his mouth and nose. Meditating in that state, he experienced bliss. At midnight, numerous women folded their hands in prayer before the lama and then said to him, "Please, now, don't let your mind rush off." The lama's mind descended and he meditated in that state. He recovered a bit and the winds were drawn back into place. After that happened, just as the sun's rays [shone], he was beset again as before, and again he meditated and recovered. [Gampopa] has said he thought [Mila] was not [actually] harmed, but appeared to be harmed through the transgression of his [i.e., Gampopa's] pledges.

Then while he resided at the place called Drakmar Poto, between Drin and Nyenam, he composed the songs of the soaring vultures below and so forth. So [Gampopa] has said.

At another time, while the lama resided in a wooded hollow, a patron approached and then left. The lama called [him], so [the patron] returned and asked, "Where were you sitting just then? I didn't see the lama, but sat beside a stūpa."

At another time, a patron looked around without bowing down and then left. The lama called [him] and he returned. [The lama asked,] "Why did you not bow down just now?" [The patron replied,] "Because the lama was not in his chamber." So it is said.

The Precious One [Gampopa] asked the lama, "What did you do at that time [to make yourself invisible]?"

[Mila] replied, "I didn't do anything. [In a similar way,] it is said that a person can see Dipaṃkara circumambulating the pinnacle of the Ütsé [temple] of Samye. [In that case,] has he done anything?"

[Gampopa] said, "Although he hasn't done anything, by means of dependent origination it appeared within people's perception as though he did. Consequently, the two form bodies appear according to the perception of others. [In actuality,] however, there are no miraculous deeds."

At another time, he reached the place called Tashi Tsering of Drin and then set off in the company of a group of disciples. [Along the way] the lama dropped off of a steep cliff. The attendant disciples wept as he tumbled downward. When they reached the edge of the cliff, the lama had risen back up. The group of disciples then asked, "Why is it that when the lama dropped off of a cliff as steep as that one he didn't perish?"

The lama replied, "If I were anyone else, his body would be smashed to pieces. I, however, rather enjoyed it."

At another time, he turned himself into a crystal stūpa and then departed into space. So it is said.

At another time, a man from Rong Khazhi in the Kathmandu Valley came to have a look at Mila. He had no faith in the lama and said, "You, yogin Mila, there is little substance to your great fame. The one called a [real] *geshé* is named Bari Lotsawa. Do you have a ceremonial umbrella? A fine conch shell? Are you the sort that whoever meets you gives you gold?" And then he departed.

In several days' time, the people of Rong Khazhi reported that each evening the lama appeared three times, riding through the sky upon a lion. When the man saw this happen, he developed great faith and paid him much respect. The lama's group of disciples said [to the man], "It is said you are a man of the cliffs. Why do you now venerate him?"

He replied, "I have faith in him because the lama came out three times each night, flying in the sky."

The Precious One [Gampopa] has said, "That was the year before I arrived."[3]

One woman asked, "What qualities does your lama have?"

"He has the qualities of deep *samādhi*, clairvoyance, and freedom from conceptuality," replied [his disciple[4]].

The woman said, "You have an understanding of your lama's qualities." This satisfied the disciple, but the woman added, "While that is so, do you just know about them or have you seen them?"

The woman then removed a goat's horn from the crook of her arm and said, "The lama appeared in here three times each night while I was praying, so I make offerings to the lama."

[Gampopa] has said the woman was a *ḍākinī*.

One time he departed from Drinkyi Chakdrang Lung accompanied by a group of disciples. A great snow fell and the lama flew off, but the entourage did not make it. So it is said. The Precious One [Milarepa[5]] was asked [about this] and he replied, "It's not that I flew. Rather, I lifted my feet a little, pushed down the winds a little, and went off. Thus, I left nothing but a mere bird's trail [in the sky] behind."

The Precious One [Gampopa] remained [with Mila] for thirteen months, and when he left, he resided at the home of the patroness Leksé. He said, "There is no need for us to carry provisions to the lama."

"Just how much did he take with him?" she asked.

"He took six measures [of grain]," he said.

"How much will he need?" she asked.

"One handful of grain each month will suffice," he said.

[Leksé] considered asking if [the lama's] previous lack of hunger had been real or faked. She returned [to him] from a place one day's journey away. The lama said, "You have returned?" and he boiled some tea and served it to her.

Then she asked [her question], to which [Mila] replied, "When the lady was not here, *ḍākinīs* fed me various kinds of pure food and drink, so I barely touched my ring finger to my mouth and for five or six days at a time I even forgot to eat. For a few days I slipped into *samādhi* and did not eat at all."

The lama also said, "That [same result] will occur whether I meditate for many days up in the high cliffs or on top of a tall castle."

News arrived that an individual named Darma Ten had gone away and died, and his relations cried. The lama asked, "What is wrong?"

[Leksé] said, "News arrived that Darma Ten died, and then they began to weep."

[Mila] replied, "He hasn't died, he is presently on his way."

[Leksé] said, "In that case, should I report this to them?"

"You should," he replied.

When she told them, they believed it and stopped crying. Then [Darma Ten] showed up. So [Gampopa] has said.

These, and many others, are the inestimable qualities [Mila] possessed. He was undistracted from *samādhi*. For him there was no difference between periods of resting in meditation and postmeditation. He was an emanated being who saw the truth of reality.

Later, when he passed away, his corpse was cremated at both Tisé and Drin. So [Gampopa] has said.

❉ ❉ ❉

This has described just a little of the qualities of Mila's realization and his activities. May I quickly attain the state of the Sugatas. Auspiciousness.

APPENDIX 2

TEXT COLOPHONS

ENGLISH TRANSLATIONS
AND TIBETAN TRANSCRIPTIONS

THE TWELVE GREAT DISCIPLES (BU CHEN BCU GNYIS)

1. COLOPHON TO TSHE RING MA CHAPTER 1
BCO, 129a.6; BCN, 162b.4 [cf. NG, 467, 515; C, 310, 353]

Ngendzong Tönpa Bodhiraja recorded, with an indelible memory, the songs sung as the questions and answers of the glorious Zhepa Dorjé, the precious lord whose qualities are difficult to express, and the five worldly ḍākinī spirits. This is the earlier cycle on questions and answers. Oṃ āḥ hūṃ.

> These songs of beautiful poetry—
> Sung as the kindness of questions and answers
> Between the *repa* who won great accomplishment,
> Lord, precious jewel, most kind one,
> And the five *ḍākinī* maidens,
> Low worldly spirits—
> Are words strung with garlands of flowers.
> This outpouring of crossing-over (*thod dgal*) experience
> Should not be recorded in writing, but
> For fear I might forget them,
> And in order to inspire and delight
> Future holders of the family line,
> I have written it according to the lama's speech.
> Three times I sought permission;
> Displeased, [the lama] did not grant it. But then
> He said, "In order to restrain the *ḍākinīs*' displeasure,

I've not acted rashly or with presumption.
For meditators who appear in the future,
Don't show the words of this text to those
Without authentic experience of the practical instructions."
This is sealed by the lord guru's command.
If you transgress this command
You'll incur the ḍākinīs' punishment.
Therefore I ask, don't spread these words, keep them hidden.

Touching the dust of the lotus feet of the lord yogin of activity, everywhere known by the name Mila, Ngendzong Tönpa three times requested [permission] from the lama Jetsün; it being granted, he put this into writing. This concludes the poetic song called "A Strand of Pearls."

rje rin po che mtshan brjod par dka' ba'i dpal bzhad pa'i rdo rje dang/ 'jig
rten mig bsgyur gyi mkha' 'gro ma lnga'i zhus lan mgur du bzhengs pa
rnams/ ngan rdzong ston pa bo dhe ra tsas mi brjed pa'i gzung du bskod
pa'o/
rje nor bu rin po che sku drin can//
dngos grub rnyes ba'i ras pa dang//
'jig rten mig sgyur gdol pa mo//
sman shar lnga'i mkha' 'gro dang//
dris pa'i lan dang bcas pa'i drin//
yid phrog snyan ngag glu blangs pa//
me tog phreng pas rgyus pa'i tshig//
thod rgal nyams kyi skyugs pa 'di//
yi ger bskod par mi rigs kyang//
bdag nyid brjed pas 'jigs pa dang//
ma 'ongs gdung rgyud 'dzin pa rnams//
mos shing spro ba bskyed pa'i phyir//
bla mas gsungs bzhin yi ger bris//
lan gsum bar du zhu phul nas//
dgyes bzhin gnang ba ma lags pa//
mkha' 'gro ko long sdom pa'i phyir//
gzu lum ras chod ngas ma byas//
slad nas 'byon pa'i bsgom chen la//
dmar khrid nyams tshad ma byas par//
dpe rgyud yi ge ma bstan gsungs//

bla ma rje'i bka' rgyas btab//
gal te bka' las 'das gyur na//
mkha' 'gro'i bka' chad 'byung ba'i phyir//
yi ge mi spel sba bar zhu//
rje spyod pa'i rnal 'byor pa/ mtshan yong su grags pa'i mi la zhes bya ba
de nyid kyi zhabs kyi padmo'i rdul la reg pa/ ngan rdzong ston pas/ bla
ma rje btsun la lan gsum zhus nas gnang ba yi ger bskod pa/ snyan ngag
gi glu mu tig gi phreng ba zhes bya ba rdzogs so//

2. COLOPHON TO TSHE RING MA CHAPTER 2
BCN, 174b.2; BCO, 136b.4 [cf. NG, 489; C, 330]

These were the songs sung as the questions and answers on the mind
generation of the supreme path, between the glorious Zhepa Dorjé, the
great *repa* whose qualities are difficult to express, and the five worldly
ḍākinī spirits headed by Lady Tashi Tseringma. The worthy and well-
trained Repa Zhiwa Ö verified [this account] directly with the sister
Tashi Tseringma herself, repeatedly asking her about it, atop the mountain peak of Tashi Palgi Todingri, on the left side of the Dingma Drin
market. Afterward, he met with the great Jetsün three times and, displeased, he reluctantly [provided] points of clarification. In the isolated
place of the glorious grove of Omchung, Ngendzong Tönpa Bodhirāja
and the yogin Zhiwa Ö discussed [the lama's] speech, and without addition or subtraction, overstatement or understatement, put the rosary of
words into well-arranged writing. This concludes the [chapter] called
"Rosary of Nectar Light."

ras pa chen po mtshan brjod par dka' ba'i dpal bzhad[1] pa rdo rje dang/
jo mo bkra shis tshe ring mas dbu mdzad pa'i/ 'jig rten mig bsgyur[2] gyi
mkha' 'gro ma lnga'i[3] theg pa mchog gi sems bskyed pa'i drin lan/ mgur du
bzhengs pa'o// tshong dus ding ma brin g.yon zur bkra shis dpal gyi tho
'ding ri'i[4] rtse la/ skal ldan sbyangs pa can gyi ras pa zhi ba 'od kyis/ sring
mo bkra shis tshe ring ma nyid la dngos su nyams bdur[5] <bsdur> zhing dri
rmed yang dang yang du byas pa la/ phyis rje btsun chen po nyi kyi zhal
mngar lan gsum gtugs nas/ dgyes bzhin du gnang ba ma gtogs/ rang dga'
ma yin pa'i gsung don rnams/ dben gnas 'om chung dpal gyi nags 'debs tu/
ngan rdzong ston pa bo de ra tsa dang/ rnal 'byor ba zhi ba 'od gnyis kyis[6]
bka' bsgros la lhag chad dang phri <dbri> bsnan med par nan tan du byas
te/ ngag brjod pa'i tshig gi phreng ba bsdebs legs yi ger dkod pa/ bdud rtsi
'od kyi phreng ba zhes bya ba rdzogs so//

3. TSHE RING MA CHAPTER 3

BCO, 136b.4 [missing]; BCN, 187b.6 [cf. NG, 517; C, 354]

These songs of symbolic meaning were sung as questions and answers regarding the *bardo*, the precipitous path of liberation, between the glorious Zhepa Dorjé, the great lord *repa* whose qualities are difficult to express, and the five worldly *ḍākinī* spirits. Ngendzong Tönpa Bhodirāja and Repa Zhiwa Ö, who made the request, set them down, with an indelible memory for words, in writing that clarifies [the intended meaning].

rje ras pa chen po mtshan yongs su grags brjod par dka' ba'i dpal bzhad pa rdo rje dang/ ' jig rten mig sgyur mkha' 'gro ma lnga'i 'phrang sgrol gnad kyi par <bar> do dris pa lan dang bcas pa brda' don klu <glu> blangs pa rnams ngan rdzongs ston pa bho dhe ra tsa dang/ zhu byas ras pa zhi ba 'od gnyis mi brjed pa'i tshig gi gzungs gsal byed yi ger bkod pa rdzogs so/

4. TSHE RING MA CHAPTER 4

BCO, 145b.2; BCN, 189b.5 [cf. NG, 520; C, 361]

These songs of questions and answers on *mudrā* practice between the glorious Zhepa Dorjé, the powerful individual who was able to attract nonhuman consorts (*karmamudrā*), and the Lady of the valley, Tashi Tseringma, are called the "Rosary of Bliss-Emptiness Wisdom Clouds." The worthy ones known as Ngendzong Tönpa Bodhirāja and Repa Zhiwa Ö offered a ritual feast and a maṇḍala, made supplications, and set them down in writing.

mi ma yin las kyi phya rgyar 'gugs nus pa'i skyes bu chen po nus pa can/ dpal bzhad pa rdo rje dang/ ljongs kyi bdag mo bkra shis tshe ring ma gnyis kyi phyag rgya dris lan gyi mgur/ bde stong ye shes sprin gi[7] phreng ba zhes bya ba/ ngan rdzong ston pa bo dhe ra tsa dang/ ras pa zhi ba 'od zhes bya ba'i skal ldan gyis/ tshogs dang maṇḍal phul zhing gsol ba btab ste yi ger bkod pa'o// ithi//

5. *THE TWELVE GREAT DISCIPLES* FINAL COLOPHON

BCO, 191b.3; BCN, 243b.1 [cf. NG, 515; C, 353]

For the benefit of fortunate meditators, this Life has been set down in writing by the twelve great *repa* disciples, such as Ngendzong Tönpa Bodhirāja.

In general, the Jetsün had an inconceivable number of disciples. Among the twenty-five yogins and yoginīs who achieved spiritual attainment, there were the ones known as the nine sons and four sisters. His four heart sons were Rechungpa, Seban Repa, Ngendzong Repa, and Drigom Repa. The eight close sons were Repa Zhiwa Ö, Repa Sangyé Kyap, Repa Dorjé Wangchuk, Shengom Repa, Drongsok Repa, Karchung Repa, Nyengom Repa, and Khyira Repa. The six who were pupils just before Milarepa's death were Dakpo Lharjé, Lokor Chakriwa, Lotön Dendun, Kyotön Shakgu, Dampa Gyapuwa, and Droban Tashi. The four spiritual sisters were Leksé Bum, Padar Bum, Salé Ö, and Rechungma.

> This transmission wish-fulfilling jewel
> Of the Cakrasaṃvara aural tantra
> Has been put into writing according to the lama's words,
> For fear it might be forgotten by those of inferior minds,
> For future holders of the family line.
> I pray for patience of the lama and ḍākinīs.
> Except for individuals of future generations, supports [for the teachings],
> Who delight in initiation, blessing, gaṇacakra feasts,
> And making offerings to hero and heroine protectors,
> This is sealed by the lord guru's command.
> If you transgress this command
> The ḍākinīs will show great displeasure.
> Therefore I ask, don't spread these words, keep them secret.

The transmission wish-fulfilling jewel. Ḍaki samaya.

rnam thar 'di skal ldan bsgom chen rnams kyi don du/ ngan rdzong ston pa bho dhe ra tsa la sogs pa'i ras pa bu chen bcu gnyis kyi yi ger bskod[8] pa'o/ spyir rje btsun de la/ slob ma bsam gyis mi khyab ste/ grub pa thob pa'i rnal 'byor pho mo nyi shu rtsa lnga la/[9] de'i nang nas/ bu[10] dgu/ sring bzhi zhes grags so/ de la thugs kyi sras bzhi ni/ ras chung ba pa dang/ se ban ras pa/ ngan rdzong[11] ras pa/ 'bri sgom ras pa dang bzhi'o/ nye ba'i sras brgyad ni/ ras pa zhi ba 'od/ ras pa sangs rgyas skyabs/ ras pa rdo rje dbang phyug/ gshen sgom ras pa/ rong chung[12] ras pa/ mkhar chung ras pa/ gnyen[13] sgom ras pa/ khyi ra ras pa dang brgyad do/ sku gshegs kha'i slob ma drug ni/ dag po lha rje/ lo skor chag ru[14] pa/ lo ston dge 'dun/ skyo ston shag 'gu/ dam pa rgya[15] phu ba/ 'bro ban bkra shis dang drug go/ sring bzhi ni/ legs se 'bum/ dpal[16] dar 'bum/ gsal le 'od/ ras chung ma dang bzhi'o/ snyan rgyud bde mchog 'khor lo yi[17]// rgyud pa yid bzhin nor bu 'di//

ma 'ongs gdung rgyud 'dzin pa rnams//
blo dman rjed[18] pas 'jigs [19]pa'i phyir//
bla ma'i gsung bzhin yi ger bkod//
bla ma mkha' 'gro'i[20] bjod par gsol//
phyi rabs[21] rten gyi gang zag rnams//
dbang bskur byin brlabs tshogs 'khor dang[22]//
dpa' bo dpa' mo mchod la sogs//
dgyes shing gnang ba ma gtogs pa[23]//
bla ma rje'i bka' rgyas btab//
gal te bka' las 'das gyur na//
mkha' 'gro ko longs dam pas na//
ye ge ma spel gsang bar zhu//
rgyud pa bzhin nor bu ḍa ku sa ma ya//

[Scribe's colophon in N 244a.3] rje mi la ras pa'i rnam thar 'di bzhings <bzhengs> pa'i thugs rje nus mthu byin brlab la brten nas 'jig rten 'di nas pho zhing dus la 'das pa tshe dbang skyabs/ rta mgrin skyabs/ ka 'bum skyabs/ snying mo yags/ snying mo skyid/ bo cog byams/ de la sogs pa'i tshe 'das rnams kyi sangs rgyas kyi sa thob par gyur cig/ rgyu sbyin pa'i bdag po tshe dang ldan pa ngag dbang chos 'dzin/ 'phrin las bsam 'grub/ chos ldan rgya mtsho/ mgon po skyabs/ tshe brtan rdo rje/ phyag rdor skyabs/ chos 'phel rgya mtsho/ gnam sman byams/ snying mo skyid/ dpal mo yags/ sman cog/ lha mo mtsho/ tshe sman rgyal la sogs pa'i sbyin bdag rnams kyi par chad thams cad nye bar zhi bar gyur cig/ bsam don thams cad chos dang ldan pa yid bzhin tu 'grub par gyur cig// dge'o// yags so//

THE BLACK TREASURY
(INDIA/SMITH VERSIONS) COLOPHONS

6. THE BLACK TREASURY FINAL COLOPHON
DNM-I, 553.2; DNM-S, 308a

This compilation of the great Jetsün Milarepa's biography, vajra songs, and spiritual songs [has three sources]: 1) the Dharma Lord Karmapa said, "Most of [the songs] are present within the some one hundred compilations of the great Jetsün's collected songs I have seen. Then, the Dharma Lord Rangjung Dorjé wrote the most excellent *Black Treasury*, personally researched and based upon authoritative sources; 2) [a text] said to be a compilation of seventeen different collected songs excellently completed in the Gungtang Pelgyi Tsuklakhang; 3) [a text] said to be a compilation [made] having seen one hundred and twenty-seven different biographies of the Jetsün. These [versions] have been compiled and supplemented with as many of the Jetsün's song collections as could be found. Through the merit of completing this well, may the precious teachings of the Practice Lineage flourish and expand in every direction and during all periods, and may it endure for a long time.

> May whoever practices, reads, writes, or rejoices in
> The sayings of the great Jetsün Zhepa Dorjé,
> As many as could be found, which I've collected here,
> Abide on the level of the vajra holders.

> Through the roots of virtue from composing this authentic Dharma,
> When the appearances of this life begin to fade,
> May sentient beings of the six migrations, headed by my mother and
>   father,
> Encounter the great Jetsün Zhepa Dorjé
> In the pure realm of Abhirati to the east
> And then swiftly achieve buddhahood.

The collected songs of Mila Zhepa Dorjé, powerful lord among yogins, embellished with historical anecdotes, called *A River of Blessings Relieving the Anguishing Heat of the Mental Afflictions*, is complete. *Sarva maṅgalam.*

rje btsun chen po mi la ras pa'i rnam thar rdo rje'i glu dang 'gur 'di rnams phyogs bcu bcig bstus pa 'di/ chos kyi rje karma pa'i zhal nas/ rje btsun chen po'i gsung 'gur phyogs cig tu bsgrigs pa brgya tsa[24] gzigs pa'i nang nas kyang/ 'di mang shos du[25]'dug gsung te[26]/ chos rje rang byung rdo rje nyid kyi[27] phyag[28] bris mdzad pa khung btsun zhing[29] thugs rtsis shin du che ba'i mdzod nag ma zhes bya ba dang/ 'gur 'bum rigs mi cig pa bcu bdun bsags nas gung thang dpal gyi[30] gtsug lags khang chen por legs[31] par bsgrub[32] zer ba dang/ rje btsun[33] gyi[34] rnam thar rig[35] mi cig pa brgya dang bnyis shu tsha bdun gzigs te[36] phyogs gcig du sgrigs pa yin zer ba dang/ de rnams phyogs cig du bsdus pa la/ gzhan yang rje btsun gyi[37] 'gur ma'i tshogs brnyed tshad kyis kha bskang te[38] legs par bsgrubs[39] pa 'di'i bsod nams kyis/ sgrub rgyud kyi[40] bstan pa rin po che phyogs dus gnas skabs thams cad du[41] dar zhing rgyas la yun ring du gnas par gyur cig//

rje btsun chen po bzhad pa rdo rje yi//
gsung sgros chi snyed dag gis bsags pa 'dis//
nyams len bris klog yi[42] rang gang byas rnams//
rdo rje 'dzin pa'i sa la gnas par shog//
dam chos 'di bzhengs dge ba'i rtsa ba 'dis//
[43]pha ma thogs drangs 'gro drug sems can rnams//
tshe 'di'i[44] snang ba nub par gyur tsal na//
shar phyogs mngon par dga' ba'i zhing khams su//
rje btsun chen po bzhed <bzhad> pa'i rdo rje dang//
mjal nas myur du sangs rgyas thob par shog//
rje rnal 'byor gyi[45] dbang phyug mi la bzhed <bzhad> pa'i rdo rje'i 'gur
tshogs lo rgyus kyis spras pa/ byin rlabs kyi chu rgyun gyis nyon mongs
pa'i tsha gdung sel bar byed pa zhes bya ba re shig rdzogs s.ho//

APPENDIX 3

TEXT OUTLINES AND CONCORDANCES

PROTO-SONGS

Lama Zhang's *Biography of Lama Milarepa*
(Bla ma mi la ras pa'i rnam thar)

1. monastic dispute
2. La phyi episode/Song of La phyi gangs
3. journey to Spa gro[1]/Song of the Staff
4. death rites and horse offering
5. meeting three disciples
6. near-death episode
7. meeting with Legs se
8. song of vultures at Brag dmar spo mtho
9. invisible lama episode
10. falling off a cliff
11. crystal stūpa transformation
12. doubter/lion riding/horn stūpa
13. snow falling/flying
14. fasting

Don mo ri pa's *Biography of Jetsün Milarepa*
(Rje btsun mi la'i rnam thar)
Episodes or episode fragments copied from the earlier Sgam po pa/
Lama Zhang traditions are in small capitals.

1. meditation at Brag dkar rnam gsum
2. meeting demoness at Ling ba'i brag, then to Rkyang dpal in Rag ma

3. meditation at Byang chub rdzong
4. meditation at Sna phu'i Brag rta so nam mkha' rdzong, song of the dark cloud hovering in the south (*lho sprin smug po lding ba'i mgur*)
5. journey to Sing ga'i nags in Nepal, meeting with bandits
6. *gaṇacakra* at Su tu ri charnel ground
7. meeting female goat herders/*ḍākinī*s
8. meeting pigeon at Phug ron phug
9. meditation at Rtsum gyi tsig ma phug
10. meeting disparaging attendants on Sa dkar pass, song of lineage (*rus mgur*)
11. MONASTIC DISPUTE in So du rgyan re in Ron phu
12a. meeting Ras chung pa at Za 'og phug
12b. journey to Dpal thang and Phug tag phug with Ras chung pa
13. patroness and Gshen sgom ras pa look for Mi la, see only fire
14. journey to Co ro 'bring tshangs and Tsho' rnga 'dre chu, five women sing of Gangs dkar ti se
15. meeting Ngan rdzong byang chub, SONG OF THE WHITE IRON STAFF (*sba lcags dkar po'i mgur*)
16. invitation to Glo by king Rtse lde
17. prophecy about Li khor phya ru's mother
18a. meeting patroness Rngag rdor mo
18b. LA PHYI EPISODE, SONG OF LA PHYI SNOW RANGES (*la phyi gangs kyi mgur*)
19. meeting Dam pa rgyags bu at La phyi sna g.yon
20. DEATH RITES AND HORSE OFFERING
21. MEETING THREE DISCIPLES
22. NEAR-DEATH EPISODE
23. meeting tantrika's consort with offerings in Brin
24. journey to Gnya' shing phug and Rta rdzong phug, meeting three patrons
25. SONG OF VULTURES AT BRAG DMAR SPO MTHO (*thang kar rgod po lding bya ba'i mgur*)
26. INVISIBLE LAMA EPISODE A
27. INVISIBLE LAMA EPISODE B
28. FALLING OFF CLIFF EPISODE
29. CRYSTAL STŪPA EPISODE
30a. DOUBTER/LION-RIDING EPISODE
30b. HORN STŪPA EPISODE
31. SNOW FALLING/FLYING EPISODE
32. taming Tshe ring ma sisters[2]
33. PROPHECY ABOUT DAR MA STAG'S NONDEATH

Rgyal thang pa's *King of Jetsüns*
(Rje btsun gyi rgyal po mi la ras pa'i rnam thar)
Episodes or episode fragments found in versions discussed above are
in small capitals.

verses 18–19:	1. MEDITATION IN LA PHYI
verse 20:	2. MEDITATION IN SENG GE GLING FOREST
verse 21:	3. meeting with aunt, description of beating
verse 22:	4. MEETING WITH TSHE RING MA
verse 23:	5. meeting with dying Bon po
	6. meeting with the logician Dar lo
	7. MEETING WITH UNRULY MONKS
verse 24:	8. vase empowerment and consecration
	9. meeting with Legs se
	10. Vajrapāṇi initiation
	11. feast of the 84 *siddhas*
verse 25:	12. overview of places and disciples

The Kagyu Garland of Wish-fulfilling Jewels
(Bka' brgyud yid bzhin nor bu yi 'phreng ba)
Numbers in parentheses refer to the order found in the *The Twelve
Great Disciples* and *The Black Treasury*.

I. [start of rnam thar:] yang rdo rje 'chang snam par snang mdzad du
sprul/ rnam snang 'jam dpal du sprul/ de nyi sprul nas/ bsgrub pa
la nan tan dgos pa'i brda bsten te/

II. ting nge 'dzin dang 'brel ba nyams su myong ba'i yon tan la/ yon tan
bcu bdun yod pa las/

1. 'khor ba snying po med par mkhyen pa'i yon tan (1)
2. rmi lam brtar shar ba'i yon tan (2)
3. dga' ba bde 'drod 'phro ba'i yon tan (3)
4. zas gos 'dun pa rang grol gyi yon tan (4)
5. nyams myong bde bar shar ba'i yon tan (5)
6. snang ba mthun rkyen du shar ba'i yon tan (7)
7. rtogs pa lam mkhan du shar ba['i yon tan] (6)
8. nye 'brel chos brgyad rang grol gyi yon tan (8)
9. drin lan bsab ba'i yon tan (10)
10. lha'i lhar gyur pa'i yon tan (12)
11. rtsod pas mi rdzi ba'i yon tan (9)

12. sbyod pa che ba'i yon tan (11)
13. nus pa che ba'i yon tan (14)
14. byin brlab che ba'i yon tan (15)
15. ting nge gyi che ba'i yon tan (16)
16. phyag rgya chen po ngo 'phrod pa'i yon tan (17)

Although the text specifies seventeen "qualities," only sixteen appear in the body of the biography. Following *The Twelve Great Disciples* and other compendia, the missing section would be "the quality in which the lamp of wisdom is born" (*ye shes sgron me bltam pa'i yon tan*).

Zhwa dmar Mkha' spyod dbang po's *Cloudbank of Blessings*
(Chos rje dpal ldan mi la ras chen gyi rnam par thar pa byin rlabs kyi sprin phung)

1. meeting with demoness at Ling ba brag
2. meditation at Byang chub rdzong
3. meditation at Sing gha la'i nags
4. *gaṇacakra* at Su lu dhi pa charnel ground
5. meeting pigeon at Phug ron phug
6. meditation at Brag djar rnam gsum and Mang yul gyi brag; sister offers cloth
7. meeting Ras chung pa at Za 'og phug
8. meeting with patroness at Mchog dkar gyi brag
9. La phyi episode
10. taming Tshe ring ma sisters
11. meditation at La phyi chu bzang
12. vision of Mar pa at Brag dmar spo mthon
13. meeting with seven a tsa ra
14. meeting with Dam pa sangs rgyas
15. meeting with Zhi ba 'od at Rgyal gyi shri ri
16. dispute at 'Om chung dpal gyi dgon
17. song of impermanence (*mi rtag pa gtso bo'i mgur*)
18. decision to go to Ti se
19. meeting with Gsal le
20. song of cutting the rope of pretense
21. song to twelve forgettings (*brjed pa bcu gnyis*) to patroness Bkra shis rtsegs pa
22. song atop the Ko ra pass to male and female disciples

23. journey to Co ro 'bring tshangs and Tsho' rnga 'dre chu, five women sing of Gang dkar ti se
24. songs to Ras chung pa
25. Ras chung returns from India, song of Yak horn, Mi la burns Ras chung pa's texts
26. Mi la plans to go to Nepal, but changes his mind
27. song to Ras chung pa
28. meeting with a nun
29. meeting with dying Bon po
30. meeting with Ston pa Dar lo
31. Mi la locked inside temple
32. explanation of disciples' visions
33. meditation at Brin gyi la so'i brag phug
34. Mi la's illness
35. arrival of eight women while at Brag dmar chen po
36. song to Lama Lha rje (Sgam po pa)
37. song on intermediate state to Lama Lha rje (Sgam po pa)
38. song at Mon gyi ri
39. offerings [from the King of Bhaktapur]
40. meeting with Dharmabodhi
41. vase initiation and consecration
42. episode on how to make dedication, with a vision of Tārā
43. song in response to Lcam lhan cig skyes pa'i sgron me
44. song of seven suitable things (ran pa bdun gyi mgur) at La phyi sna g.yon
45. Tshe ring ma sisters manifest as girls, come to meet Mi la

COMPENDIA OUTLINES

Outlines for the Newark and Oxford Editions of the *Twelve Great Disciples* (Bu chen bcu gnyis)

Newark Edition

2a.3	I. rigs dang 'brel ba dka' ba sbyad pa'i yon tan
15a.2	II. ting nge 'dzin dang 'brel ba nyams su myong ba'i yon tan
15a.4	i. 'khor ba la snying po med pa'i yon tan
15a.4	(1) snga ma bar ma gnyen 'dun gyi skor
17b.2	ii. rmi lam brdar shar ba'i yon tan

102b.3	(28) brag steng rta sga'i skor
105a.1	(29) ngom lung brag gseb kyis skor
106b.6	(30) brag dkar rta so'i skor
108b.2	(31) thog la'i skor
110b.3	(32) khyi gra ras pa'i skor
114b.4	(33) rtsang g.yag ru'i 'gron khang gi skor
117a.2	xiv. nus pa che ba'i yon tan
117a.2	(34) bring gi la so'i skor
119a.4	(35) a phyi snang ma'i skor
121a.4	xv. byin brlab che ba'i yon tan
121a.4	(36) chu mig dngul bum gyi skor
131b.2	(37) zhi ba 'od kyi skor
132b.5	(38) gung thang lho sgo'i skor
136a.3	(39) legs se 'bum mes skor
139a.3	(40) skyid rong rab chad rgan rgon gyi skor
140b.4	(41) gshin rdor mo'i skor
142b.6	(42) mang yul gung thang gi skor
143b.6	(43) sba 'gur gyi skor
147a.2	(44) lha rje g.yang nge'i skor
149b.1	(45) gcong rong bring gi skor
151a.4	xvi. ting nge 'dzin gyi rtsal rdzong pa'i yon tan
151a.4	(46) snye nams lung chung gi skor
153a.5	xvii. phyag rgya chen po ngo sprod <'phrod> pa'i yon tan
153a.5	(47) [Tshe ring ma 1] zhus lan gong ma'i skor
163a.6	(48) [Tshe ring ma 2] bdud rtsi 'od kyi phreng ba
174b.6	(49) [Tshe ring ma 3] bar do 'phrang sgrol
188a.2	(50) [Tshe ring ma 4] bde stong ye shes sprin gyi phreng ba
190a.1	(51) bring gi lha grong gi skor
195a.2	(52) ras chung dbus bzhud kyi skor
200a.3	(53) dbus gtad par pa'i skor
201b.5	(54) dbus gtad 'og ma te nya ma'i skor
204b.4	(55) lha cig ldem bu dang/ rong sogs tse'i skor dang skor gnyis so
210a.6	(56) mchod khang zhal mjal gyis skor
212a.3	(57) dag po lha rje 'byon pa'i ma 'ongs lung bstan gyi skor
213a.6	(58) rje ras pa chen po mi la dang/ mnyam med dag po rin po ches yab sras gnyis kyi zhus dang lan gyi skor
221a.3	(59) lha cig lcam me'i bsngo ba'i skor
222a.6	(60) snyen chung tsar ma'i skor

223b.6	(61) dbus gtad zhal lta'i skor
226b.2	(62) bring gi smon lam gyi skor
231b.2	[passing into nirvana]
243b.2	[list of disciples/final verses]

Oxford Edition

Song cycles not found in the Newark edition or in *The Black Treasury* works are in small capitals.

2a.3	I. rigs dang 'brel pa dka' ba spyad pa'i yon tan
12b.6	II. ting nge 'dzin dang 'brel pa nyams su myong ba'i yon tan
13a.1	i. 'khor ba la snying po med pa'i yon tan
13a.1	(1) lnga la gong ma gnyen ' dun gyi skor
14b.6	ii. rmi lam brda shar ba'i yon tan
14b.6	(2) 'di rnams snga ma la 'ogs/ de thams cad la lnga lnga ma bskor gsum
19b.1	iii. bde drong ngo 'phrod yon tan
19b.1	(3) spo ri spo thon gyi bskor
21a.3	(4) brag dmar mchong gling gi bskor
23b.1	(5) la phyi chu bzang gi bskor
25b.4	(6) shin dor mo'i skor
26b.7	iv. zas gos 'dun pa dang bral ba'i yon tan
26b.7	(7) gangs 'gur gyi bskor
29b.7	v. nyams myong bde bar shar ba'i yon tan
29b.7	(8) ras chung zhal 'jal gyi skor
31b.7	vi. rtogs pa lam du shar ba'i yon tan
31b.7	(9) mon gyi shing ri'i bskor
33b.6	(10) sing ga la'i nags gseb kyi bskor
35a.7	(11) dpal gro stag tshang gi bskor
37a.3	vii. snang ba 'thun rkyen du shar ba'i yon tan
37a.3	(12) skyid phug nyi ma'i rdzong gi bskor
38b.5	(13) gung thang ling ba'i brag de la/ ras pa dang/ brag srin mo gnyis kyi zhu ba zhu lan/ ling ba'i bskor de bskor che ba'o
44a.2	viii. chos rgyad rang grol tu shar ba'i yon tan
44a.2	(14) gnye 'dun rang sar grol ba'i skor
45b.3	(15) chos brgyad rang grol ba/ snye nam grod phug gi bskor
46b.7	ix. rtsod pas mi rdzi ba'i yon tan
46b.7	(16) dar lo'i skor
50b.6	(17) te pu'i bskor

56b.2	(18) zhal lta yo bde'i bskor
59a.4	(19) g.yag ru'i bskor
62a.6	(20) rkyang mgur gyi skor
65b.6	(21) mchong lung gi bskor
67a.1	x. drin lan bsab pa'i yon tan
67a.1	(22) pha ma'i drin lan bsab pa'i skor
69a.7	xi. spyod pa chen ba'i yon tan
69a.7	(23) sgyu 'phrul rig pa'i bskor
72b.2	(24) lcam me'i bskor
73a.7	xii. lha'i lhar gyur pa'i yon tan
73a.7	(25) 'om chung nags 'dabs ma'i bskor
74b.4	(26) bal yul nags ma'i bskor
76b.3	(27) phug ron sngon mo'i bskor
78a.4	xiii. ye shes sgron me ltam pa'i yon tan
78a.4	(28) brag steng rta sga'i skor
79b.7	(29) ngom lung brag seb kyi bskor
81a.7	(30) brag dkar rta so'i skor
82b.3	(31) thog la'i skor
84a.4	(32) khyi ra ras pa'i skor
87a.3	(33) gtsang g.yag ru 'gron khang gi bskor
88b.4	xiv. nus pa che ba'i yon tan
88b.4	(34) bring gi la so'i skor
90a.5	(35) a phyi snang ma'i bskor
91b.6	xv. byin brlabs che ba'i yon tan
91b.6	(36) chu mig dngul bum gyi bskor
99a.4	(37) zhi ba 'od kyi bskor
100a.4	(38) gung thang lho sgo'i skor
102b.4	(39) legs se 'bum me'i bskor
104b.6	(40) skyid rong rab chad rgan rgon gyi bskor
105b.6	(41) gshen rdor mo'i bskor
107a.6	(42) mang yul gung thang gi skor
108a.3	(43) sba mgur gyi bskor
110a.6	(44) lha rje yang nge'i skor
111b.7	(45) gcong rong bring gi ksor
112b.7	xvi. ting nge 'dzin gyis rtsal rdzogs pa'i yon tan
112b.7	(46) snye nam lung chung gi bskor
114a.3	(47) BZANG RGYUD PHYAG TSHANG GI BSKOR[3]
114a.3	bza' grangs kyi le'u ste dang po
115b.1	ji ltar na ba'i le'u ste gnyis pa

115b.6	mo 'debs cis kyi le'u ste gsum pa
116a.1	mo ngan srog cha bzlog pa'i le'u ste bzhi pa
116a.5	grags pa byed pa bon gyi le'u ste lnga pa
116b.4	gtang rags gi le'u ste drub pa
117a.2	bla sngor gyi le'u ste bdun pa
117b.2	ston mo'i le'u ste brgyad pa
118a.6	bshad pa btang ba'i le'u ste dgu pa
118b.5	(48) A PHYI RGAN MO'I SKOR[4]
119b.4	(49) 'GUR PHRAN[5]
124b.7	xvii. phyag rgya chen po ngo 'phrod pa'i yon tan
124b.7	(50) [Tshe ring ma 1] snyan ngag gi glu mu tig gi phreng ba
129b.3	(51) [Tshe ring ma 2] bdud rtsi 'od kyi phreng ba
136b.4	(52) [Tshe ring ma 3] [Bar do 'phrang sgrol]
144b.1	(53) [Tshe ring ma 4] bde stong ye shes phrin gyis phreng ba
145b.2	(54) bring gi lha grong bskor[6]
150b.7	(55) ras chung dbus bzhud kyi bskor
155a.6	(56) dbus gtad bar ma'i skor
156b.1	(57) dbus 'og ma ste nya ma'i bskor
157b.1	(58) lha lcam ldem bu'i skor dang/ rong sogs rtse gong gi skor dang gnyis
162b.5	(59) chod khang zhal 'jal gyi bskor
164a.1	(60) dags po 'byon pa'i ma 'ongs lung bstan gyis bskor
164b.7	(61) dags po zhal mjal gyi bskor
172a.4	(62) dags po dbus bzhud kyi bskor
176a.7	(63) lcam me'i bsngo ba'i bskor
177a.4	(64) snye nam rtsar ma'i skor
178a.2	(65) [dbus gtad zhal lta'i skor][7]
180b.1	(66) brin gyi smon lam gyi bskor[8]
182b.6	[passing into nirvana]
191b.4	[list of disciples]
192b.1	[concluding verses]

Outlines for Versions of The Black Treasury

The Black Treasury—Lhasa Edition (DNM-Lhasa)
Song cycles not found in The Twelve Great Disciples are in small capitals.

2a.1	I. rigs dang 'brel ba dka' ba sbyad pa'i yon tan
17b.4	II. ting nge 'dzin dang 'brel ba nyams su myong ba'i yon tan

18a.1	i. 'khor ba la snying po med pa'i yon tan
18a.1	(1) snga mas gong ma gnyen 'dun gyi skor
20b.7	ii. rmi lam brdar shar ba'i yon tan
20b.7	(2) snga ma'i skor gsum mo/ dge'o bkra shis par gyur cig/ 'di rnam lnga ma la gong ma te/ de thams cad snga snga ba la skor gsum
30a.6	iii. bde drod ngo 'phrod pa'i yon tan
30a.6	(3) spo ri spo mthon gyis skor
33a.2	(4) brag dmar mchang gling gis skor
36b.5	(5) la phyi chu bzang gis skor
40a.5	(6) gshen rdor mo'i skor
42a.1	iv. zas gos kyi 'dun pa dang bral ba'i yon tan
42a.1	(7) gang 'gur gyis skor
44b.6	v. nyams myong bde bar shar ba'i yon tan
44b.6	(8) ras chung zhal mjal gyis skor
50a.1	vi. rtogs pa lam du shar ba'i yon tan
50a.1	(9) mon gyi shing ri'i skor
52b.6	(10) sing gha'i nag gseb gyis skor
55a.3	(11) dpal gro stag tshangs gis skor
57b.3	vii. snang ba mthun rkyen du shar ba'i yon tan
57b.3	(12) skyid phug nyi ma rdzong gis skor
60a.4	(13) brag skya rdo rje rdzong gis skor
61a.1	(14) gung thang leng ba'i brag de la ras pa dang/ brag srin gnyis kyis zhus len/ ling ba'i skor ro: skor che ba'o//
69b.3	viii. chos brgyad rang grol ba'i yon tan
69b.3	(15) gnyan 'dun rang grol ba'i skor
72a.4	(16) chos brgyad rang grol ba'i snyen nam grod phug gis skor
74a.7	ix. rtsod pa mi brdzi ba'i yon tan
74b.1	(17) dar lo'i skor
81a.3	(18) ti pu'i skor
93b.4	(19) shal lta yo bde'i skor
95a.3	(20) g.yag ru'i skor
100a.6	(21) rkyong 'gur gyis skor
105b.2	(22) mchang lung gi lungs bstan gyis skor
107a.4	x. drin len bsab pa'i yon tan
107a.4	(23) cad phā mā la drin len bsab pa'i skor
110b.6	xi. spyod pa che ba'i yon tan
110b.7	(24) sgyu 'phrul rig pa'i skor
115b.3	(25) lcam me'i skor

117a.2	xii. lha'i lhar gyur pa'i yon tan [1594]
117a.2	(26) 'om chung nag 'dabs ma'i skor
119a.3	(27) bal yul nag gseb ma'i skor
122a.5	(28) phug ron sngon mo'i skor
124b.4	(29) RJE MI LA RAS PA DANG DBU MO YID PHROG MA GNYIS KYIS ZHUS LEN 'GUR DU GSUNG PA'I SKOR[9]
132a.3	xiii. ye shes sgron me lta bu'i yon tan
132a.3	(30) brag steng rta sga'i skor
134b.3	(31) ngom lung brag gseb gyis skor
136b.6	(32) brag dkar rta so'i skor
138b.4	(33) [thog la'i skor][10]
[140–143]	(34a) khyi ra ras pa'i skor[11]
145a.3	(34b) YANG LO RGYUS GCIG LAS . . . [KHYI RA RAS PA VERSION 2][12]
147b.4	(35) LUG RDZI'I SKOR[13]
149b.2	(36) gtsang g.yag ru mgron khong gis skor
152a.2	xiv. nus pa che ba'i yon tan
152a.2	(37) bring gis la so'i skor
154b.2	(38) a phyi snang ma'i skor
156b.5	xv. byin brlabs che ba'i yon tan
156b.5	(39) chu migs dngul 'bum gyis skor
169a.4	(40) [zhi ba 'od kyi skor]
[170]	(41) gung thong lho sgo'i skor
174a.7	(42) legs se 'bum me'i skor
177b.6	(43) skyi rang rab chad rgan rgog gis skor
179b.2	(44) gshen rdor mo'i skor
181b.5	(45) mang yul gang thong gis skor
183a.1	(46) sba 'gur gyis skor
189a.7	(47) lha rje yang nge'i skor
189b.7	(48) ljang rang bring gis skor
191b.2	xvi. ting nge 'dzin gyis rtsal rdzogs pa'i yon tan
191b.2	(49) snyen nams lus chung gis skor
193b.1	xvii. phyag rgya chen po'i ngo sprod 'phrod pa'i yon tan
193b.1	(50a) [Tshe ring ma 1] colophon (202a.4)
202b.4	(50b) [Tshe ring ma 2] colophon (213b.4)
214a.5	(50c) [Tshe ring ma 3] colophon (227b.3)
227b.5	(50d) [Tshe ring ma 4] colophon (229b.1)
229b.5	(51) brin lha grang gyis skor[14]
238b.4	(52) ras chung dbus bzhud kyis skor

244a.4	(53) dbus gtad bar ma'i skor
246a.3	(54) [dbus gtad 'og ma te nya ma'i skor]
[249–257]	(55) [lha cig ldem bu dang/ rong sogs tse'i skor dang skor gnyis so?][15]
	(56) mchang <mchod> khang zhal mjal gyis skor
258a.1	(57) dbus gtad zhal lta dang/ dags po dbus bzhud kyi skor
283a.1	(58) lcam me'i skor
284b.1	(59) snen nam rtsar ma'i skor
286a.3	(60) dbus gtad zhal ta'i <lta'i> skor
288b.6	(61) brin gyis smon lam kyis skor
293b.2	[passing in to nirvana]

The Black Treasury—Rangjung Dorjé Edition (DNM-RD)
Song cycles lacking in other versions or significantly changed are in small capitals.

3.2	I. rigs dang 'brel ba dka' ba sbyad pa'i yon tan
43.2	II. ting nge 'dzin dang 'brel ba nyams su myong ba'i yon tan
43.6	i. 'khor ba la snying po med par rtogs pa'i yon tan
43.6	(1) snga ma las gong ma gnyen 'dun gyi skor
49.4	ii. rmi lam brdar shar ba'i yon tan
49.4	(2) snga ma las 'og ma ste de thams cad snga ma'i skor gsum
63.6	iii. bde drod ngo 'phrod pa'i yon tan
63.6	(3) spo ri spo mthon gyis skor
69.4	(4) brag dmar mchong gling gis skor
77.1	(5) la phyi chu bzang gis skor
83.5	(6) gshen rdor mo'i skor
86.6	iv. zas gos kyi 'dun pa dang bral ba'i yon tan
86.6	(7) gangs mgur gyi skor
96.1	v. nyams myong bde bar shar ba'i yon tan
96.1	(8) ras chung zhal mjal gyi skor
101.5	vi. rtogs pa lam du shar ba'i yon tan
101.5	(9) mon gyi shing ri'i skor
106.6	(10) sing gha la yi nags gseb kyi skor
111.4	(11) dpal gro stag tshang gi skor
117.2	vii. snang ba mthun rkyen du shar ba'i yon tan
117.2	(12) skyid phug nyi ma rdzong gi skor
122.1	(13) BRAG SKYA RDO RJE RDZONG GI SKOR[16]
123.4	(14) gung thang lung pa'i brag de la mi la ras pa dang brag

356.1	(43) a phyi snang ma la sogs pa'i skor
365.3	(44) SBA MGUR SKOR[24]
375.3	(45) CHU MIG DNGUL 'BUM GYI SKOR[25]
376.2	xv. byin rlabs che ba'i yon tan
403.6	(46) zhi ba 'od kyi skor
406.6	(47) gung thang lho sgo'i skor
415.4	(48) GUNG THANG GI SKOR[26]
417.6	(49) 'bum me'i skor
428.6	(50) mang yul gyi skor
434.3	(51) gzhin rdor mo'i skor
439.1	(52) GANGS TI SE NA NA RO BON CHUNG BTUL BA'I SKOR[27]
450.4	(53) ti se la sogs pa'i skor
463.4	(54) brag dmar spo mtho'i skor
470.3	(54) ston pa shākya gu la sogs pa'i skor
477.6	(55) sbyin gtong drug ma dang lha rje g.yang nge la sogs pa'i skor
485.2	(56) gcong rong brin gyi skor
491.1	xvi.[28] ting nge 'dzin gyi rtsal rdzogs pa'i yon tan[29]
491.1	(57) nam lung chung gi skor
496.4	xvii.[30] phyag rgya chen po ngo 'phrod pa'i yon tan
496.4	(58) de thams cad bkra shis tshe ring ma'i skor. colophon (515.1) mkha' 'gro'i bka' chad 'byung ba'i phyir/ yi ge mi spel sba bar zhu/ rje spyod pa'i rnal 'byor pa mtshan yongs su grags pa mi la zhes bya ba de nyid kyi zhabs kyi padmo'i rdul la reg pa/ ngan rdzong ston pas bla rje btsun la lan gsum zhus nas gnang ba yi ger bkod pa dris pa'i lan snyan ngag gi glu mu tig gi phreng ba zhes bya ba rdzogs so//
572.1	(59) mtsho rna del chung gi skor
584.6	(60) brin gi lha grong gi skor
602.4	(61) ras chung pa'i rmi lam lung bstan gyi skor
606.1	(62) ras chung dbus bzhus kyi skor
616.6	(63) dbus gtad bar ma'i skor
620.4	(64) dbus gtad 'og ma dang nya ma'i skor
629.6	(65) lcam ldem bu'i skor
651.1	(66) mchod khang zhal mjal gyi skor
655.2	(67) dwags po 'byon pa'i ma 'ongs lung bstan gyi skor
658.2	(68) dwags po zhal mjal gyi skor
687/6	(69) rje btsun chen po mi la ras pa dang mnyam med dwags po rin po che yab sras kyi zhus pa dang lan gyi skor

703.3	(70) ni dbus gtad zhal lta dang/ dwags po dbus bzhud kyi skor
706.6	(71) chu bar gyi skor
716.3	(72) lcam me'i shol bgos ba'i skor
717.4	(73) snye nam rtsar ma'i skor
724.2	(74) dbus gtad zhal ta'i skor
730.2	(75) RONG SOG RTSE GONG GI SKOR[31]
733.5	(76) brin gyi smon lam gyi skor
743.3	xviii. tshe gcig gis zungs jug rdo rje'i sku 'grub cing lus su yal ba'i tshul bstan pa'i yon tan

The Black Treasury—India and Smith Editions (DNM-I/S)

Song cycles lacking in earlier versions or significantly changed are in small capitals. Page numbers = (I / S)

v.1, 2.1 / v.1, 2	Introductory verses
6.2 / 3.2	I. rigs dang 'brel pa dka' ba spyad pa'i yon tan
115.6 / 64.6	II. ting nge 'dzin dang 'brel ba nyams su myong ba'i yon tan
115.7 / 64.6	i. 'khor ba la snying po med pa'i yon tan
115.7 / 64.6	(1) snga ma bar ma gnyen bdun gyi skor
126.5 / 71.2	ii. rmi lam brtar shar ba'i yon tan
126.5 / 71.2	(2) snga ma skor gsum
161.6 / 91.4	iii. bde drod ngo phrod pa'i yon tan
161.6 / 91.4	(3) spo ri spo thon gyi skor
161.6 / 96.4	(4) brag dmar chong gling sogs gyi skor
182.2 / 103.8	(5) la phyi chu bzang gyis skor
190.1 / 108.2	(6) gshen rdor mo'i skor
193.7 / 110.2	iv. zas gos kyis 'dun pa dang bral ba'i yon tan
193.7 / 110.2	(7) C: la phyi gangs 'gur gyi skor; I: gongs 'gur gyi bskor
211.1 / 119.5	v. nyams myong bde bar shar ba'i yon tan
211.1 / 119.5	(8) ras chung zhal 'jal gyi skor
219.6 / 126.1	(9) mon shing ri'i skor
225.7 / 129.5	(10) RAS CHUNG PA LA GDAM PA'I SKOR[32]
229.7 / 130.1	vi. rtogs pa lam tu shar ba'i yon tan
229.7 / 130.1	(11) C: sing ga la'i nag gseb kyi skor; I: Sing ga la'i skor
235.4 / 133.4	(12) dpal gro stag tshang gi skor
256.3 / 146.7	vii. snang ba 'thun skyen tu shar ba'i yon tan
256.3 / 146.7	(13) skyid phug nyi ma'i rdzong gi skor

262.1 / 150.4	(14) rje ras pa chen po [C: dpal bzhed pa rdo rje] dang/ brag srin mo gnyis kyis zhu ba zhus pa len [I: ling] ba'i skor de bskor chen po'o
281.7 / 162.8	viii. chos brgyad rang grol tu shar ba'i yon tan
281.7 / 162.8	(15) gnyen bdun rang sar grol ba'i skor
288.5 / 167.3	(16) chos brgyad rang grol ba snye nam drod phug sogs kyi skor
301.7 / 175.5	ix. btsod pas mi rdzi ba'i yon tan
301.7 / 175.5	(17) ston pa dar lo'i skor
331.1 / 195.3	(18) te pu ba'i skor
354.6 / 207.8	(19) zhal lta yo bde'i skor
365.6 / 212.8	(20) g.yag ru'i bskor
382.2 / 223.1	(21) rkyang 'gur gyi skor
404.2 / 236.2	(22) I: brag dmar chong lung gis bskor; C: mchong lung gi skor
407.7 / 238.5	x. drin lan bsabs pa'i yon tan[33]
407.7 / 238.5	(23) pha ma la drin len bsab pa'i bskor
417.7 / 244.8	xi. spyod pa che ba'i yon tan
417.7 / 244.8	(24) sgyu 'brul rigs pa'i skor
431.1 / 258	(25) thog la'i skor[34]
444.2 / 255.8	(26) lca me'i skor
447.3 / 262.7	xii. lha'i lhar gyur pa'i yon tan
447.3 / 262.7	(27) 'om chung nag 'dab kyi skor
452.4 / 265.7	(28) bal yul nags ma'i skor
464.3 / 272.4	(29) phug ron [C: phu ron] sngon mo'i skor
469.5 / 275.5	(30) C: rje ras pa chen po dpal bzhed pa'i rdo rje dang/ pu yo yid 'phrog ma gnyis kyi zhu ba zhus len de sing 'phrog ba'i bskor; I: rje ras pa chen po dpal gzhed pa'i rdo rje'i dang/ yid phrog ma gnyis kyi zhus len gyis bskor
486.4 / 285.6	xiii. ye shes sgron me bltam pa'i yon tan
486.4 / 285.6	(31) brag steng rta sga'i sogs kyi skor
508.4 / 297.7	(32) dom lung brag gseb kyi skor
513.6 / 300.7	(33) brag dkar rta so'i skor
518.2 / vol. 2, 3.5	(34a) khyi ra ras pa la gsung tshul ma'i 'dra gnyis kyi skor
v.2, 15.7 / 16.8	(34b) [khyi ra ras pa version II]
26.5 / 22.8	(35) ra rdzi ras pa dang lug rdzi ras pa gnyis kyi skor
30.7 / 25.5	(36) gtsang gi g.yag ru mkhron khang gi skor

39.6 / 30.3	xiv. nus pa che ba'i yon tan
39.6 / 30.3, ends 36.7	(37) brin gyi la sogs kyi skor[35]
51.1 / 36.7	(38) I: a phyi snang ma'i skor; C: a phyi snang ma dang mgon mo lcam la sogs kyi skor
61.6 / ends 46.4	(39) JO MO GSAL LE SGRON GYI SKOR[36]
65.5 / ends 53.2	(40) A PHYI SNANG MA DANG MGON MO LCAM LA SOGS KYI KYI SKOR[37]
77.5 / 53.2	(41) GANG TI TSE'I SKOR[38]
92.5 / 61.8	(42) RGYU STON KYI SKOR[39]
100.1 / 65.7	(43) NUS PA CHE BA'I SKOR[40]
118.6 / 77.6	xv. BYIN BRLAB CHE BA'I YON TAN
118.6 / 77.6	(44) CHU MIG DNGUL 'BUM GI SKOR[41]
149.6 / 95.7	(45) ZHI BA 'OD GYI SKOR[42]
153.7 / 98.3	(46) NYA MA DPAL DAR 'BUM GYIS ZHU BA ZHUS LEN GUNG THANG GI SKOR[43]
171.3 / 108.3	(47) legs se 'bum me'i skor
179.4 / 112.6	(48) skyid rong rab chad rgan gnyis [I: rgan rgon] kyi bskor
183.6 / 114.8	(49) gshen rdor mo'i skor
189.6 / 118.1	(50) mang yul gung thang gis bskor
192.7 / 120.5	(51) ngan rdzong phug 'bar la gsung pa'i sba 'gur gyis bskor
204.5 / 126.4	(52) lha rje yang nge la gsung pa'i skor[44]
C132.2	(53) lcong ngo phring gis bskor
218.6 / 134.4	xvi. ting nge 'dzin gyis rtsal rdzogs pa'i yon tan
218.6 / 134.4	(54) snye nam lung chung gis bskor
222.6 / 136.6	(55) LO RGYUS YOD MED 'THOR BU'I SKOR[45]
260.6 / 158.2	xvii. phyag rgya chen po ngo sprod pa'i yon tan
260.6 / 158.2	(56a) [Tshe ring ma 1][46]
281.3 / 169.8	(56b) [Tshe ring ma 2] rje ras pa chen po pal gzhad pa'i rdo rje dang jo mo bkra shis tshe ring mas dbu mdzad pa'i 'dzin 'jig rten mig bsgyur gi mkha' 'gro ma lnga'i theg pa mchog gis sems bskyed pa'i dris lan 'gur du bzheng pa bdud rtsi 'od kyis phreng ba zhe ba ba 'om chung dpal gyi nab ldab su bkod pa'o
307.2 / 184.5	(57) [Tshe ring ma 3] rje ras pa chen pod pal bzhad pa'i rdo rje dang 'jig rten mig bsgyur gyis mkha' 'gro lnga'i

	'phrang xxx gnad kyis xxx la dri sa chen dang bcas pa'i xxx glu ru blang sa snams so/
I337.5	(58) [Tshe ring ma 4] rje ras pa chen pod pal gzhad pa'i rdo rje dang jo mo bkra shis tshe ring ma gnyis kyis zhu ba zhus len gyis bskor snams ngam rdzong ston pa bho dhi ra dza dang ras pa zhi ba 'od gnyis kyis tshogs dang mandal phul gsol ba btab nas yi gir bkod pa'o/ de thams cad bkra shis tshe ring ma'u bskor ste bskor che ba'o/⁴⁷
I342.5	(59) GCOG RO 'BRI 'TSHAMS KYI MTSHO SNGA SDE CHUNG GI SKOR⁴⁸
357.4 / ends 209.8	(60) JO BO BON RI'I SKOR⁴⁹
367.4 / ends 223.1	(61) brin gyi lha brong gyi skor
370.7 / 223.1	(62) ras chung dbus gzhud kyi skor
386.6 / 232.3	(63) dbus gtad bar ma'i skor
390.4 / 234.7	(64) dbus gtad 'og ma snye nya ma'i skor
403.5 / 242.6	(65) LHA LCAM LDEM BU'I SKOR⁵⁰
416.3 / 339.1	(66) mchod khang zhal mjal gyi skor
421.1 / 253.6	(67) dag po 'byon pa'i ma 'ongs lung bstan gyi skor
427.1 / 257.4	(68) dag po zhal mjal gyi skor
453.4 / 277.5	(69) rje ras pa chen po dang mnyam med dag po rin po che yab sras kyis zhus pa dang len gyi skor
478.2 / 290.1	(70) dbus gtad zhal da dang dag po dbus gzhud kyi skor
481.7 / 292.5	(71) snye nam tser [I: rtsed] ma'i skor
491.5 / 299.1	(72) dbus gtad zhal da'i skor
497.2 / 302.5	(73) RANG [I: RA] SOGS RTSE GANG GI SKOR⁵¹
/502.6 / 306.2	(74) lcam me'i bsngo ba'i bskor
504.1 / 307.1	(75) brin gyis smon lam bkra shis kyis bskor
517.1 / missing	xviii. tshe gcig gis zung 'jug rdo rje'i sku 'grub cing 'ja' lus su yal ba'i tshul bstan pa'i yon tan⁵²
551.4 / 335.3	[list of disciples]
553.2 / 336.2	[colophon]
I554.7	[I: scribal colophon]

NOTES

INTRODUCTION

1. The broader corpus of Mi la ras pa's biographical tradition also includes a host of visual and ritual materials that, while relevant to the present study, are far too numerous to address here.

2. Tibetan historians and biographers have proposed a wide range of dates for the yogin's birth and death. Many sources agree that he was born in a dragon year and lived 84 years. The dates most commonly cited in scholarship are 1052–1135 and 1040–1123. Another opinion, supported by several prominent Tibetan scholars, places his birth a full twelve-year cycle earlier, thus giving 1028–1111. I have elsewhere examined these various traditions in detail. See Quintman forthcoming.

3. On the biographical traditions of India and South Asia, see Callewaert and Snell 1994, Schober 1997, and Mallison 2001. For studies of biography and autobiography in the cross-cultural context of South and East Asia, see Granoff and Shinohara 1988, 1992, and 1994. On Jain biography in particular, see the extensive body of literature by Phyllis Granoff, including 1979, 1988a, 1988b, 1992, 1994, 2001. For a discussion of twentieth-century hagiography in India, see Rinehart 2000. Recent studies of Buddhist biography in China include Shinohara 1988, 1992, 2003; Kiechnick 1997; and Jørgensen 2005.

4. See Schaeffer 2011a, who notes that the available statistical data—here drawn from the Tibetan Buddhist Research Center's catalogue database—is both preliminary and incomplete.

5. TTC, s.v. "rnam thar." *skyes bu dam pa'i mdzad spyod lo rgyus kyi gzhung ngam/ rtogs pa brjod pa'i bstan bcos/*

6. The Bka' 'gyur preserves a series of *avadāna* collections, including the *Divyāvadāna*, and the *Avadānaśataka*. Kṣemendra's eleventh-century *Bodhisattvāvadānakalpalatā* was included in the Bstan 'gyur and became "one of the most famous books in Tibetan Buddhism." See Tucci 1949, 437ff. For an important new study of Kṣemedra's *Bodhisattvāvadānakalpalatā* and its reception and dissemination in Tibet, see Lin 2011.

7. Another Tibetan genre of life writing based on Indian literary models is *skyes rabs* (or the honorific *'khrung rabs*), literally "succession of lives," used to render the

Sanskrit *jātaka* in works such as the *Jātakamālā*. As with *rtogs brjod*, Tibetans also wrote indigenous works titled *skyes rabs*. Some of these include semimythological accounts, such as those recounting the former lives of king Srong btsan sgam po in the *Hundred-Thousand Pronouncements of Maṇi* (*Maṇi bka' 'bum*) and Atisha's disciple 'Brom ston pa in the text known as the *Son's Dharma* (*Bu chos*). The latter work, which together with the *Father's Dharma* (*Pha chos*) comprises the well-known *Bka' gdams legs bam*, records some twenty stories said to have been narrated by Atisha himself and apparently modeled in the style of the Indian *jātaka*. See Vostrikov 1970, 94n303. Other types of *sykes rabs* take the form of collective biographies. These were well suited to the Tibetan tradition of recognized incarnation lines (*sprul sku*) and chronicled such lineages, which were often affiliated with a particular religious institution.

8. Franklin Edgerton, *Buddhist Hybrid Sanskrit Dictionary* (reprint ed., Motilal Banarsidass, 1998), s.v. "*vimokṣa*." One version of the life story examined in chapter 3 directly compares Mi la ras pa to the figure of Sudhana.

9. See Gyatso 1998, 281n8.

10. See, for example, Willis 1985, Decleer 1992, Gyatso 1998.

11. Such a reading of life as *bios* is suggested in Averintsev 2002. This is illustrated, for example, in the song attributed to Mi la ras pa in which he extols the virtuous power his life example can have on his followers. He makes statements such as "Those who've seen my face or heard my speech, / Remembered my life story (*rnam thar*), / Or those who've heard of it or of my name"; and "Those who ask for, teach, or listen to it, / Read it or pay it veneration, / And those who emulate my life's account (*rnam thar*)." These passages are discussed in chapter 1.

12. See Vostrikov 1970, 187ff.

13. For a discussion of secret biography and autobiographical life writing, see Gyatso 1998.

14. Cited from *The Black Treasury*. See chapter 4 and appendix 2.6.

15. Cited from *The Twelve Great Disciples*. See chapter 4 and appendix 2.5.

16. de Filippi 1931, 224.

17. Ibid.

18. de Kőrös 1834, 184. Mi la ras pa's name is listed in a chronological table translated from the *Vaiḍūrya dkar po*, an astrological treatise written by Sde srid Sangs rgyas rgya mtsho (1653–1705), regent to the Fifth Dalai Lama. The chronology indicates the number of years elapsed from various historical moments up to the year 1687. 647 years are listed as having passed since the time of Mi la ras pa's birth.

19. Jäschke 1869.

20. Jäschke 1881, 413.

21. Das 1881; Rockhill 1884; Sandberg 1899, 1906; Laufer 1901, 1902.

22. Waddell 1895, 64–66.

23. Sandberg 1899, 613.

24. These ideas are more fully explored in Almond 1988; Lopez, ed. 1995; and Lopez 1998.

25. Sandberg 1906, 250.

26. Bell 1931, 80.

27. Tucci, 1949, 98.

28. Ibid., 151.

29. See Bosson 1967, who reproduces the Mongolian xylograph together with a translation and analysis of the translator's colophon.

30. Bacot 1925, 19.
31. Dawasamdup Kazi, Headmaster, Bhutia Boarding School, ed., *Translation of the Seventh Chapter of Jetsün Kahbum (Biographical History of Jetsün Mila Repa)* (Gangtok: Darjeeling Branch Press, 1914).
32. On Dawa-Samdup's life, see the brief descriptions in Fields 1981, 285–87 and Winkler 1982.
33. Cuevas 2003, 3.
34. W. L. Campbell to Evans-Wentz, 14 July 1919, Bodleian Library, Ms. Eng. Lett. c. 577.
35. The Capuchin missionary Francesco Orazio della Penna (1680–1745) is reported to have translated a number of Tibetan works in the eighteenth century, including Tsong kha pa's *Lam rim chen mo*, although they have not been preserved. See de Jong 1974, 65. Evans-Wentz's *Tibetan Book of the Dead* was published prior to Mi la ras pa's biography, although the former does not constitute a Tibetan book so much as a broad doctrinal cycle.
36. Kawaguchi Ekai, *Himāraya-san no hikari* (Tokyo, 1931; reprint ed. 1998); Wang Yinuan, *Xizang sheng zhe Milareba de yi sheng* (Shanghai, 1949; reprint ed. 1982).
37. In addition to his work on Milarepa, he wrote an exploration of transsexuality based on his own life titled *Self: A Study in Endocrinology and Ethics* (London: Heinemann, 1946). He later published an account of his study of Buddhism and life in a Ladakhi monastery in *Imji Getshuli* (London: Routledge, 1962). Dillon tried several times, unsuccessfully, to take full monastic ordination. He was denied because, in the eyes of his Buddhist teachers (including the British Theravada monk Sangharakshita and the Tibetan Denma Locho Rinpoche), he was not a male—one of the prerequisites for receiving the vows of a *bhikṣu* or fully ordained monk. Dillon's life is recounted in Pagan Kennedy's *The First Man-Made Man: The Story of Two Sex Changes, One Love Affair, and a Twentieth-Century Medical Revolution* (New York: Bloomsbury, 2007).
38. Don grub rgyal, TLG, 52.
39. See, for example, the introduction to Evans-Wentz 1928.
40. Radu Varia, *Brancusi* (New York: Rizzoli, 1986).
41. Comic-book versions of the life story have appeared in numerous languages. For the Tibetan and English, see Ri ga Blo bzang bstan 'dzin, ed., *Rnal 'byor gyi dbang phyug rje btsun mi la ras pa* (Dharamsala, India: Tibetan Cultural Printing Press, n.d.), and Eva van Dam, *The Magic Life of Milarepa: Tibet's Great Yogi* (Boston: Shambhala, 1991). Audio recordings of Mi la ras pa's poetry include *The Songs of Milarepa: Tibetan Music from the Mahayana Buddhist Nunnery* (New York: Lyrichord, 1970–9?); *Songs of Milarepa* (New York: Lovely Music, 1983); and *Mila's Journey Inspired by a Dream* (New York: Lovely Music, 1987). Eliane Radigue's *Jetsun Mila* (New York: Lovely Music, 1986, 1987) records a selection of music "inspired by the life of the eleventh-century Tibetan yogi and poet Milarepa," its pieces approximating a musical biography: "Prelude," "Birth and Youth," "Misdeeds," "Meeting the Guru," "Ordeals," "Practice," "Visiting the Homeland," "Retreat," "Realization/Meditation," "Death/Nirvana." Philip Glass was commissioned by the Italian Sagra Musicale Umbra Festival to orchestrate several of the yogin's songs (Dunvagen Music Publishers, 1997). Modern poetry inspired by or dedicated to Mi la ras pa has appeared in various publications, including the spoken-word recording *Milarepa Gatha* by Jackson Mac Low and Sharon Mattlin (Cavriago, Reggio Emilia, Italy: Pari & Dispari, 1976), and perhaps most famously in Allen Ginsberg's *Milarepa Taste* (Detroit: Alternative

Press, 1971). The life story has been novelized in Heather Hughes-Calero's *Shaman of Tibet: Milarepa—From Anger to Enlightenment* (Carmel, CA: Coastline Publishing, 1987), a book otherwise notable chiefly for its grandiosely naïve portrayal of life in a "Tibetan monastery for the black arts." Iris Murdoch refers, on several occasions, to Mi la ras pa in her Booker Prize-winning *The Sea, the Sea* (New York: Penguin Classics, reprint ed. 2001). Noted French author and playwright Eric-Emmanuel Schmitt's stage adaptation *Milarepa* (Paris: A. Michael, 1997) has been translated into more than a dozen languages and performed throughout Europe. A recent Google search for "milarepa" returned well over one million results; in addition to various Tibetan Buddhist meditation centers, these include a Costa Rican bungalow resort, the American musician Swami Anand Milarepa (so named by Bhagwan Shree Rajneesh), and the eponymous political action group cofounded by Adam Yauch of the Beastie Boys, famed for staging a series of "Tibetan freedom concerts."

42. *Smashing the Evil and Revealing the Proper* 1980.

43. The first film, *Milarepa: Magician, Murderer, Saint* (2006), was directed by the well-known Bhutanese teacher Neten Chokling Rinpoche and screened at the 2006 Berlin Film Festival. The second film, simply titled *Milarepa* (2006)—written, directed, filmed, and edited by Tulku Sonam Rinpoche—was a low-budget project shot in Tibet and produced in Taiwan. A recent performance of the Karmapa's stage play was recorded in India as *The Life of Milarepa* (2010).

44. George Plimpton, "The Curious Case of Sidd Finch," *Sports Illustrated*, April 1, 1985. Plimpton later reworked the story into a full-length novel under the same name (Four Walls Eight Windows, 2004).

45. See Schmid 1952.

46. de Jong 1959.

47. Smith 1969.

48. A corresponding study of editions of the *Songs* appears in Eimer and Tsering 1990 and Eimer 1996, 2000.

49. Spanian 1982. This study, which deserves wider recognition, anticipates some of the findings presented in this book, although it came to my attention only recently. Thanks to Françoise Robin for providing the reference.

50. Eimer and Tsering 1990; Eimer 1996, 2000.

51. Draghi 1980.

52. Urubshurow 1984.

53. Tiso 1989.

54. Roberts 2001; 2007.

55. Martin 1982.

56. Decleer 1994.

57. See Larsson 2009 and DiValerio 2011. The former has recently been published in Larsson 2012.

58. See, for example, de Montmillin 1985, 1990; Tiso 1996, 1997.

59. See de Jong 1974, 58ff. The story of Barlaam and Josaphat has been studied and recounted in numerous publications, most recently Ikegami 1999, Calomino 1990, and Hirsch 1986.

60. Their works are reviewed in de Jong 1974, 78ff. See also Reynolds 1976; Reynolds and Hallisey 1987.

61. Reynolds 1976, 38.

62. de Jong 1974, 82.
63. See Thomas 1927.
64. Strong 2000, 2.
65. Reynolds 1976, 39.
66. Faure 1986, 198.
67. Kurtis Schaeffer (2004) was the first to suggest the applicability of Geary's approach to the study of Tibetan biographical literature. In what follows, I explore its implications in greater detail.
68. Delehaye 1955, 3.
69. Geary 1994, 9.
70. Snell 1999, 1.
71. Tucci 1947, 150–51.
72. van Tuyl 1974, 21.
73. Tiso 1996, 13–14.
74. Aris 1989.
75. Ibid., 4.
76. Gyatso (1998, 125) describes 'Jigs med gling pa's exoteric biography by noting, "it can be assumed that the many 'outer' events the text describes are largely factual, for they conform to what we do know of Jigme Lingpa's life from other sources and reflect typical patterns of interaction in eighteenth-century Tibetan Buddhist society." She goes on, however, to acknowledge that even such "prosaic, chronicle-like" works have their own "self-serving rhetorical strategies, which are not unlike those at work in the secret autobiographies."
77. Gyatso (1998, xii–xiii) has similarly argued for the usefulness of reading Tibetan autobiographical works not only for the content of their immediate concerns but also as a means for better understanding the production of life writing as a broad literary form in other cultural contexts.
78. On the question of defining hagiography and its position vis-à-vis history and historiography, see de Certeau 1988, 269–84; Heffernan 1988, 35–71; Lifshitz 1994; Kleinberg 1997.
79. Graus 1965.
80. Geary 1994, 12.
81. Ibid.
82. Geary 1994, 12.
83. Geary 1994, 13.
84. Geary 1994, 17.
85. More recently, Carl Yamamoto (2012) has explored Lama Zhang's life through the lenses of political authority and religious charisma. To this list may be added the recent doctoral dissertations by William Gorvine (2006) and Sara Jacoby (2007). Gorvine examines the ways in which Tibetan life writing "reflects and shapes images of sanctity within the cultural dynamics of religious partisanship in twentieth century Bön religion" (x). Jacoby combines the formal analysis of the literary style of Sera Khandro's autobiography with a close reading of the text as a source of understanding the community dynamics of Tibetan treasure revealers (*ster ston*) and tantric consorts.
86. On the Tibetan practice of diary writing, see Gyatso 1997. On the notion of biographical culture, see Quintman 2013, which also discusses the role of

biographical supplications in the consecration of Tibetan scroll painting. Yamamoto 2012 examines the importance of supplication prayers and eulogies in Lama Zhang's biographical tradition.

87. Geary 1994, 17.
88. Geary 1994, 18.
89. Ibid.
90. Geary 1994, 23.
91. Lifshitz 1994, 95.
92. Geary 1994, 27.
93. Reynolds and Capps 1976, 30.
94. Heffernan 1988, 30.
95. See Gyatso 1998.
96. Jorge Luis Borges, "Kafka and His Precursors," in *Selected Non-Fictions: Volume 3* (New York: Penguin, 1999), 365.
97. TTC, 911: *gtso bo'am mchog ste gzhan thar lam du khrid mkhan gyi ded dpon lta bu yin pas na rje dang/ sgo gsum gyi mi dge bas gtan nas ma gos pas na btsun pa zer/.*
98. Smith 2001, 288n181.
99. See publication data under Zhi byed ri pa in the bibliography.
100. See Dpal brtsegs Bod yig dpe rnying zhib 'jug khang JMS and LMS.

1. EARLIEST SOURCES: A BIOGRAPHICAL BIRTH

1. This is the chapter titled: *bde mchog snyan brgyud dang ras chung snyan brgyud kyi skabs.* See BA, vol. 1, 511–38, Roerich 1949, 427–51. This chapter falls between the biographies of Mar pa and Sgam po pa. On 'Gos Lotsāwa's confusion in naming these two aural transmission lines, see Torricelli 2000, 361n10.

2. See his autobiography entitled *Nyid kyi rnam thar shes rab grub pa ma* (Zhang g.yu brag pa brtson 'grus grags pa'i gsung 'bum [Kathmandu: Sherab Gyaltsen, 2004], vol. ka, 316–66) describing his life as dictated to the disciple Shes rab grub pa. The figure of Lama Zhang and his literary corpus has recently been studied in Yamamoto 2012.

3. Gyatso 1998, 101.

4. Gtsang smyon Heruka records, however, that Mi la ras pa recited the life story of his guru Mar pa to several disciples, who later served as the principal sources for the Gtsang smyon's *Life of Mar pa.* See note 17 below.

5. Several sources, however, claim otherwise. First, the tradition of *The Black Treasury* (discussed in chapter 3) preserves a record stating that Mi la ras pa wrote short diary notes that were left in his retreat locations. Second, Gtsang smyong Heruka's teacher Sha ra rab 'byams Sangs rgyas seng ge is said to have used a copy of Mi la's handwritten notes (*zin bris*) on instructions to Nāropa's yogic practices. See chapter 4.

6. See Ricard 1994. In his introduction, Zhabs dkar himself describes how he originally kept diary notes recording his daily activities, which he passed on to a close disciple. Later, he dictated a detailed account of his life story to a group of pupils who set some of what they heard in writing. Finally, at the repeated insistence of his followers, Zhabs dkar himself felt "inclined to write down the events of my life from my birth until the present" (7).

7. BCO, 13a; BCN, 15b. Cf. Gtsang smyon's version in DJ, 114.18. *kye ma kye ma kyi hud kyi hud ang/ 'khor ba'i chos la blo gtad byas pa rnams/ bsams shing bsams shing yi mug yang yang ldang/ spyad cing spyad cing sdug bsngal gting nas 'khrungs/ bskor zhing bskor zhing 'khor ba'i gting la 'phen/.*

8. BCO, 13b; BCN, 16a. Cf. DJ, 112.1. *kye ma 'khor ba'i chos la snying po med/ mi rtag mi rtag snying po med/ 'gyur zhing 'gyur zhing snying po med/ mi nges mi nges snying po med/*

9. Stein 1979, 4.

10. Sgam po pa, MMN, 25. *da lta su yin cha yod dam/ da lta su yin ma shes na/ nga la mi la rnal 'byor yin/.*

11. Gtsang smyon also includes this song with minor variations. Cf. NG, 324ff; C, 160.

12. BCO, 92a.4; BCN, 121b.5. *'o na khye'u chung bzhin legs po// khyod rtogs 'dod can de tshur la nyon// mi nga ngo khyod kyi <kyis> mi shes na// nga rang mi la ras pa yin// lte ba gung thang smad du bcad// slob gnyer dbus gtsang gnyis na byas// pha gyer ston dang ngag mis dbu mdzad pa'i// rong ston lha rga yan chad kyi// drin can bla ma bcu tsam yod// chos ni rgyud sems mngon gyur nyan// khong lta dgongs phugs nas mkhyen pa mthong// khyad par lha rje gnub chung la// drags sngags gza' gdong dmar nag zhus// khong phrin las bsgrubs pa bzhed lags kyang// ngad rung spros pa cung ma chod// rje na ro dang mi tri'i byin brlabs zhugs/ sems chos nyid ma dang ngo sprod byas// lus rten 'brel gnad du bsnun ba cig// lho bro bo lung na bzhugs so skad// pha lo ts.tsha'i snyan pa rgyang nas grags// mtshan thos pa tsam gyis ba spu g.yo// lam dka' ba spyad de spyan mngar mchis// zhal mthong ba tsam gyis snang ba 'gyur// khong tshe rabs kyi bla ma yin bar nges// rje 'gran gyi do med lho brag pa// sku drin can gyis <gyi> rje btsun la// zang zing dngos po bdag la med// lus ngag go zhags rtogs <tog> rdul du brlag// rgyud zab mo dgus pa rdo rje thob// khyad par na ro'i thabs lam zhus// dpal byin brlabs can gyi bde mchog la// rmi lam dbang bzhi rdzogs par zhus// shos phyag rgya chen po'i ngo sprod byas// don gnyug ma'i sems kyi ngo bo mthong// bzhi chos nyid spros dang bral bar rtogs// spyir snyan rgyud chu bo rnam bzhi la// gdam ngag che dgu spus thus byas// gnang zab dgu cud kyi yang snying phyung// bsgom ni rtsa rlung thig le bsgom// don rlung sems gnyis la rang dbang thob// nga de phyir nam mkha' rnal 'byor pa// nad 'du ba rnam bzhi dbyings su 'dres// 'byung ba chu la nyam nga med// nga bsgoms sa rgyal gyi rtsibs ri yin// gdugs da nang gung thang stod nas 'ongs// do nub gar 'gro nges pa med// nga rnal 'byor gyi byung tshul de ltar lags// bu khye'u chung skyid do gang bder bzhud//.*

13. BCO, 182a; BCN, 229b. Cf. DJ, 170.21; Quintman 2010, 187. *bdag gi zhal mthong gsung thos dang// rnam thar yid la dran pa dang// mtshan nam thar thar thos tshad dang// mngon dga'i zhing du mjal bar shog// gang zhig bdag gi rnam thar la// spyod cing sgrub pa byed pa dang// 'bri zhing 'chad nyan byed pa dang// rnam thar tshul bzhin skyong rnams dang// mngon dga'i zhing du mjal bar shog// . . . chos phyir dka' thub spyod pa la// bsod nams dpag tu med pa yod// de la 'jug cing bskul ba la// bka' drin dpag tu med pa yod// mi kho bo'i rnam thar thos pa la// byin rlabs dpag tu med pa yod// dpag med gsum gyi byin rlabs kyis// thos pa tsam gyis grol gyur nas// bsams pa tsam gyis 'grub par shog/.*

14. I use the word "cult" here in its literal sense, emphasizing its Latin roots meaning "1. Worship; reverential homage rendered to a divine being. 2. A system of religious worship, esp. as expressed in ceremonies, ritual, etc. 3. Devotion or homage paid to a person or thing" (*Shorter Oxford English Dictionary*).

15. Heffernan 1988, 35.

16. His name is alternately recorded as Ngam rdzong and the Sanskritized Ngan rdzong bo dhi rā dza; he is also known as Ngan rdzong ston pa (the teacher) to indicate his

great intellect and Ngan rdzong ras pa to demark his status as a follower of Mi la ras pa's yogic path.

17. Ngan rdzong was instrumental in the initial recording of the life of his spiritual grandfather, Mar pa Chos kyi blo gros. The colophon to Gtsang smyon Heruka's early sixteenth-century publication of Mar pa's *rnam thar* states: "Thus, this *Life of Rje btsun Mar ston Chos kyi blo gros, Meaningful to Behold* was transmitted orally and in detail by Rje btsun Mi la and Mar pa mgo legs to Ngan rdzong ston pa. Rje btsun Mi la also gave it to Ras chung. Ras chung pa and Ngan rdzong ston pa Byang chub rgyal po discussed it and the original biography they compiled remains here as the principal text" (*De ltar rje btsun mar ston chos kyi blo gros kyi rnam par thar pa mthong ba don ldan 'di nyid/ rje btsun mi la dang/ mar pa mgo legs gnyis kyis/ ngan rdzong ston pa la zhib rgyas zhal nas snyang du brgyud pa dang/ rje btsun mi la ras chun ba la yang gnang bas/ ras chung pa dang ngan rdzong ston pa byang chub rgyal po gnyis bka' bgros nas bsgrigs pa'i rnam thar phyi mo'i gtso bor bzhugs pa las/*). Cf. Nālandā Translation Committee 1986, 204.

    Ngan rdzong also played a role in recording the life of at least one of Mi la ras pa's senior disciples, the female meditator Sa le 'od. The colophon to the chapter on her meeting with Mi la from Gtsang smyon's version of the *mgur 'bum* states: "Sa le 'od meditated without leaving mountain retreat and thereby became one of the Rje btsun's four female disciples, a self-liberated yoginī benefiting both the teachings and beings. Her story was recorded by Ngan rdzong ston pa Byang chub rgyal po through his indelible memory" (NG, 577). Chang's translation (420) leaves out mention of the author's memory, discussed below.

18. The biography is preserved as the first text in the Ngan rdzong's collected works. See Dam pa ras can, NDN. *rje dam pa ras chen gyis mdzad pa la/ rnal sbyor <'byor> rgod tshang pas cung zad rgyan par bkod pa'o/* (17). Structurally, the biography is divided into two main sections: the history of his practicing austerities together with an account of his family line; and receiving blessings and the dawning of realization. *rigs dang 'brel ba dka' ba spyod pa'i lo rgyus dang/ byin rlabs zhugs zhing rtogs pa shar ba'i yon tan gnyis . . . /* (2–3). This will become an important clue in the following chapter's discussion of Mi la ras pa's early biographical compendia.

    The name Dam pa ras can is not listed as Ngan rdzong's disciple in either the BA (which mentions only Gung thang ras pa and Gnyal pa Gsung bcad pa) or the LRC (which mentions only Ras pa Seng ge grags pa and Lho brag Mi bskyod rdo rje, who composed a *yig cha* for Ngan rdzong's *snyan brgyud*). However, one Dam pa ras chen is mentioned as the direct recipient of Ngan rdzong's aural transmission lineage in Gtsang smyon Heruka's *Bde mchog mkha' 'gro snyan rgyud kyi bzhung 'brel sa bcad dang sbrags pa* (*Gzhung 'brel nor bu skor gsum*), where the transmission succession runs from Mi la ras pa through the early 'Brug pa masters: *rje btsun nas ngan rdzong ston pa byang chub rgyal po/ dam pa ras chen/ gling ras/ rgya ras/ dbon ras pa/ rgod tshang pa/. . . .* See Gtsang smyon Heruka, BMMG, vol. 1, 91–93; vol. 2, 167–69. It seems reasonable to place Dam pa ras chen's birth in the late eleventh or, more likely, the first decades of the twelfth century. Ngan rdzong's biography, therefore, would have been written by the late 1100s.

19. According to 'Gos Lotsawa, he was born in Mdo khra lcim lung. BA, 555; Cf. Roerich 1949, 449. The LRC has Lcim lung, in Ding ri'i mgo. The BC also uses the spelling Lcim lung.

20. Tshe dbang rgyal, LRC, 151. Mar pa mgo yag was himself a disciple of Mi la's guru Mar pa, from whom he received the aural transmissions (LRC, 71). The *snyan rgyud/ brgyud* is discussed below, but here, this indicates that Ngan rdzong was already introduced to the teachings of Mi la ras pa's lineage prior to his meeting with the yogin.

21. Dam pa ras chen, NDN, 4ff.

22. In Gtsang smyon Heruka's account, the story appears as an addendum to the chapter on the "Song of the Staff" (NG, 353; C, 190). The chapter begins with a separate account in which Mi la ras pa meets a wealthy farmer of Lcim lung named Byang chub 'bar, to whom he sings the famed "Song of the Staff." After leaving the farmer, he meets his future disciple Ngan rdzong who, in contrast to the original account, initially appears arrogant and condescending. The source for the first story of Gtsang smyon's chapter is found in Mi la ras pa's early biographical compendia (BCN, 144a.1; BCO, 108a.3; DNM-Lhasa, 183a.1; DNM-I, 192.7; DNM-S, 120.5), where the farmer is, somewhat confusingly, also given the clan name Ngan rdzong. This serves as a good example of how Gtsang smyon Heruka formed a single chapter using narrative elements from various sources; in this case, most likely combining them to clarify any confusion about the two individuals named Ngan rdzong. This editorial "cut and paste" tactic was widespread among Mi la ras pa's biographical literature, and will be examined in following chapters.

23. Dam pa ras chen, NDN, 8.

24. Dam pa ras chen, NDN, 2. *dang por sbyangs pa mthar phyir <phyin> mkhas pa'i gtso/ der rjes sgom pa mthar phyin grub pa'i gtso/ mkhas grub mi rjed gzungs thob bo ji'i mtshan/ ngan rdzong ston pa'i zhabs la gus phyag 'tshal/.*

25. Dam pa ras chen, NDN, 15.4. *snang ba dbang du 'dus nas gdul nas gdul bya phrin las bsam gyi mi khyab pa mdzad/ mi rjed pa'i gzungs thob nas/ rje btsun chen po mi la ras pa'i gsung sgros bka'i bsdu ba mdzad pas sems can la phan btags/.* The term used to describe Ngan rdzong's abilities (*mi brjed pa'i gzung*), literally "the memory (or retention) that does not forget," is here rendered as "indelible memory." The Tibetan *gzung*—defined as "retaining the words and the meaning of Dharma without forgetting them" (TTC, *chos kyi tshig don mi brjed par 'dzin pa*)—was also used by Tibetan translators to render the Sanskrit *dhāraṇī*. The word is frequently understood as referring to a kind of magic formula, ranging in length from a single syllable to the entire Sanskrit alphabet, and often devoid of any clear semantic meaning. In that context, a *dhāraṇī* is believed to capture and retain the essence of an element of the Buddhist teaching or a text describing it, a function illustrated by the term's foundation in the verbal root "to hold" (*dhṛ*). *Dhāraṇīs* are also believed to serve as a form of protection, in which case they may be compared with the *paritta* of the Pāli canon, although they are most frequently discussed in relation to mantra, found in the literature of both the sūtras and the tantras. For a discussion of the literature pertaining to *dhāraṇī* and mantra, and the relationships between the two, see Gyatso 1992, 198n11.

In a broader sense, however, the term *dhāraṇī* refers to a form of memory. According to the *Akṣayamatinirdeśa*,

> *Dhāraṇī* is to keep, retain in memory and not forget, to truly retain by remembrance the eighty-four thousand multitudes of religion. . . . Again, *dhāraṇī* is that by which one retains the sayings of all the bodhisattvas, pratyekabuddhas,

śrāvakas and all living beings, that by which one retains all good sayings without remainder. (cited in Braarvig 1985, 18)

The *Bodhisattvabhūmi* classifies four types of *dhāraṇī*: dharma *dhāraṇī*, meaning *dhāraṇī* (*arthadhāraṇī*), mantra *dhāraṇī*, and forbearance *dhāraṇī* (*kṣāntidhāraṇī*) (cited in Braarvig 1985, 19–20). Of these, the first refers to the mnemic ability to retain in memory the formulation of oral or written Dharma, such as a sermon or a book, for an infinite period of time. The second category identifies the ability to retain the meaning of those teachings, not just the syntactic formation of their words. Mantra *dhāraṇī* refers to the verbal formula employed by a bodhisattva for the benefit of beings; it is both the formula retained in the mind and the efficacy retained by the formula. Forbearance *dhāraṇī* refers to the bodhisattva's realization, gained through the use of a *dhāraṇī* formula, that the ultimate nature lies beyond verbal expressions. Thus, if in this context *dhāraṇī* might be translated as "the power of retaining in memory . . . through memory of extraordinary power," the term describes both the faculty of memory and the remembrance itself.

26. TTC, s.v. "*snyan brgyud*." These two terms are occasionally used interchangeably.

27. The text, translated by Mar pa together with Nāropa, is preserved in the Bstan 'gyur, Toh. 2338. See Torricelli 1998 for a study and critical edition.

28. An overview of this system is provided in Zhang Lotsāwa, TY, and is further discussed in Torricelli 2001 and Serensi 2004, 2011a. On the content and systematization of the *snyan rgyud/brgyud*, see also Torricelli 2000. For a list of translations of related *snyan rgyud* texts preserved in the Tibetan canon, see Roberts 2001, appendix B.

29. For references to biographical literature in which these instructions appear, see Torricelli and Naga 1995, 74n62. The nine verses are frequently presented as:

    1. Maturation and liberation: sever mind's tangled knots (*smin grol sems kyi rgya mdud bshig*)
    2. Commitments: look into your own mind, a mirror (*dam tshig rang sems me long ltos*)
    3. Channels and their energies: animate the networks and centers (*rtsa rlung drwa mig 'khor lo bskor*)
    4. Great bliss: keep the precious gem of speech (*bde chen gsung gi rin chen zung*)
    5. Pristine cognition: look with the lamp of primordial awareness (*rig pa ye shes sgron me ltos*)
    6. Self-liberation: attend to the Great Seal (*rang grol phyag rgya chen po ltos*)
    7. Sacramental substance: bask in realization's sun (*dam rdzas rtogs pa'i nyi ma lde*)
    8. Action: strike the water with a sword (*spyod pa chu la ral gri rgyob*)
    9. Equal taste: gaze into the mirror of externals (*ro snyoms phyi'i me long ltos*)

30. A brief account of Mi la ras pa's conferral of the *snyan brgyud yid bzhin nor bu* upon his close disciples is recounted in the chapter of the *Songs* entitled "Empowerment and Consecration" (NG, 700–3; C, 549–51). Here both Ras chung pa and Ngan rdzong are mentioned by name. According to this account, Mi la ras pa has a vision of Vajrayoginī, who grants him permission to waive the command-seal prohibiting him from passing the *snyan brgyud* instructions to more than a single disciple. The mechanics and historical context of the *chig brgyud* ("single transmission") is discussed in Sernesi 2004. At least one text of the *Ras chung snyan brgyud* cycle implicitly describes this scene as beginning the *snyan brgyud*'s literary tradition, as

opposed to its strictly oral, unwritten (*yi ge med par*) tradition. See *Dpal bde mchog snyan brgyud las bum dbang dang 'brel ba'i nyams len thun mong yid bzhin nor bu'i khrid yig rje mi las mdzad pa* in DND, vol. 5, 263–84. 'Jam mgon kong sprul Blo gros mtha' yas also identifies an aural transmission of instructions on the Nā ro chos drug stemming from Zhi ba 'od, one of Mi la's close disciples who also collaborated with Ngan rdzong in his biographical writings regarding their guru.

31. BA, 524; Cf. Roerich 1949, 437.

32. Dam pa ras chen, NDN, 8. The biography, however, continues, "Some say that Rje btsun Ras chung pa was given each [of the instructions], while others say that he was not given them." This statement is repeated in the *Blue Annals*. See Roerich 1949, 450. *khyad par snyan rgyud yid bzhin nor bu'i gdam pa 'di nga ma yin pa bzhan su la yang ma gnang ba yin/ rje btsun ras chung pa la res gnang ba skad kyang gsung/ res ma gnang ba skad kyang gsung gin gda' gsung ngo/.*

33. Dam pa ras chen, NDN, 16. *gzhan la ma grags pa'i khyad chos snyan rgyud yis bzhin nor bu'i gdams ngag rnams kyang rje btsun chen po'i gsung las phri bsnan med par zin bris mdzad pas/ ngan rdzong snyan rgyud zhes yongs su grags/.*

   In his biography of Ras chung pa, Rgod tshang ras pa offers a different solution to the disputed *snyan brgyud* lineage, in which Ras chung pa receives the complete transmission:

   > [Mi-la ras-pa] thought that when the appointed time came, he would give to Dwags-po-rin-po-che the abridged instructions on the major points . . . ; to the Revered Ngam-rdzong-pa an intermediate method; to the Revered Ras-chung-pa the complete [transmission] without exceptions. (Sernesi 2004, 259)

34. NG, 812; C, 672. *sras nams kyis mi brjed pa'i gzungs su bzung zhing yi ger bkod pa . . . /.*

35. Gtsang smyon, however, rearranged the original order of these chapters/colophons.

36. Chang (688) described the text in relation to these chapters as revealing an "outstanding difference, flavor, and superior quality." See van Tuyl 1972; 1974; 1975 for detailed analyses of these chapters, their content, and their literary style, where he notes their influence by early Bon po themes and terminology. Although he correctly deduced, without access to the early literature, that these chapters formed some of the earliest biographical writings in the tradition, his assumption that they were first incorporated into the *Collected Songs* by Gtsang smyon Heruka has now been disproved since they appear in all of the early biographical compendia, including the earliest version, *The Twelve Great Disciples*.

37. These colophons, recorded by Gtsang smyon Heruka and translated in Chang 1962, follow those in *The Twelve Great Disciples* with some emendations, although Chang occasionally misses the intended meaning.

38. van Tuyl 1974, 22.

39. BCN, 162a.4; BCO, 129b.6. Cf. NG, 515; C, 353.

40. *tshe ring ma'i chos skor rnams la 'chad pa po dpal bzhad pa rdo rje'i bka' rgya/ zhu ba po mkha' 'gro mched lnga'i gsang ba'i rgya/ sdud pa po a tsa rya bo dhi rā dza dang/ ras pa zhi ba 'od gnyis kyi dam tshig gi rgya ste/ . . .* (NG, 521; C, 361). Chang misses the intended meaning, translating: "The story of the Lady of Long Life and Milarepa, including several preachings of Mila and the requests of the five Dakinis, was compiled and preserved by Ahtsarya Bodhi Radsa and Repa Shiwa Aui."

41. 'Jam mgon kong sprul, DND, vol. 5, 425–42.

42. Several texts list Sgam po pa among a group of disciples who entered Mi la ras pa's tutelage late in the yogin's life. The *Twelve Great Disciples* (BCO, 188b; BCN, 243b), for example, uses the heading "students who [met Mi la] on the verge of his passing" (*sku gzhegs kha'i slob ma*); the *Lho rong chos 'byung* (107) has "the six teachers who were born during [Mi la's] old age" (*sku bgres khar 'khrungs pa'i ston pa drug*).

    For accounts of Sgam po pa's life and works, see Stewart 1995 and Sherpa 2004. An account of Sgam po pa's meeting with Mi la ras pa, from Mi la's biographical tradition, is translated in C, 463–97. Ulrich T. Kragh is reportedly working on a comprehensive study of Sgam po pa's writings.

43. Padma dkar po, KSY, 311. *gzhan gyis byas nges pa 'dir bcug pa sogs snang bas logs su dpyad rgyur bzhag/.*

44. Tibetan text cited in Jackson 1994, 10n17. *'on kyang 'di dag gi bka' 'bum rnams su slob ma mkhas pa dang mi mkhas pa du mas zin bris nyag nyog mang po bcug 'dug pa la yid brtan mi snang ngo//.*

45. Jackson 1990b, 2.

46. Bsod nams lhun grub also authored Sgam po pa's extensive biography, printed at Dwags lha sgam po (called Ri bo shanti in the text) and included in most editions of the *Collected Works.*

47. This accords with several other sections in the *Collected Works*, which contain records of question-and-answer (*zhu lan*) sessions between Sgam po pa and his principal disciples, including Dus gsum mkhyen pa, Phag mo gru pa, and Dwags po sgom tshul. The former contains Sgam po pa's own autobiographical sketches. See Sherpa 2004.

48. These divisions are not explicitly marked in the text, although they are strongly suggested by context and abrupt changes in narrative flow.

49. Sgam po pa, MMN 1974, 30.

50. The chapel adjacent to Mi la ras pa's tower (Sras mkhar dgu thog) in Lho brag has enshrined as one of its relics a large stone butter lamp, described as the one from this story.

51. Lord 1960, 124.

52. See Roberts 2007, 50 for a note correcting the dates of early members of this transmission lineage.

53. Ibid.

54. Byang chub bzang po, RMN, 97. *dang po rigs dang 'grel <'brel> ba dka' ba spyad pa'i yon tan dang/ ting nge 'dzin dang 'bral <'brel> ba nyams su myong pa'i yon tan/.*

55. Zhang Lotsāwa was an important figure in the early aural transmission stemming from Ras chung pa. He is named as the author of numerous texts in Byang chub bzang po's *yig cha* collection, including a biography of his guru (and Ras chung pa's direct disciple) Khyung tshang pa Ye shes bla ma. In contrast to earlier biographies in the series, this attribution seems plausible given that Zhang Lotsāwa's name is attributed to at least a dozen texts in the collection, and he may have formed an earlier *snyan brgyud* compilation around which Byang chub bzang po constructed his work. On his life, see Roerich 1949, 445–48. In his study of Mi la ras pa's life, Zhi byed ri pa repeatedly cites a Mi la *rnam thar* by Zhang Lotsāwa as one of his main sources, although this text has not yet come to light.

56. Zhang Lotsāwa, TY, 2. *rgyud pa'i bka' ma chad pa las byung ba ni/ rnam thar gyi rim pa ye shes mkha' 'gro nas rtsa ba' bla ma'i bar du'o/.* Torricelli 2001 discusses this short work in detail.

57. Gtsang smyon Heruka, DKN, 19. *slob mas bla ma'i rnam thar yon tan ma thos shing ma mthong na/ brtan pa la 'jug pa dang zhugs nas smin grol gyi go 'phangs mi thob pas/ brgyud pa dang gdams ngag la yid ched shing khungs btsun pa'i 'du shes skye pa dang/ rgyud byin gyis brlabs pas slob ma'i mtshan nyid rnams brtsol med du rgyud la skye bar bya ba'i phyir/ bla ma brgyud pa'i rnam par thar pa rags mdo tsam zhig brjod par bya'o/*

58. Nālandā Translation Committee 1980, 329. This note is particularly ironic since the passage in question is an extensive quotation from an early biographical compendium, discussed in chapter 3.

59. Urubshurow 1984, 16.

60. Tiso 1989, 247.

61. Kunga and Cutillio 1991, xvi.

62. A rare copy of the original print in the Royal Archives of Nepal indicates the print was completed by Lha btsun Rin chen rnam rgyal at Brag dkar rta so in 1550. The brief colophon reads: *nam mo gu ru/ rje btsun chen po mi la ras pa'i mgur ma/ rnam mgur par ma na cher mi bzhugs pa'i/ mgur ma 'ga' yar 'di nyid kyis mgo bzham 'brig par/ lha'i btsun pa rin chen rnam rgyal gyis/ lcags pho khyi'i lo'i sbyar zlar ba'i yar tshes bzang po la/ gnas chen brag dkar rta sor par du sgrubs pa'i dge bas/ pha ma'i gtso byas 'gro kun gyis/ gdong na gnas pa'i sku gsum mngon gyur shog/ e vam// dge'o//.* See Lha btsun Rin chen rnam rgyal, DJG, in the bibliography.

    The work is clearly a synthetic text composed of materials assembled from various sources, some of which appear to have been known to Gtsang smyon Heruka, left out of his publications. The work begins with a brief overview of the life story, followed by the so-called "six vajra songs" (*rdo rje mgur drug*). The remainder contains a variety of songs, some with independent introductions and minicolophons, although most contain very little prose narrative, unlike the chapters of Gtsang smyon Heruka's standard versions. The final section describing Mi la's death is copied verbatim from Gtsang smyon's *Life*. Sections of the text have been translated into English in Kunga and Cutillo 1978, 1986. For a translation of the six vajra songs and a discussion of their doctrinal background, see Sernesi 2004.

2. PROTO-LIVES: FORMATIONS OF A SKELETAL BIOGRAPHY

1. BA, 828. Cf. Roerich 1949, 707. *phag mo grur gcen po'i rgyags skyel du byon pas/ rje btsun mi la'i rnam thar gsung ba dang thub/ de 'dra ba cig ngas kyang bya snyam nas chos grwa der mgo lcogs lan gsum byas/.* Rgyal tsha was at Phag mo gru sometime between his twenty-fifth and fifty-fourth years (BA, 828; Roerich 1949, 707. Cf. MD, 406–7). If Kun ldan made this journey when he was eighteen, Rgyal tsha would have been forty-seven; this would have taken place in 1165, toward the end of Phag mo gru pa's life.

    Rgyal tsha Rin chen mgon was also the founder of the monastery at Khro phu. Kun ldan ras pa likewise served as a disciple of Phag mo gru pa and later assumed great responsibilities at his guru's monastery, constructing a shrine hall (*gtsug lag khang*) and spending time in a retreat cell there. See MD, 51.

2. See Petech 1978; Vitali 1996, 372ff.

3. Sgam po pa founded a seat at Dwags lha sgam po in 1121; Lama Zhang established a center for the Tshal pa bka' brgyud, Tshal gung thang, around 1175. Phag mo gru pa laid the foundations for Gdan sa mthil in 1158. These were followed by 'Bri gung (1179), Stag lung (1180), and Mtshur phu (1189) monasteries.

4. van der Kuijp 1996, 46.

5. See Smith 1970.

6. It should be noted, however, that several examples of Mi la ras pa's instructions were later recorded outside biographical sources, as part of the aural transmission literature. See, for example, the *snyan brgyud* collections codified by Byang chub bzang po (DKN, vol. 1, 371–73; vol. 2, 467–69, 393–401, 481–97), Padma dkar po (DNK, vol. 1, 449–53), and 'Jam mgon kong sprul (DND, vol. 5, 66–67, 109–20, 120–21, 263–84, 286–317, 344–61).

7. The literature on these traditions is extensive. See, for example, Kapstein 2006; Guenther 1969, 1993; R. Jackson 1996, 2004; Kvaerne 1977; Schaeffer 2005; Templeman 1994. Beginning with the early twentieth-century discovery of seminal *dohā* and *caryā* texts in the Nepalese Royal Archives by Hariprasad Sastri, Bengali scholars have also made pioneering contributions to the study of these traditions; see, among others, Bagchi (1934, 1938, 1946, 1956) and Shahidullah (1928, 1940, 1960).

8. R. Jackson 1996, 372.

9. R. Jackson 1996, 373.

10. R. Jackson 1996, 373.

11. The word *'bum* in the second term is used figuratively, its implication being that all extant or relevant materials have been included. This is true also for the terms *bka' 'bum* ("one hundred thousand pronouncements") and *gsung 'bum* ("one hundred thousand teachings"), which generally refer to an author's oeuvre and are often rendered "collected works." Traditional sources have enumerated and classified Mi la ras pa's songs in several different ways. First, Lha btsun Rin chen rnam rgyal, Gtsang smyon's disciple and publisher of the *Miscellaneous Songs*, states in the beginning of that work:

    > [Mi la ras pa] perfected the practice of *samādhi* one-pointedly and sang 2,800 songs born of his experience and realization headed by 18, 21, or 40 major song cycles. Two thousand of these are said to have been carried away by ḍākinīs and no longer exist in the human realm. To this day, yogins recite the remaining 800 and make use of them in their practice.

    (DJGR, 3, *ting nge 'dzin gyi sgrub pa rtse gcig tu mthar phyin te nyams dang rtogs pa 'khrungs pa'i mgur ma skor tsho chen po bco brgyad dam/ nyer gcig gam/ bzhi bcu rtsa lngas thog drangs pa'i nyis stong brgyad brgya gsungs na'ang/ nyis stong po de mkha' 'gro ma rnams kyis khyer nas mi yul na med ces grags/ brgyad brgya po de da lta rnal 'byor pa rnams kyis gsung 'don dang nyams len mdzad pa'i nang nas/*) Cf. Kunga and Cutillio 1978, 32.

    An anonymous manual of liturgical procedures (*khog dbubs*) to the *Ocean of Kagyu Songs* (*Bka' brgyud mgur mtsho*), a well-known collection of spiritual songs by Bka' brgyud masters written circa 1542 by the Eighth Karmapa, Mi skyod rdo rje (1507–54), provides another enumeration. The text (*Bka' brgyud mgur mtsho'i go don khog dbubs spyi chings rnam par bshad pa skal bzang yid kyi ngal so*), published in the Rumtek edition as an appendix to the main work, states: "It is said that the great Rje btsun Mi la sang sixteen thousand great songs, ten thousand of which were taken to Akaniṣṭa by ḍākinīs; six thousand were left for the benefit of future generations of disciples in his lineage." (6a, rje btsun chen po mi las mgur chen khri tsho gcig dang drug stong gsungs pa'i khri phrag gcig po mkha' 'gros 'og min du spyan drangs/ stong tsho drug phyi rabs slob brgyud kyi don du bzhags skad na/) See also Nālandā Translation Committee 1980, 10.

After classifying Mi la ras pa's songs into topical cycles, Zhi byed ri pa states, "In short, he is famed to have sung a great 111,108 [songs], which are made clear in the histories of Lords Khyung tshang pa and Mnga' ris Zhang Lotsāwa. However, I, Zhi bye ri khrod pa, have seen only some ten thousand." (NDO, 25, mdor na 'bum che gcig dang khri tsho gcig dang/ stong tsho cig dang brgya rtsa brgyad gsungs par grags te/ rje khyung tshag <tshang> pa dang mnga' ris zhang lo ts.tsha ba'i lo rgyus la gsal zhing nga zhi byed ri khrod pas kyang/ khri tsho gcig tsam mthong lags so/)

In his historical survey of Tibetan song (mgur glu), modern Tibetan author Don grub rgyal (1953–85) notes that Gtsang smyon's standard version of the Collected Songs records 384 songs of varying length, 62 of which were sung by nonhumans, ḍākinīs, disciples, and so forth, leaving 322 attributed to Mi la ras pa himself. See Don grub rgyal, BGL, 459.

12. It is, perhaps, ironic that a modern Chinese reprint of Gtsang smyon's standard works presents his two texts in their earlier, conjoined format under the title The Life and Songs of Mi la ras pa (Mi la ras pa'i rnam mgur). The xylographic edition carved and printed in the famous Derge publishing house apparently served as a model for this. See the introduction to NG.

13. Heffernan 1988, 55.

14. Laurie Aikman, "Religious Biography," in Encyclopedia of Life Writing: Autobiographical and Biographical Forms, ed. Margaretta Jolly (London: Fitzroy Dearborn Publishers, 2001), 741. This point is emphasized by Nirmala S. Salgado's "Buddhism and Life Writing" in the same publication: "Life writing in Buddhist culture is not conceived on the basis of the individual in the Western sense, for an individual life is always regarded as one of many lives and is usually connected to a probable past life . . . as well as a future life" (155). The fallacy of this statement is made painfully clear in Gtsang smyon's standard biography, which explicitly condemns the view of Mi la ras pa as an emanation or reincarnation.

15. Heffernan 1988, 30.

16. Brooks 1984, xx. The former is a classical definition after Aristotle; the latter is Brooks' own.

17. Janet Gyatso (1998) has argued extensively and persuasively for an individuality of lives represented in (at least some) Tibetan autobiography. Here, I am thinking particularly of her use of Charles Taylor's work, which asserts that "an emphasis upon ordinary, everyday details in autobiography can indicate an individualistic self-conception, whereas life stories that fixate on the ideal norm would relate details only if they have didactic value." See Gyatso 1998, 112; Taylor 1989.

18. Pertinent texts include: Bla ma mi la ras chen gyi rnam thar lags pa gda'o, by Mar pa's disciple Rngog gzhung Chos kyi rdo rje (1023–90), DK, 1567 (phyi ra 190, #017697, 14 folios, 19 x 11 cm.); and Dpal ldan mi la bzhad pa'i rnam par thar pa, by the the first Karma pa's disciple Sangs rgyas ras chen dpal grags (1148–1218), DK, 1503 (phyi ra 2, #016937, 16 folios, 29 x 8 cm.)

19. Zhi byed ri pa, NDO, 41. *spyir mid la ras chen gyi rnam thar la mdzad pa mi cig pa brgya dang nyi shu rtsa bdun tsam mthong ba dang/ khyad par du rje khyung tshang ba dznya na gu ru dang/ lnga rig zhes bya'i gnas la ma rmongs pa/ chos rje zhang lo tshā ba grub pa dpal zang po dang/ de rnams kyi gsung gros la gzhi blangs nas byas pa lags cing/*. For a detailed study of this text and its author, see Quintman 2012, and Childs and Quintman 2012.

20. On his life, see Roerich 1949, 441–43.

21. Roerich 1949, 435.

22. I have made use of two editions of the *Collected Works*: 1972 and 2004. The latter was redacted from numerous editions, including several in the microfilm collection of the Nepal-German Manuscript Preservation Project in Kathmandu. For a brief overview of Lama Zhang's life and discussion of his religious writings, see Jackson 1990 and Martin 1992 and 2001, the latter of which also contains a useful bibliographical essay. Lama Zhang's life and activities have recently been examined in greater detail in Sørensen and Hazod 2007 and Yamamoto 2012. Toward the end of his life, Lama Zhang established the monastery of Tshal Gung thang, outside Lhasa. As will be discussed in the next chapter, this was later the site for the production of an influential, although as yet undiscovered, Collected Songs of Mi la ras pa. References are generally to the 2004 edition unless noted.

23. See Schaeffer 2000.

24. It is interesting to note that in the process of preparing the 2004 publication of the Tibetan text, editors changed the sentence "Since [in their family], there were none but father and son" (*yab sras gnyis las med pa pa la/*) to instead read "there were none but *mother* and son" (46), bringing the narrative in line with the later, accepted version. The impulse to read Mi la's early biographical works "under the influence" of Gtsang smyon's standard version remains strong, even among learned Tibetan editors and scholars.

25. Roberts (2007, 70) lists two other "incidents that reveal flaws or limitations in Mi-la Ras-pa" missing in Lama Zhang's text, episodes he feels were cut in order to cover up Mi la's purported inadequacies. Both occur in the proto-Songs section: mistaking the calls of the search party for the cries of animals (Sgam po pa §2); and being unaware of the miraculous manifestations that others perceive on seeing him (Sgam po pa §9). While Lama Zhang does indeed alter these accounts, I read them in their original context not as recording flaws or limitations, but as providing dramatic tension (in the first case) and as a karmic explanation for the appearance of miraculous deeds (in the second). Moreover, in the second story, only the additional explanation recording a conversation between Sgam po pa and his guru was removed, not the incident itself. Both of these episodes are retained in the biography by Don mo ri pa, analyzed in the next section, so it seems doubtful that their original Tibetan audiences read them as describing inherent flaws or inadequacies, but rather as describing the difficulties or "messiness" of sustained spiritual practice.

26. Zhang, LMN, 148. *de ltar mang yul gyi ri yun ring du bzhugs/.*

27. Zhang, LMN, 148. *ri khrod la sgom pa yan chad kyis lo dgu'i bar du ting nge 'dzin ye ma skyes nas/ thugs shin tu mug par byung ste/ dgon pa zhig tu bsdad nas nga'i lus 'di 'dir bskams nas shi bar gyur kyang/ ting nge 'dzin ma skyes kyi bar du stan 'di las mi 'gul bar bya'o snyam nas/.*

28. Literally "beat a small drum" (*te te brdungs*). The TTC glosses *te te* with *'rnga chung/ sems dga' nas te te rdung bzhin 'khrab/.*

29. Zhang, LMN, 149. *a ne da ni nga la drod cig 'ong bar 'dug go gsung pas/ khong gnyis na re drod bya ba ci la zer la/ drod bya ba gos mi dgos pa zhug 'ong ba yin te gsung pas/ nged kyi ming po grub pa thob par 'dug a ri <re> dga' zer nas te te brdungs so/ de nas cher ma lon par bde drod dang mi rtog pa 'ur gyis 'bar/ gnyug ma lhan cig skyes pa'i rtog pa lhag gis shar te/ de snga phan chad 'khrul ba'i snang ba la yang dag tu zhen te bslus nas 'dug snyam nas/ sring mo dang ne ne gnyis phrad du shog/ khyod la ston ma myong ba zhig bstan du yod gyis gsungs pas/ khong gnyis byung ba dang/ gcer bur 'dug nas gsang ba'i gnas thams cad mi sbed par bstan to/ khong gnyis na re nged kyi ming po smyo nas 'dug zer nas ngus so/.*

30. Here following 1972; 2004 has *brjed drug*, "six forgettings."

31. Here following 1972. *de nas dus rgyun du ras yug sku la bsnams/ res phrag la 'gel/ res gcer bur bzhugs/ gtsang btsog dang ngo tsha dang bral bar bzhugs pas/.*

32. Here following 1972, 150. *gnas gzhi tshan gcig dang yul mi tshan gcig gis/ mi'i na chung mdzes ma rgyan gyis brgyan pa gsum bzhi tsam la rngan pa byin nas/ bu mo rnams kyis bla ma grog po dben pa zhig tu khrid nas/ bu mo rnams kyis bla ma'i pho rtags mnyes pas/ dang po je gnyen la song/ de nas ne thung la song/ tha mar sbubs su nub par gyur to/ der sde pa dang yul mi thams cad shin tu dad pa skyes nas ngo mtshar skyes so/.* Roberts (2007, 70) comments that, in this instance, Mi la "arranges for a group of girls to masturbate him." It is clear, however, that the meeting was orchestrated by skeptical locals in order to test the powers of his yogic realization. Rgyal thang pa makes a statement to this effect toward the end of his work: "Many beautiful women surrounded him, inappropriately seeking to demean him, but he was not moved to desire." (Rgyal thang pa, JGM, 259, *bud med mdzes ma mang pos mtha' skor te tshul bzhin ma yin pa' sgo nas snyad tsal <rtsal> yang 'dod chag la g.yo 'gul med pas/ nyon mongs pa'i bdud bcom/*) The passage also makes a direct reference to one of the thirty-two major marks (*lakṣaṇa*) of a buddha's body: a retractable (or sheathed) penis, capable of withdrawing entirely out of sight.

33. See, for example, the *Twelve Great Disciples* (BCO, 18a; BCN, 21b) translated in chapter 3, and also Gtsang smyon Heruka's version (DJ, 145; Quintman 2010, 155), although the accompanying song has been moved to chapter 9 (DJ, 162.25; Quintman 2010, 178).

34. DJ, 142; Quintman 2010, 153.

35. Zhang, LMN, 158. *de la sogs te mtha' yas mchog/ ting nge 'dzin las mi g.yo ba dang/ mnyam bzhag dang rjes thob med pa dang/ chos nyid kyi bden pa gzigs pa dang/ sprul pa'i gang zag yin gsung so/.*

36. This was published as the *Great Biographies of the Kagyu: A Treasury of Jewels, the Source for All Wishes* (*Bka' brgyud kyi rnam thar chen mo rin po che'i gter mdzod dgos 'dod 'byung gnas* [Bir, India: D. Tsondu Senghe, 1985]). A partial (and fairly loose) English translation appears in Könchog Gyaltsen 1990.

37. Dates for Rdo rje mdzes 'od, Don mo ri pa, and the text have been persuasively argued in Roberts 2007, 10ff. The biographies authored by Don mo ri pa include: Vajradjara and the Buddha (13), Tilopa (53), Nāropa (86), the Tibetan religious kings (*mes dbon rgyal po*, 127), Mar pa (137), Mi la ras pa (176), Atisha (218), Sgam po pa (306), Phag mo gru pa (340), 'Jig rten mgon po (394), and the first part of a biography of his guru, Ri khrod dbang phyug (427). Rdo rje mdzes 'od completes the latter work and adds brief biographies of Don mo ri pa (under the title *dus gsum mkhyen pa*, 489), and Don mo ri pa's disciples 'Jig rten blos btang (504), 'Od sku brtse ba (here only named, 505), Rdzong gong ma (505), and Chun 'dor ba (507).

38. Don mo ri pa, JMN, 472–73.

39. It occurs in Don mo ri pa, JMN, 205, which favors Lama Zhang's version of proto-Songs story 12 over Sgam po pa's.

40. Don mo ri pa, JMN, 178. Translating the term *lo rgyus* as "historical" in this context is provocative, and admittedly problematic. *Lo rgyus* has also been translated as "chronicle" and "annals," although in some cases it is better rendered more generally as "story" or "account." In the present context, however, *lo rgyus* seems to imply a historiographic content beyond a mere temporal narrative, especially when read in contrast to the works of Sgam po pa and Lama Zhang, which are almost entirely lacking in chronological movement. I have discussed this topic further in Quintman 2012.

41. Rdo rje mdzes 'od, NTC, 137. *lung bstan thob pa'i yon tan dang/ rigs dang 'brel pa dka' ba spyad pa'i yon tan dang/ ting nge 'dzin dang 'brel ba nyams su myong ba'i yon tan . . . /.* The latter two sections are used as the principal divisions for Mi la's life story in the version by O rgyan pa (discussed later in this chapter) and Rgyal thang pa's biography of Ras chung pa, as well as all of the later biographical compendia. It is as yet unclear when a formal two-part division into early life and subsequent realization was first used in the context of Bka' brgyud biography. As noted earlier in chapter 1, these two sections appear in the *rnam thar* of Ngan rdzong ras pa, first written in the mid-twelfth century, but the structure may have been appended by Rgod tshang pa a century later. O rgyan pa's version may have been written in the mid-thirteenth century, contemporary with those of Rgod tshang pa and Don mo ri pa, but likely already reflects developments from the later compendia.

42. Don mo ri pa, JMN, 178. *de'i rnam thar ram lo rgyus la bzhi ste/ dang po rje mar pa dang mjal ba'i dus kyi rnam thar dang/ rje mar pa dang mjal nas thugs mnyes pa'i zhabs tog phul nas chos dang gdams ngag zhus pas gnang lugs dang/ chos dang gdams ngag thob nas bla ma'i zhabs tog tu bsgrub pa mdzad pas mchog thun mong gi yon tan brnyes lugs dang/ gdul bya snod ldan smyin par mdzad lugs so/.*

43. Here "Tibet" is designated by the Tibetan term *bod*. To this day, residents of many southern Tibetan border areas refer to Dbus Gtsang as Tibet (*bod*).

44. Don mo ri pa, JMN, 179ff. *ru khu lung bya ba de na lha rje ye shes gzungs bya ba la gshin rje ma lus par zhus/ drag sngags gza' gdong dmar nag bstan srung du zhus so/ lo brgyad bsgrubs pas rtags thon/ de nas nyang stod kho rer byon nas/ ba mi bho de ra tsa bya ba la sgyu 'phrul gsan/ de nas nyang stod rgyan khar du dgyer ston dbang nge bya ba la rdzogs chen gsan/ yang rong gi g.yu' phug bya ba der 'bre ston dbang nge bya ba la yang rdzogs chen gsan/ de nas yar 'brog dor byon nas mar pa 'byung nge bya ba la mdo sems phyogs gsan/.* Subsequent texts, beginning with Zhi byed ri pa, reverse the final two teachers so that Mi la's early training concludes with 'Dre ston lha dga' of Rong (a.k.a. Rong ston). Gtsang smyon would emphasize this latter individual in his standard work. See Zhi byed ri pa, NDO, 5; Padma dkar po, DCJ, 357; Si tu Paṇ chen, CSK, 71.

45. Of course, it may also have drawn upon early textual sources that have not yet come to light, such as those by Khyung tshang pa and Zhang Lotsāwa.

46. Don mo ri pa, JMN, 215. *de'i dus su mthun snang du sku'i bkod pa gsum las gcig bkra shis tshe ring ma'i bla mchod du gshegs/ gcig rgya gar du gshegs pa yang sung ngo/.* The description of Mi la ras pa visiting India is later echoed several times by Zhi byed ri pa.

47. The collection was published as *Rwa lung dkar brgyud gser 'phreng: Brief Lives of the Successive Masters in the Transmission Lineage of the Bar 'Brug-pa Dkar-brgyud-pa of Rwa-luṅ* (Palampur, India: Sungrab Nyamso Gyunpel Parkhang, 1975–78). The Mi la ras pa biography appears in volume 1, 167–216. Mention should be made of another, somewhat later, golden rosary collection recording the lineage of the Mdo chen Bka' brgyud sub-branch of the 'Brug pa that florished in the Skyid grong region of southwestern Tibet. This is the *Bka' brgyud kyi rnam thar thog mar rdo rje 'chang gi rnam thar na rim par zhugs so/ Bka' brgyud gser 'phreng*, a manuscript microfilmed by the Nepal-German Manuscript Preservation Project in Nepal (reel nos. L481/4, L481/5). Franz-Karl Ehrhard (2008, 99) has dated this work to the fifteenth century, and it is unclear what relationship, if any, its Mi la biography has to Sangs rgyas 'Bum's work.

48. The original blocks were prepared through the patronage of the sixteenth Sde srid of Bhutan, Chos rgyal bsod nams lhun grub (ruled ca. 1768–72), and the colophon is signed by the twelfth Rje mkhan po Kun dga' rgya mtsho (served 1769–71).

49. Sangs rgyas 'Bum, MNT, 135: *sdom bu'i rnal 'byor pa sangs rgyas 'bum gyi <gyis> rnam thar lnga'i gung gcig tu bsgrigs pa shog drang nyer gcig/.*

50. Sangs rgyas 'Bum, MNT, 10.5.

51. On Sangs rgyas 'Bum's life see BA, 716; Sørensen and Hazod 2007, 41–45, 100–101, 228ff. Tshal Gung thang monastery is also mentioned in the colophon of a larger *Black Treasury* compendium, where it is described as the place in which a compilation of seventeen different *mgur 'bum* was created. That statement does not seem to be referring to Sangs rgyas 'Bum's text under discussion here, although it is possible that the author also compiled an extended *mgur 'bum* that has not yet come to light. See the discussion in chapter 3.

52. Sørensen and Hazod (2007, 228) call this date into question.

53. The second part is alternatively titled "the biographical account of how he gained experience and exhibited good qualities" (*nyams myong skyes tshul yon tan bsten <bstan?> pa'i rnam thar*).

54. Sangs rgyas 'Bum, MNT, 172.

55. Sangs rgyas 'Bum, MNT, 205. It is possible that this refers to another of Sangs rgyas 'Bum's works. See note 51.

56. This was published as *Dkar brgyud gser 'phreng: A Thirteenth-Century Collection of Verse Hagiographies of the Succession of Eminent Masters of the 'Brug-pa dkar-brgyud-pa Tradition* (Tashijong, India: Sungrab Nyamso Gyunphel Parkhang, 1973). The complete Tibetan title is *Dpal dwags po bka' brgyud las/ don brgyud dpal ldan dbyar rnga pa'i bstan pa rin po cher byon pa'i 'brug ra lung gdan rabs chos rje dbon ras dang/ rgod tshangs pa yan gong ma grub thob gser ri'i phreng ba'i rnam par thar pa mdor tshang rags bsdud le tshan rnam phyogs bsgrigs/* The poetic name used above is derived from this. E. Gene Smith has placed the text generally in the thirteenth century. Roberts 2007 (14–15) suggests a narrower, but tentative, dating between 1258 and 1266.

57. Tiso (1989) has made an initial translation of this work.

58. Rgyal thang pa, JGM, 194. *rje btsun bla ma mid la ras pa rje// gang la gang 'dul sprul pa mchog gi sku// tha mal tshul bzung dka' spyad sna tshogs skyis// yon tan dpag med brnyes mdzad gus phyag 'tshal//.*

59. Rgyal thang pa, JGM, 194. . . . *sangs rgyas kyi rnam 'phrul kho na yin/.*

60. Rgyal thang pa, JGM, 195. *yin pa nga sangs rgyas rang gis lung stan cing/ sangs rgyas nyid rang gi rnam 'phrul du 'byon pa/ slob dpon 'phags pa klu sgrub snying po zhes bya ba bcig*

yod pa/ de'i skye ba'i rnam 'phrul gcig nga yin gsung/ des nas rje btsun gyi rgyal po mid la
ras pa 'di nyid/ sangs rgyas kyi sprul pa klu sgrub snying po dngos yin te/ de yang/ nga da
lta tha mal pa rnams kyi snang ngor/ tha mal pa'i skur sprul nas/ tha mal pa rnams kyi don
la byon pa'o/.

Rgyal thang pa may not have been the first to identify Mi la ras pa with
Nāgārjunagarbha. Zhi byed ri pa (47) notes "Some people, including the 'Bri gung
pa of Lama Kyu ra Rinpoche, say that Rje btsun Mi la ras pa was born as master Ārya
Nāgārjunagarbha, a physical birth of the Bhagavan Amoghasiddhi, but Lord Khyung
tshang pa and Zhang Lotsāwa don't clarify the matter." (*yang bla ma kyu ra rin po che'i*
'bri khung pa la sogs pa kha gcig ni/ bcom ldan 'das don yod grub pa'i sku'i skye ba slob dpon
'phags pa klu grub snying po yin la/ de'i sku'i skye ba rje btsun mid la ras chen yin gsung ba
yang 'dug la/ rje khyung tshang ba dang/ zhang lo ts.tsha ba'i zhal gsal ni mi 'dug/) Kyu ra
(also spelled Skyu ra) is a clan name closely associated with the 'Bri gung Bka' brgyud,
and according to Dung dkar's encyclopedic dictionary, Skyu ra Rinpoche should be
identified as 'Bri gung skyob pa himself, i.e., 'Jig rten mgon po (1143–1217), Phag
mo gru pa's disciple and founder of the 'Bri gung Bka' brgyud (DKT, 257). This quote
implies that the statement was made prior to Khyung tshangs pa's text, perhaps by
'Jig rten mgon po himself. Mi la ras pa's identification as a specific incarnation thus
seems to have appeared within a century following his death.

61. Rgyal thang pa, JGM, 213. *dpon slob sdongs nas mar pa'i drung du byon// las sgrib zad*
    nas gdams pa'i snod dang ldan// gdam ngag chos rnams kun gyi bdag por gyur// rje btsun
    lung du stan la phyag 'tshal stod//.

62. Rgyal thang pa, JGM, 214. *mar pa'i zhal nas shin du yang legs so/ na ning nas nga mid*
    la la chos mi ster ba de/ nga thugs rje chung ba yang yin/ kho'i rgyud la sdig sgrib dpag tu
    med pa 'dug pas/ de rnams sbyang ba'i phyir/ khru slog pa dang/ mkhar rtsig pa la sogs pa
    la bkol ba yin/ spyir mid la khyod snod ldan pa'i gang zag gcig 'dug/ gdam ngag gi snod du
    rung ba yin/ khyod kyi sngon 'gro sdib sbyong la sogs pa yongs su tshar yod/ da dngos gzhi
    gdam ngag phog pas chog par yod pas/.

    This is in contrast to the standard account in Gtsang smyon Heruka's version, in
    which Mi la does not complete all nine stories of the tower. Mar pa interprets this
    as an indication that Mi la has not eradicated all traces of his karmic past, which
    then becomes a rationale for the many years of hardship in meditation the yogin is
    forced to endure. See DJ, 81; Quintman 2010, 82.

63. For a discussion of the geography described here, see Quintman 2008.

64. Rgyal thang pa, JGM, 259. *yon tan drug dang ldan.* These are identical to the *legs pa'i*
    yon tan drug, described as the six great qualities of the Bhagavan (*bcom ldan 'das kyi*
    che ba'i yon tan drug). See TTC, 2801.

65. Rgyal thang pa, JGM, 260. *sgyu ma gzugs kyi phung po 'di/ dus pa da lo mi rtag pa'i tshul*
    ston pa yin gsung/.

66. Only later, in Gtsang smyon Heruka's standard version, would this figure be
    described as a *dge bshes* logician.

67. Roberts 2007, 17. See also Roerich 1949, 602.

68. O rgyan pa, KGW, 174. *yang rdo rje 'chang rnam par snang mdzad du sprul/ rnam snang*
    'jam dpal du sprul/ de nyid lar sprul nas/ bsgrub pa la nan tan dgos pa'i brda' bsten te/.

69. They record the principal Karma Bka' brgyud lineage from Tilopa to the author's
    guru, the Fourth Karmapa, Rol pa'i rdo rje (1340–83), and includes a brief
    autobiographical account.

70. Mkha' spyod dbang po, CBB, 188. *'phags pa'i yul gyi bdag nyid chen po 'jam dpal bzhes gnyen gyi rnam 'phrul/ byang phyogs kha ba can gyi ljongs na 'gran zla thams cad dang bral ba/ rje btsun mi la ras pa chen po de nyid . . .*

71. Mkha' spyod dbang po, CBB, 188. *de ltar bla ma rje btsun chen po 'di bcom ldan 'das rigs kyi bdag po dngos yin kyang/ bod kha ba can gyi gdul bya rnams la thabs sna tshogs kyi sgo nas lam ston pa'i phyir/ dang por 'jig rten gyi bya ba dang mthun par yum la sring zhu mdzad/ de'i bzhed pa yongs su rdzogs par mdzad pa dang/ gzhon du nor bu bzang po dang/ bdag nyi chen po nā ro zhabs ltar lus srog la 'phangs pa bcung <cung> zad kyang med pa'i sgo nas bla ma dam pa sten pa dang/ phyi rabs kyi gdul bya'i skye bo rnams la sgrub rgyud <brgyud> kyi bka' srol mi nyams par bya ba'i phyir/ lto gos la ltos pa med par ri bo'i khrod na ri bo'i khro du gshegs shing sgrub pa kho na snying por mdzad pa dang/ bka' rgyud <brgyud> gong ma'i lung bstan gyi dgongs pa yongs su rdzogs par bya ba'i phyir/ snod ldan gyi slob ma rnal 'byor dang rnal 'byor ma rnams la gdam ngag gi dmar khrid rdzogs par mdzad de/.*

72. Davidson 2005.

73. Davidson 2005, 2.

74. Davidson 2005, 2.

75. The parallel between the Indian biographical genre of *paṭṭāvali* among Jain authors and Tibetan golden rosary works, first noted by Schaeffer (2000b, 362), is of interest since it points to a precedent for this type of literature on the subcontinent. As Schaeffer notes, however, such works have not yet been found among the extant Indian Buddhist literature. See Granoff 1998 for the original discussion of *paṭṭāvali*.

3. BIOGRAPHICAL COMPENDIA: LIVES MADE FLESH

1. For an overview of the division into four major and eight minor subsects see, for example, Smith 1970.

2. On Rwa Lotsawa's biography see Decleer 1992, 1994–95. On Atisha's biographical works, see Eimer 1982; Decleer 1996, 1997, 1998. For sources on Nyang ral's text, see Martin 1997, 32. Recent scholarship has called the authorship, and thus the dating, of the first two works into question.

3. Precedent for understanding the Collected Songs as a biographical network may be found in the traditions of some early Greek and Roman Lives (*bios*), frequently "occupied with the description of a character over the coherently chronological narrative," in which *bios* is understood to mean "way of life" as much as the life itself (Averintsev 2002, 21–2). Western biographical writing has, of course, also made use of alternate narrative modes. Nabokov's study of Nikolai Gogol's life (*Nikolai Gogol*, 1961) famously inverts the usual chronology, beginning with the author's death and concluding with his birth. Michael Ondaatje's study of Billy the Kid (*The Collected Works of Billy the Kid: Left Handed Poems*, 1970) dispenses with strict chronology—and, for that matter, narrative prose—altogether.

4. The few exceptions to this rule found within specific episodes contrast sharply with Gtsang smyon Heruka's standard version, where the author frequently forms explicit chronological links between chapters.

5. Cyrus Stearns, unpublished survey of *The Twelve Great Disciples* (n.p., n.d.); Jackson 2003, 150.
6. Smith 1969, 77, 288n. 175.
7. L, xxx.
8. Tiso 1996; Roberts 2007.
9. See Newark Museum Association 1971; Reynolds 1978; Pal and Meech-Pekarik 1988. The 1971 catalogue lists this work under the title *Mid la ras pa'i rnam thar*, and did not make note of the fact that it preserved an early version of the life story.
10. Padma dkar po, KSY, 310. . . . *rje btsun gyi rnam mgur ngam rdzong pa dang/ ras pa bcu gnyis kyis bsgrigs pa gnyis la tshad mar byed pa/*.
11. The Stockholm edition was first acquired by Swedish Tibetologist Toni Schmid in the early 1960s and remained in her private collection until her death in 1972, when it passed to the Folkens Museum Ethnografiska in Stockholm. Unfortunately, the text was separated from the rest of the Tibetan collection and is currently unavailable. The text was inadvertently misplaced when it was added to the museum's textile collection due to its traditional cloth covering (personal communication, Hakan Wahlquist, Senior Curator of the Asian Collections, National Museum of Ethnography, Stockholm, Sweden, January 4, 2001). Roberts (2007, 22) notes that a partial photocopy exists, but I have not been able to access it for the present study.
12. The Oxford edition (a handwritten *dbu can* ms. on two-ply paper in 193 folios, 4 × 22.75 in.) reached the Bodleian Library in 1905, one of many books collected under the supervision of L. A. Waddell during the expedition to Tibet led by Colonial Francis Younghusband the previous year.
13. The Newark edition (a handwritten *dbu can* ms. in 244 folios, 4 × 23 in.) was first acquired from Labrang monastery in A mdo by the Christian missionary Carter D. Holton, and arrived at the Newark Museum in 1936 (Reynolds 1978, 13).

    This text preserves an exceptional example of an illuminated edition of Mi la ras pa's Life and Songs and its illustrations deserve an extensive discussion, which lies beyond the scope of the present study. I plan to return to these illustrations, in the context of Mi la ras pa's iconographic tradition, in the future, but will briefly introduce them here. The text incorporates more than three hundred individual color images and related inscriptions. Pratapaditya Pal (1988, 178) referred to the manuscript as "almost casually illustrated with haphazardly distributed vignettes." Closer examination, however, indicates that tremendous care was taken in the planning and execution of the illustrations.

    The opening two folio sides visually record the early Bka' brgyud lineage: in the center of the first page sits Vajradhara (incorrectly identified as Vajrasattva in the inscription); to his right and left, respectively, sit Mi la and Ras chung pa, dressed in white robes, hands to their ears in the gesture of singing. The next folio shows Sgam po pa on the left and Mar pa on the right, but here both wear the robes and scholar's hat of a Dge lugs pa monk (discussed in a later note). The lineage depicted here emphasizes the relationship between Mi la and Ras chung pa: an indirect reference, perhaps, to the aural transmissions that passed between them and to which this text is closely aligned.

    The early life consists primarily of decorative motifs such as royal insignia and auspicious symbols, although several objects related to the story also appear, such as the magic dagger used by Mi la's mother and the copper pot he offers to his guru. Later images record static figures of Mi la and his disciples, but they also illustrate active scenes describing the literary narrative. The illustrations serve two main functions. They frequently mark the beginning of songs; this is true of the symbols in the early Life, and it also occurs later in the Songs, where Mi la, or his disciple, is frequently depicted in singing posture. This forms a natural pause in the reading, allowing for the transition from prose to poetry. The vignettes also illustrate the story's central action, making clever use of space on the folio page. One good example is the account of Mi la ras pa's conversion of the hunter, his dog, and deer, frequently reproduced in both statues and paintings (*Khyi ra ras pa'i skor*, 110b.3). The story unfolds over six folio sides: the first scene illustrates the deer approaching the yogin from across the page; next, the dog approaches the place where Mi la and the deer are seated; then, the hunter appears, enraged at seeing all three together; next the hunter approaches close to Mi la, his body taut, bow and arrow drawn, ready to kill; the penultimate scene depicts the hunter's conversion, kneeling in devotion. The final image shows the hunter seated with dog and deer, having cast off his weapons and traded his worldly clothes for the white robe of Mi la's yogic tradition. The inscription reads "hunter and assembly become awakened" (*khyi gra 'khor bcas sangs rgyas pa*). In a cave off to one side, the animal carcasses and broken weapons are visible, described by the text as relics that remained up to the time of writing. Each of these multipart illustrations carefully tracks the text, appearing next to the words that describe it. The result is a dynamic space in which images literally run across, and through, the text, reminiscent of a flip-style animation booklet. Text and images are fully integrated and equally serve the story's narrative goals.

14. DK, 1514. This is text *phyi ra* 49, #017070.
15. Personal communication, Karma Bde legs and Shes rab bzang po, May 11, 2005.
16. Roberts 2007, 22. The printer's colophon bears a similar title: *Gangs stod mid la ras chen gyi bka' 'bum chen mo grub thob ras pa bcu gnyis kyis bsgrigs pa.*
17. Roberts 2007, 238n65. *shar dags <dwags> po'i rnal 'byor pa gangs stod kyi ras chen guna matis/ sham bu gangs dkar mo'i dben gnas su bsgrubs pa/*. While little is known of this individual, his name (a Sanskritized form of Yon tan blo gros) appears in Chos kyi dbang phyug's historical study of Brag dkar rta so. There the author notes, among the sources for his summation of Mi la ras pa's life, an encomium (*bstod pa*) called the *'Jam dpal bshes gnyen ma* that he describes as very well known. He determined the author to be "the great cotton-clad Guṇamati Yon tan blo gros of Gangs stod" (*gangs stod ras chen guṇamati yon tan blo gros*), clearly a reference to the same person mentioned in the Stockholm edition colophon. The title of this work underscores the close identification of Mi la ras pa with Mañjuśrīmitra ('Jam dpal bshes gnyan), discussed in detail in chapter 4. See Chos kyi dbang phyug, DTL, 23b.
18. This region became a major religious center for the G.ya' bzang Bka' brgyud, a tradition founded by Skal ldan ye shes (d. 1207) and Chos kyi smon lam (1167–1233) in the lineage of Mi la ras pa, Sgam po pa, and Phag mo gru pa. Mi la's disciple Ras chung pa, who established a meditation center in the area, is also credited with first opening the pilgrimage circuit around the mountain. For a study of the region and its ties to the G.ya' bzang Bka' brgyud, see Gyalbo, et. al. 2000.

There is no mention of this work in either of the extant biographies of Lha btsun Rin chen rnam rgyal (1473–1557), Gtsang smyon Heruka's disciple who founded a monastery and printing center at Brag dkar rta so and was responsible for flurry of block-print biographies of Bka' brgyud masters. See Anon., CRD, 52a; and Smith 2001, 75–77, which catalogue these works. Although the library of Brag dkar rta so was severely damaged during the Cultural Revolution, many original wood blocks remain on site. However, in several visits between 1994 and 2007, I was unable to locate blocks for *The Twelve Great Disciples*. There appeared to be no living oral tradition of the text there, as the current residents of the retreat center had no previous knowledge of *The Twelve Great Disciples* when I offered a copy in 1997.

19. These variations are indicated in the translations that follow.

20. He was born in Reb gong in eastern Tibet, and later trained at Dga' ldan monastery in Lhasa before returning to A mdo, where he spent much of his life in retreat. He was also the first in a line of incarnate lamas, the Rong po grub chen, extending to the present day. For a detailed treatment of Skal ldan rgya mtsho's life and collected songs, see Sujata 2003 and more recently, Sujata 2005.

21. Sujata 2003, 84ff. It is particularly interesting that Chos pa Rinpoche is identified as a reembodiment not only of Mi la ras pa but also of several early Bka' brgyud masters, including Mi la's pupil and contributor to *The Twelve Great Disciples*, Zhi ba 'od (although how he might simultaneously take rebirth as both guru and disciple is left unexplained). In the context of this text, then, he is both biographical subject and biographer, an unusual situation that will be reexamined through the figure of Gtsang smyon Heruka in chapter 5. Moreover, Chos pa Rinpoche's incarnation line is asserted to begin with Mañjuśrīmitra, the figure associated with Mi la ras pa throughout his early biographical tradition. Both of these points will provide evidence for why *The Twelve Great Disciples* was favored over the standard version in the discussion that follows.

    Skal ldan rgya mtsho repeatedly described himself as following Mi la ras pa's example of solitary yogic practice, on many occasions signing transcriptions of his songs Skal ldan ras pa (Sujata 2003, 102–3). He also authored a brief *guruyoga* (*bla ma'i rnal 'byor*) manual centered around the figure of Mi la ras pa. See Skal ldan rgya mtsho, MLN.

22. See for example the block-print illustration reprinted in D. Jackson 1996, 319, fig. 173; and the mural reproduced in Sujata 2003. These images consciously blend symbols of Dge lugs scholasticism (monastic robes, scholar's hat) and of Mi la ras pa's hermetic life (singing posture, meditation belt, snow mountain environment).

23. Sujata 2003, xvii. This hermitage is located four hours west of Reb gong in A mdo.

24. The scribe's colophon to the Newark manuscript (244a) mentions neither the date nor the place of its production. The text includes prayers for the enlightenment and the removal of obstacles for a number of patrons, most of which bear A mdo ba names. As has been well attested across Asian Buddhist cultures, this is one illustration of how the production of texts often reflected private concerns, such as merit-making and liberation, as much as the desire to promulgate doctrinal content. The complete scribal colophon is listed in appendix 2.5.

25. The text makes numerous visual references to Dge lugs monastic culture. The second folio (2b) depicts both Mar pa (usually as a householding lay teacher) and Sgam po pa in the garb of fully ordained monks, complete with yellow scholar's cap after the Dge lugs fashion. A more direct reference is found in the story of Zhi ba 'od's conversion. While the text makes no mention of his ordination status,

the chapter opens (131b) with a portrait of Zhi ba 'od wearing the robes of a fully ordained monk. The episode concludes (132b) with a depiction of the disciple, once again in monk's dress, but now with his hand to his ear in the gesture of singing—nearly identical to Skal ldan rgya mtsho's representation, but here, no doubt a subtle commemoration of Chos pa Rinpoche's status as incarnation of both Mi la and Zhi ba 'od. As with the portrait of Skal ldan rgya mtsho, these images are not (or not merely) a blanket attempt to convert the cast of Mi la ras pa's life story to their own tradition. Rather, they illustrate a visual mapping of the themes and qualities of the life story, as embodied in this particular version, to the lives of the great teachers of their time.

26. The Oxford edition lacks a title on the outside cover.

27. BCO, 191b. *dpal bzhad pa'i rdo rje'i rnam thar/ mgur chings dang bcas pa rdzogs so//.* The term "song-outline" translates the unusual Tibetan compound *mgur chings*, unattested in other texts of the tradition except for *The Black Treasury*, which copies this entire colophon. The TTC defines *chings* in this context as "an outline or concise text that essentializes important points" (*sa bcad dam don gyi 'gag mdo dril ba'i sdom tshig*), and as an illustration lists the word *spyi chings*, perhaps translated as "general summary." It is clearly not the songs themselves that are summarized in *The Twelve Great Disciples*, as was often the case in the proto-works. The term *mgur chings* predates any known use of the word *mgur 'bum* in the tradition, and is replaced in later compendia with references to "collected songs" (*mgur 'bum*). It is tempting, therefore, to understand *mgur chings* as an early description of the burgeoning literary genre of collected songs—a "song survey" summarizing the entirety of the yogin's teaching in verse. It is also possible that the term refers to the division of the Songs into seventeen discrete units, which, as noted earlier, form a brief outline of Mi la ras pa's spiritual career from first awakening to final liberation—thus "song outline." Gtsang smyon Heruka also used this term in the colophon to his version of the *Life*, where it appears to refer specifically to his eleventh chapter (discussed in the next chapter) that summarizes the *Collected Songs* in their entirety. Each of these readings agrees with the description of the Songs as a narrative network, glossing the entirety of Mi la ras pa's teaching career.

28. BCO, 191b.4; BCN, 243b.1. *rnam thar 'di skal ldan sgom chen rnams kyis don du ngan rdzongs ston pa bho dhi ra dza la sogs pa'i ras pa bu chen bcu gnyis kyi yi ger bkod pa'o//.* The twelve great disciples (*bu chen*) referred to here are likely those listed in the colophon under two headings: the four heart sons (*thugs kyi sras bzhi*), Ras chung pa, Se ban ras pa, Ngan rdzongs ras pa, 'Bri sgom ras pa; and the eight close sons (*nye ba'i sras brgyad*), Ras pa Zhi ba 'od, Ras pa Sangs rgyas skyabs, Ras pa Rdo rje dbang phyug, Gshen sgom ras pa, Rong chung ras pa, Mkhar chung ras pa, Gnyen sgom ras pa, and Khyi ra ras pa.

29. Roberts (2007, 22) calls the attribution of this text to the twelve disciples "erroneous," pointing out that both the Newark and Oxford editions use the genitive particle *kyi*, as opposed to the instrumental *kyis*, forcing a literal translation: "has been set down in the words *of* Ngan rdzongs." (He claims the Stockholm edition also follows this reading, but in note 144 states that this particular passage was unavailable.) Apart from the fact that these manuscripts regularly confuse genitive and instrumental particles, it should be noted that several versions of *The Black Treasury* compendia copy this colophon in its entirety, using the instrumental

particle. And as mentioned above, both Padma dkar po and the edition listed in the 'Bras spungs dkar chag also record the attribution in the instrumental case. These points of grammatical minutia may, in the end, make little difference in the way these texts are understood.

30. See for example Gyatso 1998, 103, who describes such a process in the context of autobiography.

31. As noted in chapter 1, Dam pa ras chen's biography of Ngan rdzong used a narrative structure very similar to *The Twelve Great Disciples*, although it is unclear whether this was itself an innovation or a replication of his guru's literary works.

32. Chapter 2 pointed out, for example, Don mo ri pa's use of structural division in the formulation of his biographical works; his *Life of Mar pa* employs an outline nearly identical to *The Twelve Great Disciples*.

33. There is at least one clear illustration of this. O rgyan pa's text follows *The Twelve Great Disciples* in dividing the Songs into seventeen sections, one of which is called "the quality of the god of gods" (*lha'i lhar gyur pa'i yon tan*). In the compendium, this title is clearly taken from a line in a song Mi la sings, describing the King of Bhaktapur, a song that is lacking in O rgyan pa's text. Thus it appears that O rgyan pa retained the name of the quality while leaving out the song upon which it is based. It is difficult to imagine the process working in the opposite direction.

34. See appendix 2.1 for the full citation.

35. BCO, 191b.3; BCN, 243b.1. See appendix 2.5 for Tibetan transcription and complete translation.

36. I read *brgyud* for *rgyud* here for reasons that follow.

37. BCO, 1b; BCN, 2a.

38. BCO, 2b; BCN, 2a.

39. BCO, 3b; BCN, 3a.

40. BCO, 4b; BCN, 4a.

41. BCO, 4b; BCN, 4b.

42. BCO 5a; BCN, 4b.

43. BCO, 5a; BCN, 5a.

44. BCO, 6b; BCN, 6b.

45. In this version, Mi la receives the copper kettle from Mar pa's disciple Rngog ston, to use as an initiation offering. This stands in contrast to the standard version, in which Mi la earns it himself during his begging rounds and offers it to his guru soon after arriving at Mar pa's home. There, Gtsang smyon Heruka transforms the verse into prose dialogue. See Quintman 2010, 84.

46. BCO, 9a; BCN, 10a.

47. In the early compendia, Mar pa sings this song based upon his prophetic dream and then offers his own commentary. This contrasts with the standard version, in which Mi la sings the original song (much earlier in the narrative), which is then clarified by Mar pa. Cf. Quintman 2010, 95–100.

48. BCO, 11b; BCN, 13b.

49. BCO, 12a; BCN, 14a.

50. The Newark edition records 62 cycles, the Oxford edition 66. The term "cycle" is frequently used, somewhat loosely, to render the Tibetan word *skor* (in this context, literally "class" or "group") in compounds such as *chos skor*, "Dharma cycle," and *gdams ngag gi skor*, "instruction cycle," that refer to a collection of writings on a

particular theme or topic. In the present context, however, "cycle" precisely captures the intended meaning, in reference to the technical term used in Western classical music traditions, "song cycle," defined as "a series of songs set as a rule to a number of poems with a connected narrative or some other unifying feature" (*Everyman's Dictionary of Music*, Kessinger Publishing, 2005). Used in reference to nineteenth-century musical works of Beethoven, Schubert, and Schumann, the sense is that each cycle contains a group of related songs structured through a narrative frame so as to tell a story; this closely approximates the smallest functional unit of Mi la ras pa's Collected Songs, in both the early compendia and the standard version.

51. The first section is named for the song of essencelessness, also recorded in many of the early proto-texts, sung upon Mi la's return to his homeland where he finds his home in ruins, his mother dead, and his sister gone off begging; the second derives its name from a dream that inspires the yogin to persevere in his practice.

52. BCO, 182b; BCN, 231b.

53. BCO, 183a; BCN, 231b.

54. BCO, 183a; BCN, 232a. Cf. Quintman 2010, 192–93.

55. Kurtis Schaeffer (2007) notes this contrast occurring within the standard version of Mi la ras pa's Life. At the time, Schaeffer did not have access to *The Twelve Great Disciples* and thus argued that this narrative tradition began with Gtsang smyon Heruka. It is clear from the following examples, however, that the template for this tradition was formed much earlier and was well established by the time Gtsang smyon began his project.

56. In this story, Devadatta plots to murder the Buddha with poison secreted under his fingernails. Inevitably, the scheme fails and Devadatta falls into hell, whereupon the Buddha dispatches his disciples Śāriputra and Maudgalyāyana to help assuage his suffering. The episode is translated in Rockhill 1991 [1884], 107. For descriptions of the Buddha's death from the Tibetan translation of the *Mahāparinirvāṇa Sūtra*, see Rockhill 1991; the Pāli version is translated in several sources, including Walshe 1987.

57. BCO, 186a; BCN, 235b.

58. Rgyal thang pa, JGM, 264. *gdung rus sen mo tsam gcig dang spyan drang rgyu ma byung bar/ dpa' bo dang mkha' 'gro rnams kyis spyan drang nas/.*

59. Some versions of *The Black Treasury* and, later, Gtsang smyon Heruka's standard version would bring this episode in line with the Buddha's life by having the cremation pyre lie dormant until Ras chung pa's arrival.

60. BCO, 187b; BCN, 237b.

61. BCO, 188b; BCN, 239b.

62. BCO, 189a; BCN, 239b.

63. BCO, 190a; BCN, 241b.

64. BCO, 190b; BCN, 242a.

65. Relying on the oral commentary of a Tibetan informant, Roberts (2007, 32) suggests translating the title as *Dark Treasury*, in reference to the practice of keeping secret texts in a darkened room. This seems particularly apt here since the early compendia are identified with the carefully guarded aural transmission instructions.

66. DNM-D, 513.3 ff. The sequence of events described here closely parallels those mentioned in the four colophons signed by Ngan rdzong ras pa and Zhi ba 'od, although the relationship between the two is uncertain. See appendix 2.

67. According to the BA (544), he is also known as Rin chen bzang po. Si tu Paṇ chen (DCS, vol. 1, 512–515) records his name as Sog dbon Rin chen bzang po.

68. DNM-D 515.

69. See Chan 1994, 749.

70. Shes rab bzang po, personal communication, May 9, 2005.

71. According to the *Blue Annals*, the Fifth Karma pa, De bzhin shegs pa (1384–1415), who was born in the Kong po region, received both his novice and full ordination vows at Rtse lha sgang, and later received teachings there from the Second Zhwa dmar, Mkha' spyod dbang po (1350–1405) (Roerich 1947, 507–8). It also records a visit by the Sixth Karma pa, Mthong ba don ldan (1416–53), in 1452 (Roerich 1947, 516). According to Si ti Paṇchen's DCS (348), *sprul sku* Karma Chos skyong (seventeenth century), a disciple of the Tenth Karma pa, Chos dbying rdo rje (1604–74), was appointed to oversee the establishment, whose name is recorded as Rtse lha sgar. Thanks to Gene Smith for this reference. According to Smith, the name Rtse lha sgar also appears in a verse biography of the Tenth Karma pa attributed to the Seventh Zhwa dmar, Ye shes snying po (1631–94), noting that the Karma pa visited the location on his way from Dwags lha sgam po (personal communication, March 9, 2006). An anonymous history of *sprul sku* lines compiled between 1814 and 1820 records the following lineage of Rtse la'i sprul sku of Rtse la sgang together with their ages at death: (1) Bstan 'dzin rdo rje, 73; (2) Rgod tshang sna tshogs rang grol, 74; (3) Kun bzang legs grub, 39; (4) Kun bzang mthu stobs dbang po, 47; (5) Kun bzang bde chen rgya mtsho, 48; (6) Kun bzang bde chen. It notes that the sixth incarnation, Kun bzang bde chen, was seven years old at the time of writing. The first incarnation, Bstan 'dzin rdo rje (1534–1608?) is considered the incarnation of Vairocana (TBRC database P4688). The second incarnation is Rtse le Sna tshogs rang grol (b. 1608), the famed disciple of the Tenth Karma pa (TBRC database P1687). See Anon, KDZ, 333–34. There appear to have been several institutions located in the vicinity of Rtse la sgang, and further research is needed to sort out their history.

72. Kaḥ thog Si tu Chos kyi rgya mtsho, DLY, 523. *'di nas mar ring du song bas nyang po nas nyang chu/ lang po nas lang chu/ 'brug la phyogs sam brag gsum phyogs te nyang lang gtsang po 'dzoms sar rnam sras dgon gong der karma pa'i mdzod nag de'u 'bur yod/.* Modern-day Sman gling rdzong is situated near the confluence of these two rivers.

73. Shes rab bzang po, personal communication, May 9, 2005.

74. It is possible that other texts have also been designated by this name. For example, Dezhung Rinpoche is said to have seen a version of *The Black Treasury* authored by Zhi byed ri pa. That text (Zhi byed ri pa, NDO), discussed earlier in this study, does not use such a title. Dezhung Rinpoche claimed he had never heard of *The Black Treasury* written by Rang byung rdo rje (Cyrus Stearns, personal communication, May 1994).

75. Full bibliographic information for these works is given in the bibliography. Two manuscript versions of *The Black Treasury* have recently come to light but cannot be included in the discussion here: a manuscript recently acquired by the British Library (Shelfmark OR 16756); and a manuscript currently held in a private

collection, which upon preliminary analysis appears to fit within the later stratum, perhaps similar to the DNM-D.

76. The text's catalogue entry identifies the manuscript as *The Biography of Jetsün Mila Dorjé Gyaltsen* (*Rje btsun mi la rdo rje rgyal mtshan gyi rnam par thar pa*) and its author as Rangjung Dorjé (DK, 1515, entry 017082, 42 × 82 cm., 309 folios, 17 missing pages). The cover page bears the classification number inscribed by the 'Bras spungs archivists: *phyi ra* 42, the letter *ra* referring to historical works (*chos 'byung/lo rgyus*), the category under which all biographies were catalogued. The catalogued title is unusual in its use of Milarepa's first ordination name (Rdo rje rgyal mtshan), given by Marpa during the conferral of lay vows, instead of his tantric initiation name, Bshad pa rdo rje, by which the yogin and his biographies are more commonly known. Moreover, the account in which Mi la ras pa receives the name Rdo rje rgyal mtshan is recorded in neither this version of *The Black Treasury* nor the earlier *The Twelve Great Disciples* upon which it is largely based. That story first appears in DNM-I/S, discussed below, an indication that this manuscript, or at least its title, was likely produced at a later date. The Lhasa manuscript also contains many illustrations, although the artwork is generally of limited aesthetic value.

77. DNM-Lhasa, 308a.

78. DNM-Lhasa appends at least three new song cycles and reconfigures several others. For instance, the section recording Mi la ras pa's meeting with the hunter Khyi ra Mgon po rdo rje incorporates an alternative account (145a) that would be expanded in later versions of *The Black Treasury*. It also adds a central plot point to the death scene, describing Ras chung pa's vision of his master's passing (297a), that was absorbed into later versions.

79. DNM-Lhasa, 308b. *chos kyi rje mi pham mgon po'i zhal nas// rje btsun mi la chen po'i 'gur 'bum mtha' med pa cig yod pa 'dra zhing phyogs gcigs du// sgrigs pa brgya tsams mthong ba'i nang nas mang shos su 'dug cing/ rje rang byung rdo rje nyid kyis phyag bris mdzad pa yin pas// khung btsun gsung nas thugs rtsis shin tu legs mdzad 'du ba zhes yongs su grags pa'i glegs bam 'di yin no/.*

80. The title listed in the Collected Works is *Songs of the Powerful Lord of Yogins Mila Zhepa Dorjé Called The Black Treasury, Compiled by Karmapa Rangjung Dorjé* (*rnal 'byor gyi dbang phyug mi la bzhad pa rdo rje'i gsung mgur mdzod nag ma zhes pa karma pa rang byung rdo rjes phyogs gcig tu bkod pa*).

81. DNM-RD, 773.

82. The scribe records that the original manuscript was produced in Padma skod, with work commencing in a water-tiger (*chu stag*) year and completed the following water-hare (*chu yos*) year.

83. Smith's edition contains twenty-four pages of illustrations, half devoted to Mi la ras pa's disciples and half depicting a lineage of masters passing through Sgam po pa, Phag mo gru pa, and the early masters of the Upper 'Brug pa lineage. It is hoped that a closer analysis of the later individuals may allow for a more precise dating of the manuscript.

84. This title echoes Don mo ri pa's text in its reference to "historical accounts" (*lo rgyus*), although in this case, the term appears more ambiguous. The emphasis is on the collection of songs (*'gur tshogs*). As the title lacks the term "biography" (*rnam thar*), it is unclear whether the "historical" anecdotes refer to the biography proper as a means of contextualizing the Songs, to the narrative frames within each song

cycle, or to the many unusual stories preserved throughout the text. As will be shown, many narrative episodes differ significantly from earlier versions, and it seems reasonable to read the term *lo rgyus* as asserting the veracity of these stories while noting their function as embellishments to the central narrative traditions.

85. For the complete transcription and translation, see appendix 2.6.

86. See, for example, Lama Zhang's brief biography in RA, 127 and his *Collected Works* (2004, vol. ka, 8).

87. This song cycle first appears in *The Twelve Great Disciples* and is copied in DNM-Lhasa with the addition of an alternate ending. DNM-I/S is the only version to extend the alternate account into a complete narrative cycle; it is also the first work to locate its action at the sacred mountain of Rtsib ri in western Tibet, and incorporates an introductory song of praise to the site. The *Lho rong chos 'byung* preserves an abbreviated version of the story, likewise located at Rtsib ri. See Tshe dbang rgyal, LRC, 89. We shall later see evidence that the LRC elsewhere glosses and refines elements drawn from DNM-I/S, especially in the context of Mi la's death. In line with this, it has been observed that the LRC was based on "an enormous corpus of biographical and autobiographical literature. . . . [Its author] must have had access to an exceptionally fine library with a very large number of texts that have yet to become available" (van der Kuijp 2001, 69). It appears that later versions of *The Black Treasury* were among such texts.

88. The text significantly reorganizes later sections of the early life: part 1 is expanded to include elements of the first song cycle from *The Twelve Great Disciples*, as are the first cycles of part 2. This results in some ambiguity and repetition in the narrative where, for example, Mi la's famed song of essencelessness is recorded twice, further evidence that the text remains unpolished.

89. O rgyan pa, KGW, 175. *bu 'go yags bya ba yod.*

90. DNM-S, 2a.7; DNM-I, 8.3. *pha na re/ nga'i rgyud thams cad kyi mgo yag pas mgo yag ming thog gcig zer/ ma na re/ nga'i bu 'di chos byed gcig 'ong bas/ chos rgyud kyi mgo yag pa yin pas mgo yag ming thog zer ro/.*

91. Don mo ri pa, JMN, 179. *mi chos kyi mtshan mid la thos pa dgar btags so.*

92. DNM-S, 3a; DNM-I, 12. *grong pas ston mo ci byed pa la sprang zhing/ glu ldab ldib shes pa yang len/ skabs skabs su yul pa'i ba ra yang 'tshos/ de' dus su/ nga' lag du thog pa'i 'ur rdo 'di// sgom thag gon pa cig yin na ang// nga yi rgyab du gyon pa'i go cog 'di// ras gos rkyang cig yin na ang// zhes pa la sogs pa'i bsgrub pa la yid smon pa'i glu mchid dpag tu med pa len cing// glu'i sdeb sbyor dang gtam rgyud sogs la shin tu mkhas la/ sgrung mang po shes pa yang nyal brang dang 'phang ra thams cad du byed pas kun dga' nas/ mi la thos pa dga' ming btags/.*

93. This contradicts the explanation offered by Rgyal thang pa (JGM, 199) and later adopted in the standard version, in which it is the news of Mi la's birth that is "delightful to hear," not the sound of his singing voice.

94. This is the only known example of an early mundane song sung by Mi la ras pa, and appears to serve as the source for the comment in the *Lho rong chos 'byung* (73) that he sang songs about his slingshot, clothing, and so forth. Regarding this early collection of folk songs, Zhi byed ri pa provides a "history of songs and tales sung by Mi la thos pa dga' in his early life" (*thog mar mi la thos pa dgas/ glu sbrungs blangs pa'i lo rgyus*), including a lineage of song books (*glu yig*) that were apparently quite widespread among the followers of his tradition. These refer specifically to

traditional songs (*glu*) and tales (*sgrungs*), and not to the songs of realization (*mgur*) for which he is famed.

95. Unsure passage.

96. DNM-S, 21.7, *de nas bu tsa rnams kyi bslab pa'i lam de la song nas drung du phyin te/ sngags rgan tshon po bang ring rakṣa'i phreng ba ring po mgul du bskon nas yang rko yin 'dug pa dang mjal/ the tsom pas de la phrin gcig zhu dgos byas nas/ 'di na mar pa lo ts.tsha bya ba gzig bzhugs zer ba de dang len gcig mjal bar zhu gyis byas pa la/ bla ma lots.tsha ba chen pos yang la rim mo mdzad nas 'di phan chad de rkos dang ngas 'phrin bya'o gsungs nas tshig su bcad pa 'di gsungs so// bla ma dam pa'i gdams ngag gis// rtsa khams dbu mar bsdus byas te// nyon mongs kyi tha ba 'dul lags na// 'bras bu myur du smin te mchi// ces gsungs so/ mi las ye ma go nas de bar mrkos pa la bla ma mgu nas rnal 'byor pa las 'ong ba gcig 'dug gsungs/ yang nga 'phrin zhu byas pa la/ yang yang la ri mo gcig mdzad nas 'di bar rkos dang ngas 'phrin bya'o gsungs nas yang tshig bcad 'di gsungs so// rgyud ldan bla ma byin rlabs kyis/ sems nyis lhug pa'i ngo bor gnas// dran pas tha ba 'dul lags na// ston thog 'bras bu myur du smin/ zhes gsungs la/ mi la'i bsam pa la ban rgan khas blas byed pa gcig 'dug bsam ba gcig byung skad/ de nas bla mas bang pa'i gseb nas chang tho lom chen po cig gi gang byung bas/ dang po bla ma chen po khong rang gi thog chen po gcig gsol/ de 'phro mi la thos pa dga' la gnang ba mi la thang chad pas 'jang pa la ngom tshad gcig byung skad/ de nas yang bla ma chen po tshig bcad 'di gsungs so// bde ba chen po chang gi dngos// yang dag don chen gsang ba 'di// yang dag gi tha ba 'dul lags na// ston thog 'bras bu smin te mchi/ zhes gsungs pa la/ mi las kyang chos tshig tu 'dug te/ ban rgan chang gi bzi nas ci zer ma tshor ba yin snyams pa byung skad/ de'i dus su rje mar pas mi la thos dga' la phyag rgya chen po dbang po rab 'bring gis <gi> chos sgom khrid byas pa yin te/ ma go bar 'dug skad/ de yang ri mo gnyis mdzad pa de zhabs tog gi dka' blas gcig/ sgom brgyag nyon mongs kyi dka' blas gcig/ de'i rjes la chang ngom tshad gcig gnang ba de ni dngos grub nyam rtog glo bur du skye ba'i brda'o// de nas bla ma chen pos thos dga' la da rnal 'byor pa khyod de sdod dang ngas 'phrin bya'o gsungs nas/ rta mo dang sel po thos dga' la khur bcug nas bla ma chen po khyim du bzhud/ mi la der bsdad pas/ jo mo 'bod byung bas da shor zer te khrid nas khyim du phyin tsa na/.*

97. Interestingly, the text later has Mar pa declare to Mi la that he met Rngog ston and his other close disciples in a similar manner.

98. DNM-S, 22b.6; DNM-I, 73. *tshe cig la mchog gi dngos grub thob par lung bstan pa'o/.*

99. DNM-S, 32b.1. *de'i nub mo drod skyes nas bzhugs thabs ma byung bas gangs kyi rtse la yar byon/ de phyin tshar nas 'dod pa'i yon tan lnga ni char bzhin du bab/ mchog thun mongs gyi dngos grub mthar thug pa ni thob/.*

100. DNM-S, 33a.8; DNM-I, 114. *de ltar rje mi la ras pa de nyid dus gsum sangs rgyas thams cad dang dbyer med cing mnyam nyid bde ba chen po'i ngang la ma g.yos kyang/ kun slob tu rtsod dus kyi gdul bya gyi snang ba la/ tha mal du byon nas dang po dka' ba du ma'i sgo nas bla ma'i zhabs ston mdzas cing snyan rgyud kyi gdams ngag rin mo che mnos/ bar du lus dka' thub dang sgrubs pa la ldem rkyang med par mdzad cing/ 'gro ba'i don mdzad cing mthar mnya ngan las 'das pa'i tshul bstan to/ de yan chad thams cad dka' spyad snying rus kyi skor ro/ snga ma gong ma'i skor ro//.*

101. Mi la's presence at Kailāsa is mentioned in works as early as Sgam po pa's (where he is said to have been cremated) and Rgyal thang pa's (where he is said to have visited the mountain). This, however, is the first detailed record of his activities there. In his standard version, Gtsang smyon Heruka describes the yogin's famed contest of miracles with the Bon po priest Na ro bon chung, and his subsequent

"conversion" of the sacred site, with an impressive sweep of dramatic narrative. In this case, however, much of the song cycle (*gang ti tse'i skor*) is devoted to the journey to and from the mountain, and the actual contest of miracles is recorded in a most perfunctory manner:

> Mi la reached the snows of Ti tse and, having opened the entrance gate to the sacred site, thereby had a visionary encounter with Cakrasaṃvara and his divine assembly on the Ti tse snows. Previously, Bon pos ruled over this sacred site, but the Rje btsun said, "This sacred site is a Buddhist location. It is the place where the Blessed One, accompanied with an assembly of five hundred arhats, once came and taught Dharma. These snows are Cakrasaṃvara's palace."
>
> An accomplished [Bon po] master called Na ro bon chung who lived there said, "This sacred site is a place blessed by the Bon po teacher Gshen rab and its snows, the divine face of Ge god. You yogin, don't stay around here." He then laid down a wager on the site (*gnas skug*) and drew the Rje btsun into a contest of miracles. But due to the power of [Mi la's] mastery of miraculous display, [Na ro bon chung] was not able to [defeat him] and offered the site to the Rje btsun.

DNM-S, 181a.4; DNM-I, 88.4. *der ti tse'i gang la byon te gnas kyi sgo phyes <phye> pas/ ti tse'i gang la 'khor lo bde mchog lha tshogs zhal gzigs/ gnas de nyid sngar bon pos bdag po byed pa la/ rje btsun gyis bnas 'di nged nang pa sangs rgyas pa'i gnas yin/ sngon bcom ldan 'das dgra bcom ba lnga brgya 'khor dang bcas pa byon nas chos gsungs pa'i gnas yin/ gang 'di 'khor lo bde mchog gi pho brang yin gsungs pas/ der na ra [I: ro] bon chung bya ba'i grub thob gcig 'dug pa des/ gnas 'di nged bon po'i ston pa gshen rab kyi [I: kyis] byin gyi brlabs pa'i gnas yin cing/ gang 'di ge god kyi lha zhal yin/ rnal 'byor pa khyod 'dir ma 'dug zer ba la/ de na gnas skug la bzhag nas rje btsun dang rdzu 'phrul 'dren pas khong rdzu 'phrul la mnga' brnyes pa'i stobs kyis khos ma thub te/ gnas rje btsun la phul lo//.*

102. This perhaps anticipates Gtsang smyon Heruka's own chapter of miscellanea, incorporated toward the end of his version of the *Collected Songs*. See NG, 678; C, 523.

103. DNM-S, 311b.2; DNM-I, 531. *slob ma ras pa rnams la ting nge 'dzin khyad par can rgyud la skyes/ khyad par du bla ma ras chung pa la dag pa'i snang ba dpag tu med pa shar/ de'i tshe rje btsun gyi gdung khang gi rlung sgo gcig la bla ma'i gsungs gi sgra grags pa/ kho bo dpral ba'i dkyil na gdung sha ri ram sran rdog [I: bdun] tsam gcig 'ong bar gda'/ de lha sman rgyal mo tshe ring ma mos pa'i rten du 'khyer bar 'dug/ gdung thal rnams phyed g.yas ru [C: su] gtsang [C: rtsang] po la phos/ phyed bong [C: bang] chu la phos/ chus khyab tshad kyi sems can thams cad ngan song las thar pa yin gsung/.* This entire section was later incorporated into the *Lho rong chos 'byung* (LRC, 100–101), where certain passages appear to have been edited and glossed (providing further evidence that DNM-I/S predates the LRC).

104. The G.yas ru gtsang po refers to the major river of southern Tibet (Gtsang po, Brahmaputra) as it passes through one of the four geographic divisions of central Tibet (*ru*): G.yas ru, which comprises half of Gtsang province. The Bong chu is a river running near Ding ri and Shel dkar to the south of the Rtsib ri massif in Gtsang, southwest Tibet. (See map 2 in Wangdu et. al. 1996). The text is somewhat ambiguous about the site of Mi la ras pa's cremation, mentioning that Ras chung pa arrives first near "the place where the Rje btsun passed away" (*rje btsun 'das*

pa'i sa), and then at Tshar ma (modern Tashigang, Nyelam) before reaching the cremation site in an unmentioned location. Although the biographical tradition generally agrees that the principal cremation took place at Chu bar in the border region of Rong shar—and the *Lho rong chos 'byung* emends its version to include that toponym—the text may refer to a location significantly farther north. However, this "alternate" account concludes with the statement, repeated by Zhi byed ri pa (writing in 1373), the *Lho rong chos 'byung*, and Gtsang smyon Heruka, "The letters oṃ āḥ hūṃ and the six syllables [oṃ maṇi padme hūṃ] appeared on a stone of the funerary chamber which still exist at Chu bar today" (*gdung khang gi rdo la oṃ aḥ hūṃ dang yig drug byon pa da lta chu bar na yod do/*). This tradition continues, as I was shown such a stone during visits to Chu bar in 1997 and 1998.

105.   As noted earlier, the implements of Mi la ras pa's daily life—his staff, shawl, flint, striker, and the like—also assume the role of sacred objects as metonymic relics through their association with his daily life. There is ample evidence that objects associated with his life continued to be venerated as relics. In his rare memoir, Bstan 'dzin Chos kyi nyi ma, the Fourth Khams sprul incarnation (1730–79/80), records that as of early 1756, a number of Mi la ras pa's possessions were kept as "religious supports" (*nang rten*) at 'Pel rgyas gling monastery in Rdzong dkar, the administrative center for Mang yul, Gung thang, and Skyid grong near the yogin's birthplace (Chos kyi nyi ma, RTL, 222a). These include the *Ratnakūṭa Sūtra* scriptures that figure in the story of Mi la ras pa's youth. The Brag dkar rta so incarnation Chos kyi dbang phyug noted that he saw the remains of this *Ratnakūṭa Sūtra* as a child, nearly half a century later, and that they were apparently taken to Tashilhunpo monastery during the Tibet-Gorkha wars (Chos kyi dbang phyug, DTL, 17b), although they were still present when Rdo ring Paṇḍita Bstan 'dzin dpal 'byor (b. 1760) passed through in 1789 (Bstan 'dzin dpal 'byor, GZN, 504). Chos kyi nyi ma also describes seeing Mi la ras pa's meditation belt (*sgom thag*), and a dagger (*phur ba*) of his magic teacher, Gnub khu lung pa Yon tan rgya mtsho. The latter is particularly interesting, as it seems to agree with the version of Mi la's early life as recorded in all three of the early compendia (in which the mother destroys her brother-in-law's house by means of a magic dagger). Zhi byed ri pa reports that it is said that Mi la ras pa's staff and his cotton robes offered by the Nepalese king were held at Ri bo che monastery in Khams, although he hadn't seen them himself (Zhi byed ri pa, NDO, 47). Mi la ras pa's possessions continue to circulate within the Tibetan Buddhist world: among the principal relics kept at Ras chung phug in central Tibet is the walking staff said to have belonged to him. Moreover, a relic pill offered to me in 1995 by the resident lama of Mar pa's seat at Gro bo lung was described by its inventory list as containing a portion of Mi la ras pa's robe.

106.   The biographical tradition is not, however, unanimous in maintaining that Mi la ras pa's corporeal relics were completely lost. Zhi byed ri pa (NDO, 42) records that the funerary ashes were divided into four parts, and used in the following manner: (1) for a statue first housed in La phyi, then moved to Bkra shis sgang in Nyelam; (2) for a statue housed in Chu bar; (3) taken by Mi la's repentant murderer dge bshes Tsag phu ba and housed in a chapel constructed by the patrons of Sding ma [Brin]; and (4) split among the disciples for individual reliquaries. A twentieth-century pilgrimage guide to the regions of Rong shar and La phyi, including some of Mi la ras pa's most famous hermitages, by Bstan 'dzin Chos kyi blo gros (1868–1906),

likewise records that the Bla ma lha khang of the Chu bar monastery housed the yogin's funerary ashes, as well as a statue of him made by Ras chung pa from clay mixed with his nasal blood (LNY, 38). A tradition of Mi la ras pa's corporeal relics also appears to have survived up to the present day. The recent international tour of Buddhist relics sponsored by contemporary Tibetan teacher Lama Zopa and The Maitreya Project lists within its treasury relics of Mi la ras pa, received by Lama Zopa from a Chinese disciple. Although it does not specify what form these relics take, the description is accompanied by a photograph of the small white pearls (*ring bsrel*) often associated with the cremation relics of Tibetan masters (see http://www.maitreyaproject.org/en/relicgallery/g-milarepa.html).

107. Nadel 1984, 207.

4. A NEW STANDARD: TSANGNYÖN HERUKA'S *LIFE* AND *SONGS OF MILAREPA*

1. On the activities of Byang chub rgyal mtshan, see van der Kuijp 1991, 2001.
2. On this conflict, and the war between Gu ge and Glo bo that followed, see Vitali 1996, 530ff.
3. See Shakabpa 1984, 73–91.
4. Smith 1969, 60.
5. See Smith 1969, Larsson 2009, 2012, and DiValerio 2011 for a discussion of this tradition. Ardussi and Epstein 1978 present a broader, more anthropological view of the phenomenon. Ehrhard 2010b examines the political relationships of Gtsang smyon Heruka's contemporary and fellow religious madman Dbus smyon Kun dga' bzang po (1458–1532).
6. See Guillory 1990.
7. Heffernan 1988, 35.
8. Three versions of Gtsang smyon Heruka's biography are known to exist, each composed by one of his disciples: 1) Dngos grub dpal 'bar, *Rje btsun gtsang pa he ru ka'i thun mong gi rnam thar yon tan gyi gangs ril dad pa'i seng ge rnam par rtse ba,* xylograph completed in 1508 at Bsam gtan gling; 2) Rgod tshang ras pa Sna tshogs rang grol (1482?–1559?), *Gtsang smyon her ru ka phyogs thams cad las rnam par rgyal ba'i rnam thar rdo rje theg pa'i gsal byed nyi ma'i snying po,* written perhaps in 1512 and xylograph completed in 1547; 3) Lha btsun Rin chen rnam rgyal (1473–1557), *Grub thob gtsang pa smyon pa'i rnam thar dad pa'i spu slong g.yo ba,* xylograph completed in 1543 at Brag dkar rta so. A rare copy of the first biography exists in the microfilm collection of the Nepal-German Manuscript Preservation project in Kathmandu. This work was completed immediately following Gtsang smyon's death, based on a number of primary sources, including the notes, diaries, and oral accounts of Gtsang smyon Heruka's closest disciples. It clearly served as a major source for both later works. Rgod tshang ras pa's biography is the most extensive of the three. On Rgod tshang ras pa's biography and literary oeuvre, see Smith 1969 and especially Ehrhard 2010a. Ehrhard has reviewed the possible dates for Rgod tshang ras pa's birth and death (2010a, 130n3) and proposes 1482–1559 as the most likely (132n6).

Ehrhard further suggests that the completion of Rgod tshang ras pa's biography of Gtsang smyon (which took place in a monkey year) corresponds to 1512 (145). The sources for Gtsang smyon Heruka's life and activities are discussed in further detail in Larsson 2009, 2012 and DiValerio 2011. A rare, and so far unstudied, xylograph copy of Gtsang smyon Heruka's collected songs, *Rje btsun gtsang pa he ru ka'i mgur 'bum rin po che dbang gi rgyal po tham cad mkhyan pa'i lam ston* by Rgod tshang ras pa, is also housed in the NGMPP archives (reel no. 567/2, 28 folios).

9. Rgod rtsang ras pa records Gtsang smyon's age as eighteen. Lha btsun, TNL, 9; Rgod tshang ras pa, TNG, 20.

10. Rgod tshang ras pa, TNG, 22.

11. Rgod tshang ras pa, TNG, 22.

12. Lha btsun, TNL, 13. Rgod tshang ras pa, TNG, 25. The former lists the Ras chung snyan rgyud and the Bde mchog snyan rgyud; the latter elaborates on this: the Bde mchog snyan rgyud, the Mkha' 'gro snyan rgyud, the Ras chung snyan rgyud, the Ngan rdzong snyan rgyud, and the Dags po snyan rgyud.

13. Lha btsun, TNL, 15.

14. Lha btsun, TNL, 16. On the sacred site and its related pilgrimage traditions, see Huber 1999.

15. Rgod tshang ras pa here uses an alternate spelling for the region's name, based on a different etymology. See Huber 1999, 82–83.

16. Rgod tshang ras pa, TNG, 37. . . . *sku gcer bur ro thal kyis byugs zhing/ khrag gi thig le/ zhag go zo ris/ mi gcig shi ba'i ro yi rgyu ma rnams do shal dang/ phyag zhabs kyi rgyan du mdzad/ rkang lag gi sor mo rnams gcad nas srang bu la rgyus ba'i 'phreng bas dbus skra bcings/ gcig gis rus pa'i rgyan ka rags med pa gcig phul ba sku la gsol/ res rgod res ngu/ khyad par khrom gseb du gyam tho sna tshogs mdzad pas/ rtsa ri ba mi sbyong shin tu rtsub ba kyang nus pas zil byi <gyis> mnan zhing thugs rjes dbang du 'dus pas shin tu mos shing kun kha 'cham par mtshan gtsang pa smyon par gsol nas phyogs kun du nyi zla ltar grags so/.*

17. Rgod tshang ras pa, TNG, 48. This passage is translated in DiValerio 2011, 125. The latter episode describes one of Buddha's thirty-two physical marks, a retractable (or sheathed) penis, also attributed to Milarepa by Lama Zhang as seen in chapter 2.

18. Lha btsun, TNL, 37, 27. Rgod tshang ras pa, TNG, 38.

19. See Vitali 1996, 533–34.

20. See Ehrhard 1991.

21. See Larsson 2012, chapter 9.

22. Smith 1969, 61. Gtsang smyon's version of Mar pa's Life has been translated into English in Nālandā Translation Committee 1986. The separate volume of Mar pa's songs has not yet been studied, but a rare copy of the Brag dkar rta so xylograph exists in the archives of the Nepal-German Manuscript Preservation Project in Kathmandu.

23. Although the following passage from Rgod tshang ras pa's text is undated, Lha btsun (TNL, 54) notes that Gtsang smyon began a year-long retreat in Chu bar in 1481 at age thirty, after which he makes the trip to Kailāsa and then Gung thang.

24. Ruins of this building remain in the village, and are still known as the Lha khang dmar po. It is interesting to note here that this temple would enshrine and commemorate Mi la ras pa's consummate sinful activity: the murder of his entire paternal family.

25. Thanks to Kurtis Schaeffer for pointing out this reference. Rgod tshang ras pa, TNG, 72. *de nas rje btsun mi la'i 'khrungs yul kyi snga rtsa na/ lha khang dmar chung bya ba dang po rje mi la rang gi a khu'i shul la/ phyi lha khang bzos shing rje btsun mi la'i sku byin rlabs can zhig yod pa mjal du phebs tshe/ sku gnyer ngab che rtsan <brtsan> phyug na re/ rje rin po che lags khyed kyis rje mi la'i rnam thar gsol 'debs zhig rtsom pa zhu zhus pas/ rje yi zhal nas khyod rang mar me stag <brtags> bgyis shig/ legs byung na ngas rtsom pa yin no gsung/.*

26. Rgod tshang ras pa, TNG, 73. *de nas rje yang thugs spro bzhin rje btsun gzhad <bzhad> pa rdo rje'i rnam par thar pa la mdzad pa bcu gnyis kyi sgo nas bstod pa'i gsung rtsom mdzad/.*

27. A praise to the Buddha's twelve deeds (*Dvādaśakāranayastotra, Mdzad pa bcu gnyis kyi tshul la bstod pa*) attributed to the Indian Buddhist philosopher Nāgārjuna (ca. second century C.E.) is translated and preserved in the Tibetan Bstan 'gyur (Toh. 1135). For a recent English translation, see Tyler Dewar, "In Praise of the Twelve Deeds of the Buddha," *Bodhi* 8, no. 1 (2004): 33–34. Accounts of the Buddha's life structured around twelve great acts are further recorded among the earliest known Tibetan histories, including Nyang ral Nyi ma'i 'od zer's twelfth-century *Chos 'byung me thog snying po sbrang rtsi'i bcud*, and Mkhas pa Lde'u's thirteenth-century *Rgya bod kyi chos 'byung rgyas pa*. Rdo rje mdzes 'od's biographical collection, discussed in chapter 2, contains a Life of the Buddha by Don mo ri pa that uses the twelve deeds as a narrative structure. Praises to the Buddha's twelve deeds were written by authors within Gtsang smyon Heruka's own Bka' brgyud tradition at least as early as the late twelfth and early thirteenth centuries. See, for example, the *Praise to the Muni's Twelve Deeds* (*Thub pa'i mdzad pa bcu gnyis*) by the 'Bri gung Bka' brgyud founder 'Jig rten mgon po (1143–1217) preserved in the *Rtsib ri par ma* (vol. 27, Darjeeling: Kargyud Sungrab Nyamso Khang, 1978–85). For an English translation, see Akester 2001–2.

28. Lha btsun, TNL, 96. */brod <grod> phug bzhugs tshe nā ro paṇ chen gyis/ /dngos su zhal stan <bstan> bzhad pa rdo rje yi/ rnam thar brtsom bar bskul zhing tshe ring mas/ /phrin las grub par khas blangs khyod la 'dud/ /ces pa ste/.*

29. Lha btsun, TNL. *//de nas la bye mtshams gnya' nang brod <grod> phug na bzhugs pa'i dus su zla bag cig gi bar dug sung ngag bcad de chos nyid ji lta ba nyid kyi chub o rgyun gyi ting nge 'dzin la snyoms par bzhugs pa'i tshe/ mnal dang 'od gsal 'gres pa'i gzigs snang la dpal nā ro pa chen po'i sku'i mdzad spyod sngar rna bar thos ching rmi lam du mthong ba las kyang tshes mngo mtshar ba'i sku bongs che ba gzi brjid 'od du 'bar ba sku bcer bu la rus ba'i rgyan drug gis brgyan cing/ seng ge dkar mo nyal ba'i gnang la za 'og sngo phra bkab ba'i steng su phyag gnyis chos 'chad kyi phyag rgya dang zhabs gnyis rgyal po rol ba'i stabs kyis bzhugs lha dang mi'i 'khor dpag tu med pas bskor nas chos gsung zhing 'dug pa la/ phyag dang maṇḍal phul chod drug gcig gsol ba btab pas/ saṃskri ta'i skad du gsungs byung pa shin du snyan pa gcig byung kyang/ [97] tshig 'bru ma go bar slar yang phyag dang maṇḍal phul nas gsol ba btab pas rdo rje tshig rkang cig rgya bod kyi skad 'gres mar gnang ba'i rje su/ /byang phyogs mun pa'i smag rum na/ /gangs la nyi ma shar 'dra ba'i/ /thos pa dga' zhes bya ba yi// skye bu de'i gsung ba'i 'tshams nas saṃskri ta'i skad du mang po zhig gsung zhing 'dug ma mgo bas thams cad mig phar cher tshur cher du 'dug/ rgya bod kyi lo tsa shes pa'i rgya gar paṇḍita'i cha byad can cig 'dug pa des rje btsun mi la ras pa 'khrungs nas sangs rgyas ba'i bar gyi rnam thar khrigs chags kyi mgur 'bum sgrigs la bar rkos te/ par 'gyed gyis sangs rgyas kyi bstan pas gar khyab tu mi la ras pa la gsol ba 'debs pa cig yong gsungs ba'i rgya skad yin zer ba la/ grub thob kyis de lta bu'i yon bdag mi 'byor gsungs bas/ rje btsun nā ro pa rgya skad cig gsung*

zhing phyag 'dzub glob o gung thang las stod phyogs la gtod pa cig gzigs/ lo tsa ban a re
de rnams khyed kyi sbyin bdag yin gsung pa'i brda' mdzad pa yin gsung par shing rkos mkhan
yig mkhan sogs ngas mi shoms gsungs pas/ yang phyag 'dzub bud med lnga sgrigs 'dug pa la
gtang song pa/ bud med lnga po langs nas 'di dag gi phrin las rgyun du bdag rnams kyis sgrub
pa zhu zer saṃskri ta'i skad kyis glu len zhing 'dug/ rje paṇ chen nā ro pa'i zhal mthong chos
thos lung stan thob snyams pa'i dga' spro'u thugs rtog gcig 'khrungs pa'i tshe/ paṇ chen nā ro
la sogs pa'i snang ba rnams yal ba dang slar yang snang med 'od gsal gyi ngang du bzhugs so/.

30. Gtsang smyon Heruka's *Life* describes Nāropa's verse of homage recited to Mar pa
during the translator's third journey to India. Mar pa's request for the the aural
transmissions and yogic instructions on ejection and transference (*'pho ba grong*
'jug) elicited the following exchange:

> Nāropa asked, "Did you remember [to request the transference of conscious-
> ness] yourself, or did you receive a revelation?"
>
> Mar pa replied, "I neither received a revelation, nor did I think of it myself.
> I have a student called Thos pa dga' who received a revelation from a *ḍākinī*."
>
> Nāropa said, "How wonderful! In the dark country of Tibet there is a being
> like the sun rising over the snow." Nāropa placed his joined palms on top of
> his head, saying:
>
>> In the gloomy darkness of the north
>> Is the one called Thos pa dga'
>> Like the sun rising upon the snows.
>> To that individual I bow down.
>
> He closed his eyes and bowed his head three times. All the mountains,
> trees, and greenery in India bowed three times. Even now the mountains and
> trees of Phullahari bow toward Tibet. (DJ, 90. Cf. Quintman 2010, 94)

Gtsang smyon Heruka repeats this passage in his biography of Marpa. See
Gtsang smyon Heruka, TDY, 107; Nālandā Translation Committee 1986, 89.

31. Rgod tshang ras pa, TNG, 137. *rje yi thugs la da lta gangs can kyi ljongs 'di na rje btsun*
gzhad <bzhad> pa rdo rje'i rnam thar dang mgur 'bum mang dag 'dug na'ang/ thung mon
ma yin pa'i rnam thar 'di rgyun chad 'dug pas gsal bar bya ba dang kho bo rang gi gdul
bya skal bar ldan pa rnam la ni/ zab rgyas kyi tshad dang gdams ngag bstan nas grol bar
byas zhing byed mod/ bsod nams ba bsags par kha 'cham la/ dam pa'i chos tshul bzhin du
bya ba'i long med pa'i rgyal po dang/ blon po dang/ mi che bar rlom pa'i dpon po so so nas
dmangs phal pa'i bar rnams dang/ chos byed par rlom zhung byed pa'i long yod la byas na
yod kyang/ zab mo'i gnad nyams su len mi shes par/ tha snyad tshig gi rbu <lbu> ba'i rjes
su rnyog pa las/ tshe gcig gi sangs rgyas kyi sar 'khrid pa'i thabs khyad par can yid bzhin
gyi nor bu las/ phyi rol du gyur pa'i dge shes su rlom pa rnams la rnam dkar kyi rigs sad
par bya ba la/ rje btsun gzhad <bzhad> pa rdo rje'i rnam thar 'di nyid mig lam du gyur na
'dod yon dang tshe 'di la zhen pa rnams la dka' thub sdug khur gyi mig rkyen/ g.yeng ba
la dga' ba rnams brtse cig bsgrub pa'i mig rkyen/ tshe cig gis sangs rgyas thob pa la the
tshom za zhing/ zab mo sgom pa'i dus min par 'dod pa rnams la/ de dag yin pa'i mthun dpe
rnam dag du gyur nas/ des don dam pa'i chos la yid ches zhing/ rab kyi tshe 'di 'am 'chi kha
bar do tshun la grol ba dang/ 'bring gis rang gis nyams su ma myong kyang/ nyams su len
pa'i skyes bu rnams la dad cing mos te mthun rkyen sgrub/ smon lam rnam par dag pas
mtshams sbyar ste/ tshe phyi mar nyams su blangs nas rten de la grol bar bya ba dang/
tha ma rnams kyis kyang log lta spangs te dad pa thun mong ma yin pa skyes nas/ 'khor ba

mtha' can du gyur pa cig nges par byed dgos pa 'dug cing/ de yang spar du bsgrubs nas 'gro ba mtha' dag la phan pa cig bya'o dgongs pas/.

32. This is perhaps clearest in the transformation of Mi la ras pa's poisoner from a Bon po priest in the compendia to a *geshe* philosopher in the standard version.

33. This likely refers to Mi la's famed retreat site Shel phug chu shing rdzong, near the village of 'Brin in the Rongshar valley of southern Tibet.

34. Lha btsun, TNL, 98. *mdang gi lung stan de yang bzang de ring tshes brgyad yang yin 'grub sbyor yang tshang bas mchod brjod kyis rtsom pa'i mgo btsugs/ rnam mgur gyi dge rnams phal che ba shin du dar bas btsal sla bar snang mod/ kha mthor ba 'ga' zhig shin du btsal dka' na yang mgur re re'i phyir yang grwa ba rnams kha gtor te/ mnga' ris dbus gtsang dang dags skong tshun nas dka' ba dpag med kyis btsal te zang zing gis rdzas phang med gnang/ par shing bcod pa'i zhal lta yig mkhan par mkhan rnams 'bod pa la phogs phyogs su rdzangs ste shel phug du phebs nas gdan phab <pheb> rnam thar kyi rkos legs par grub 'tshams/.*

35. Brag dmar is another of Mi la ras pa's famed retreat locations near 'Brin in the Rongshar Valley, several hours' walk from Shel phug.

36. Rgod tshang ras pa, TNG, 139. *de nas ston spar shing rnams spyad cing de nas spar gyi cha rkyen la dgongs nas/ 'bul ba sdud dang bsod snyom mdzad de'i sos nam na 'dum shel phug du bu slob kun 'dus shing spar rnams gzhengs pa'i dbu tshugs te/ rgyu dngos dang longs spyod pa 'phangs pa med par bsgrubs tshe/ slongs <slong> dang bdud kyi bar chad kyi rnam pas sku shin tu snyung nas brag dmar du sku mtshams mdzad/ de dus tho rangs kha cig rnal lam du tshe rings mched lngas spar 'di sogs bka' brgyud kyi bstan pa'i bya ba rnams mthar phyin pa'i 'phrin las kho mo lcag <cag> gi bsgrub pas thugs las mi dgos zer ba'i ngang la rnal sad do/ bu slob kun gyis kyang gsol 'debs gdan <brtan> gzhugs la'ang pa myur du snyung ba las grol te shel phug du phebs so/.*

37. Gtsang smyon Heruka echoes this statement himself, in his colophon to the original print edition of the *Life*, where he notes that many of his disciples offered gold, silver, and other resources at their disposal.

38. Ibid., 148. *de dus slob ma 'ga ' zhig gis/ rang re'i nor rdzas sngar ji tsam zhig zad da dung la stod lho'i dus zings <zing> chen po 'di dang bcas bas/ spar 'di grub pa'i nges pa med lags pas gshol <bshol> nas dbon slob rnams bsgrub pa la gzhugs na rtogs ldan ji tsam zhig thon/ de bas gshol <bshol> ba legs pa 'dug zhus tshe/ rje yi gsung gis nga la bud med lngas the tshe gcug <the btsugs?> yong bas grub par nges khyed rang rnams kha tshum/ rtsams <btsams> ting shol ba'i skabs med gsung ma gshol <bshol> bar sgrubs pas/ la stod lho dus shin du mi bde bar yang/ rje btsun rang gi bka' gnang ltar mtshe <'tshe> ba med cing/ kun gyi mchod gnas dang skyabs mgon du gyur pa'i ngang nas grwa pa 'ga' shas kyi spar gyi do dam mdzad cing/ rje dpon slob rnams kyi gung 'brog sogs la 'bul bsdud la phebs/ de nas nor rdzas stobs che ba dang bcas slar log phebs te lo gnyis la spar rnams mthar phyin par grub/.*

39. See DJ, 210.7.

40. A copy of Gtsang smyon's original block print has not yet come to light. However, two manuscripts preserved in the archives of the Nepal-German Manuscript Preservation Project in Kathmandu appear to have been copied from this first printing and preserve Gtsang smyon Heruka's own printer's colophon.

41. For a survey of print and manuscript culture in Tibet, see Schaeffer 2009.

42. Schaeffer 2009, 9–10. See also Jackson 1983, 1989, 1990a; Fushimi 1999.

43. See Schaeffer 2009, 63. On these early prints, see Sernesi 2011b.

44. See Smith 1969, 70–73; and Eimer and Tsering 1990 for a detailed analysis of this version's printing history.

45. Chos kyi dbang phyug DTL, 23a. He adds that the original set of blocks carved under the direction of Lha btsun Rin chen rnam rgyal had become worn with use and were recarved. Ron kyi 'od gsal phug is a meditation cave of Mi la ras pa near the provincial center of Rdzong dkar. This edition was completed in 1538 with Rin chen rnam rgyal's assistance.

46. I am currently completing an updated study of the xylograph editions of Mi la ras pa's *Life* and *Songs*.

47. See Guillory 1995, 237. For an overview of the printing projects of Gtsang smyon Heruka and his disciples, see Schaeffer 2011b.

48. Lha btsun, TNL, 99. *par mang po btab sbus gtsang phyogs la par 'gyed lan gsum bzhi tsam gnang/ mnga' ris lho byang sogs phyog mtha' dag tu mgur 'bum rnam thar dang bcas pa mang bar gnang bas/.*

49. Rgod tshang ras pa, TNG, 162.

50. Rgod tshang ras pa, TNG, 162.

51. See Chos dbang grags pa, JMT and its commentary by the first 'Bri gung Chung tshang, Chos kyi grags pa (ZNT). On Nam mkha' bsam grub rgyal mtshan's praise, see Smith 1969.

52. Gtsang smyon Heruka's production of biographical paintings previously received brief mention in Smith 1969, 66; and D. Jackson 1996, 371.

53. Recent studies include Brown 1997, Davis 1997, Kinnard 1999, Sharf 2001, and Rotman 2009. For an influential, though much criticized, study on the power of images in European traditions, see Freedburg 1989.

54. See, for example, Kossak and Singer 1999, plate 27.

55. See Heller 2001, plate 64.

56. Rgod tshang ras pa, TNG, 147.

57. Rgod tshang ras pa, TNG 158. *rje mi la'i rnam par mthar <thar> pa 'di dang mthun pa'i rnam thar thang kha gcig rnal 'byor dbang phyug gi mdzad yod 'dug pa/*

58. Rgod tshang ras pa, TNG 158, 161. *de nas rje mi la'i rnam thar dang mthun pa'i rnam thar thang ka 'di nyid sngar bod du ma grags zhing/ ma dar 'dug pas 'di nyid dar zhing rgyas pa cig byung na dgongs pa thugs la shar te/ rnam thar thang ka'i bris sku cig gung thang dang klo bo sogs stod la snang <gnang> te mang du dang/ gcig phyag rang du gzhugs te la stod lho phyogs su mang du dar bar mdzad/ gcig rgyal po don yod rdo rjes gsol ba btab cing zhal gyi bzhes pa ltar dbus gtsang sogs snang phyogs rnams su dar bar gzhed de/ thug srad bsod nams grub pa la bu khyod kyi <kyis> rnam thar thang ka 'di bzhengs pa'i zhal bkod dang/ dbus gtsang rtswa ri sogs la spar 'gyed dang 'gro don la 'gro dgos gsung tshe/.*

59. A series of three paintings, published in Dollfus 1991, are identified by inscription as Lha btsun's own work, although the paintings themselves appear to be the work of a later hand. The life story was later expanded to a widely copied series of individual paintings. See Schmid 1952; Bachhofer 1986.

60. The TTC glosses this as Jo mo glang ma ri, or Mount Everest, although in local tradition it refers to Mount Gaurishankar on the border of the Rongshar Valley in Tibet, where it is considered the abode of either one or all five of the Long Life Sisters, who figure prominently in Mi la's life story.

61. Bstan 'dzin dpal 'byor, GZN, 484. . . . *nyin gcig sman btsun tshe ring mched lnga'i pho brang gangs mthon mthing rgyal mo mthong bas rkyen byas 'gro mgon rin po che mi la ras chen gyi mdzad pa dang rnam thar dran te mig mchi mas brnangs bzhin du rje btsun chen po'i rnam mgur gyi don bsdu gsol 'debs dang Æbrel ba sho lo ka brgyad cu gya bdun yod pa*

zhig de 'phral brtsams te skye ba nas tshe rabs kun tu 'bral med rjes 'dzin yong ba'i smon 'dun gang shes byas/.

62. Bstan 'dzin chos kyi nyi ma, RTL, 130b. *de nas rje btsun mi la'i rnam mgur gtsang bsgrigs zhig 'dug pa zhag kha shas g.yar nas bltas/ sngar phru gu'i sgabs su klog sbyangs la tshar mang po klog myong kyang de skabs tshor 'di yin ci yang ma byung/.*

63. These stories contrast with an episode from the childhood of 'Bri gung master Nam mkha' rgyal mtshan (b. 1372), Gtsang smyon's contemporary and author of the famed Mi la encomium. In this story, which occurs prior to Gtsang smyon's literary activities, he draws inspiration not from the written Life and Songs but from the oral tradition:

> When he was seven or eight years old (1378/9) he saw several *ras pas* singing songs of Mi la ras pa. This aroused inconceivable faith and respect toward Mi la ras pa and he shed many tears. He had the single-minded intention, "Now, I shall definitely become a holder of Mi la's lineage. I shall renounce karmic activity and act as Mi la did."

> (Nam mkha' bsam grub rgyal mtshan, NGN, 11. *dgung lo bdun brgyad tsam gyi dus nas ras pa 'ga' zhig mi la ras pa'i mgur ma len pa gzigs pa'i rkyen byas nas/ mi la ras pa la dad gus bsam gyis mi khyab pa 'khrungs shing/ spyan chab mang du shor/ da ni nges par mi la'i brgyud 'dzin cig las rab tu byung nas mi la lta bu zhig byed dgongs pa sha stag byung bas/)* Gtsang smyon later met Nam mkha' rgyal mtshan at La phyi. See Rgod tshang ras pa, TNG, 105ff.

64. Tucci 1949, 151.

65. Stein 1962, 276.

66. Vostrikov 1970, 189.

67. Smith 1969, 3.

68. White, 1987, 24.

69. Davis 1987, 3. See especially 147n5 for a review of the literature discussing fiction in this way.

70. Nadel 1984, 9.

71. Nadel 1984; see especially chapter 1.

72. Nadel 1984, 7.

73. Nadel 1984, 7.

74. Nadel 1984, 7. The term first appeared in Virginia Woolf's "The Art of Biography."

75. Nadel 1984, 155.

76. Nadel 1984, 156.

77. Nadel 1984, 8.

78. Most subsequent editions followed this format, printing Life and Songs as independent texts. The Derge edition, however, published them as a single work, as did the modern Chinese reprint based on that edition, ironically returning to the compendia's original format. See Smith 1969, 71; Don grub rgyal, TLG, 51.

79. The words *lam ston* in the title could also be understood as "guide," creating the title A Guide for Liberation and Omniscience, further emphasizing the point above.

80. Mi la ras pa's autonarration concludes partway through chapter 11, after which Gtsang smyon as author and narrator states, "Up to this point I have recorded the Rje btsun's own sayings just as they were. I shall expand a little on this summarized description, taught by the Rje btsun himself, of the deeds that will benefit the

teachings and sentient beings through the results of his practice" (DJ, 157.29, *de yan chad rje btsun rang gi gsung ji lta ba yi ger bkod pa lags shing/ sgrub 'bras kyis bstan pa dang sems can la phan gdags pa'i mdzad pa rje btsun rang gi zhal nas gsungs pa mdor bstan lus rnam bzhag lta bur gyur pa 'di la cung zad cig rgya par phye na . . ./*).

81.   DJ, 26.5. *bla ma rje btsun rin po che sngar 'das pa'i sangs rgyas rnams kyis kyang mdzad pa bcu gnyis la sogs pa'i rnam thar pa bsam gyis mi khyab pa sems can gyi don du gsungs pa . . ./.*

82.   DJ, 22.23; 208.20.

83.   See Ricard 1996.

84.   Don grub rgyal, BGL, 457.

85.   DJ, 161.18. *de dag mgur 'bum gyi skabs su shin tu rgyas par phye nas ston to/*

86.   Rgod tshang ras pa, TNG, 162. *rje btsun bzhad pa rdo rje'i rnam thar/ de'i nang nas mchog gi mdzad pa brgyad par phye ba mgur 'bum/.*

87.   NG, 812. Chang 1969 mistranslates this passage, referring to Mi la ras pa's "eight deeds."

88.   Heffernan 1988, 31.

89.   Don grub rgyal, BGL, 457. *gal te mi la ras pa'i «rnam thar» la slob sbyong byed na «mgur 'bum» med tshe go ba zab mo zhig len mi thub pa dang/ de mtshungs mi la ras pa'i «mgur 'bum» klog skabs «rnam thar» ma shes na'ang mgur de dag gi lo rgyus kyi rgyab ljongs zhes mi thub pa lta bu'o/.*

90.   Gtsang smyon grouped together all four cycles on the Tshe ring ma sisters, previously enumerated individually in the compendia. Chang 1969 has counted them separately, accounting for his 61 chapters.

91.   Reynolds 1997, 24.

92.   Zhi byed ri pa, NDO, 47. *yang bla ma kyu ra rin po che'i 'bri khung pa la sogs pa kha gcig ni/ bcom ldan 'das don yod grub pa'i sku'i skye ba slob dpon 'phags pa klu grub snying po yin la/ de'i sku'i skye ba rje btsun mid la ras chen yin gsung ba yang 'dug la/ rje khyung tshang ba dang/ zhang lo ts.tsha ba'i zhal gsal ni mi 'dug/.* It should be noted, however, that elsewhere, Zhi byed ri pa (27) states, "Some say Rje btsun Mi la is an emanation of Buddha Amoghasiddhi, or master Ārya Nāgārjuna. But most assert that he attained *siddhi* due to perseverance in practice during his lifetime." (*kha gcig na re sangs rgyas don yod grub pa'i sprul pa/ slob dpon 'phags pa klu grub yin la/ de'i sprul pa rje btsun mi la yin bya ba yang 'dug/ phal che bas ni sku tshe 'di rang la brtson 'grus kyi grub pa thob par 'dod pa mang ba 'dug/*). This is a curious statement, since many works prior to Zhi byed ri pa's do assert Mi la's status as an emanation. It is possible that by "most" Zhi byed ri pa is referring principally to the works by Khyung tshang and Zhang Lotsāwa, two of his principal sources that, as noted in the preceding quote, were apparently silent on the matter. This is also perhaps the earliest mention of the yogin's liberation in one lifetime and a single body, and demonstrates that the two competing versions of Mi la's status—miraculous emanation and ordinary human— existed side by side for some time.

93.   Nāgārjunagarbha is recognized as the author of several works preserved in the Bstan 'gyur: Toh. 2225, 2278, 2640 (tantra section), the latter is a *sādhana* based on the *Heart Sūtra* (see Lopez 1996); Toh. 3839 (madhyamaka section); and Toh. 4307 (medicine section). Perhaps more relevant here is the fact that the name also appears in lists of eight "knowledge holders" (S. *vidyādhara*, T. *rig 'dzin*) as enumerated in Rnying ma sources. Also listed among these eight figures is Mañjuśrīmitra, an

individual more commonly described as Mi la ras pa's former manifestation, as will be described below. The TTC glosses the name Nāgārjunagarbha as an alternative reference to Ārya Nāgārjuna.

94. BA, 522, *rje btsun chen po 'di ni slob dpon 'jam dpal bshes gnyen yin no zhes grub pa'i skyes bu chen po dag gsung ngo/*; Roerich 1949, 436.

95. Chos kyi dbang phyug, DTL, 23b. This was written by the individual also responsible for the Stockholm xylograph print of *The Twelve Great Disciples*.

96. See Karma chags med, JZN, 93.

97. For a traditional account of Mañjuśrīmitra's life, see Dorje and Kapstein 1991, 490–96; and Norbu and Lipman 1987. For an account of the mental class transmissions, see Dorje and Kapstein 1991, 438ff; Roerich 1949, 168ff.

98. Davidson 1981, 5.

99. Dorje and Kapstein 1991, 922.

100. See Martin 1982. Roerich 1949, 428 freely translates one passage, "Then Mid-la received from sNub-chung numerous instructions in the Guhyagarbha, etc." The original text, however literally has "illusory display" (*sgyu 'phrul*), although this appears to have been used as a general equivalent of the *Guhyagarbha tantra*. See BA, 513. On the Guhyagarbha tradition, see Germano 1994.

101. Jacob Dalton, personal communication, November 29, 2005.

102. Martin (1982, 73n62) has also suggested this possibility, although the source he worked from (Padma dkar po's *Chos 'byung*) does not mention Mar pa 'byung nge's relation to the mental class teachings. That information is only supplied in earlier accounts.

103. See Dorje and Kapstein 1991, 701ff; Roerich 1949, 160ff, 383ff.

104. Gtsug lag 'phreng ba, KGT, 866.

105. Chos kyi dbang phyug, DTL, 11b. *de dag thams cad kyi nang nas gtso bor gyur pa slob dpon chen po manju sri mi tra 'jam dpal bshes gnyen gyi rnam par 'phrul pa ni rne btsun chen po mi la yin te/*

106. This author is also known as 'Ja' tshon snying po (1585–1656).

107. Chos kyi dbang phyug, DTL, 11b. *mkha' ri'i zhus lan las/ slob dpon chen pos chos rgyal khri srong lde btsan la bka' stsal pa/ makā ra ja/ lo pan mang po byon yong/ bod nas kyang lo tsa ba mang po yong/ khyad par nag po'i sprul pa 'brog mi zhes bya ba dang/ dom bhi he ru ka'i spril pa mar pa lo tsa zhes bya bas nyan bshad bsgom gsum dar bar byed/ bdag gi bla ma 'jam dpal bshen gnyen gyi sprul pa mi lar grags pas bsam btan pa dar ba yong/ . . . las phro gling pa'i gter byon thugs che chen po ngan song rang grol gyi lung bstan dngul dkar me long las/ de tshe shrī simha'i sprul pa ni: mar pa blo brag phyogs nas 'byung: bod khams grub thob chu mgo de yi 'jugs: de nas 'jam dpal bshe gnyen sprul pa ni: mi la zhes bya rgya bod yong la grags: zhes dang/ . . . gzhan yang klong gsal mkha' 'gro snying thig sogs du ma zhig nas lung ri snyil ba ltar mang kyang 'dir yi ge'i 'jigs zhing/.*

108. See Chos kyi dbang phyug, DKS, 20b; 25b.

109. Ricard 1994, 471.

110. Ricard 1994, xx.

111. Zhi byed ri pa, NDO, 43. *da lta 'og min chos kyi pho brang na byang chub sems dpa' sems dba' chen po kun dga' blo gros zhes bya ba'i mtshan bzung nas chos sku dri bral rtogs pa dang ldan par dag pa ye shes kyi sa thob nas/ sangs rgyas bcom ldan 'das drug pa rdo rje 'chang chen po'i drung du dam pa' chos gsan cing bzhugs pa nyid yin te/ de yang sngon longs sku lus med ma dang/ te lo pa dang/ na ro pa la sogs pa gong ma rnams kyi lung bstan*

dang/ rje btsun lho brag mar pa pa chen po'i zhal bzhes dang/ rje btsun chen mo mid la ras chen rang gi zhal nas gsung ngag khyad par 'phags pa rnams dang/ thugs kyi sras mchog ras chung rdo rje grags pa la sogs pa'i bu chen rnams kyis kyang gsungs la/ khyad par du rje khyung tshang pa dznyā na gu ru dang/ lnga rig shes bya'i gnas la ma rmongs pa/ chos rje zhang lo ts.tsha ba'i gsung la gsal bar bzhugs cing/ dpal phag mo grub <gru> pa rdo rje rgyal po'i skyes rabs las kyang gsal bar bstan pa nyid do/ longs sku sprul slu gnyis kyi sku ni bsam gyis mi khyab la/ da lta yang longs sku lus med mkha' 'gro 'i snyan rgyud yid bzhin nor bu 'dzin pa'i sprul sku rnams dang/ nā ro chos drug mgo rtsa ma log par 'dzin pa'i gang zag nam pa rnams ni/ bla ma mid la ras chen gyis <gyi> sprul sku lags so/.

112. See 'Jam mgon kong sprul, YSJ, 517. Kong sprul is commenting on a biographical verse of praise written by the Eighth Karma pa, Mi skyod rdo rje, recorded in his (Kong sprul's) Mi la *guruyoga sādhana* ('Jam mgon kong sprul, YPB). Kong sprul notes that Mi la attained complete awakening, manifested innumerable emanations including Mañjuśrīmitra, and then, though the power of his aspirations, took birth in Tibet.

113. Nam mkha' rgyal mtshan, NGN, preface.

114. Pabongka Rinpoché 1991, 331. According to the TBRC catalogue entry (P3460), this individual was also known as Lho brag pa, identifying his association with the homeland of Mi la's guru Mar pa. He studied under Atisha (b. 972/982) and thus would have lived perhaps one generation before Mi la ras pa.

115. Chos kyi dbang phyug, DTL, 22a. *nges pa'i don du tshe gcig lus gcig gi mngon par rdzogs par sangs rgyas na slar yang sprul pa'i rnam rol mkha' khyab tu 'gyed cing/ bod yul 'dir yang/ 'bri khung skyob pa rin chen dpal dang/ lo ras dar ma dbang phyug/ rgod tshang pa mgon po rdo rje dang/ phyi ma'i dus 'dir grub thob gtsang smyon pa sogs sprul pa'i mtshan gi rnam grangs lang gu bstan par grags so/.*

116. Chos kyi dbang phyug, DTL, 22a. See previous note.

117. Quintman 2010, 165.

118. Quintman 2010, 166.

119. Quintman 2010, 166–67.

120. Smith 1969, 60.

121. Smith 1969, 60.

122. Smith 1969, 61.

123. See Lha btsun, TNL, 48.

124. This statement appears in the context of a prophecy Mi la receives from his guru, Mar pa, regarding the sacred mountain site of Tsā ri. Gtsang smyon has Mar pa tell Mi la ras pa, shortly before the yogin's departure for a life of solitary practice: "Together in the east lie the great sacred site of Devīkoṭa and Tsāri. It is not, at present, time to open them. In the future your spiritual descendants will establish themselves there" (DJ, 103; cf. Quintman 2010, 109. *shar phyogs na gnas chen de wi ko ṭa dang/ tsā ri 'brel nas yod de/ de da lta zhal byed ma ran/ ma 'ongs pa na khyod kyi bu rgyud kyis 'dzin pa zhig 'ong ba yin/*). "Spiritual descendants" no doubt refers to, among others, Gtsang smyon himself.

125. See Ehrhard 1991.

126. Bstan 'dzin chos kyi blo gros, LNY, 34; Rgod tshang ras pa, TNG, 214 (who repeatedly uses the spelling 'O 'byung). 'Om chung is noted in the colophon to Ngan rdzong's second Tshe ring ma chapter as the place where he and Zhi ba 'od recorded the episode. According to Bstan 'dzin chos kyi blo gros, after Mi la ras pa, the site

passed to Gnyos rgyal ba Lha nang, and then to the acclaimed yogin and poet Ko brag pa Bsod nams rgyal mtshan (1170–1249). Following a period of stewardship by the 'Bri gung Bka' brgyud, the site was then passed to Gtsang smyon.

127. See Smith 1969 and Schaeffer 2009.

128. Lha btsun's anonymous biography CRD describes how many of his compositions were inspired by visionary experiences in which he meets Gtsang smyon Heruka in the form of a great lineage master. After waking, he would typically record the experience in a painting before putting its content in writing. One evening, for example, he experiences a vision of Gtsang smyon Heruka in the form of Tilopa riding a white lion. The master teaches the instructions of the *Rdo rje gzhung chung*, after which Lha btsun fashions a cloth painting (*ras bris*) and produces his writings on that text. He later has a vision of Gtsang smyon in the form of Nāropa riding a golden tiger, after which he crafts another painting before writing his biography of the Bengali *siddha*. He also has visions of Gtsang smyon in the forms of Sha wa ri pa and Mar pa. Anon., CRD, 44b, 45a, 46a, 46b.

129. However, since the aural transmissions, principally the Ras chung snyan brgyud, did not survive as an independent tradition but were absorbed into and transmitted by the 'Brug pa Bka' brgyud, Gtsang smyon is often referred to as a 'Brug pa master.

130. Quintman 2010, 167.

5. THE YOGIN AND THE MADMAN: A LIFE BROUGHT TO LIFE

1. The depiction of Gtsang smyon Heruka's death, and its possible relationship to the tradition of Mi la ras pa's own passing, has been discussed in Schaeffer 2002.

2. See Ehrhard 2010a, 154.

3. Jäschke 1881, xxii; Das 1902, xxix.

4. Bacot 1925, 19.

5. Evans-Wentz 1928, 306, 309. The former quotation pertains to a mistranslation of Gtsang smyon's reference to Sgam po pa's own biography, calling it instead Sgam po pa's biography of Mi la ras pa.

6. Evans-Wentz 1928, 31.

7. Tucci 1949, 98.

8. DJ, 11.

9. C, 688.

10. Smith 1969.

11. L, xxx. Emphasis added. Lhalungpa's reference to the *Life* as an autobiography and later, a "genuine autobiography," fits well with the discussion above.

12. Don grub rgyal, 45. *gtsang smyon gyis rang gi mthong thos su gyur pa'i mi la'i rnam thar thor bu rnams phyogs gcig bsgrigs te/ nyams pa sor chud dang ma nyams gong du spel ba'i phyir/ ma dag rgyud 'byams su song sba rnams dag par bcos/ mi bden lhad kyis zhugs pa rnams bden par bcos/.*

13. Don grub rgyal's view, echoing that of many readers both inside Tibet and out, stands somewhat ironically in contrast to the usual polemic pitting hagiography against what is considered historical truth.

14. See, for example, Nadel 1988.
15. Rear cover, A. J. A. Symon, *Quest for Corvo* (NYRB Classics, reprint ed., 2001).
16. Nadel 1988, 27.
17. Heffernan 1988, 75.
18. Heffernan 1988, 76.
19. Heffernan 1988, 76.
20. Although his *Illuminating Lamp* repeatedly refers to some 127 different versions of the life story, the author also documents in detail his position as a direct recipient in the transmission lineage of Mi la ras pa's teachings, his songs, and his biographical traditions.
21. Smith 1969, 61.
22. Smith 1969, 61–62. This passage occurs in Rgod tshang ras pa, TNG, 132.
23. Lha btsun, TNL, 7.
24. Lha btsun, TNL, 45. *de nas rje nyid dgung lo nyer drug pa la yar bod la byon nas/ brin gyi brag dmar mchong lung du zla ba gcig tsam chu bo rgyun ting nge 'din la snyoms par bzhugs pas/ rje btsun mi la ras pa de nyid res 'ga' rnam thar gsung ba/ res 'ga' thugs brtse ba'i zhal bkod gnang ba/ res 'ga' chos gsung ba/ res rdzu 'phrul sna tshogs ston pa la sogs te. . . .*
25. The narrative seems to momentarily slip into the first person here.
26. Lha btsun, TNL, 45. *de nas zhag 'ga' song ba dang mnal dang 'od gsal 'gres pa'i ngang la/ nam mkha' 'ja' 'od kyi dbus su rje btsun bzhad pa rdo rje sku gzi mdangs shin du cho ba phyag na shel gyi ka pā la bdud rtsis gang ba bsnams ba cig 'dug pa'i zhal nas/ kha sang gi brda de tsho la gsang mtshan stan pa'i dbang zer ba yin/ rtsa mdud 'grol ba gsang ba'i dbang/ khyab byed kyi rlung dbang du 'dus pa/ shes rab ye shes kyi dbang gnyis cig char du bskur ba la yid ches pa gyis 'khor lo lngar ye shes skyes pa'i 'gro ba 'di lta bu cig yong gsung/ bdud rtsi ka pā la nga'i kha ru blug byung/ lces ro ji ltar myong ba ltar de ni lus kyi bspu'i bug kha re res kyang zag med kyi bde bas ra ro ba'i ting nge 'dzin gyi ngang la song ngo/.*
27. Lha btsun, TNL, 49.
28. Lha btsun, TNL, 51. *de nas dbyar de la phyi la gzhan phan gyi sgrub pa la bzhugs pa'i dus su rje mi la'i zhabs rjes la gser chab gsol bas sa chen po lan gsum gyi bar du g.yos shing/ zhabs rjes la oṃ āḥ hūṃ gsum 'bur du byon nas.*
29. Lha btsun, TNL, 77. *tho rangs ting nge 'dzin shin du dangs ba'i ngang la nam mkhar 'ja' 'od kyi gur phub ba'i nang na rje btsun bzhad pa rdo rje de nyid sku'i bkod pa mtha' dag nas bsal zhing gzi brjid 'od du 'bar ba phyag g.yas chos 'chad g.yon mnyam gzhag gi stengs na ka pā la bdud rtsis gang ba bsnams ba/ zhabs dkyil dkrungs phyed pas padma stong ldan lta bu'i 'ja' 'od kyi steng na bzhugs pa cig gzigs pa la/ mos gus tshad med pa'i gdung shugs drag pos phyag mang du btsal la byin brlabs zhu bar rtsams pa na/ phyag g.yas pas rje nyid kyis dbul byam bil du ma mdzad nas khyod la ming gnyis yod pa'i dang ma la bde ba skyong da lta mthu stob dbang phyug bya ba yin no gsung nas 'ja' ltar yal song/.*
30. Rgod tshang ras pa, TNG, 148. *da lta la stod lho na rje mi la'i sprul pa rnal 'byor gyi dbang phyug gtsang smyon pas rje mi la'i rnam thar mgur 'bum spar du bzheng zhing 'dug. . . .*
31. Rgod tshang ras pa, TNG, 152. *de nas spar rnams gnya' nang grod phug du gdan grangs <drangs> sde pa tsha 'da' ba sogs dad can gyi yon bdag tha dad nas ci dgos kyi zhabs rtogs <tog> yang dag phul/ spar khang bzhis <gzhis> kha dpar mrgyun <brgyun> chags dang bcas bstan pa rin po che'i gsal byed dang sems can ma lus ba'i bde skyid kyi 'byung gnas su gzhugs su gsol lo/ de dus kun gyis rje dpon slob rnams la bsnyen bkur bzang po phul zhing khyad par du gnya' nang dgon gsar ba bla chen ngag dbang grags pas tshogs 'khor 'bul ba dang bcas pa yang dag mdzad rjes/ rje rin po che lags khyed kyi mdzad pa gang la ltas rung sangs rgyas*

byang chub sems dpa' gang rung ba cig gi rnams <rnam> sprul las 'os mi 'dug cing mi rnams gyi zer lugs la rje btsun ras chung pa/ ngan rdzong ston pa sogs gang gi sprul pa yin la kha mi 'cham zhing zer lugs sna tshogs pa gcig 'dug pa gang lags pa/ gang gi sprul pa yin dang rje btsun mi la'i rnam thar na yod [?] pa'i thun mong ma yin pa'i slob dpon su yin rnams <nam> gsung du gsol zhus tshe/ rje yi gsung gi nga su'i sprul pa yin la phyi ras chen phug gi zhabs rjes la ltas pas shes/ thun mong ma yin pa'i slob dpon nga shi nas sngon <mngon> yong gsung/.

32. The account in the *Songs* in which Mi la leaves these footprints occurs in *Sal le 'od kyi skor* of Gtsang smyon's version (NG, 574; C, 416) where Mi la flies from Brag dmar to Ras chung phug, leaving his footprints in the rock as he lands.

33. See Rgod tshang ras pa, TNG, 214 for Chos grags rgya mtsho's praise of Gtsang smyon's literary activity and his efforts in restoring the *mahācaitya* of Swayambhū.

34. Mi nyag pa likely refers to Mi nyag pa Rdo rje seng ge (b. 1462), who received teachings from the Fourth Zhwa dmar Chos grags ye shes (1453-1524). See TBRC database (P463).

35. Rgod tshang ras pa, TNG, 161. *de dus sprul sku rin po che zhwa dmar spyod <cod> paṇ 'dzin pa'i dpon po mi nyag bya ba dang/ chos rje rtsa ri rab 'byams pa dpon slob 'ga' rje yi snyan pas yid grogs <'phrogs> te zhabs drung du byon pa/ dbang dang gdams pas rjes su bzung te sgom zhing yong pa las/ dpon po mi nyag pa la tho rangs kha zhig gi rmi lam na rgyan du mas dgeg [?] cing ras gos gon pa'i bu mo mdzes ma lnga byung nas/ khyod mi la ras chen la chos e zhu zer/ los zhu gang na gshugs byas pas pha bong dkar lab na gzhugs zer/ bu mo de rnams dang sdongs <sdong> nas phyin pas pha bong gi steng na rje rin po che rus pa dang dur khrod kyi chas kyi rgyan nas phyed dkyil <skyil> log ge phyag g.yon pa sa ka rtsugs <gtsugs> nas g.yas chos 'chad kyi tshul du gzhugs 'dug pas/ 'di ni pha rin po che yin/ mi la ras pa ga na gzhugs sam mnyam pa la/ bu mo rnams na re 'di ka mi la ras pa yin/ khyod rang gis ngo ma shes 'dug pa da chos zhus zer khong rnams phyags 'tshal zhing 'dug/ dpon po bas kyang phyag phul nas sa la sdad pas/ drang nge kyi chos mang po snang zhing sems la phan par byung te/ rnal sad tshe sngar dang mi 'dra ba'i mos gus kyis dungs <gdung> shugs skyes/ rje btsun mi la dngos su byon par yid ches shing blo thag chod do/.*

36. Dngos grub dpal 'bar, TNN, 26b. *grwa pa bu slob yon bdag dang bcas pa rnams/ snyigs dus mi la ras pa rang dngos su 'jal ba yin pas/ las dang skal ba bzang/ da dung mi la'i rnam thar la ltos la/ tshe dang sgrub pa snyoms/.*

37. Lha btsun, TNL, 128.

38. See Thu'u bkwan, CRN, 38–39. Smith 1969 pointed this out for the first time.

39. Rgod tshang ras pa, TNG, 8.

40. Rgod tshang ras pa, TNG, 8.

41. Rgod tshang ras pa, TNG, 13. *de yang rje btsun rnal 'byor gyi dbang phyug dpal ldan gzhad pa rdo rje de nyid/ ngo mtshar rmad du byung ba'i mdzad pas tshe gcig gis bcu gsum rdo rje 'dzin pa'i sa sgrod <bgrod> kyang/ tshad med pa'i thugs skyed dang smon lam gyi dbang gis/ 'dul bya gang la gang 'dul gyi sku dang mdzad pas/ sangs rgyas kyi zhing rab 'byams thams cad khyab cing/ srid mthar 'gro ba'i don mdzad pa las/ lnga brgya tha ma snyings <snyigs> ma lnga sngo <bdo> ba'i dus 'dir/ byang phyogs gi zhing 'dir 'og min lhun gyi grub pa'i zhing khams nas/ mkhyen rtse <brtse> ye shes kyi 'od zer spros pa las/ sprul sku chen po yum gyi ltums su zhugs te/.*

42. Chos kyi dbang phyug, DTL, 22a.

43. Chos kyi dbang phyug, DTL, 23a. *mna ngan las 'da 'khar gra bu slob yon bdag dang bcas pa rnams snyigs dus kyi mi la ras pa dang dngos su mjal ba yin pas dga bar gyis/ zhes gsung pa 'dis rje btsun nyid kyi sprul par zhal gyi bzhes pa yin tshul slob brgyud rnams bzhed/.*

44. Thrangu Rinpoche 1999, 7.
45. As discussed in chapter 3, Rgyal thang pa's text presents one exception in which the first chapter is largely devoted to describing Mi la ras pa's miraculous origins. Zhi byed ri pa's work begins with a record of the yogin's family history and lineage, although it incorporates a fair amount of detail.
46. DJ, 23; Quintman 2010, 11.
47. Kazi Dawa-Samdup's translation in the Evans-Wentz edition (1928, 41) captures the intended meaning, "At one time, so I have heard," although Lhalungpa strangely leaves this reference out. Traditional commentators and scholars of Buddhist literature have variously understood the phrase *evaṃ mayā śrutam* and its Tibetan equivalent *'di skad bdag gis thos pa dus gcig na* as meaning both "thus did I hear at one time," and "thus did I hear: at one time." For a discussion of these two readings and the divergence of the Tibetan rendered from Sanskrit sources, see von Staël-Holstein 1933, Brough 1950, Galloway 1991, and Lopez 1988, 1996. Galloway 1991, 92 critiques the earlier scholarship and specifically addresses the common Tibetan variant "*thos pa'i dus gcig,*" used by Gtsang smyon Heruka, and argues for the translation used in the passage above.
48. There is, however, little uniformity regarding the definition of this term and the following one. For a discussion of their various interpretations, see Galloway 1991, 98; Lopez 1996, 47n1.
49. This definition is from Haribhadra's *Abhisamayālaṃkārāloka*. Cited in Lopez 1996, 47n1. Cf. Sparham 2006, 174.
50. Lopez 1996, 19.
51. Questions arose, for example, as to whether Ānanda—a "pre-Mahāyāna" follower— was capable of also understanding the words of the *Prajñāpāramitā* as he heard them. More pertinent here, though, are the historical implications of locating Ānanda in texts written many centuries after the Buddha's death. This became a major hermeneutical enterprise for Mahāyāna Buddhist commentators, who sought to defend their works as existing coeval with the Buddha and his great disciples, thereby maintaining the status of those works as *buddhavacana*. See Lopez 1988, 33–41; 1996, 19–46. The Mahāyāna strategies for determining scriptural authenticity have been described at length and in detail in MacQueen 1981, 1982; Lamotte 1984; Davidson 1990; and Lopez 1996.
52. Brough 1950, 423.
53. DJ, 210; Quintman 2010, 234. *rje btsun gyi rnam thar du ma mthong na'ang/ thun mong ma yin pa'i slob dpon gyi zhal nas byung ba ji lta ba bzhin dur khrod nyul ba' rnal 'byor pa rus pa'i rgyan can gyis/ . . . dag cing rdzogs par yi ger bkod pa. . . .* Lhalungpa (203) misconstrues this passage slightly, translating instead, "It was transmitted to me by my lama according to the secret oral tradition, although I have seen other accounts of Jetsün's traditions." In this passage, however, the emphasis is not merely that the transmission was an oral one (and the original Tibetan makes no mention of a secret tradition), but rather that it was taught directly by the "extraordinary master."
54. Gtsang smyon Heruka opens the *Life* by referring to Mi la ras pa as the "great heruka," perhaps quietly acknowledging his own identification with the yogin.

6. CONCLUSIONS

1. Lamotte 1988, 665.
2. These "rules" were derived from E. Gene Smith's *Among Tibetan Texts* (Boston: Wisdom Publications, 2001) by Kurtis Schaeffer for circulation at the memorial for Smith's passing on February 12, 2011. They are reproduced here with permission.

EPILOGUE

1. Cited in Reynolds and Hallesy 1987, 322.
2. BA 518; Roerich 1949, 432. *de yan chad cung zad zhib par bris te/ bcos ma mang po mthong bas 'di tsam zhig 'thad pa yin no snyam nas bgyis so/.*
3. Cited in the pilgrimage guide to the Kathmandu Valley by the fourth Khams sprul, Bstan 'dzin chos kyi nyi ma (1730–79), written in 1756. See Macdonald 1989, 123. For the Tibetan text, see Macdonald 1975. *gzhan yang mchan don dang ldan pa'i thams cad mkhyen pa chen po kun mkhyen padma dkar po'i gsung las kyang/ gu ru padma 'byung gnas lta bu ni skad cig bskal pa dang bskal pa skad cig tu bsgyur nus pa'i rdzu 'phrul gyi cho 'phrul can yin pas kha cig tu brdzus te skye ba dang la lar mi'i mnal nas skye ba sogs 'gal ba ltar snang ba'i rnam thar rgya mtsho lta bu la nges bzung byar med pas gang dang gang bshad pa thams cad 'thad cing yin par ces dngos zhes. . . .*
4. Nikos Kazantzakis, *Zorba the Greek* (1952; reprint, New York: Simon & Schuster, 1996), 64.

APPENDIX 1

1. This is an excerpt of Sgam po pa's *Lives of Lord Marpa and Jetsün Mila* (*Rje mar pa dang rje btsun mi la'i rnam thar*). Four readily available editions of the *Collected Works* have been consulted for the translation. See Sgam po pa, MMN, in the bibliography. Sherpa 2004 lists several other editions of the *Collected Works*, unavailable to me.
2. Khenpo Shedup 2004, 34.2 has *yum* (mother) where the previous editions have *yab* (father), an example, perhaps, of editing the text under the influence of Gtsang smyon's standard version.
3. Sgam po pa's text includes the following brief passage, whose meaning was unclear even for several knowledgeable Tibetan informants. Lama Zhang's text elides the entire passage. *mngon par shes pa'i sha ro bstan/ ma chung gang sdoms pas sngar ma 'thungs/ bud med gzhon nu ma la bu skye gsungs/ mgur mo'i mkhar ston gyis srang du phyin pa la/ kho na re nga'i rig pa 'di yin zer/.*
4. The subject here is made clear in Zhang 2004, 157.
5. The subject here is made clear in Zhang 2004, 158.

APPENDIX 2

1. O: gzhad
2. N: sgyur
3. N: lnga yis
4. N: tho tho ri
5. N: bsgyur
6. O: kyi
7. O: phrin gyis
8. N: bkod
9. N: la/ lacking
10. N: bu lacking
11. N: rdzongs
12. N: drong sogs
13. N: snyan
14. N: chags ri
15. N: brgyag
16. N: dpa'
17. N: 'khor lo yi > 'di
18. N: brjed
19. N: inserts: pa bsal
20. O: 'gro la
21. O: rab
22. N: rnams
23. N: par
24. I: brgyad
25. I: su
26. I: nas
27. I: kyis
28. I: phag
29. I: shing
30. I: gyis
31. I: lags
32. I: sgrub
33. I: chen po
34. I: gyis
35. I: rigs
36. I: nas
37. I: gyis
38. I: nas
39. I: sgrubs
40. I: kyis
41. I: 'ang
42. I: yid
43. C: bsod nams mchog gi
44. I: yis
45. I: gyis

APPENDIX 3

1. Compare with Sgam po pa, which has "journey to Nepal (Bal po)."
2. This episode is a summary, without songs, of the third Tshe ring ma chapter recorded in the biographical compendia, as well as Gtsang smyon Heruka's standard version, under the title *bar do 'phrang grol.*
3. Lacking in BCN or DNM.
4. Lacking in BCN.
5. Lacking in BCN.
6. More extensive than BCN.
7. Missing final folio.
8. Missing beginning folio.
9. Lacking in BC.
10. Missing final pages.
11. Missing beginning pages; starts at BCO 86a.5; BCN 113b.4.
12. Lacking in BC.
13. Lacking in BC.
14. Extended introductory section. BC version begins at 233a.1.
15. Folios 249–257 missing.
16. Lacking in DNM-Lhasa and DNM-I/S.
17. Lacking in DNM-Lhasa and DNM-I/S.
18. Moved to § 25 in DNM-I/S.
19. Lacking in DNM-Lhasa and DNM-I/S.
20. Lacking in DNM-Lhasa.
21. Lacking in DNM-Lhasa.
22. DNM-I/S combines §38–39 into a single cycle.
23. Lacking in DNM-Lhasa and DNM-I/S.
24. Lacking in DNM-Lhasa and DNM-I/S.
25. Moved from the following section in DNM-Lhasa.
26. Lacking in DNM-Lhasa and DNM-I/S.
27. Lacking in DNM-Lhasa and DNM-I/S.
28. The text mistakenly reads xvii.
29. The heading for section xvii appears to be missing.
30. The text mistakenly reads xviii.
31. Lacking in DNM-Lhasa.
32. Newly added. DNM-S missing two folios.
33. DNM-S mistakenly labels it number 11.
34. Moved from its position in DNM-Lhasa §32. DNM-S has some pages out of order here.
35. DNM-S has pages out of order here; possible missing pages or repeats.
36. Newly added.
37. Newly added.
38. Newly added.
39. Newly added. DNM-S missing final few lines and chapter title.
40. Newly added. DNM-S missing final few lines and chapter title.
41. Moved from its position in DNM-Lhasa §38.
42. Moved from its position in DNM-Lhasa §39.

43. Newly added.
44. DNM-I missing pages 211–16.
45. Newly added.
46. The DNM-I/S version of the first two Tshe ring ma episisodes diverges slightly from the BC and DNM-Lhasa in that it combines the first two accounts into a single song cycle, eliding the colophon to the first episode.
47. DNM-S has some repeats and some folios out of order here.
48. Newly added.
49. Separated from DNM-Lhasa §53.
50. Separated from DNM-Lhasa §57.
51. Separated from DNM-Lhasa §57.
52. DNM-S missing 4 folios.

BIBLIOGRAPHY

TIBETAN LANGUAGE SOURCES

DNM-D   *Mi la'i gsung mgur mdzod nag ma.* Khren tu'u: si khron mi rigs dpe skrun khang, 2008. 2 vols. Also published in *'Bri gung bka' brgyud chos mdzod chen mo.* Lhasa: S.N., 2004, vols. 7–8.

DNM-I   *Rnal ' byor gyi dbang phyug mi la bzhad pa rdo rje'i gsung mgur ma mdzod nag ma zhes pa ka rma pa rang byung rdo rjes phyog gcig tu bkos pa.* Dalhousie: Damchoe Sangpo, 1978. 2 vols.

DNM-Lhasa   *Rje btsun mi la rdo rje rgyal mtshan gyi rnam par thar pa'i dbu phyogs lags.* Unpublished *dbu med* manuscript in the archives of 'Bras spung Monastery. *'Bras spung dkar chag: phyi ra* 42, 017082, 309 folios.

DNM-RD   "Mi la bzhad pa rdo rje'i gsung mgur mdzod nag ma zhes pa karma pa rang byung rdo rjes phyogs gcig tu bkod pa." In *Karma pa rang byung rdo rje'i gsung 'bum.* Zi ling: Mtshur phu mkhan po lo yag bkra shis, 2006. Vol. ga, 5–778.

DNM-S   *Rje rnal sbyor gyi dbang phyug dpal bzhad pa' i rdo rje'i 'gur 'tshogs tshad phyogs gcig du bsgrig pa lo rgyus kyis sbas pa zhes bya ba bzhugs so.* Unpublished *dbu med* manuscript in the collection of E. Gene Smith.

KDZ   *Bod dang bar khams rgya sog bcas kyi bla sprul rnams kyi skye 'phreng deb gzhung.* In *Bod yig gal che'i lo rgyus yig cha bdams bsgrigs.* Gangs can rig mdzod 16. Sinkiang: Bod ljongs bod yig dbe rnying dpe skrun khang, 1991, 281–369.

CRD   *Dpal ldan bla ma dam pa mkhas grub lha btsun chos kyi rgyal po'i rnam mgur blo ' das chos sku' i rang gdangs.* Kathmandu, Nepal. NGMPP Reel no. L11/20, 54 folios.

Bstan 'dzin Chos kyi blo gros (1868–1906)

LNY   *Gsang lam sgrub pa'i gnas chen nyer bzhi'i ya gyal gau dā wa ri'am/ 'brog la phyi gangs kyi ra ba'i sngon byung gi tshul las tsam pa'i gtam gyi rab tu phyed pa nyung ngu rnam gsal.* Gangtok: Sherab Gyaltsen, 1983.

Bstan 'dzin Chos kyi nyi ma (1730–79/80)

RTL   *Rang tshul lhug par smra pa ma bcos gnyug ma'i rang grol.* Unpublished *dbu med* manuscript.

Bstan 'dzin dpal 'byor, Rdo ring Paṇḍita (b. 1760)

GZN   *Dga' bzhi ba'i rnam thar.* Lhasa: Bod ljongs mi dmangs dpe skrun khang, 1988.

Byang chub bzang po (sixteenth century)

DKN   *Bde mchog mkha' snyan rgyud (ras chung snyan rgyud).* Reproduced from the rare manuscript in the library of Apho Rinpoche. 2 vols. Delhi, 1973.

RMN   [*Mi la ras pa'i rnam thar*]. In Byang chub bzang po (ca. sixteenth century), ed., *Bde mchog mkha' 'gro snyan rgyud (ras chung snyan rgyud).* Reproduced from the rare manuscript in the library of Apho Rinpoche. Delhi, 1973. Vol. 1, 97–125. Attributed to Ras chung pa.

Chos dbang grags pa (1404–69)

JMT   *Rje btsun mi la ras pa la bstod pa'i tshigs su bcad pa ka la ping ka'i sgra dbyangs. Sbrang char* 31. 1988–89.

Chos kyi dbang phyug, Brag dkar rta so sprul sku (1775–1837)

DKS   *Dpal ldan gzhung 'brug pa bka' brgyud gser phreng.* Written 1820. Kathmandu, Nepal. NGMPP reel no. L381/1, 55 folios. *Dbu med* manuscript.

DTL   *Grub pa'i gnas chen brag dkar rta so'i gnas dang gdan rabs bla ma brgyud pa'i lo rgyus mdo tsam brjod pa mos ldan dad pa'i gdung sel drang srong dga' ba'i dal gtam zhes bya ba bzhugs so.* Written in 1816. Kathmandu, Nepal. NGMPP reel no. 940/8, 52 folios. *Dbu med* manuscript.

Chos kyi grags pa, 'Brin gung Chung tshang 1 (1595–1659)

ZNT   *Rje btsun bzhad pa rdo rjer snyan ngag gi bstod pa ka la pingka gsal byas pa.* In *The Collected Works (gsun 'bum) of Kun-mkhyen Rig-pa 'dzin-pa Chen-po Chos-kyi-grags-pa.* Dehradun: Drikung Kagyu Institute, 1999. Vol. 15, 157–68.

Chos kyi rgya mtsho, Kaḥ thog Si tu (1880–1925)

DLY   *An Account of a Pilgrimage to Central Tibet During the Years 1918 to 1920,* being the text of *Gangs ljongs dbus gtsang gnas bskor lam yig nor bu zla shel gyi se mo do.* Tashijong, India: Sungrab Nyamso Gyunphel Parkhang, 1972.

Dam pa ras chen (ca. early twelfth century)

NDN   *Rgyud pa yid bzhin nor bu las rje btsun ngan rdzong ras pa'i rnam thar 'khrul med.* In *Ngam rdzong snyan brgyud kyi skor.* Bir: D. Tsondu Senghe, 1985, 1–17.

Dngos grub dpal 'bar (sixteenth century)

TND   *Rje btsun gtsang pa he ru ka'i thun mong gi rnam thar yon tan gyi gangs ril dad pa'i seng ge rnam par rtse ba*. Microfilm. Kathmandu, Nepal. NGMPP reel no. L834/2, 31 folios.

Don grub rgyal (1953–85)

BGL   *Bod kyi mgur glu byung 'phel gyi lo rgyus dang khyad chos bsdus par ston pa rig pa'i khye'u rnam par rtsen pa'i skyed tshal*. In *Dpal don grub rgyal gyi gsung 'bum*. Beijing: Mi rigs dpe skrun khang, 1997. 6 vols. Vol. 3, 316–601.

TLG   *«Mi la ras pa'i rnam thar» gyi rtsom pa po'i lo rgyus*. In *Dpal don grub rgyal gyi gsung 'bum*. Beijing: Mi rigs dpe skrun khang, 1997. 6 vols. Vol. 3, 27–53.

Don mo ri pa (b. 1203)

JMN   *Rje btsun mi la'i rnam thar*. In *Rdo rje bdzes 'od, Bka' brgyud kyi rnam thar chen mo rin po che'i gter mdzod dgos 'byung gnas*. Bir, India: D. Tsondu Senghe, 1985, 176–218.

Dpal brtsegs bod yig dpe rnying zhib 'jug khang

DK   *'Bras spungs dgon du bzhugs su gsol ba'i dpe rnying dkar chag*. Beijing: Mi rigs dpe skrun khang, 2004.

JMS   *Rje btsun mi la ras pa'i gsung 'bum*. 5 vols. Beijing: Krung go'i bod rig pa dpe skrun khang, 2011.

LMS   *Lho brag mar pa lo tsā'i gsung 'bum*. 7 vols. Beijing: Krung go'i bod rig pa dpe skrun khang, 2011.

Dung dkar Blo bzang 'phrin las (1927–97)

DKT   *Dung dkar tshig mdzod*. Bejing: Krung go'i bod rig pa dpe skrun khang, 2002.

'Gos Lotsāwa Gzhon nu dpal (1392–1481)

BA   *Deb gter sngon po*. Chengdu: Si khron mi rigs dpe skrun khang, 1984. 2 vols.

Grags pa 'byung gnas and Blo bzang mkhas grub

MD   *Gangs can mkhas grub rim byon ming mdzod*. Lanzhou: kan su'u mi rigs dpe skrun khang, 1992.

Gtsang smyon Heruka (1452–1507)

DKN   *Bde Mchog Mkha' 'Gro Snyan Rgyud (Ras Chung Snyan Rgyud): Two Manuscript Collections of Texts from the Yig Cha of Gtsang Smyon Heruka*. 2 vols. Leh, Ladakh: S. W. Tashigangpa, 1971.

NG   *Rnal 'byor gyi dbang phyug chen po mi la ras pa'i rnam mgur*. Zi ling: Mtsho sngon mi rigs dpe skrun khang, 1981.

TDY   *Sgra bsgyur mar pa lo tsa'i rnam par thar pa mthong ba don yod.* Indian edition, n.d., n.p., 1970.

Gtsug lag 'phreng ba, Dpa' bo II (1504–64)

KGT   *Chos 'byung mkhas pa'i dga' ston.* 2 vols. Beijing: Mi rigs dpe skrun khang, 1986.

'Jam mgon kong sprul Blo gros mtha' yas (1813–99)

DND   *Ddams ngag mdzod.* Delhi: N. Lungtok and N. Gyaltsan, 1971. 12 vols.

YPB   *Rje btsun ras pa chen po la brten pa'i rnal 'byor tshogs mchod dang bcas pa ye shes dpal 'bar.* N.d., Rumtek ed.

YSJ   *Rje btsun ras pa chen po la brten pa'i bla ma'i rnal 'byor gyi zin bris ye shes gsal byed.* In *Rgya chen bka' mdzod.* 20 vols. Vol. 1, 493–527.

Karma chags med (1613–78)

JZN   *Grub pa'i dbang phyug rje btsun bzhad pa rdo rje'i rnam thar.* In *Brief Verse Biographies of Various Bka' brgyud pa and Rnying ma pa Masters of the Tibetan Buddhist Tradition.* Tashijong, India: Khampa Gar Sungrab Nyamso Gyunphel Parkhang, 1985, 93–102.

Lha btsun Rin chen rnam rgyal (1473–1557)

DJGN   *Rje btsun Mi la ras pa'i rdo rje mgur drug sogs gsung rgyun tho bu 'ga'.* Microfilm. Kathmandu, Nepal. NGMPP reel no. L251/2, 109 folios. Brag dkar rta so xylograph.

DJGR   *Rje btsun Mi la ras pa'i rdo rje mgur drug sogs gsung rgyun tho bu 'ga'.* Rumtek edition. N.p., n.d.

TNL   *Grub thob gtsang pa smyon pa'i rnam thar dad pa'i spu slong g.yo ba.* In *Bde mchog mkha' 'gro snyan rgyud (Ras chung snyan rgyud): Two Manuscript Collections of Texts from the Yig cha of Gtsang-smyon He-ru-ka.* Leh, India: S. W. Tashigangpa, 1971, 1–129.

Mkha' spyod dbang po, Zhwa dmar II (1350–1405)

CBB   *Chos rje dpal ldan mi la ras chen gyi rnam par thar pa byin rlabs kyi sprin phung.* In *The Collected Writings (Gsuṅ 'bum) of the Second Źwa-dmar Mkha'-spyod-dbaṅ-po.* Gangtok, Sikkim, India: Gonpo Tseten, 1978. Vol. 1, 188–317.

Mon rtse Kun dga' dpal ldan (1408–75)

MRN   *Rje btsun mi la ras pa'i rnam par thar pa.* In *Dkar brgyud gser 'phreng: A Golden Rosary of Lives of Eminent Gurus.* Leh: Sonam W. Tashigang, 1970, 104–65.

Nam mkha' bsam grug rgyal mtshan (fifteenth century)

NGN   *Rje la phyi chen po nam mkha' rgyal mtshan gyi rnam thar gsal bar byed pa dri med zla ba'i phreng ba.* Dehra Dhun, India: 'Bri gung bka' brgyud gstug lag slob gnyer khang, 1999.

Ngan rdzongs ston pa Byang chub rgyal po (b. late eleventh century), et al.

BC   *Bu chen bcu gnyis.*

Editions:

BCN   Newark edition. Cover title: *Rje btsun chen po mid la ras pa'i rnam thar zab mo.* N.p., n.d. 244 folios. *Dbu can* manuscript in the collection of the Newark Museum, microfilm master negative No. 0001, *Tibetan Book Collection,* Folio 36.280, *Biography of Milarepa,* IIB R 16.

BCO   Oxford edition: No cover title. No title page. N.p., n.d. *Dbu can* manuscript in the Bodlean Library Microfilm Reel No. SN 1207 ms. Tib. a. 11a.

Nyang ral Nyi ma'i 'od zer (1124/36–1192/1204)

CMN   *Chos 'byung me tog snying po sbrang rtsi'i bcud.* Gang can rig mdzod series no. 5. Lhasa: Bod ljongs mi dmangs dpe skrun khang, 1988.

Nyima Dondrup

YNY   *Sbas yul spyi dang bye brag yol mo gangs ra'i gnas yig.* Kathmandu: Khenpo Nyima Dondrup, 2003.

LGN   *Sbas yul yol mo gangs rar rgyal bstan ji ltar dar tshul lo rgyus brjod pa nor bu'i me long.* In *Sbas yul spyi dang bye brag yol mo gangs ra'i gnas yig,* ed. Nyima Dondrup. Kathmandu: Khenpo Nyima Dondrup, 2003, 52–145.

O rgyan rin chen dpal (1229/30–1309)

DYN   *'Bri gung dkar brgyud yid bzhin nor bu yi ' phreng ba, A Rosary of Wish-fulfilling Jewels [containing life stories of] the Drigung Kagyu Masters.* Leh: S. W. Tashigangpa, 1972, 174–245.

Padma dkar po (1527–92)

DCJ   *'Brug pa'i chos 'byung.* Gang-can rig-mdzod series no. 19. Lhasa: Bod ljongs Bod yig Dpe rnying Dpe skrun khang, 1992.

DNK   *Bde mchog snyan brgyud nor bu skor gsum (Yig Rnying) [Tibetan title: Snyan Rgyud Yig Rnying Gzhung].* 2 vols. Tashijong, India: Gsunrab Nyamso Gyunphel Parkhang, 1985.

KSY   *Bka' rgyud kyi bka' 'bum gsil bu rnams kyi gsan yig (Record of Teachings Received from the Fragmented Teaching Collections of the Bka' brgyud).* In *Collected Works (gsun 'bum) of Kun mkhyen Padma dkar po.* Darjeeling: Kargyud Sungrab Nyamso Khang, 1973. Vol. nga (4), 309–496.

PCM   *Phyag chen po gnad kyi man ngag dang/ bsam gyis mi khyab pa la sogs dho ha'i mgur brgyad.* In *Bdem mchog snyan brgyud nor bu skor gsum yig rning.* Tashijong: Sungrab Nyamso Gyunphel Parkhang, 1985, 7–18.

Rdo rje mdzes 'od (active fourteenth century)

NTC   *Bka' brgyud kyi rnam thar chen mo rin po che'i gter mdzod dgos 'byung gnas.* Bir, India: D. Tsondu Senghe, 1985.

Rgod tshang ras pa Sna tshogs rang grol (1482?–1559?)

TNG   *Gtsang smyon her ru ka phyogs thams cad las rnam par rgyal ba'i rnam thar rdo rje theg pa'i gsal byed nyi ma'i snying po. The Life of the Saint of Gtsaṅ.* Ed. Lokesh Chandra. New Delhi: Śata piṭaka Series Indo Asian Literatures, Volume 79, 1969.

Rgyal thang pa Bde chen rdo rje (ca. thirteenth century)

JGM   *Rje btsun gyi rgyal po mid la ras pa'i rnam thar.* In *Dkar brgyud gser 'phreng: A Thirteenth-Century Collection of Verse Hagiographies of the Succession of Eminent Masters of the 'Brug-pa Dkar-brgyud-pa Tradition.* Tashijong, India: Sungrab Nyamso Gyunphel Parkhang, 1973, 189–265.

Sangs rgyas 'bum (b. twelfth century)

MNT   *Mi la ras pa'i rnam thar.* In *Rwa lung dkar brgyud gser 'phreng: Brief Lives of the Successive Masters in the Transmission Lineage of the Bar 'Brug-pa Dkar-brgyud-pa of Rwa-luṅ.* 1:167–216. Palampur, India: Sungrab Nyamso Gyunpel Parkhang, 1975–78.

Sgam po pa Bsod nams rin chen (1079–1153)

MMN   *Rje Mar pa dang mi la'i rnam thar.*

          Editions:

          In *Selected Writings of Sgam po pa Bsod nams rin chen with the Biography written by his descendant Sgam po pa Bsod nams Lhun grub.* Lahul: Topten Tshering, 1974, 18–30.
          In *Collected Works of Gampopa.* New Delhi: Khedrup Gyatso Sashin, 1975. Vol. 1, 16–26.
          In *Dwags po Lha rje bka' 'bum. The Collected Works of Gampopa.* Darjeeling: Kargyud Sungrab Nyamso Khang, 1982, 23–42.
          In *Khams gsum chos kyi rgyal po dpal mnyam med sgam po pa 'gro mgon bsod nams rin chen mchog gi gsung 'bum yid bzhin nor bu bzhugs so.* 2nd ed. New Delhi: Khenpo Shedup Tenzin and Lama Thinley Namgyal, 2005, 47–68.
          "Unidentified" xylograph added at the end of O rgyan Rin chen dpal DYN.

Si tu Paṇ chen Chos kyi 'byung gnas (1700–74) and 'Be lo tshe dbang kun khyab

DCS   *Karma kam tshang brgyud pa rin po che'i rnam par thar pa rab 'byams nor bu zla ba chu shel gyi phreng ba.* 2 vols. New Delhi: D. Gyaltsan and Kesang Legshay, 1972.

CSK   *Karma kam tshang brgyud pa rin po che'i rnam par thar pa rab 'byams nor bu zla ba chu shel gyi phreng ba'i kha skong.* In *Si tu Chos kyi 'byung gnas kyi bka' 'bum.* Vol. Da. Kangra, India: Sherab Ling Institute, 1990.

Skal ldan rgya mtsho (1607–77)

MLN
Rje mi la la brten pa'i bla ma'i rnal 'byor. In *Mdo smad sgrub brgyud bstan pa'i shing rta ba chen po phyag na padmo yab rje bla ma skal ldan rgya mtsho'i gsung 'bum.* Reb gong: Kan su'u mi rigs dpe skrun khang, 1999. Vol. 2, 269–71.

Thu'u bkwan Chos kyi nyi ma (1737–1802)

CRN
Lcang skya rol pa'i rdo rje'i rnam thar. Lanzhou: Kan su'u mi rigs dpe skrun khang. 1989. 2nd ed., 1991.

Tshe dbang nor bu, Kaḥ thog rigs 'dzin (1698–1755)

MMD
Mar mi dwags po jo bo rje yab sras sogs dam pa 'ga' zhig gi rnam thar sa bon dus kyi nges pa rjod pa dang ldan pa nyung gsal. In *Selected Writings of Kaḥ thog Rig 'dzin Tshe bgang nor bu.* Dargeeling: Kargyud Sungrab Kyamso Khang, 1973. Vol. I, 669–705.

SDN
Mar mi dwags po jo bo rje yab sras sog dam pa 'ga' zhug gi rnam thar sa bon dus kyi nges pa brjod pa dag ldan nyung gsal. In *Selected Writings of Kaḥ thog Rig 'dzin Tshe dbang Nor bu.* 6 vols. Darjeeling: Kargyu Sungrab Nyamso Khang, 1973. Vol. 1, 669–705.

Tshe dbang rgyal (ca. fifteenth century)

LRC
Dam pa'i chos kyi byung ba'i legs bshad lho rong chos 'byung ngam rta tshag chos 'byung zhes rtsom pa'i yul ming du chags pa'i ngo mtshar zhing dkon pa'i dpe khyed par chan. Khangs can rig mdzod 26. Lhasa: Bod ljongs bod yig dpe rnying dpe skrun khang, 1994.

Tshal pa Kun dga' rdo rje (1309–64)

RA
Deb gter dmar po. Beijing: Mi rigs dpe skrun khang, 1981.

Zhang G.yu brag pa Brtson 'grus grags pa (1123–93)

LMN
Bla ma mi la'i rnam thar.

Editions:

In *Writings (Bka' Thor Bu) of Zhang g.yu-brag-pa Brtson-'grus grags-pa.* Tashijong, India: Sungrab Nyamso Gyunpel Parkhang, 1972, 333–43. In *Dpal tshal-pa bka'-brgyud-kyi bstan-pa'i mña-bdag zhañ gyu-brag-pa brtson-'grus grags-pa'i gsuñ-'bum rin-po-che.* 9 vols. Kathmandu: Sherab Gyaltsen, 2004. Vol. 1, 146–58.

KGN
Dkar rgyud rnam thar. In *Bka' thor bu of Zhang g.yu brag pa brTson 'grus grags pa.* Tashijong: Sungrab Nyamso Gyunpel Parkhang, 1972, 307–93.

Zhang Lotsāwa Grub pa dpal bzang (b. 1237)

TY
Zhang lo'i thim yig. In *Bde mchog mkha' snyan rgyud (ras chung snyan rgyud),* ed. Byang chub bzang po. Reproduced from the rare manuscript in the library of Apho Rinpoche. 2 vols. Delhi, 1973, 1–5.

Zhi byed ri pa (fourteenth century)

NDO   *Rje btsun mid la ras pa'i rnam par thar pa nyi zla'i 'od zer sgron ma*. Manuscript in the archives of 'Bras spung Monastery. *'Bras spungs dkar chag: phyi ra* 72, 017188, 105ff, 45 x 8 cm (pagination refers to computer printout).

        Editions:

        In *'Bri gung bka' brgyud chos mdzod chen mo*. Lhasa: s. n. 2004. Vol. 9: 251–498.

        In Dpal brtsegs bod yig dpe rnying zhib 'jug khang, *Rje Btsun Mi la ras pa'i gsung 'bum*. Beijing: Krung go'i bod rig pa dpe skrun khang, 2011. Vol. 5, 154–331.

WESTERN LANGUAGE SOURCES

Akester, Matthew. 2001–2. *Buddhist Himalaya* 11.

Almond, Phillip C. 1988. *The British Discovery of Buddhism*. Cambridge: Cambridge University Press.

Ardussi, John and Lawrence Epstein. 1978. "The Saintly Madmen in Tibet." In *Himalayan Anthropology*, ed. James F. Fisher, 327–37. The Hague: Mouton.

Aris, Michael. 1979. *Bhutan: The Early History of a Himalayan Kingdom*. Warminster, England: Aris and Phillips.

——. 1980. "Notes on the History of the Mon-Yul Corridor." In *Tibetan Studies in Honor of Hugh Richardson*, ed. M. Aris and A. S. S. Kyi, 9–20. New Delhi: Vikas Publishing.

——. 1989. *Hidden Treasures and Secret Lives: A Study of Pemalingpa (1450–1521) and the Sixth Dalai Lama (1683–1706)*. London: Kegan Paul International.

Averintsev, Sergei S. 2002. "From Biography to Hagiography." In *Mapping Lives: The Uses of Biography*, ed. P. France and W. St. Clair, 19–36. Oxford: Oxford University Press.

Bachhofer, Joss. 1986. *Verrückte Weisheitt, Leben und Lehre Milarepas*. Haldenwang: Schangrila.

Bacot, Jacques. 1925. *Milarépa: Ses Méfaits, Ses Épreuves, Son Illumination*. Paris: Éditions Bossard.

Bagchi, Prabhodha Chandra. 1934. "Some Aspects of Buddhist Mysticism in the Caryāpadas." *Calcutta Oriental Journal* 1 (5): 201–14.

——. 1938. "Materials for a Critical Edition of the Old Bengali Caryāpadas." *Journal of the Department of Letters, University of Calcutta* 30.

——. 1946. "The Dohakosa of Tillapada, Commentary to Verse No. 25." *Journal of the Department of Letters, University of Calcutta* 38.

——. 1956. *Caryāgīti-kośa of Buddhist Siddhas*. Calcutta: Visva-bharati.

Bajrācārya, Dhanavajra and Tekbhadur Shresta. 1975 (2032 B.S.). *Nuwākoṭako aitihāsik rūparekhā*. Kathmandu: Tribhuvan University.

Bell, Charles. 1931. *The Religion of Tibet*. Oxford: Cambridge University Press.

Blondeau, Anne-Marie. 1980. "Analysis of the Biographies of Padmasambhava According to Tibetan Tradition: Classification of Sources." In *Tibetan Studies in Honor of Hugh Richardson*, ed. M. Aris and A. S. S. Kyi, 45–52. Warminster, England: Aris and Phillips.

——. 1984. "Le 'Découvreur' du Maṇi Bka'-'bum était-il Bon-po?" In *Tibetan and Buddhist Studies Commemorating the 200th Anniversary of the Birth of Alexander Csoma de Körös*, ed. L. Ligeti, 77–123. Budapest: Akadémiai Kiadó.

Bosson, James Evert. 1967. *Mila yin Namtar: The Biography of Milaraspa in Its Mongolian Version by Siregetü Güüsi Corjiva*. Taipei: N.p.

Braarvig, Jens. 1985. "*Dhāraṇī* and *Pratibhāna*: Memory and Eloquence of the Bodhisattvas." *Journal of the International Association of Buddhist Studies* 8:17–29.

Brough, John. 1950. "'Thus Have I Heard. . . .'" *Bulletin of the School of Oriental and African Studies* 13 (2): 416–26.

Buffetrille, Katia. 1996. "One Day the Mountains Will Go Away: Preliminary Remarks on the Flying Mountains of Tibet." In *Reflections of the Mountain: Essays on the History and Social Meaning of the Mountain Cult in Tibet and the Himalaya*, ed. A.-M. Blondeau and E. Steinkellner, 77–90. Wien: Verlag der Österreichischen Akademie der Wissenschaften.

Callewaert, Winand M. and Rupert Snell. 1994. *According to Tradition: Hagiographical Writing in India*. Wiesbaden: Harrassowitz.

Calomino, Salvatore and Rudolf. 1990. *From Verse to Prose: The Barlaam and Josaphat Legend in Fifteenth-Century Germany*. Potomac, Md.: Scripta Humanistica.

de Certeau, Michel. 1988. *The Writing of History*. New York: Columbia University Press.

Chan, Victor. 1994. *Tibet Handbook*. Hong Kong: Moon.

Chang, Garma C. C., trans. (1962) 1999. *The Hundred Thousand Songs of Milarepa*. Boston: Shambhala.

Childs, Geoff. 2003. "Polyandry and Population Growth in a Historical Tibetan Society." *History of the Family* 8:423–44.

Childs, Geoff and Andrew Quintman. 2012. "Marriage, Kinship, and Inheritance in Zhi byed ri pa's Account of Mi la ras pa's Early Life." *Revue d'Etudes Tibétaines* 23 (Avril): 43–49.

Cox, Collett. 1992. "Mindfulness and Memory: The Scope of *Smṛti* from Early Buddhism to the Sarvāstivādin Abhidharma." In *In the Mirror of Memory: Reflections on Mindfulness and Remembrance in Indian and Tibetan Buddhism*, ed. J. Gyatso, 67–108. Albany: State University of New York Press.

Csoma de Körös, Alexander. 1834. *A Grammar of the Tibetan Language*. Reprint ed. Budapest: Akadémiai Kiadó, 1984.

Cuevas, Bryan J. 2003. *The Hidden History of the Tibetan Book of the Dead*. Oxford: Oxford University Press.

Das, Sarat Chandra. 1881. "Dispute Between a Buddhist and a Bonpo Priest for the Possession of Mount Kailāsa and the Laka Mānasa." In "Contributions on the Religion, History, &c. of Tibet," *Journal of the Asiatic Society of Bengal* 50, part 1: 206–11. Reprinted in *The Religion and History of Tibet* (Delhi: Cosmo, 1988).

——. (1902) 1983. *A Tibetan-English Dictionary*. Calcutta. Revised compact edition, Kyoto: Rinsen.

Davidson, Ronald M. 1981. "The *Litany of Names of Mañjuśrī*: Text and Translation of the *Mañjuśrīnāmasaṃgīti*." In *Tantric and Taoist Studies in Honor of R. A. Stein*, ed. M. Strickmann. 1–69. Bruxelles: Institut Belge des Hautes Étuded Chinoises.

——. 1990. "An Introduction to the Standards of Scriptural Authenticity in Indian Buddhism." In *Chinese Buddhist Apocrypha*, ed. R. E. Buswell. 291–325. Honolulu: University of Hawaii Press.

———. 2002. "Gsar-ma Apocrypha: Gray Texts, Oral Traditions, and the Creation of Ortho-doxy." In *The Many Canons of Tibetan Buddhism*, ed. H. Eimer and D. Germano. Leiden: Brill.

Davis, Natalie Z. 1987. *Fiction in the Archives*. Stanford: Stanford University Press.

Dayal, Har. 1932. *The Bodhisattva Doctrine in Buddhist Sanskrit Literature*. New Delhi: Motilal Banarsidass.

Decleer, Hubert. 1992. "The Melodious Drumsound All-pervading, Sacred Biography of Rwa-Lotsawa: About Early Lotsawa rnam thar and chos byung." In *Tibetan Studies: Proceedings of the 5th IATS Seminar*, ed. S. Ihara and Y. Zuiho, 2 vols., vol. 1: 13–28. Narita: Naritasan Shinshoji.

———. 1996. "Master Atiśa in Nepal: The Tham Bahīl and Five Stūpas' Foundations According to the 'Brom ston Itinerary." *Journal of the Nepal Research Center* 10:27–54.

———. 1997. "Atisha's Arrival in Nepal." *Buddhist Himalaya: Journal of Nagarjuna Institute of Exact Methods* 8 (1&2): 1–15.

———. 1998. "Atisha's Arrival in Nepal/Vijayasimha's Death." *Buddhist Himalaya: Journal of Nagarjuna Institute of Exact Methods* 9 (1&2): 1–20.

de Filippi, Filippo, ed. 1931. *An Account of Tibet: The Travels of Ippolito Desideri of Pistola, S.J., 1712-1727*. Rev. ed. London: Oxford University Press.

DeVilario, David. 2011. "Subversive Sainthood and Tantric Fundamentalism: A Historical Study of Tibet's Holy Madmen." Ph.D. diss., University of Virginia.

Diemberger, Hildegard. 2007. *When a Woman Becomes a Dynasty: The Samding Dorje Phagmo of Tibet*. New York: Columbia University Press.

Doctor, Andreas. 2006. *Tibetan Treasure Literature: Revelation, Tradition, and Accomplishment in Visionary Buddhism*. Ithaca, N.Y.: Snow Lion.

Dolfuss, Pascale. 1991. "Peintures Tibétaines de la vie de Mi-la-ras-pa." *Arts Asiatiques* XLVI:50–71.

Donaldson, Ian. 2002. "National Biography and the Arts of Memory." In *Mapping Lives: The Uses of Biography*, ed. P. France and W. St. Clair, 37–66. Oxford: Oxford University Press.

Dorje, Gyurme and Matthew Kapstein, trans. and ed. 1991. *The Nyingma School of Tibetan Buddhism: Its Fundamentals and History*. 2 vols. Boston: Wisdom.

Draghi, Paul. 1980. "A Comparative Study of the Theme of the Conversion of a Hunter in Tibetan, Bhutanese, and Medieval Sources." Ph.D. diss., Indiana University.

Ehrhard, Franz-Karl. 1991. "Further Renovations of the Svayambhunath Stupa (from the 13th to the 17th Centuries)." *Ancient Nepal* 123–125:10–20.

———. 2008. *A Rosary of Rubies: The Chronicle of the Gur-rigs mDo-chen Tradition from South-Western Tibet*. München: Indus.

———. 2010a. "Editing and Publishing the Master's Writings: The Early Years of rGod tshang ras chen (1482–1559)." In *Edition, éditions: l'écrit au Tibet, évolution et devenir (Collectanea Himalayica 3)*, ed. Anne Chayet, Cristina Sherrer-Schaub, Françoise Robin, and Jean-Luc Achard, 129–61. München: Indus Verlag.

———. 2010b. "The Holy Madman of dBus and His Relationships with Tibetan Rulers of the 15th and 16th Centuries." In *Geschichten und Geschichte: Historiographie und Hagiographie in der asiatischen Religionsgeschichte*, ed. Peter Schalk, 219–46. Uppsala: Uppsala University.

Eimer, Helmut. 1982. "The Development of the Biographic Tradition Concerning Atisha (Dipaṃkaraśrījñana)." *Journal of the Tibet Society* 2:41–51.

——. 1996. "Two Blockprint Fragments of Mi la ras pa's Mgur 'bum Kept in the Wellcome Institute." *Zentralasiatische Studien* 26:7–20.

——. 2000. "Welche Quelle benutzte Berthold Laufer für die Bearbeitung einiger Kapital aus Mi la ras pa *mGur 'bum*?" In *Vividharatnakaraṇḍaka: Festgabe für Adalheid Mette*, ed. C. Chojnacki, J.-U. Hartmann, and V. M. Tschannerl. Swisttal-Odendorf: Indica et Tibetica Verlag.

Eimer, Helmut and Pema Tsering. 1990. "Blockprints and Manuscripts of Mi la ras pa's *Mgur 'bum* Accessible to Frank-Richard Hamm." In *Frank-Richard Hamm Memorial Volume*, ed. H. Eimer, 59–88. Bonn: Indica et Tibetica Verlag.

Evans Wentz, W. Y., ed. (1928) 1969. *Tibet's Great Yogī Milarepa: A Biography from the Tibetan*. London: Oxford University Press.

Faure, Bernard. 1986. "Bodhidharma as Textual and Religious Paradigm." *History of Religions* 25 (3): 187–98.

Fields, Rick. 1981. *How the Swans Came to the Lake*. Boston: Shambhala.

Flood, Gavin. 1996. *An Introduction to Hinduism*. Cambridge: Cambridge University Press.

Freedberg, David. 1989. *The Power of Images: Studies in the History and Theory of Response*. Chicago: University of Chicago Press.

Foucher, Alfred. (1949) 1963. *The Life of the Buddha According to the Ancient Texts and Monuments of India*. Trans. S. B. Boas. Middletown, Conn.: Wesleyan University Press.

Fushimi, Hidetoshi. 1999. "Recent Finds from the Old Sa-skya Xylographic Edition." *Wiener Zeitschrift für die Kunde Südasiens und Archiv für Indische Philosophie* 43:95–108.

Galloway, Brian. 1991. "'Thus Have I Heard: At One Time. . . .'" *Indo-Iranian Journal* 34:87–104.

Geary, Patrick. 1996. "Saints, Scholars, and Society: The Elusive Goal." In *Saints: Studies in Hagiography*, ed. Sandro Sticca. Binghamton, N.Y.: Medieval and Renaissance Texts and Studies.

Germano, David. 1994. "Architecture and Absence in the Secret Tantric History of the Great Perfection (*rdzogs chen*)." *Journal of the International Association of Buddhist Studies* 17 (2): 203–336.

Goodman, Steven D. 1992. "Rig-'dzin 'Jigs-med gling-pa and the *kLong-Chen sNying-thig*." In *Tibetan Buddhism: Reason and Revelation*, ed. S. D. Goodman and R. M. Davidson, 133–46. Albany: State University of New York Press.

Goodman, Steven D. and Ronald M. Davidson, eds. 1992. *Tibetan Buddhism: Reason and Revelation*. Albany: State University of New York Press.

Gorvine, William. 2006. "The Life of a Bönpo Luminary: Sainthood, Partisanship, and Literary Representation in a Twentieth-Century Tibetan Biography." Ph.D. diss., University of Virginia.

Granoff, Phyllis and Koichi Shinohara, eds. 1988. *Monks and Magicians: Religious Biographies in Asia*. Oakville, Ont.: Mosaic Press.

——. 1992. *Speaking of Monks: Religious Biography in India and China*. Oakville, Ont.: Mosaic Press.

——. 1994. *Other Selves: Autobiography and Biography in Cross-Cultural Perspective*. Oakville, Ont.: Mosaic Press.

Granoff, Phyllis. 1979. "Holy Warriors: A Preliminary Study of Some Biographies of Saints and Kings in the Classical Indian Tradition." *Journal of Indian Philosophy* 12:291–303.

——. 1988a. "Jain Biographies of Nagarjuna: Notes on the Composing of a Biography in Medieval India." In *Monks and Magicians: Religious Biographies in Asia*, ed. P. Granoff and K. Shinohara. Oakville, Ont.: Mosaic Press.

——. 1988b. "The Biographies of Arya Khapatacarya: A Preliminary Investigation Into the Transmission and Adaptation of Biographical Legends." In *Monks and Magicians: Religious Biographies in Asia*, ed. P. Granoff and K. Shinohara. Oakville, Ont.: Mosaic Press.

——. 1992. "Jinaprabhasūri and Jinadattasūri: Two Studies from the Śvetāmbara Jain Tradition." In *Speaking of Monks*, ed. P. Granoff and K. Shinohara. Oakville, Ont.: Mosaic Press.

——. 1994. "Biographical Writings Amongst the Śvetāmbara Jains in Northwestern India." In *According to Tradition: Hagiographical Writing in India*, ed. W. M. Callewaert and R. Snell. Wiesbaden: Harrassowitz.

——. 1998. *The Forest of Thieves and the Magic Garden: An Anthology of Medieval Jain Stories.* New Delhi: Penguin.

——. 2001. "From Detachment to Engagement: The Construction of the Holy Man in Medieval Śvetāmbara Jain Literature." In *Constructions Hagiographicques Dans Le Monde Indien: Entre mythe et histoire*, ed. F. Mallison. Paris: Champion.

Grapard, Allan G. 1982. "Flying Mountains and Walkers of Emptiness: Towards a Definition of Sacred Space in Japanese Religions." *History of Religions* 21 (3): 195–221.

Graus, Frantisek. 1965. *Volk, Herrscher und Heiliger im Reich der Merowinger*. Praha: Nakladatelství Československé akademie věd.

Guenther, Herbert V. 1969. *The Royal Song of Saraha: A Study in the History of Buddhist Thought*. Seattle: University of Washington Press.

——. 1993. *Ecstatic Spontaneity: Saraha's Three Cycles of Dohā*. Ed. P. L. Swanson. Nanzen Studies in Asian Religions. Berkeley, Calif.: Asian Humanities Press.

Guillory, John. 1995. "Canon." In *Critical Terms for Literary Study*, ed. Frank Lentricchia and Thomas McLaughlin, 233–49. Chicago and London: University of Chicago Press.

Gusdorf, Georges. 1980. "Conditions and Limits of Autobiography." In *Autobiography: Essays Theoretical and Critical*, ed. J. Olney, 28–48. Princeton: Princeton University Press.

Gyalbo, Tsering, Guntram Hazod, and Per K. Sørensen. 2000. *Civilization at the Foot of Mount Sham-po: The Royal House of lHa Bug-pa-can and the History of g.Ya'-bzang*. Wien: Verlag der Österreichischen Akademie der Wissenschaften.

Gyatso, Janet B. 1986. "Signs, Memory and History: A Tantric Buddhist Theory of Scriptural Transmission." *Journal of the International Association of Buddhist Studies.* 9 (2): 7–35.

——. 1989. "Down with the Demoness: Reflections on a Feminine Ground in Tibet." In *Feminine Ground: Essays on Women and Tibet*, ed. J. D. Willis, 33–52. Ithaca, N.Y.: Snow Lion.

——. 1992. "Genre, Authorship, and Transmission in Visionary Buddhism: The Literary Traditions of Thang-stong rGyal-po." In *Tibetan Buddhism: Reason and Revelation*, ed. R. M. Davidson and Steven Goodman, 95–106. Albany: State University of New York Press.

——. 1993. "The Logic of Legitimation in the Tibetan Treasure Tradition." *History of Religions* 33 (1): 97–134.

——. 1996. "Drawn from the Tibetan Treasury: The *gTer ma* Literature." In *Tibetan Literature: Studies in Genre*, ed. J. I. Cabezón and R. R. Jackson. Ithaca, N.Y.: Snow Lion.

——. 1997. "Counting Crow's Teeth: Tibetans and Their Diary-Writing Practices." In *Les Habitants du Toit du Monde*, ed. Samten Karmay and Philippe Sagant, 159–77. Paris: Societe d'ethnologie.

——. 1998. *Apparitions of the Self: The Secret Autobiographies of a Tibetan Visionary*. Princeton: Princeton University Press.

Gyatso, Janet B., ed. 1992. *In the Mirror of Memory: Reflections on Mindfulness and Remembrance in Indian and Tibetan Buddhism*. Albany: State University of New York Press.

Hallisey, Charles. 1995. "Roads Taken and Not Taken in the Study of Theravāda Buddhism." In *Curators of the Buddha: The Study of Buddhism Under Colonialism*. Chicago and London: University of Chicago Press.

Harrison, Paul. 1978. "*Buddhānosmṛti* in the *Pratyupanna-buddha-sammukhāvasthita-samādhi-sūtra*." *Journal of Indian Philosophy* 6 (1): 35–57.

——. 1990. *The Samādhi of Direct Encounter with the Buddhas of the Present*. Studia Philogica Buddhica, Monograph Series V. Tokyo: International Institute for Buddhist Studies.

——. 1992. "Commemoration and Identification in *Buddhānosmṛti*." In *In the Mirror of Memory: Reflections on Mindfulness and Remembrance in Indian and Tibetan Buddhism*, ed. J. B. Gyatso, 215–38. Albany: State University of New York Press.

Heffernan, Thomas J. 1988. *Sacred Biography: Saints and Their Biographers in the Middle Ages*. Oxford: Oxford University Press.

Heller, Amy. 1999. *Tibetan Art: Tracing the Development of Spiritual Ideals and Art in Tibet 600–200 A.D.* Milano: Jaca.

Hirsch, John C. and Cambridge University Library. 1986. *Barlam and Iosaphat: A Middle English Life of Buddha*. London: Oxford University Press.

Huber, Toni. 1999. *The Cult of Pure Crystal Mountain: Popular Pilgrimage and Visionary Landscape in Southeast Tibet*. Oxford: Oxford University Press.

——, ed. 1999. *Sacred Spaces and Powerful Places in Tibetan Culture: A Collection of Essays*. Dharamsala, India: Library of Tibetan Works and Archives.

Ikegami, Keiko. 1999. *Barlaam and Josaphat*. New York: AMS Press.

Jackson, David. 1983. "Notes on Two Early Printed Editions of Sa-skya-pa Works." *The Tibet Journal* 8 (2): 5–24.

——. 1989. "More on the Old dGa'-ldan and Gong-dkar-ba Xylographic Editions." *Studies in Central and East Asian Religions* 2:1–18.

——. 1990a. "The Earliest Printing of Tsong-kha-pa's Works: The Old Dga'-ldan Editions." In *Reflections on Tibetan Culture: Essays in Memory of Turrell E. Wylie*, ed. L. Epstein and R. F. Sherburne. Lewiston, N.Y.: Edwin Mellon Press.

——. 1990b. "Sa-skya Pandita the 'Polemicist': Ancient Debates and Modern Interpretations." *Journal of the International Association of Buddhist Studies* 13 (2): 17–117.

——. 1994. *Enlightenment by a Single Means: Tibetan Controversies on the "Self-Sufficient White Remedy" (Dkar po chig thub)*. Wien: Verlag der Österreichen Akademie Der Wissenschaften.

——. 1996. *A History of Tibetan Painting: The Great Painters and Their Traditions*. Wien: Verlag der Österreichischen Akademie der Wissenschaften.

——. 2003. *A Saint in Seattle: The Life of the Tibetan Mystic Dezhung Rinpoche*. Boston: Wisdom.

Jackson, Roger. 1996. "'Poetry' in Tibet: *Glu, mGur, sNyan ngag* and 'Songs of Experience.'" In *Tibetan Literature: Studies in Genre*, ed. José Ignacio Cabezón and Roger R. Jackson. Ithaca, N.Y.: Snow Lion.

——. 2004. *Tantric Treasures: Three Collections of Mystical Verse from Buddhist India*. Oxford: Oxford University Press.

Jacoby, Sarah. 2007. "Consorts and Revelation in Eastern Tibet: The Auto/biographical Writings of the Treasure Revealer Sera Khandro (1892–1940)." Ph.D. diss., University of Virginia.

Jäschke, H. A. 1869. "Probe aus dem tibetischen Legendenbuche: die hundert tausand Gesänge des Milaraspa." *Zeitschrift der Deutschen Morgenländischen Gesellschaft* 23:543–58.

——. (1881) 1972. *A Tibetan-English Dictionary*. London: Routledge and Kegan Paul.

de Jong, J. W. 1959. *Mi la ras pa'i rnam thar: Texte Tibétain de la vie de Milarépa*. The Hague: Mouton.

——. 1974. "A Brief History of Buddhist Studies in Europe and America." *The Eastern Buddhist* 7 (1–2): 55–106.

Jørgensen, John J. 2005. *Inventing Hui-neng, the Sixth Patriarch: Hagiography and Biography in Early Ch'an*. Leiden: Brill.

Kadar, Marlene, ed. 1992. *Essays on Life Writing: From Genre to Critical Practice*. Toronto: University of Toronto Press.

Kapstein, Matthew. 1985. "Religious Syncretism in 13th-Century Tibet: *The Limitless Ocean Cycle*." In *Soundings in Tibetan Civilization*, ed. B. N. Aziz and M. Kapstein, 358–71. New Delhi: Manohar.

——. 1992. "Remarks on the Maṇi Bka' 'bum and the Cult of Avalokitesvara in Tibet." In *Tibetan Buddhism: Reason and Revelation*, ed. R. M. Davidson and S. D. Goodman, 79–94. Albany: State University of New York Press.

——. 2006. "An Inexhaustible Treasury of Verse: The Literary Legacy of the Mahāsiddhas." In *Holy Madness: Portraits of Tantric Siddhas,* ed. Rob Linrothe, 49–61. Chicago: Serindia.

Kieschnick, John. 1997. *The Eminent Monk: Buddhist Ideals in Medieval Chinese Hagiography*. Honolulu: University of Hawai'i Press.

Kinnard, Jacob N. 1999. *Imaging Wisdom: Seeing and Knowing in the Art of Indian Buddhism*. Curzon Critical Studies in Buddhism. Surrey: Corzon.

Kleinberg, Aviad. 1997. *Prophets in Their Own Country: Living Saints and the Making of Sainthood in the Later Middle Ages*. Chicago: University of Chicago Press.

Kunga Rinpoche. 1978. *Drinking the Mountain Stream*. Trans. Brian Cutillo. Novato, Calif.: Lotsawa.

——. 1986. *Miraculous Journey*. Novato, Calif.: Lotsawa.

Konchog Gyaltsen. 1990. *The Great Kagyu Masters: The Golden Lineage Treasury*. Ithaca, N.Y.: Snow Lion.

Kossak, Steven Miles and Jane Casey Singer. 1998. *Sacred Visions: Early Paintings from Central Tibet*. New York: The Metropolitan Museum of Art.

van der Kuijp, Leonard W. J. 1991. "On the Life and Political Career of Ta'i-si-tu Byang chub rgyal mtshan (1302?–1364)." In *Tibetan History and Language: Studies Dedicated to Uray Géza on His Seventieth Birthday*, ed. E. Steinkellner, 277–327. Wien: Arbeitskreis für Tibetische und Buddhistische Studien Universität Wien.

——. 1996. "Tibetan Historiography." In *Tibetan Literature: Studies in Literature*, ed. J. I. Cabezón and R. R. Jackson, 39–56. Ithaca, N.Y.: Snow Lion.

——. 2001. "On the Fifteenth-Century *Lho rong chos 'byung* by Rta tshang Tshe dbang rgyal and Its Importance for Tibetan Political and Religious History." *Lungta* 14 (Spring): 57–76.

Kværne, Per. 1977. *An Anthology of Buddhist Tantric Songs: A Study of the Caryāgīti.* 2nd ed. Bangkok: White Orchid Press.

Lamotte, Étienne. (1958) 1988. *History of Indian Buddhism: From the Origins to the Śāka Era.* Trans. Sara Webb Boin. Louvain la neuve: Université Catholique de Louvain, Institut Orientaliste.

Larsson, Stefan. 2009. "The Birth of a Heruka: How Sangs Rgyas Rgyal Mtshan Became Gtsang Smyon Heruka: A Study of a Mad Man." Ph.D. diss., Stockholm University.

——. 2011. "What Do the Childhood and Early Life of Gtsang myon Heruka Tell Us About His Bka' brgyud Affiliation?" In *Mahāmudrā and the bKa´-brgyud Tradition [PIATS 2006: Proceedings of the Eleventh Seminar of the International Association for Tibetan Studies, Königswinter 2006],* ed. Rodger R. Jackson and Matthew Kapstein, 425–52. Halle (Saale): International Institute for Tibetan and Buddhist Studies.

——. 2012. *Crazy for Wisdom: The Making of a Mad Yogin in Fifteenth-Century Tibet.* Leiden: Brill.

Laufer, Berthold. 1901. *Zwei Legenden des Milaraspa. Archiv für Religionswissenschaft* 4. Band: 1–44.

——. 1902. *Aus den Geschichten und Liedern des Milaraspa.* Wien.

——. 1922. *Milaraspa: Tibetische Texte in Auswahl übertragen.* Hagen i. W. und Darmstadt: Folkwang Verlag.

Levine, Nancy E. 1988. *The Dynamics of Polyandry: Kinship, Domesticity, and Population on the Tibetan Border.* Chicago: University of Chicago Press.

Lhalungpa, Lobsang P., trans. (1977) 1984. *The Life of Milarepa.* Boston: Shambhala.

——. 1986. *Mahāmudrā: The Quintessence of Mind and Meditation.* Boston: Wisdom.

Lin, Nancy. 2011. "Adapting the Buddha's Biographies: A Cultural History of the *Wish-Fulfilling Vine* in Tibet, Seventeenth to Eighteenth Centuries." Ph.D. diss., University of California, Berkeley.

Lifshitz, Felice. 1994. "Beyond Positivism and Genre: 'Hagiographical' Texts as Historical Narrative." *Viator: Medieval and Renaissance Studies* 25:95–113.

Lord, Albert. (1964) 2000. *Singer of Tales.* Cambridge, Mass.: Harvard University Press.

Lopez, Donald S. 1992. "Memories of the Buddha." In *In the Mirror of Memory: Reflections on Mindfulness and Remembrance in Indian and Tibetan Buddhism,* ed. J. B. Gyatso, 251–96. Albany: State University of New York Press.

——. 1995. "Foriegner at the Lama's Feet." In *Curators of the Buddha: The Study of Buddhism Under Colonialism,* ed. D. S. Lopez, 251–96. Chicago: University of Chicago Press.

——. 1996. *Elaborations on Emptiness: Uses of the Heart Sūtra.* Princeton: Princeton University Press.

——. 1998. *Prisoners of Shangri-la.* Chicago: University of Chicago Press.

Lopez, Donald S., ed. 1995. *Curators of the Buddha: The Study of Buddhism Under Colonialism.* Chicago: University of Chicago Press.

Macdonald, Alexander W. 1975. "A Little Read Guide to the Holy Places of Nepal, Part I." *Kailash* 3 (2): 89–144.

——. (1965) 1984. "The Tamang as Seen by One of Themselves." In *Essays on the Ethnology of Nepal and South Asia,* ed. A. W. Macdonald, 2 vols., 1:129–68. Kathmandu: Ratna Pustok Bhandar.

——. 1989. "A Little-Read Guide to the Holy Places of Nepal, Part II." In *Essays on the Ethnology of Nepal and South Asia,* ed. A. W. Macdonald, 2 vols., 2:100–35. Kathmandu: Ratna Pustak Bhandar.

——. 1990. "Hindu-isation, Buddha-isation, Then Lama-isation or: What Happened at La-phyi." In *Indo-Tibetan Studies: Papers in Honour and Appreciation of Professor David L. Snellgrove's Contribution to Indi-Tibetan Studies*, ed. T. Skorupski, 199–208. Tring: Institute of Buddhist Studies.

MacQueen, Graeme. 1981. "Inspired Speech in Early Mahāyāna Buddhism I." *Religion* 11:303–19.

——. 1982. "Inspired Speech in Early Mahāyāna Buddhism II." *Religion* 12:49–65.

Mallison, Francoise, ed. 2001. *Constructions Hagiographicques dans Le Monde Indien: Entre mythe et histoire*. Paris: Champion.

Martin, Dan. 1982. "The Early Education of Milarepa." *The Journal of the Tibet Society* 2:53–76.

——. 1992. "A Twelfth-Century Tibetan Classic of Mahāmudrā, *The Path of Ultimate Profundity: The Great Seal Instructions of Zhang*." *Journal of the International Association of Buddhist Studies* 15 (2): 243–319.

——. 1997. *Tibetan Histories: A Bibliography of Tibetan-Language Historical Works*. London: Serindia.

——. 2001a. "Meditation is Action Taken: On Zhang Rinpoche, A Meditation-Based Activist in Twelfth-Century Tibet." *Lungta* 14:45–56.

——. 2001b. *Unearthing Bon Treasures: Life and Contested Legacy of a Tibetan Scripture Revealer, with a General Bibliography of Bon*. Leiden: Brill.

Massey, Doreen. 1994. *Space, Place, and Gender*. Minneapolis: University of Minnesota Press.

Mathes, Klaus-Dieter. 2001. "The High Mountain Valley of Nar (Manang) in the 17th Century According to Two Tibetan Autobiographies." *Journal of the Nepal Research Center* 12:167–89.

McDermott, James P. 1984. "Scripture as the Word of the Buddha." *Numen* 31 (1): 22–39.

Mette, Adelheid. 1976. "Beobachtungen zur uberlieferingsgeschichte einiger lieder des Mi la ras pa'i mgur 'bum." *Indo Iranian Journal* 18:255–72.

de Montmollin, Marceline. 1988. "Some More on the *sa ba sa khyi 'cham*—a Bhutanese *'cham* on the Conversion of the Hunter mGon po rDo rje by Mi la ras pa." In *Tibetan Studies*, ed. Helga Uebach and Jampa Panglung, 293–300. München: K25, Bayerische Akademie der Wissenschaft.

Nadel, Ira Bruce. 1984. *Biography: Fiction, Fact and Form*. London: Macmillan.

——. 1988. "The Biographer's Secret." In *Studies in Autobiography*, ed. J. Olney, 24–31. Oxford: Oxford University Press.

——. 1994. "Biography as Cultural Discourse." In *Biography and Source Studies, I*, ed. F. R. Karl, I:73–84. New York: AMS Press.

Nālandā Translation Committee, trans. 1980. *The Rain of Wisdom*. Boulder, Colo.: Shambhala.

——. 1986. *The Life of Marpa the Translator*. Boston: Shambhala.

Newark Museum Association. 1971. *Catalogue of the Tibetan Collection*. Vol. 3. Newark, N.J.: Newark Museum Association.

Newman, John. 1996. "Itineraries to Shambhala." In *Tibetan Literature: Studies in Genre*, ed. J. I. Cabezón and R. R. Jackson, 485–99. Ithaca, N.Y.: Snow Lion.

Norbu, Namkai and Adriano Clemente. 1999. *The Supreme Source: Fundamental Tantra of the Dzogchen Semde Kunjed Gyalpo*. Ithaca, N.Y.: Snow Lion.

Norbu, Namkai and Kennard Lipman, trans. 1987. *Primordial Experience: An Introduction to rDzogs chen Meditation*. Boston and London: Shambhala.

Olney, James. 1980. "Some Versions of Memory/Some Versions of *Bios*: The Ontology of Autobiography." In *Autobiography: Essays Theoretical and Critical*, ed. J. Olney, 236–67. Princeton: Princeton University Press.

——. 1998. *Memory and Narrative: The Weave of Life-Writing*. Chicago: University of Chicago Press.

Olney, James, ed. 1980. *Autobiography: Essays Theoretical and Critical*. Princeton: Princeton University Press.

Pabonka Rinpoche. 1991. *Liberation in the Palm of Your Hand*. Boston: Wisdom.

Pal, Pratapaditya and Julia Meech-Pekarik. 1988. *Buddhist Book Illuminations*. Hurstpierpoint, England: Ravi Kumar Publishers.

Patrul Rinpoche. 1995. *Words of My Perfect Teacher*. Trans. Padmakara Translation Group. New York: HarperCollins.

Petech, Luciano. 1978. "The 'Bri-gun-pa Sect in Western Tibet and Ladakh." In *Proceedings of the Csoma de Körös Memorial Symposium*, ed. L. Ligeti, 313–25. Budapest: Akademiai Kiado.

Prats, Ramon. 1984. "Tshe Dban-Nor-Nu's Chronological Notes on the Early Transmission of the *Bi ma Sñyin Thig*." In *Tibetan and Buddhist Studies Commemmorating the 200th Anniversary of the Birth of Alexander Csoma de Körös*, ed. L. Ligeti, 2 vols., 2:197–209. Budapest: Adadémiai Kiadó.

Quintman, Andrew. 2008. "Toward a Geograhic Biography: Milarepa's Life in the Tibetan Landscape." *Numen* 55 (4): 363–410.

——. 2010. *The Life of Milarepa*. New York: Penguin Classics.

——. 2012. "Between History and Biography: Notes on Zhi byed ri pa's *Illuminating Lamp of Sun and Moon Beams*, a Fourteenth-Century Biographical State of the Field." *Revue d'Etudes Tibétaines* 23 (Avril): 5–41.

——. 2013. "Life Writing as Literary Relic: Image, Inscription, and Consecration in Tibetan Biography." *Material Religion* 9 (4), forthcoming.

——. Forthcoming. "Wrinkles in Time: Notes on the Vagueries of Milarepa's Dates."

Reynolds, Frank E. 1976. "The Many Lives of the Buddha: A Study of Sacred Biography and Theravāda Tradition." In *The Biographical Process: Studies in the History and Psychology of Religion*, ed. Frank E. Reynolds and Donald Capps, 37–62. The Hague: Mouton.

——. 1997. "Rebirth Traditions and the Lineages of Gotama: A Study in Theravāda Buddhology." In *Sacred Biography in the Buddhist Traditions of South and Southeast Asia*, ed. J. Schober, 50–63. Honolulu: University of Hawai'i Press.

Reynolds, Frank E. and Charles Hallisey. 1987. "Buddha." In *Encyclopedia of Religion*, 2:319–32. New York: Macmillian.

Reynolds, Valrae. 1978. *Tibet: A Lost World*. Bloomington: Indiana University Press.

Ricard, Matthieu. 1994. *The Life of Zhabkar: The Autobiography of a Tibetan Yogin*. Albany: State University of New York Press.

Rinehart, Robert. 1999. *One Lifetime, Many Lives: The Experience of Modern Hindu Hagiography*. Atlanta, Ga.: Scholars Press.

Roberts, Peter Allen. 2001. *The Biographies of Ras-chung-pa: The Evolutions of a Tibetan Hagiography*. D.Phil. Thesis, Harris Manchester College, Oxford University.

——. 2007. *The Biographies of Rechungpa: The Evolution of a Tibetan Biography*. London: Routledge.

Rockhill, Woodville W. 1884. "The Tibetan 'Hundred Thousand Songs' of Milaraspa." *Journal of the American Oriental Society* XI, Proceedings: 207–11.

——. (1884) 1991. *The Life of the Buddha*. New Delhi: Navrang.

Roerich, Georges [and Dge 'dun chos 'phel], trans. 1949. *The Blue Annals*. 2 vols. Calcutta: Royal Asiatic Society of Bengal. Reprint ed., New Delhi: Motilal Banarsidass, 1989.

Rotman, Andrew. 2009. *Thus Have I Seen: Visualizing Faith in Early Indian Buddhism*. New York: Oxford University Press.

Sandberg, Graham. 1899. "A Tibetan Poet and Mystic." *The Nineteenth Century* XVVI (272): 613–32.

——. 1906. "The Poet Milaraspa." In *Tibet and Tibetans*, 250–72. London: Society for Promoting Christian Knowledge.

Sanderson, Alexis. 1988. "Śaivism and the Tantric Traditions." In *The World's Religions*, ed. S. Sutherland, L. Houlden, P. Clarke, and F. Hardy, 660–704. London: Routledge.

Schaeffer, Kurtis R. 2000. "The Religious Career of Vairocanavajra—A Twelfth-Century Indian Buddhist Master from Dakṣiṇa Kośala." *Journal of Indian Philosophy* 28 (4): 361–84.

——. 2004. *Himalayan Hermitess: The Life of a Tibetan Buddhist Nun*. Oxford: Oxford University Press.

——. 2005. *Dreaming the Great Brahmin: Tibetan Traditions of the Buddhist Poet-Saint Saraha.* New York: Oxford University Press.

——. 2007. "Dying Like Milarepa: Death Accounts in a Tibetan Hagiographic Tradition." In *The Buddhist Dead: Practices, Discourses, Representations*, ed. Bryan J. Cuevas and Jacqueline I. Stone, 208–33. Honolulu: University of Hawaii Press.

——. 2009. *The Culture of the Book in Tibet*. New York: Oxford University Press.

——. 2011a. "Tibetan Biography: Growth and Criticism." In *Edition, éditions: l'ecrit au Tibet, évolution et devenir*, ed. A. Chayet, C. A. Scherrer-Schuab, F. Robin, and J.-L. Achard. Munich: Indus Verlag.

——. 2011b. "The Printing Projects of Gtsang smyon Heruka and His Disciples." In *Mahāmudrā and the bKa´-brgyud Tradition [PIATS 2006: Proceedings of the Eleventh Seminar of the International Association for Tibetan Studies, Königswinter 2006]*, ed. Rodger R. Jackson and Matthew Kapstein, 453–79. Andiast: International Institute for Tibetan and Buddhist Studies.

Schmid, Toni. 1952. *The Cotton-Clad Mila: The Tibetan Poet-Saint's Life in Pictures*. Sino-Sweding Expedition (1927–1935), pub. 36. Stockholm: Statens etnografiska museum.

Schober, Juliane, ed. 1997. *Sacred Biography in the Buddhist Traditions of South and Southeast Asia*. Honolulu: University of Hawai'i Press.

Sernesi, Marta. 2004. "Milarepa's Six Secret Songs: The Early Transmission of the *bDe-mchog snyan brgyud*." *East and West* 54 (1–4): 251–87.

——. 2011a. "The Aural Transmission of Saṃvara: An Introduction to Neglected Sources for the Study of the Early Bka' Brgyud." In *Mahāmudrā and the Bka'-brgyud Tradition [Proceedings of the Eleventh Seminar of the International Association for Tibetan Studies, Königswinter 2006]*, ed. David Jackson and Matthew Kapstein 179–209. Andiast: International Institute for Tibetan and Buddhist Studies.

——. 2011b. "A Continuous Stream of Merit: The Early Reprints of gTsang smyon Heruka's Hagiographical Works." *Zentral-Asiatiche Studien* 40:179–237.

Shahidullah, Mohammed. 1928. *Les Chants Mystiques de Kânha et de Sarah. Les Dohā-koṣa (en apabhraṃṣa, avec les versions tibétaines) et Les Caryā (en vieux-bengali) aved introduction, vocabulaires et notes*. Paris: Adrien-Maisonneuve.

——. 1940. "Buddhist Mystic Songs." *The Dacca University Studies* IV (4).

——. 1960. *Buddhist Mystic Songs: Oldest Bengali and Other Eastern Vernaculars*. Karachi: Bengal Literary Society, University of Karachi.

Shakabpa, Tsepon W.D. 1984. *Tibet: A Political History*. New York: Potala.

Sharf, Robert H. and Elizabeth Horton Sharf, eds. 2001. *Living Images: Japanese Buddhist Icons in Context*. Asian Religions and Cultures. Stanford: Stanford University Press.

Sherpa, Trungram Gyaltrul Rinpoche. 2004. "Gampopa, the Monk and the Yogi: His Life and Teachings." Ph.D. diss., Harvard University.

Shinohara, Koichi. 1988. "Two Sources of Chinese Buddhist Biographies: Stupa Inscriptions and Miracle Stories." In *Monks and Magicians: Religious Biographies in Asia*, ed. P. Granoff and K. Shinohara. Oakville, Ont.: Mosaic Press.

——. 1992. "Quanding's Biography of Zhiyi, the Fourth Chinese Patriarch of the Tiantai Tradition." In *Speaking of Monks*, ed. P. Granoff and K. Shinohara. Oakville, Ont.: Mosaic Press.

——. 2003. "The Story of the Buddha's Begging Bowl: Imagining a Biography and Sacred Places." In *Pilgrims, Patrons, and Place: Localizing Sanctity in Asian Religions*, ed. P. Granoff and K. Shinohara. Vancouver: University of British Columbia Press.

Slusser, Mary. 1982. *Nepal Mandala: A Cultural Study of the Kathmandu Valley*. 2 vols. Princeton: Princeton University Press.

Smashing the Evil and Revealing the Proper: Spoken on Behalf of Living Beings. A Critique of the Hundred Thousand Songs of Milarepa. 1980. N.p.

Smith, E. Gene. 1969. "Preface" to *The Life of the Saint of Gtsang*. New Delhi: Śata piṭaka Series Indo Asian Literatures Volume 79. (Reprinted in Smith 2001, 59–79.)

——. 1970. "Introduction" to *Dkar Brgyud Gser 'Phreng: A Golden Rosary of Lives of Eminent Gurus*. *Smanrtsis Sherig Spendzod*, vol. 3. Leh: Sonam W. Tashigang. (Reprinted in Smith 2001, 39–51.)

——. 2001. *Among Tibetan Texts: History and Literature of the Himalayan Plateau*. Boston: Wisdom.

Snell, Rupert. 1999. "Introduction: Themes in Indian Hagiography." In *According to Tradition: Hagiographic Writing in India*, ed. Winand M. Callewaert and Rupert Snell. Wiesbaden: Harrowitz.

Sørensen, Per K. 1990. *Divinity Secularized: An Inquiry Into the Nature and Form of the Songs Ascribed to the Sixth Dalai Lama*. Vienna: Arbeitskreis für Tibetische und Buddhistische Studien, Universität Wien.

Sørensen, Per K. and Guntram Hazod. 2007. *Rulers on the Celestial Plain: Ecclesiastic and Secular Hegemony in Medieval Tibet: A Study of Tshal Gung-thang*, Veröffentlichungen zur Sozialanthropologie. Wien: Verlag der Österreichischen Akademie der Wissenschaften.

Spanien, Ariane. 1982. "Histoire et philologie tibétaines." In *École pratique des hautes études. 4e section, sciences historiques et philologiques. Livret 1. Rapports sur les conférences des années 1978-1979, 1979-1980, 1980-1981*, 247–50.

von Staël-Holstein, Alexander. 1933. *A Commentary to the Kāçyapaparivarta*. Peking.

Stein, Rolf A. (1962) 1972. *Tibetan Civilization*. Trans. J. E. Stapleton Driver. Stanford: Stanford University Press.

——. 1979. "Introduction to the Gesar Epic." In *The Epic of Gesar*, vol. 1. Thimphu, Bhutan: Kunsang Topgyel.

——. 1988. *Grottes-Matrices et Lieux Saints de la Déesse en Asie Orientale*. Publications de l'École Française d'Extrême-Orient, Volume CLI. Paris: École Française d'Extrême-Orient.

Steward, Jampa Mackenzie. 1995. *The Life of Gampopa: The Incomparable Dharma Lord of Tibet*. Ithaca, N.Y.: Snow Lion.

Sujata, Victoria. 2003. "A Commentary on the 'Mgur 'bum' (Collected Songs of Spiritual Realization) of Skal ldan rgya mtsho, a Seventeenth-Century Scholar and Siddha from Amdo (Tibet)." Ph.D. diss., Harvard University.

——. 2005. *Tibetan Songs of Realization: Echoes from a Seventeenth-Century Scholar and Siddha in Amdo*. Brill's Tibetan Studies Library. Leiden: Brill.

Taylor, Charles. 1989. *Sources of the Self: The Making of the Modern Identity*. Cambridge, Mass.: Harvard University Press.

Templeman, David. 1994. "Dohā, Vajragīti and Caryā Songs." In *Tantra and Popular Religion in Tibet*, ed. G. Samuel, H. Gregor, and E. Stutchbury, 15–38. New Delhi: International Academy of Indian Culture and Aditya Prakashan.

——. 1999. "Internal and External Geography in Spiritual Biography." In *Sacred Spaces and Powerful Places in Tibetan Culture*, ed. T. Huber, 187–97. Dharamsala, India: Library of Tibetan Works and Archives.

Thomas, E. J. 1927. *The Life of the Buddha as Legend and History*. London: Routledge and Kegan Paul.

Thrangu Rinpoche. 1999. *Ten Teachings from the 100,000 Songs of Milarepa*. New Delhi: Sri Satguru.

Tiso, Frances. 1989. "A Study of the Buddhist Saint in Relation to the Biographical Tradition of Milarepa." Ph.D. diss., Columbia University.

——. 1994. "The *Rdo rje 'chang rnam thar* in the *Bkha' brgyud gser 'phreng* Genre." In *Tibetan Studies: Proceedings of the 6th Seminar of the International Association for Tibetan Studies, Fagernes, 1992*, ed. Per Kvaerne. Oslo: Institute for Comparative Research in Human Culture.

——. 1996. "The Biographical Tradition of Milarepa." *The Tibet Journal* 21 (2): 10–21.

——. 1997. "The Death of Milarepa: Towards a Redaktionsgeschichte of the Mila rnam thar Traditions." In *Tibetan Studies: Proceedings of the 7th Seminar of the International Association for Tibetan Studies, Graz 1995*, ed. E. Steinkellner. Graz.

Torricelli, Fabrizio. 1998. "The Tibetan Text of the *Karṇatantravajrapada*." *East and West* 48:385–423.

——. 2000. "Padma dkar-po's Arrangement of the bDe-mchog snyan-brgyud." *East and West* 50:359–87.

——. 2001. "Zhang lo-tsā-ba's Introduction to the Aural Transmission of Śaṃvara." In *Le parole e i marmi: studi in onore de raniero gnoli nel suo 70 compleanno*, 2 vols., 2:875–96. Roma: Istituto Italiano per l'Africa e l'Oriente.

Torricelli, Fabrizio and Sangye T. Naga. 1995. *The Life of Mahāsiddha Tilopa by Mar-pa Chos-kyi bLo-gros*. Dharamsala, India: Library of Tibetan Works and Archives.

Tsuda, Shinichi. 1978. *A Critical Tantrism*. Memoires of the Research Department of the Toyo Bunko, no. 36. Tokyo: Toyo Bunko.

Tucci, Giuseppi. 1949. *Tibetan Painted Scrolls*. Rome: La Libreria Della Stato. Reprint ed., Kyoto: Rinsen, 1980.

Uebach, Helga. 1979. "Notes on the Tibetan Kinship Term Dbon." In *Tibetan Studies in Honor of Hugh Richardson*, ed. M. Aris and A. S. S. Kyi, 301–9. New Delhi: Vikas Publishing.

Ui, Hakuju, et al. 1934. *A Complete Catalogue of the Tibetan Buddhist Canons*. Sendai, Japan: Tôhoku Imperial University.

Urubshurow, Victoria K. 1984. "Symbolic Tradition on the Buddhist Path: Spiritual Development in the Biographical Tradition of Milarepa." Ph.D. diss., University of Chicago.

van Tuyl, Charles D. 1972. "An Analysis of Chapter Twenty-Eight of the Hundred Thousand Songs of Milarepa, a Buddhist Poet and Saint of Tibet." Ph.D diss., Indiana University.

——. 1974. "Mila Raspa." *Tibet Society Bulletin* 7:21–27.

——. 1975. "The Tshe ring ma Account—An Old Document Incorporated Into the Mi La Ras Pa'i Mgur 'Bum?" *Zentralasiatische Studien* 9:23–36.

Vitali, Roberto. 1996. *The Kingdoms of Gu.ge Pu.hrang.* Dharamsala, India: Tho.ling gtsug. lag.khang lo.gcig.stong 'khor.ba'i rjes.dran.mdzad sgo'i go.sgrig tshogs.chung.

Vostrikov, A. I. 1970. *Tibetan Historical Literature.* New Delhi: Indian Studies Past and Present.

Waddell, L.A. 1895. *The Buddhism of Tibet, or Lamaism, with its Mystic Cults, Symbolism and Mythology, and in its Relation to Indian Buddhism.* London: W. H. Allen & Co.

Walshe, Maurice. 1987. *Thus Have I Heard: The Long Discourses of the Buddha, Dīgha Nikāya.* London: Wisdom.

Wangdu, Pasang and Hildegard Diemberger. 1996. *Shel Dkar Chos 'Byung: History of the "White Crystal."* Wien: Verlag der Österreichischen Akademie der Wissenschaften.

Willis, Janice Dean. 1985. "On the Nature of *Rnam-thar.*" In *Soundings in Tibetan Civilization,* ed. B. N. Aziz and M. Kapstein, 304–19. Delhi: Manohar.

Winkler, Ken. 1982. *Pilgrim of the Clear Light.* Berkeley, Calif.: Dawnfire.

Yamaguchi, Zuiho. 1984. "Methods of Chronological Calculation in Tibetan Historical Sources." In *Tibetan and Buddhist Studies Commemorating the 200th Anniversary of the Birth of Alexander Csoma de Körös,* ed. L. Ligeti, 2 vols., 2:405–24. Budapest: Akadémiai Kiadó.

Yamamoto, Carl S. 2012. *Vision and Violence: Lama Zhang and the Politics of Charisma in Twelfth-Century Tibet.* Leiden: Brill.

Zangpo, Ngawang. 2001. *Sacred Ground: Jamgon Kongtrul on "Pilgrimage and Sacred Geography."* Ithaca, N.Y.: Snow Lion.

INDEX

TH refers to Tsangnyön Heruka (Gtsang smyon Heruka).

SOUTH ASIA ACROSS THE DISCIPLINES

EDITED BY MUZAFFAR ALAM, ROBERT GOLDMAN,
AND GAURI VISWANATHAN

DIPESH CHAKRABARTY, SHELDON POLLOCK,
AND SANJAY SUBRAHMANYAM, FOUNDING EDITORS

Extreme Poetry: The South Asian Movement of Simultaneous Narration by
Yigal Bronner (Columbia)

The Social Space of Language: Vernacular Culture in British Colonial Punjab
by Farina Mir (California)

Unifying Hinduism: Philosophy and Identity in Indian Intellectual History by
Andrew J. Nicholson (Columbia)

The Powerful Ephemeral: Everyday Healing in an Ambiguously Islamic Place
by Carla Bellamy (California)

*Secularizing Islamists? Jama'at-e-Islami and Jama'at-ud-Da'wa in Urban
Pakistan* by Humeira Iqtidar (Chicago)

*Islam Translated: Literature, Conversion, and the Arabic Cosmopolis of South
and Southeast Asia* by Ronit Ricci (Chicago)

Conjugations: Marriage and Form in New Bollywood Cinema by Sangita
Gopal (Chicago)

Unfinished Gestures: Devadāsīs, Memory, and Modernity in South India by
Davesh Soneji (Chicago)

Document Raj: Writing and Scribes in Early Colonial South India by Bhavani
Raman (Chicago)

South Asia Across the Disciplines is a series devoted to publishing first books across a wide range of South Asian studies, including art, history, philology or textual studies, philosophy, religion, and the interpretive social sciences. Series authors all share the goal of opening up new archives and suggesting new methods and approaches, while demonstrating that South Asian scholarship can be at once deep in expertise and broad in appeal.